MW00637173

THE BIRNBAUM EDITION

PIRKEI AVOS

פרקי אבות

RABBI BEREL WEIN

AVOS

פרקי
אבות

TEACHINGS FOR OUR TIMES

THE BIRNBAUM EDITION

PIRKEI

First edition – First Impression / April 2003
First edition – Second Impression / April 2005

Published by **SHAAR PRESS**
and Distributed by **MESORAH PUBLICATIONS, LTD.**
4401 Second Avenue / Brooklyn, N.Y 11232 / (718) 921-9000 / www.artscroll.com

Distributed in Israel by SIFRIATI / A. GITLER — BOOKS
6 Hayarkon Street / Bnei Brak 51127

Distributed in Europe by LEHMANNS
Unit E, Viking Business Park / Rolling Mill Road / Jarow, Tyne and Wear NE32 3DP / England

Distributed in Australia and New Zealand by GOLDS WORLD OF JUDAICA
3-13 William Street / Balaclava 3183, Vic., Australia

Distributed in South Africa by KOLLEL BOOKSHOP
Shop 8A Norwood Hypermarket / Norwood 2196, Johannesburg, South Africa

Printed in the United States of America by Noble Book Press
Custom bound by Sefercraft, Inc. / 4401 Second Avenue / Brooklyn N.Y. 11232

This volume of Pirkei Avos is dedicated to our beloved parents

Moshe and Malka Birnbaum לאוי״ט

Chazal tell us, one who wants to be a chasid, should study the words of Pirkei Avos. Pirkei Avos is more than just a collection of pithy maxims and anecdotes. Rather, it instructs us as Jews in a *derech,* a path of wisdom, This instruction is delivered and received through example, not just statements, just as the Rabbis quoted therein lived by their words.

שמע בני מוסר אביך ואל תטש תורת אמך

Hear my child the discipline of your father,
and do not forsake the teaching of your mother
(*Mishlei* 1:8)

Our beloved parents, in whose honor we dedicate this volume of Pirkei Avos, have instructed their children in the ways of their Avos, from Moshe Rabbeinu, who began this chain of instruction. They have taught us not just by words, but by action, in the face of adversity and a world that was torn asunder.

מוסר אביך / THE DISCIPLINE OF YOUR FATHER

Daddy survived the Holocaust, during which he suffered the loss of almost his entire family. Such a loss would have caused many others to lose faith in Hashem and our religious principles. But he would not. He did not. Instead he resolved to begin anew. He started a new life in a new country and created a whole new generation of shomrei Torah umitzvos. His initiative to pick up the Daf Yomi late in life is but one example of how he shows love of Torah and avodah. With his faith, courage, strength, and the vivid memory and teachings of his parents and grandparents — the "Avos" — he has raised his children to be dedicated to Torah and the teachings of our ancestors. Our father has guided us through his teachings, noble bearing and more importantly, through his daily conduct and dedication to Torah and Mitzvos. To us, he is the greatest of the Avos.

תורת אמך / THE TEACHING OF YOUR MOTHER

Ima's resolve to raise a true Torah — oriented family was no less palpable nor significant than that of our beloved father. She provided for the physical well being of her children, and always made sure that our home was one of Torah. A true Eishes Chayil, she walks in the ways of the matriarchs, who supported the Avos in their lifelong dedication and quest to perpetuate and disseminate the word of Hashem.

Our parents have done their part by instructing us in the paths of our ancestors. We understand that as part of that lesson, it is incumbent upon us to do our part; to impart their lessons to our children and others. For we are all links in the chain of the mesorah.

May Hashem Yisbarach grant them many more years of health and happiness to reap the nachas from their children and grandchildren; nachas that they richly deserve.

Their beloved children ...

Gitty and Ezra Birnbaum

Introduction

Few works have spawned as many other works about them as has *Pirkei Avos*. It has been translated into many languages and published in hundreds of editions. Although it is commonly known in English as "Ethics of the Fathers," the literal translation of *Pirkei Avos* is "Chapters of the Fathers." It comprises six chapters, the first five of which are the original Mishnaic tractate, in the Mishnah, while the sixth is an added collection of later *beraisos,* which are teachings from the Mishnaic era that were not incorporated into the corpus of the Mishnah.

The word *Avos* has two meanings. In addition to "Fathers," it can also be rendered "basic principles," or "fundamental ideas." For example, when listing the main categories of activities prohibited on the Sabbath, or the primary categories of torts in civil law, the Talmud refers to them as *Avos*, or the "fathers," meaning the major categories. This, then, would imply that the tractate Avos contains the basic principles and fundamental guidelines of Jewish life. Indeed, although *Pirkei Avos* is often thought of as a book of "ethics," it is really more than that. It is a handbook of the Jewish value system. Beyond being a collection of wise aphorisms and sage advice — though it certainly is that as well — Avos reflects the true spirit of Judaism. It is the skeleton, so to speak, that underlies the flesh of the great corpus of laws, customs and lifestyle of the Jewish people throughout the ages. It is about family, education, interpersonal relationships, faith, commercial behavior, history and all the other components of human life and existence.

Avos is like a medical imaging scanner that allows us to see hidden structures of God's Torah and its practical application in human life and society. Life is full of noble ideas and theories that often seem not to coincide with one another, but Judaism and its Torah is a religion of balance, of conciliation of opposites, of a practical way called halachah, which allows one to live a fulfilling and meaningful moral life despite all the vicissitudes of time, circumstance, human behavior and Godly fate. While fully cognizant of the stark reality of the human condition, Avos is a book of noble aspirations as well as realistic counsel for self-improvement and societal advancement. It is the reflection of our Sages' vision of balance in life and behavior — of the realization of Solomon's wise statement that "There is a time for everything" (*Ecclesiastes* 3:1).

The book radiates a sense of optimism and undying hope for a better person and a finer society, in spite of the foibles, weaknesses, frustrations and cruelties that are part of our human existence. It is not for naught that the Talmud recommends that "one who wishes to be a pious person (in the sense of truly fulfilling the Torah's precepts) should study carefully the words of Avos," for it is a handbook for pious and generous living. In effect, to understand and appreciate the Jewish definition of piety, one must be a student of the words of Avos. Of all the sixty-three volumes of the Mishnah, Avos is the one most studied by the masses of Israel.

The dictums of Avos were, of course, stated at certain times and places, and the lessons its authors chose to teach their particular generations undoubtedly addressed their historical circumstances. Yet, as is true of all books of Torah thought and knowledge, the ideas, sayings, outlooks and insights of the book go beyond the recorded times and places they were uttered. Torah is timeless and eternal. So is good sense, wise observations on the human condition and excellent advice on proper and holy behavior.

To truly appreciate the grandeur of its words and the sublime nature of its wisdom, one should understand Avos on two planes: on the one hand, the times when it was taught and the great authors of its teachings, and on the other hand, the universality of what they had to say. This commentary is my attempt to discuss the men and ideas in view of the milieu of the times in which the maxims were stated, considering the cataclysmic events that marked that period of Jewish history (350 BCE to 200 CE), and also to interpret these holy words in a fashion that is relevant and timely for our age as well.

It has been my distinct privilege to have taught Avos tens of times during my years as a teacher at yeshivos and as a pulpit rabbi in Chicago, Miami Beach, and Monsey. Now I teach it regularly in a yeshivah and at a synagogue here in the holy city of Jerusalem. I am continually fascinated by the freshness of this "old" book and the never-ending wells of inspiration that both the teacher and the student derive from its study; much of the material included in this book is based on lectures and classes I have delivered. Although I am very far from being any sort of scholar or expert on the subject, I am hopeful that my thoughts can benefit the broad English-speaking public desiring to gain from the wisdom and life experience of our great spiritual leaders of the Mishnah.

This book is also a very personal one. I have not hesitated to include within it favorite anecdotes and firsthand experiences, not so much as to reveal myself, as to help illustrate the actual influence of Avos in everyday human life. With this hope of making the book ever more accessible to a large section of the Jewish people, I am bold enough to embark on the task that this volume represents.

A final caveat regarding this work: After decades of researching, reading and teaching the works of the great scholars and rabbis of the previous generations, it is difficult for me to identify any particular insight or comment as being original with me. I have not footnoted this book nor have I quoted sources verbatim. But I am confident that the reader will realize that thoughts of value appearing in it are not necessarily my original creation. Almost all of this book has been culled from the commentaries and insights of others. I am naturally solely responsible for any errors or false ideas that may have crept into it. And I am also solely responsible for the actual selection of the ideas and comments of others that I have chosen to include.

Since any book that discusses and teaches Torah has a whiff of eternity attached to it, I have attempted to avoid fanciful interpretation, current political correctness and mythical, undocumented statements about the exalted authors and contents of Avos.

I am especially indebted to Rabbi Meir Zlotowitz for prodding me (none too gently) to undertake this project. Rabbi Nosson Scherman has helped me greatly with his comments and editing. Shmuel Blitz has been my friend and adviser here in Israel. Avrohom Biderman has shepherded the project from manuscript to finished book. Sheah Brander and his staff have elevated the book to a level of elegance and beauty that is not my own.

My wife and family continue to provide me patience and support, and this is especially appreciated for the times when my good humor begins to fade in the frustrations of working on a new book.

And I am humbly grateful to the God of Israel Who has preserved me until now in years and health and has allowed me to compose this work in the holy city of Jerusalem. May the work of our hands be acceptable and well established before God and Israel.

Rabbi Berel Wein

II Adar 5763 / April 2003

פרק ראשון

CHAPTER ONE

כָּל יִשְׂרָאֵל יֵשׁ לָהֶם חֵלֶק לָעוֹלָם הַבָּא, שֶׁנֶּאֱמַר: „וְעַמֵּךְ כֻּלָּם צַדִּיקִים, לְעוֹלָם יִירְשׁוּ אָרֶץ, נֵצֶר מַטָּעַי, מַעֲשֵׂה יָדַי לְהִתְפָּאֵר.״

All Israel has a share in the World to Come, as it is said: *And your people are all righteous; they shall inherit the land forever; a branch of My plantings, My handiwork, in which to take pride* (*Isaiah* 60:21).

Prologue

כָּל יִשְׂרָאֵל יֵשׁ לָהֶם חֵלֶק לָעוֹלָם הַבָּא
All Israel has a share in the World to Come

A JEW IS BORN WITH A BUILT-IN ANNUITY, FOR EVERY JEW HAS A SHARE IN the World to Come — but the proceeds are not guaranteed. It is comparable to a child receiving a large sum of money from a parent, on the condition that the money be wisely invested. The child can make great profits or lose the entire amount, depending on how wisely — or foolishly — the nest-egg is invested. The same is true regarding our share in the World to Come.

By living a Torah life, being a moral upright person, and resisting the obvious temptations and distraction of this world, one safeguards and even enhances one's share in the World to Come. Behaving in the opposite fashion, however, guarantees the diminishing or perhaps even the complete loss of that share.

This mishnah, which introduces the eleventh chapter of Tractate Sanhedrin, is the fitting introduction to Avos. We can assure the preservation of our birthright share in the World to Come by following the maxims and principles of this tractate. Thus, the importance of Avos is stressed to us by the choice of this mishnah to precede its study.

[א] **מֹשֶׁה** קִבֵּל תּוֹרָה מִסִּינַי, וּמְסָרָהּ לִיהוֹשֻׁעַ, וִיהוֹשֻׁעַ לִזְקֵנִים, וּזְקֵנִים לִנְבִיאִים, וּנְבִיאִים מְסָרוּהָ לְאַנְשֵׁי כְנֶסֶת הַגְּדוֹלָה.

Chapter One

מֹשֶׁה קִבֵּל תּוֹרָה מִסִּינַי
Moses received the Torah from [God at] Sinai

Mishnah 1 THE JUDGMENT OF WHAT IS RIGHT AND WRONG IS NOT left to man's conscience and/or intellect alone. Contrary to all the ideas and philosophies of the Enlightenment, against Kant's doctrine of man's autonomy and final authority, and in stark contrast to the moral relativism that marks the Western world's current value system, Avos proclaims the unchanging God-given principles of Sinai. This opening sentence, "Moses received the Torah from [God at] Sinai," was composed in a world dominated by Greek culture and its worship of beauty. At the beginning of Mishnaic times, the primitive forms of paganism that had marked the world of ancient Jewish history and the First Temple Era had given way to a newer and much more attractive and advanced pagan culture.

For well over a millennium, beginning in the 300's BCE, the ideas, philosophies, language, theories of astronomy and physics, forms of architecture, theater and drama, as well as the governmental structures of Greece, were the basis for much of human civilization. The Greeks, however, also had a value system and a "morality" that differed sharply from that of Jewish tradition. Paganism, sexual promiscuity, violence and abuse — especially against slaves and women — were also part of the Greek way of life. Thus, the opening sentence of Avos clearly defines the gulf that divided Greek and Jew in the ancient world. Jewish ethics, morals, values and lifestyle derive from Sinai — from the One God Who created all. That value system was and is non-negotiable. To defend their heritage and the Torah way of life, Jews, at the time of the Maccabees, would go to war against the Syrian-Greeks and their culture, and against Jews who were Hellenized and swayed by the seductive Syrian-Greek surroundings of the time. That war, won miraculously against overwhelming odds, gave us the festival of Chanukah, which remains our eternal reminder that the flame of Sinai continues to light our way through the fog of new cultures that are enticing, but false and alien.

אַנְשֵׁי כְנֶסֶת הַגְּדוֹלָה
Men of the Great Assembly

THIS WAS A GROUP OF 120 SAGES WHO LED THE JEWISH PEOPLE AT THE beginning of the Second Temple Era. They included the last prophets, among them Ezra, Mordechai (of *Megillas Esther* fame), Haggai, Zechariah, and Malachi. As the Sages put it, the Great Assembly "restored the crown of the Torah to its pristine splendor." They authorized major rabbinic decrees and measures to preserve Judaism in the face of foreign dominion and

1/1

1. Moses received the Torah from [God at] Sinai and transmitted it to Joshua; Joshua to the Elders; the Elders to the Prophets; and the Prophets transmitted it to the Men of the Great Assembly.

---

influence, instituting many of the most familiar features of Jewish practice, such as the text of much of the basic daily and Sabbath and festival liturgy. They transmitted the Oral Law of Moses and Sinai to all later generations, and facilitated its understanding and its method of analysis for the masses of Israel; they completed and established the canon of the Hebrew Bible, built the Second Temple in Jerusalem, and provided the moral and temporal leadership for the Jewish world at the beginning of the Second Commonwealth.

The Men of the Great Assembly were led by Ezra the Scribe, a man who, the Talmud comments, was so worthy that God could have given the Torah to Israel through him, had He not already given it through Moses. It was this group of great people who transmitted Judaism to the post-Biblical Jewish world and who secured the role and influence of the Oral Law in Jewish life. It was this assembly of great leaders that created a Jewish infrastructure and way of life that would enable the people of Israel, under harrowingly negative conditions, to survive and even prosper for the ensuing twenty-five centuries. The "Men of the Great Assembly" might as well have been called "The Great Men of the Great Assembly."

Judaism is a religion of personal tradition, of binding the past to the present and to the future. It is a seamless chain of experience and memory. Its knowledge and truths pass from parent to child, from teacher to student, from leaders to members of the community. It is certainly a religion of books and scholarship, but it is mainly a faith of communication between generations, between human beings. Therefore, Avos begins by describing the transmission of the Jewish tradition from Sinai and Moses to the Men of the Great Assembly. Our faith is based on the proposition that our parents were not liars, that they personally witnessed the revelation at Sinai, saw Solomon's dedication of the First Temple, heard Ezra's sermon at the beginning of the Second Commonwealth and knew and assessed all of the men who appear in the book of Avos.

It is this personal acquaintanceship and relationship with people — not just with "scholarly" books and recently concocted professorial theses — that provides Judaism with its constant vitality and strength. This is why storytelling is so much a part of Jewish life and tradition. The secret of Jewish survival is the attachment of Jews to great people of Torah, who are their teachers and role models. That is why the rabbis liken the death of a Torah Jew to a *Sefer Torah,* a Torah scroll, itself being consumed by fire. A Jew is

א/א הֵם אָמְרוּ שְׁלֹשָׁה דְבָרִים: הֱווּ מְתוּנִים בַּדִּין, וְהַעֲמִידוּ תַלְמִידִים הַרְבֵּה, וַעֲשׂוּ סְיָג לַתּוֹרָה.

---

destined to be a living *Sefer Torah*. That is the challenge of the book of Avos; properly studied and applied, it transforms us into a human embodiment of the Torah.

הֵם אָמְרוּ שְׁלֹשָׁה דְבָרִים
They said three things

THE MEN OF THE GREAT ASSEMBLY SAID MANY THINGS ON A WIDE VARIETY of subjects, of Torah knowledge and of life generally. Nevertheless, the mishnah sums up their legacy to Israel in the three lessons stated here.

In Avos, the words *they said* or *he used to say* appear constantly. They always signify that the lesson or instruction recorded was central to the life of the person or persons being quoted. Thus, the lessons of Avos are essentially the distillations of the life and teachings of the great personages who appear on its pages. It is far easier to speak for 40 minutes on a subject than to compact the same message into a 10-minute talk. But the 10-minute talk is more effective and will be better and longer remembered. Part of the genius of Avos is its ability to reduce sophisticated, philosophical, complex issues and solutions into concise, easily remembered nuggets of wisdom.

❦ ❦ ❦

Profundity of brevity

One of my favorite "rabbi stories" concerns the rabbi who delivered a 40-minute sermon. After the services, a man approached the rabbi and said, "I produce a popular magazine-type radio program. I heard your sermon and I wonder if you could possibly reduce your sermon to a three-minute message." Thrilled at the opportunity to reach millions with his words of wisdom, the rabbi eagerly replied, "Yes! Of course I could get my message across in three minutes!" To which the radio producer retorted, "Then why didn't you?"

❦ ❦ ❦

Avos is composed of trenchant sound bites, lifetimes of wisdom contracted into a few pithy words. These few words, repeated often by the wise men who uttered them throughout their lives, represent their unique and individual legacies to all future generations of Jews and all human beings generally. Since life itself is always too brief and short, its lessons should therefore be taught and phrased in a like fashion.

הֱווּ מְתוּנִים בַּדִּין
Be deliberate in judgment

THIS IS TRUE NOT ONLY REGARDING JUDICIAL PROCEDURES AND COURT decisions, but is wise advice for all areas of life. First impressions of people, events, situations, and opportunities are often erroneous. Wise shopping demands resisting impulse buying. Love at first sight creates as many bad marriages as healthy ones, probably more. Careful judgment should always

They said three things: Be deliberate in judgment; develop many disciples; and make a protective fence for the Torah.

---

precede action. Just as the conscientious judge must weigh all the evidence carefully and ponder the consequences before rendering final judgment, so too does successful living require the trait of patient consideration of the facts and probabilities of life. The overwhelming majority of smokers would like to quit, but since they began as adolescents, the years-old addiction makes that task most difficult. Decisions made when we are young are often faulty and wrong. Since patient consideration of facts and probabilities is not a common virtue of the young, parents, teachers, and counselors should always intervene to provide the patient consideration that the young must have in order to choose wisely. Abdicating parental responsibility in this matter is inexcusable.

❦ ❦ ❦

Never be hasty

Another of my favorite stories is about the elderly East European rabbi suffering an ailment. After weeks of trying, he was finally able to obtain an appointment with a great specialist, a reputed expert in the field. The rabbi was ushered into one of many small cubicles in the doctor's offices, where he sat and waited for the doctor to enter and examine him. The doctor eventually rushed into the cubicle, quickly heard out the symptoms, made a perfunctory examination of the patient, and jotted down a prescription. As the doctor hurriedly got up to go to the next cubicle, the rabbi frowned noticeably. The doctor asked what was wrong, to which the rabbi answered, "I have been a rabbi for over fifty years. Every Friday morning, women bring me bruised chickens and ask me to decide whether the chickens are kosher. I am well-versed in this field, and I have decided such questions hundreds of times in my career. But each time, I discuss the matter with each woman, and review the matter in the codes of law, even though I am convinced I know the correct answer beforehand. Now, if a dead chicken is worthy of such deliberation, isn't a still breathing, albeit old, rabbi?!"

❦ ❦ ❦

Especially for people engaged in the professions of imparting advice and knowledge to others — medical, legal, economic, counseling, education, etc. — deliberation in judgment is required behavior.

וְהַעֲמִידוּ תַלְמִידִים הַרְבֵּה
Develop many disciples

THE KEY WORD HERE IS *MANY* DISCIPLES. WE ENCOUNTER HERE THE ISSUE of balance when conflicting Torah ideals emerge, as discussed in my Introduction. The rabbis of the Talmud stated forcefully that one should not teach "a student who is not 'worthy'" but the word "worthy" was not clearly defined. Nevertheless, there was a policy in force among certain groups of the teachers of Israel, both before and after the time of the Men of the Great

[ב] **שִׁמְעוֹן** הַצַּדִּיק הָיָה מִשְּׁיָרֵי כְנֶסֶת הַגְּדוֹלָה.

Assembly, to teach only the especially talented and sincerely pious students and to exclude others. While not specifically criticizing that policy, the Men of the Great Assembly stated that the Jewish people need *many disciples*. It was left to the individual teacher and educational institution to reconcile the two opinions and to draw their line of inclusion and exclusion. The words of the Men of the Great Assembly, however, were meant to influence a policy and bias toward inclusion. This is based on the idea that one never knows which student will prove to be one of the next generation's great men.

As someone who has taught young men and women for many decades, and who also has personal recollections of his own yeshivah classmates and their later achievements in life, I can personally attest to the frequency of "sleepers" who became scholars and leaders, in spite of (or maybe because of) their apparently mediocre scholastic achievements in high school. Many ducklings turn into swans, just as, unfortunately, not every potential swan matures and develops.

In any event, the Jewish people are dependent on a learned laity, an intelligent and sophisticated folk, in order to survive and prosper. By definition, this requires many students. Unlike the medieval Church that preferred an ignorant laity, which then made the presence of priests indispensable to society at large, the Men of the Great Assembly reinforced Moses' statement, "Would that all of God's people were prophets!" Thus, their words regarding "many disciples" can be understood as a warning to the scholars not to be over-protective of their knowledge and wisdom, but to share their gifts with all the people, in order to enhance Torah and glorify it. True, not every Jewish student belongs in every Jewish school, but there should be some type of school available for every student.

וַעֲשׂוּ סְיָג לַתּוֹרָה
And make a protective fence for the Torah

THE TRILLION-DOLLAR INSURANCE AND SECURITY INDUSTRY IS TESTIMONY to this deep-felt need, for it rightfully and wisely insisted on preventive safeguards. To Jews, the Torah, its commandments, values and precepts are priceless, so it is natural that the rabbis of Israel would take measures to protect the Torah from erosion and damage. Facing the pressure of a changing and challenging world and a Greek culture that assaulted every Jewish value and mocked the observance of Jewish ritual — especially the Sabbath, circumcision, sexual morality, and personal discipline — the Sages raised a wall to surround the Torah and its rituals. They established ordinances that would impede any erosion of actual Torah law and arrest risky behavior before it could impinge upon actual Torah prohibitions. Particularly those areas of Jewish life that were most attacked by the Syrian-Greeks and their Hellenizing Jewish allies — such as Sabbath, *kashrus*, and sexual discipline — were singled out to be strengthened. The

2. Shimon the Righteous was [one] of the remnants of the Great Assembly.

---

bar of observance of Jewish commandments was raised and the fence of protection of the Torah was erected and reinforced. Unquestionably, Jewish history has proven the wisdom of the rabbinic "fences" and ordinances that protected these areas of Jewish life and preserved Israel's observance of those basic tenets.

The Sages exercised great wisdom and balance in instituting such ordinances, and they cautioned against adding to what they imposed. The Midrash teaches that erecting fences capriciously can be counterproductive. Adam's wife Eve, in the Garden of Eden, embellished upon God's commandment not to *eat* from the Tree of Knowledge, and told the serpent that she was not allowed even to *touch* the tree. The serpent thereupon pushed her against it and — presto — nothing happened! The serpent thus "proved" to her that eating the tree's fruit would also bring forth no untoward results. The rest is history.

Similarly, the Talmud criticized those who took upon themselves the vow of being a *nazir*, thus restricting themselves from drinking wine. To such a person, the Sages stated critically, "Do you consider the prohibitions of the Torah to be so insufficient that you feel compelled to add more?" Yet the very same Talmud infers from Scripture that there are times when a judicious person should take a vow to become a *nazir.* In a society of sexual promiscuity, when there is an occurrence of the process of *sotah* — the ritual testing of a wife accused by her husband of infidelity — it is permissible and even praiseworthy to become a *nazir,* as a means of erecting a personal "fence" against such loose conduct. So we see once more the exquisite sense of balance that the Torah demands.

There is no question that a fence must be erected to protect the Torah. How high that fence should be, where it should be placed, when it should be erected and the judgment as to the efficacy of erecting a fence at all is left to the leaders of Israel in every generation. These are questions of extreme complexity and delicacy.

שִׁמְעוֹן הַצַּדִּיק
Shimon the Righteous

Mishnah 2 VERY FEW PEOPLE IN THE MISHNAH OR TALMUD ARE GIVEN honorary titles, though such titles as *tzaddik,* "righteous one," have come to be used liberally in the last two centuries. Thus the appearance of the designation *tzaddik* appended to the name of Shimon is very high praise.

The noted scholar and prolific Torah author, Rabbi Reuven Margolios, explains why Shimon HaTzaddik is described as a *"survivor"* of the Great Assembly. He posits that none of the 120 members of the Great Assembly were replaced when they died, so that their numbers constantly shrank

א/ב הוּא הָיָה אוֹמֵר: עַל שְׁלשָׁה דְבָרִים הָעוֹלָם עוֹמֵד: עַל הַתּוֹרָה, וְעַל הָעֲבוֹדָה, וְעַל גְּמִילוּת חֲסָדִים.

---

due to the attrition of time and mortality. That is what is meant by Shimon being one the last remaining members of that august group.

Shimon was the *Kohen Gadol,* the High Priest, at the beginning of the Second Temple Era. The Talmud relates how he greeted Alexander the Great, when the latter reached Jerusalem in about 330 BCE. Shimon made such a profound impression upon the young conqueror of the then-known world that Alexander spared Jerusalem the destruction he visited upon the other cities occupied by his army. Besides being High Priest in the Temple, Shimon also appears to have been the temporal leader of the Jewish community. If so, then he set a precedent that two centuries later would spark civil war among the Jews. The concentration of spiritual and temporal power in the hands of one individual has always been questionable. Power corrupts. In the hands of a Shimon, who was a *tzaddik*, the situation caused no harm, and in fact was beneficial in helping the fledgling Jewish state overcome the internal and external problems it faced, since it eliminated competitive power bases and personal jealousies and pique. However, in the hands of lesser men (such as the Hasmonean king, Alexander Yannai) such concentration of power proved to be most injurious to both the temporal and spiritual well-being of the Jewish commonwealth. King Yannai was vain and impervious to the authority of the great sages. When they dared to correct his excesses, he responded with a wholesale slaughter that nearly wiped out all of the greatest Torah authorities of the age.

עַל שְׁלשָׁה דְבָרִים הָעוֹלָם עוֹמֵד
The [existence of the] world depends on three things

FUNDAMENTAL TO JEWISH THOUGHT IS THE CONCEPT THAT THE PHYSICAL world rests on spiritual supports. The prophet Jeremiah (33:25) had proclaimed in God's Name, *If not for My covenant [i.e., Torah study] day and night, I would not have established the laws of nature that govern heaven and earth.* Jewish thought, therefore, dealt with the reality that the physical, apparent, natural world that we live in is supported by invisible but necessary and vital spiritual underpinnings. The world exists and our planet revolves in its preordained orbit because there is Torah, Godly service and behavior, and human kindness. And even though there may be more darkness than light, more evil than good when measured quantitatively, the qualitative presence of Torah, Godly service and acts of human kindness on earth allow for its solid base of life.

1/2

He used to say: The [existence of the] world depends on three things: on Torah study, on the service [of God], and on kind deeds.

Judaism was always confident that the relatively few good people would outweigh the many bad ones. Sodom was destroyed not because of countless evildoers in its midst; it was destroyed because there were not ten good people in the city. Jewish tradition attributes the continuity of human life on this planet to the fact that there are thirty-six righteous people living at all times.

עַל הַתּוֹרָה
On Torah study

THIS REFERS TO THE STUDY, OBSERVANCE AND SUPPORT OF THE WRITTEN and Oral Law that, as per the previous mishnah, was transmitted to Israel at Sinai. The Jewish people's survival and vitality is the direct result of Torah within our community. Jewish history is replete with the wreckage left by Jewish groups and individuals who sought survival and success by jettisoning the "restrictions" of Torah. The cornerstone of Jewish survival was always and still is the Torah, especially its study.

וְעַל הָעֲבוֹדָה
On the service [of God]

ORIGINALLY THIS REFERRED TO THE TEMPLE SERVICE, BUT AFTER THE Destruction and exile, prayer, synagogue attendance, and ritual observance took the place of the offerings. In its broadest sense, Godly service applies to every walk of life and every circumstance of human interaction. Judaism views such service in terms of discipline, obligation, and constant effort, which is why the word *avodah* — literally *work*, *labor*, *toil* — is used to describe this concept of service. This fundamental Jewish concept of service will be discussed in greater detail later in this book as commentary to the specific *mishnayos* that deal with it.

וְעַל גְּמִילוּת חֲסָדִים
And on kind deeds

DEEDS OF HUMAN KINDNESS MEANS EXACTLY WHAT IT SAYS. A SMILE, A greeting, a cheerful and comforting word, a timely loan of money or goods, a personal gift, home and meal hospitality, visiting the sick and the homebound, helping others deal with pain, grief and sorrow, caring for those in need, charity for the poor and defenseless, providing vocational training — all of these and much more are hallmarks of the Jewish society. Every such act of human kindness, no matter how superficially inauspicious it may seem, helps in propping up our world. עוֹלָם חֶסֶד יִבָּנֶה, *the world is built on kindness* (*Psalms* 89:3); the world is built on the foundation of goodness and acts of lovingkindness to others.

[ג] **אַנְטִיגְנוֹס** אִישׁ סוֹכוֹ קִבֵּל מִשִּׁמְעוֹן הַצַּדִּיק. הוּא הָיָה אוֹמֵר: אַל תִּהְיוּ כַּעֲבָדִים הַמְשַׁמְּשִׁין אֶת הָרַב עַל מְנָת לְקַבֵּל פְּרָס; אֶלָּא הֱווּ

אַנְטִיגְנוֹס אִישׁ סוֹכוֹ
Antigonos, leader of Socho

Mishnah 3 THE INFLUENCE OF THE GREEK WORLD ON THE JEWS IS readily apparent in this name. The Jews had agreed to name their sons Alexander, in tribute to the conqueror and as an expression of gratitude to him for not destroying their capital and Temple. Thus Alexander, in all of its forms (Sender, Alex, etc.) became an accepted Jewish name. Once one Greek name became acceptable, it was only a matter of time until almost all Greek names became acceptable. Antigonos is an example, and it was this major disciple of Shimon HaTzaddik who became a preeminent leader of his generation.

Antigonos himself had two disciples, Tzadok and Baysos (another Greek name), who publicly deserted Jewish tradition. They took advantage of Antigonos' statement in this mishnah, which will be discussed below, as an excuse to create a dissident group of Jews — who denied the Oral Law and the concept of the World to Come after death — and to become increasingly more assimilated into Greek culture. This small, deviant group developed into the powerful political, social and heretical movement known as the *Tzedokim* — the Sadducees. This movement was less radical than the *Misyavnim* — the completely Hellenized Jews — and it soon became very strong, especially among the Jewish upper class. It struggled for political and religious control of Jewish society throughout the remaining time of the Second Temple, and many times the Sadducees were ascendant. It eventually faded away after a number of centuries. There is no surer method of Jewish self-destruction than to sever the ties to Torah, and the Sadducees sadly paid the price for their defection from the Oral Law, halachah, and tradition.

The rabbis of the time saw the defection of Antigonos' disciples as having been inspired by a desire, influenced undoubtedly by the surrounding Greek culture, to pursue a lifestyle that was opposed to traditional Torah discipline. Their misinterpretation of Antigonos' teaching (see below) was merely an excuse to justify their unpublicized inner desires for luxury, sexual immorality, and hedonism. How deep must have been the pain of this great teacher in Israel at the betrayal of Judaism by two of his own disciples!

אַל תִּהְיוּ כַּעֲבָדִים . . . עַל מְנָת לְקַבֵּל פְּרָס
Be not like servants . . . for the sake of receiving a reward

THE SIMPLE EXPLANATION OF THIS MAXIM IS THAT SERVING GOD IS ITS OWN reward, and there is no necessity for any further rewards. A task well done provides great satisfaction to its doer. Fulfilling one's obligation to God, so to speak, validates one's existence on this planet and therefore carries blessing all in itself, without the necessity for a further prize. This is the concept of לִשְׁמָהּ,

3. Antigonos, leader of Socho, received the tradition from Shimon the Righteous.

He used to say: Be not like servants who serve the master for the sake of receiving a reward, but rather, be like

---

for its own sake, i.e., doing the right and moral and holy thing for the sake of the action itself, without extraneous thoughts of honor, notoriety, praise, or reward entering one's motivation. This is a difficult level to achieve, but Jews are bidden to strive for it.

Noble as this ideal is, however, it needs explanation. The Talmud teaches that it is permissible, even praiseworthy, to make a "deal," so to speak, with the Lord regarding the performance of good deeds. Giving money to charity on the condition that heaven will restore a child's health and grant him long life is only one of many examples of such behavior. It is precisely this point that Antigonos addresses. God may indeed reward the donor for his good deed. The donor may even pray that God will do so. But what happens if Heaven does not respond as the donor had hoped, and tragedy strikes the child and its family? Does the father now regret his pledge to charity? Does he demand the return of his donation? Does he rebel because he suffered, despite doing a good deed? Not at all.

In effect, Antigonos preempts the age-old question, "Why should one do good, if bad things happen to good people, too?" Based on the conclusion drawn from the Book of *Job* that finite man can never understand the workings of the infinite God, Antigonos teaches that a good deed must stand on its own merit, irrespective of the apparent lack of fulfillment, so to speak, by God on His part of the "bargain." Giving charity is a good thing even if the child does not survive. The gift will undoubtedly count as a merit to the donor and thus somehow be of influence in Heaven, but the act of giving itself should be viewed as an independent action — good for the sake of good.

❦ ❦ ❦

The deal is off

I am reminded of an incident that occurred when I was a child living in the then all-Jewish Lawndale neighborhood of Chicago. A neighborhood Jewish politician of rather unsavory reputation was running for a City Council position. The primary election day fell during Chol HaMoed Pesach. Sensing the necessity for the Orthodox Jewish vote, this politician and his wife ostentatiously shopped at the local Pesach store before the holiday, even though his observance of Torah ritual until then was not exactly his strongest point. As events turned out, he was soundly trounced in the election. So, in the middle of Pesach, he publicly and pointedly threw out the remaining packages of matzah, proclaiming loudly: "Who needs these miserable crackers anyway?" Conditional matzos never taste as good as the real thing!

❦ ❦ ❦

כַּעֲבָדִים הַמְשַׁמְּשִׁין אֶת הָרַב שֶׁלֹּא עַל מְנָת לְקַבֵּל פְּרָס; וִיהִי מוֹרָא שָׁמַיִם עֲלֵיכֶם.

[ד] **יוֹסֵי** בֶּן יוֹעֶזֶר אִישׁ צְרֵדָה וְיוֹסֵי בֶּן יוֹחָנָן אִישׁ יְרוּשָׁלַיִם קִבְּלוּ מֵהֶם.

Tzadok and Baysos misinterpreted their teacher's words to somehow imply that there is no afterlife — no reward and punishment in the World to Come. Antigonos' words, however, address only reward in this world, but belief in the World to Come, in the immortality of the soul, of eventual and eternal reward and punishment after death, are all core beliefs of Judaism. Without them, Judaism is barely a culture, much less a faith. In fact, it is the belief in the existence of the World to Come that gives our lives meaning and vindication in this world.

וִיהִי מוֹרָא שָׁמַיִם עֲלֵיכֶם
And let the awe of Heaven be upon you

ANTIGONOS MEANS TO TEMPER AND COMPLEMENT HIS PREVIOUS teaching. One might be tempted to say that since there is no guarantee of good things happening to me in this world even if I do serve God, then let me jettison the whole affair and live my life as I wish, without the Torah's inhibitions and restraints. Antigonos warns that the constant awe of heaven is incumbent upon us in any event, regardless of reward and punishment. One also should not think that one's past good deeds make one a good person forever. Good deeds need continuing reinforcement. The knowledge that everything we humans do is somehow of cosmic importance and subject to Heavenly scrutiny — again, independent of reward and punishment — is an important aid and support to strengthen our good intentions and actions.

Judaism always gives practical expression to abstract ideas. The ages-old Jewish custom of males covering their head — wearing a *yarmulke,* or *kippah* — is meant to convey a constant reminder of the awe of Heaven, that there is Someone above us. By prodding us to think of what is above us, it makes the great abstract teaching of awe of Heaven real to us here on earth — literally on top of our minds. This idea of maintaining Heavenly awe is repeated constantly throughout the book of Avos. It is the pillar that supports all Jewish behavior and attitudes.

יוֹסֵי בֶּן יוֹעֶזֶר . . . וְיוֹסֵי בֶּן יוֹחָנָן
Yose ben Yoezer . . . and Yose ben Yochanan

Mishnah 4 ANTIGONOS TRANSMITTED THE TRADITION OF TORAH TO these two great men. They are the first of the *Zugos* — the "Pairs" — who led the nation during the transitional period starting from the founders of the Second Commonwealth, continuing through the Hasmoneans, and ending with the rise of the early *Tannaim* and the Roman domination over Judea and the Jews. Jewish leadership during this time was

servants who serve the master not for the sake of receiving a reward; and let the awe of Heaven be upon you.

4. Yose ben Yoezer, leader of Tz'redah, and Yose ben Yochanan, leader of Jerusalem, received the tradition from them.

---

concentrated in the offices of the High Priest and the heads of the Sanhedrin. The *Zugos*, the Pairs, were the two main leaders of the Sanhedrin, one man serving as *Nasi* (the executive authority) and the other as *Av Beis Din* (the judicial, procedural head of the court). The period of the *Zugos* extended for more than two centuries, and this system of Sanhedrin leadership provided an alternative government, to the absence of Jewish temporal authority, so to speak, for Jewish society in a very uncertain and turbulent period. Their main task was the continued transmission of Torah from Sinai to later generations and the creation of students and scholars to accomplish this. The two "Yoses" of this mishnah are the prototypes for all the later *Zugos*. They were people of integrity, wisdom, faith, and self-sacrifice. Because of their efforts and accomplishments, the great basic works of Judaism, Bible, Mishnah and Talmud survive and prosper until our very day.

❦ ❦ ❦

Yose ben Yoezer was martyred by the Greeks for teaching Torah to his students. The Midrash tells us that Yose had a nephew, Yakim Ish Tzroros, who became Hellenized and completely assimilated. Yakim was riding his horse on the Sabbath when he saw his uncle being taken out for execution, the gallows carried before him. Yakim mocked his uncle, saying, "Look at the fine horse that my master (the Greeks) gives me to ride, and look at the horse your master (the God of Israel) forces you to ride!"

Yose replied: "If the Lord rewards those who provoke Him (such as you) then how much more will He reward those who do His will."

"But who does His will more than you [yet look at your end]!" the nephew challenged. "If such is the end [in this world] for those who do His will," the uncle retorted, "then what will be the [ultimate] end for those who provoke Him?" Yose's calm and assured, yet pointed, words penetrated Yakim "like venom from a serpent." Yakim repented and died from the trauma caused to his spirit — and preceded his great uncle into Paradise and the World to Come.

❦ ❦ ❦

Other wayward nephews

It is interesting that there are a number of stories in the Talmud regarding wayward nephews and pious uncles. Perhaps the most famous one concerns Rabban Yochanan ben Zakkai, the preeminent sage and leader of the Jewish people at the time of the Second Temple's destruction, and his nephew,

א/ד

יוֹסֵי בֶּן יוֹעֶזֶר אִישׁ צְרֵדָה אוֹמֵר: יְהִי בֵיתְךָ בֵּית וַעַד לַחֲכָמִים, וֶהֱוֵי מִתְאַבֵּק בַּעֲפַר רַגְלֵיהֶם, וֶהֱוֵי

Abba Sikra, the head of the Jewish outlaws who were instrumental in the rebellion against Rome and in the eventual destruction of the Temple and the Jewish Commonwealth. Rabban Yochanan asked for a secret meeting with Abba Sikra, and tried to convince him that the rebellion was causing fatal harm to the Jewish people and was doomed to failure. Rabban Yochanan wanted Abba Sikra's help in leaving Jerusalem to meet with Vespasian, the Roman general who was besieging the city.

The nephew, feeling unable to extricate himself from a following that had become suicidal and murderous toward their own brethren, advised Rabbi Yochanan ben Zakkai to smuggle himself, in a coffin, out of the besieged city of Jerusalem. Rabbi Yochanan successfully arrived at the camp of Vespasian and convinced the Roman conqueror to grant him wishes that eventually guaranteed Jewish survival throughout the long exile that was then about to begin.

In modern Jewish history as well, the sixth Lubavitcher Rebbe, Rabbi Yosef Yitzchak Schneerson, was arrested during Stalin's reign of terror by his nephew, also a Schneerson, who was a captain in the Soviet police. It seems that the "old uncle" is always wrong and impedes progress — until eventually the "wise" nephew is taught differently by life experience and events.

❦ ❦ ❦

The first dispute: Yose ben Yoezer and his compatriot, Yose ben Yochanan, figure in the first recorded halachic dispute in Talmudic times. Apparently, the disruption in Jewish life caused by the arrival of Greek rule in Israel contributed to a lack of clarity regarding some ritual practices. (Perhaps the death of Shimon HaTzaddik and the conflicts regarding the strange new Temple of Chonyo in Egypt* contributed as well.) In any case, this first disagreement concerned a detail of a Temple-related issue — whether the required leaning with both hands on the sacrificial animal should be done on *Yom Tov*, a festival, or whether it must be done beforehand (because of the rabbinical decree against putting one's full weight on an animal on *Yom Tov*). From this time forward, numerous disagreements

---

* The Temple of Chonyo: One of Shimon HaTzaddik's direct descendants, either a son or grandson, or perhaps even a great-grandson, was denied the dynastic succession to the High Priesthood in Jerusalem. Piqued and angry, this man, named Chonyo, left the Land of Israel for Alexandria, and near there built an alternative temple to the one in Jerusalem. His temple was named after him, and he served as its founding high priest. Though the Temple of Chonyo had none of the holiness of the Temple in Jerusalem, it mimicked exactly and carefully the sacrificial service of the Jerusalem Temple, and had a considerable popular following. Chonyo's Egyptian temple lasted several centuries, much to the chagrin and disapproval of the Jerusalem rabbis and the other descendants of Shimon HaTzaddik.

1/4 Yose ben Yoezer, leader of Tz'redah, says: Let your house be a meeting place for sages; sit in the dust of their feet;

---

regarding halachic matters would dot the pages of the Mishnah and Talmud.

יְהִי בֵיתְךָ בֵּית וַעַד לַחֲכָמִים
Let your house be a meeting place for sages

ONE'S HOUSE SHOULD BE A GATHERING PLACE FOR WISE SCHOLARS. THE rabbis have taught us that even the שִׂיחַת חוּלִין, the *ordinary, mundane conversation* of scholars, requires study and attention. Having people of intellect and Torah scholarship as guests in one's home serves as an example for those living there. Such a guest becomes an inspiration and role model, an influence that lasts long after the guest has departed.

One of the great advantages I had in life was serving as a rabbi in Miami Beach, Florida for more than eight years. During those years almost all the generation's great men of Israel visited Miami Beach at one time or another. My wife and I had the honor of hosting these men, and sometimes their wives and families as well, in our home. The impression they made on me, my wife, and, perhaps most importantly, upon our children — a lifelong impression — was remarkable, inspirational, and vastly educational. What actually takes place in one's home, and whom one's guests and friends are, tells the children a great deal about their parents and themselves. Adults are always anxious to choose their children's friends. Parents should also be very careful about whom they bring into their house as their own friends.

Not everyone is fortunate enough to be a rabbi in Miami Beach and have great scholars as guests. Yet there is a vicarious way to have honored guests in one's home on a permanent basis, and that is through books. Traditionally, books were always part of a Jewish home. Now, naturally, books are there for reading and study, but even if they are not used much, their mere presence on the shelves is of comfort and instruction. Books carry with them the spirit and presence of their authors, and therefore they are not necessarily the inanimate objects they would otherwise appear to be. Judaism always preached the lesson that "books should be members of your household." When they are, then one's home automatically becomes a gathering place for the wise.

וֶהֱוֵי מִתְאַבֵּק בַּעֲפַר רַגְלֵיהֶם
Sit in the dust of their feet

RESPECT FOR TEACHERS AND WISE PEOPLE IS A CARDINAL PRINCIPLE IN Jewish life. Therefore, the instruction to be willing to wallow "in the dust of their feet" refers to the respect due them. But it also points out the necessity for a true student to possess and practice the trait of humility. Personal arrogance is the greatest enemy of both teacher and student. The greatest teacher, Moses, was characterized as the humblest of all humans. The Talmud is replete with descriptions of students who wallowed in the dust of the feet of their teachers and thereby gained greatness and future leadership

שׁוֹתֶה בַצָּמָא אֶת דִּבְרֵיהֶם.

[ה] **יוֹסֵי** בֶּן יוֹחָנָן אִישׁ יְרוּשָׁלַיִם אוֹמֵר: יְהִי בֵיתְךָ פָּתוּחַ לָרְוָחָה, וְיִהְיוּ עֲנִיִּים בְּנֵי בֵיתֶךָ,

---

roles. The arrogant student gains little from the wise teachers; since he or she is so full of himself or herself, there is almost no space left where the teacher's wisdom can be absorbed.

Since our main learning years are during our youth, adolescence and early adulthood — the years when we "know the most" — Yose's admonition about humility is most relevant and important. In the course of this discussion on *Pirkei Avos,* I will return many times to this concept of respect for teachers, for tradition, and for belief in the truths transmitted to us by our grandparents, the wise people of Israel. The revisionist historians, the new theoreticians and the currently politically correct arbiters of a changing morality have no place in Yose ben Yoezer's worldview of Judaism and Jewish life.

וֶהֱוֵי שׁוֹתֶה בַצָּמָא אֶת דִּבְרֵיהֶם
And drink in their words thirstily

IT IS ONE THING TO DRINK WATER WHEN ONE IS PARCHED AND THIRSTY. It is quite another thing, and not nearly as pleasant, to drink that same cool water when one feels satiated and full. Torah is truly appreciated only when one thirsts for it. If one is convinced that one is "full" without Torah, then a true appreciation of Torah and its beauty becomes almost impossible. The rabbis of the Midrash taught that the Torah was given in the desert, for only someone who is wandering in the desert, lonely and thirsty and unable to rely any longer on other resources to save him from his thirst, will truly appreciate the life-giving waters of Torah. Torah must be "drunk with thirst" and then it will serve as the elixir of life to those who drink it. It should be noted that throughout the Bible, the Torah is metaphorically compared to water. Therefore, thirstily drinking water is certainly the apt metaphor for the love for and commitment to Torah, the basic essential of all Jewish life.

יוֹסֵי בֶּן יוֹחָנָן
Yose ben Yochanan

Mishnah 5 THIS "MAN OF JERUSALEM," TOGETHER WITH HIS COMPAtriot, Yose ben Yoezer, mentioned above, was considered an *Ish HaEshkolos* — a person who possessed all talents and widely varied strengths. One of the great hallmarks of the authors of Avos is their broad knowledge and interests, the varieties of their life experiences, professions and social standings, and their great abilities that spanned all fields of human life and endeavor. Torah and Israel were the focus of all their lives, but they were not narrow people. They lived at a time when most Jews were already in the Diaspora, especially in the major communities of Babylonia and Egypt. Diaspora Jews sometimes have a tendency to ignore the special holiness of the Land of Israel. Therefore, Yose ben Yoezer and Yose ben Yochanan

and drink in their words thirstily.

5. Yose ben Yochanan, man of Jerusalem, says: Let your house be open wide; treat the poor as members of your

---

sponsored the rabbinic ordinance requiring that people outside the geographical boundaries of the Land of Israel are considered to be ritually impure. This rabbinic decree reinforced the holiness of the Land in Jewish thought and practice.

יְהִי בֵיתְךָ פָּתוּחַ לָרְוָחָה
Let your house be open wide

WHILE YOSE BEN YOEZER PREACHED OPENING ONE'S HOME TO SCHOLARS, Yose ben Yochanan stated that one's house should be open to all who are in need. The word *lir'vachah* in this mishnah is usually understood as "wide open," in reference to the house's doors. However, Rabbi Samson Raphael Hirsch states that the word *lir'vachah* rather describes the ultimate purpose of the home. It should be a home that offers succor and aid to all who need it. Hospitality, an open and welcoming home, is a Jewish inheritance from our father Abraham.

Yet, we must again stress, as in everything in Jewish life and Torah, that balance is necessary. Houses that are completely devoted to guests DO so at the expense of the children and other family members. In gentile culture, the familiar maxim "charity begins at home" is usually used in an exclusionary way, i.e., one should concentrate on one's own needs, and not give to outsiders. In the Torah perspective of our mishnah, the maxim has a double meaning: that an open home is the surest sign of charity and goodwill, and that our own home and family nevertheless should be the primary and justified recipients of our charity and goodness.

וְיִהְיוּ עֲנִיִּים בְּנֵי בֵיתֶךָ
Treat the poor as members of your household

THIS CAN BE SEEN AS A FURTHER EXTENSION OF YOSE BEN YOCHANAN'S original statement, regarding an open house and hospitality. Some guests are more honored and desirable in our eyes than others. The poor, therefore, should be seen as "members of your household," rather than as guests. Members of a household are accepted no matter their manners, appearance, or personality. The poor usually will not necessarily meet the standard we would like of being "guests" in our homes, so Yose ben Yochanan bids us to see them as family members. Such a view will dispel resentment and avoid any subsequent feelings of guilt caused by that almost instinctive reaction.

❦ ❦ ❦

Poorest of all

The poor are not only those poor monetarily. In my family's experience, now over a number of generations, there have always been lonely, discouraged and sometimes even depressed individuals who were well-to-do, but were certainly poor in spirit, hope, and human companionship; it may very well be that such people are the poorest of all. To make them members of

וְאַל תַּרְבֶּה שִׂיחָה עִם הָאִשָּׁה. בְּאִשְׁתּוֹ אָמְרוּ; קַל וָחֹמֶר בְּאֵשֶׁת חֲבֵרוֹ. מִכַּאן אָמְרוּ חֲכָמִים: כָּל הַמַּרְבֶּה שִׂיחָה עִם הָאִשָּׁה – גּוֹרֵם רָעָה לְעַצְמוֹ, וּבוֹטֵל מִדִּבְרֵי תוֹרָה, וְסוֹפוֹ יוֹרֵשׁ גֵּיהִנֹּם.

[ו] **יְהוֹשֻׁעַ** בֶּן פְּרַחְיָה וְנִתַּאי הָאַרְבֵּלִי קִבְּלוּ מֵהֶם.

---

one's household is possibly the greatest act of human friendship and compassion. My mother-in-law, of blessed memory, never took a Sabbath afternoon nap during her years in Detroit — though she certainly could have benefited from one — because a lonely neighbor would visit her every Sabbath afternoon for hours of conversation, a cup of tea and a strong dose of human sympathy. I imagine that in today's world, this type of relationship is called therapy. My mother-in-law thought of it as living up to Yose ben Yochanan's teaching.

❦ ❦ ❦

וְאַל תַּרְבֶּה שִׂיחָה עִם הָאִשָּׁה
And do not converse excessively with a woman

THE TORAH HAS A REALISTIC VIEW OF THE RELATIONSHIP BETWEEN MEN and women. It never underestimates the problems that invariably arise if that nature is allowed free rein. In our current century, when the role and social status of women in Western society has changed so radically, the problems of the relationship between the sexes in the workplace, school and society, generally have become deep and complex, and often very troubling. This is especially true now since the social feminist revolution has been accompanied by a blatant encouragement of hedonism by the media, the entertainment industry and the avant-garde intellectuals who always know better than anyone else what is really good for society. Without inhibitions, controls, and attitudinal commitment to probity and morality, the urges of human nature can turn very, very sour. That nature becomes the very *Gehinnom/* hell that is referred to in the concluding words of this mishnah.

Because of this very pragmatic understanding of life, the Torah bade us to drive defensively in matters of relationships between men and women. The laws of holy speech that are part of all general Jewish tradition are opposed to idle chatter and silly conversation. This attitude applies doubly so to conversation between men and women. The admonition of our mishnah is to abbreviate such conversations, to keep them from being frivolous or suggestive, to refrain from words that can in any way be misinterpreted, to take all precautions to avoid falling into any situation that is morally dangerous. Part of defensive driving is to sometimes refrain from insisting on your right of way, even when the law is on your side. It is said that the cemetery could be full of

household; and do not converse excessively with a woman. They said this even about one's own wife; surely it applies to another's wife. Consequently, the Sages said: Anyone who converses excessively with a woman causes evil to himself, neglects Torah study, and will eventually inherit *Gehinnom.*

6. Yehoshua ben Perachyah and Nittai of Arbel received the tradition from them.

---

gravestones engraved with the words, "He had the right of way!" Therefore, Jews should drive defensively in the relationship between men and women at all times. The advice against idle, unnecessary conversation applies even to the behavior between spouses themselves, in the privacy of their own home. Most marriages benefit more from comfortable periods of silence than from the constant chatter that often leads to words spoken in haste, anger or foolishness.

יְהוֹשֻׁעַ בֶּן פְּרַחְיָה
Yehoshua ben Perachyah

Mishnah 6 YEHOSHUA BEN PERACHYAH WAS THE LEADER OF THE Sanhedrin and of the Perushim, the so-called Pharisees, the preservers and guardians of the Oral Law and Rabbinic decrees, during the reign of the powerful Hasmonean king, Alexander Janneus (Yannai HaMelech). Originally a modest and unassuming private person, Yehoshua became one of the strongest leaders of the Perushim's opposition to the excesses of this volatile king. The Talmud relates to us his rueful comment about the corruption of personality caused by the exercise of power: "Originally, I wished to cast to the lions the person who proposed my name as head of the Sanhedrin. Now that I have been appointed to the post, if anyone would suggest I resign, I would pour boiling water over his head!" Realizing the possible corrupting influence of power is the first step in guarding oneself from being destroyed by it.

The rule of King Yannai was marked by a major revolt against him by the Torah scholars of Israel. The underlying cause of the civil war was the assumption by the Hasmonean rulers of both the High Priesthood and the monarchy. I have explained above the objections of the rabbis to this concentration of power, especially in such a strong and violent person as Yannai. Under the influence of the Sadducees, he accused the Perushim of treachery and disloyalty, and persecuted and killed many of them. The rabbis dispersed and fled, many to Egypt, among them Yehoshua ben Perachyah. According to a reference in *Yalkut Shimoni,* Yehoshua appears to have returned to Jerusalem and served as High Priest.

א/ו

יְהוֹשֻׁעַ בֶּן פְּרַחְיָה אוֹמֵר: עֲשֵׂה לְךָ רַב, וּקְנֵה לְךָ חָבֵר, וֶהֱוֵי דָן אֶת כָּל הָאָדָם לְכַף זְכוּת.

עֲשֵׂה לְךָ רַב ***Make for yourself a teacher***

THIS IS A STRANGE USAGE. HOW DOES ONE "MAKE" FOR ONESELF A RABBI, a teacher, a master? And, why "make"? Why not choose, appoint or search? It has taken me over forty years as a practicing rabbi to understand why Yehoshua chose the word *make* . The word implies an act of production, of creativity. I was always privileged to be in a pulpit situation where I served without a contract and with people who were able to accept my occasional lapses of judgment and disagreements with their opinions. These wonderful people *made* me their *rav.* There are no perfect people, no perfect leaders, not even perfect rabbis. Everyone has a fault. People, however, unwisely require — even demand — perfection from their leaders, especially from their spiritual leaders. One inadvertent, even innocent, comment or oversight on the part of a rabbi can sometimes spell the end of his tenure or career.

To be effective, a rabbi must have a community that is willing to make him their spiritual guide and leader, and that requires sophistication, tolerance of human faults, and, as mentioned above, creativity: the creative ability to see the whole picture and not just the narrow incident. Unfortunately, there are too few of us who are willing to make such a *rav* for themselves. In the Chassidic community, the *rebbe* remains the *rebbe.* This situation is also not without problems. But in the broader Jewish world, even in the Orthodox/ yeshivah world, this type of allegiance to a *rav* is not always present. A moral, knowledgeable, caring *rav* will be successful in a community that agrees to make him its spiritual leader. This naturally implies a drastic change in the relationship of rabbi and congregants from what is currently in vogue in many Jewish communities. The words of Yehoshua ben Perachyah, therefore, have special poignancy and urgency for our generations.

וּקְנֵה לְךָ חָבֵר ***Acquire for yourself a friend***

AVOS D'RABBI NASSAN EXPANDS UPON THIS LESSON OF YEHOSHUA BEN Perachyah, as follows: "How does one acquire a friend? A person should acquire a friend for himself by eating and drinking with him, by studying Torah and debating with him, by lodging with him, by sharing private thoughts with him — thoughts regarding Torah and life. And when they debate matters of Torah and importance, his friend will respond to him, and thus the bonds of friendship and truth will be strengthened." A friend is more than a social companion. A friend is someone with whom one can share even dark secrets and embarrassing situations. A friend is not a "yes-man," a sycophant, but rather someone with whom one shares truths, someone who criticizes and comments, supports and comforts. Friendship is always a two-way street. There must be an expenditure of time, material and emotion

1/6 Yehoshua ben Perachyah says: Make for yourself a teacher; acquire for yourself a friend; and judge everyone favorably.

---

in order to "acquire" such a friend. Friends cheaply bought are usually not friends at all.

וֶהֱוֵי דָן אֶת כָּל הָאָדָם לְכַף זְכוּת
And judge everyone favorably

WE ARE ALL PRONE TO MAKING QUICK JUDGMENTS ABOUT THE ACTIONS and motives of others, and most such judgments are less than charitable. Since we all have had difficult experiences with people whom we once trusted, or have been bruised by interpersonal relationships with others, we are unlikely easily to give people the benefit of the doubt thereafter. Such an attitude eventually punishes the suspicious person more than the one he suspects. It corrodes and hardens, and makes originally good people miserly, socially inhibited, and eventually cruel and evil. This idea will be expressed a number of times in Avos. The ability to "stand in another's shoes" is, by its very nature, almost an impossibility. Therefore, one must always be careful and considerate in judging the behavior and actions of others. Most of the time, things are not as simple as they appear.

אֶת כָּל הָאָדָם
Everyone

YEHOSHUA BEN PERACHYAH USES THE PHRASE אֶת כָּל הָאָדָם, WHICH IS usually understood to mean *everyone* or *all humankind*. In that sense, it means that all human beings are entitled initially to be given the benefit of the doubt. That is certainly true. However, the phrase can also be understood as meaning *the totality of the person*, which teaches us to judge others by the totality of their behavior and attitudes, not on the basis of an individual incident or remark. This is in line with the interpretation of the same phrase as it appears at the very end of *Koheles*/Ecclesiastes. There King Solomon sums up all of his wisdom by saying that one should fear the Lord, because this is the *totality of each person*. The rabbis interpreted the phrase to mean that a person is defined by his totality, not just by one good or bad act, but rather by his overall character.

In judging another person's behavior and actions, it is necessary to differentiate between a continuing pattern of behavior and an individual aberrational act. A good, friendly, productive and reliable person may nevertheless have an annoying personality trait or behavioral quirk. By judging the whole person, we are able to salvage the relationship and perhaps eventually correct the disturbing trait or habit as well. By dwelling on the "fault," we doom the relationship. This is true in employer-employee situations, teacher-student interaction and, most importantly and certainly, in marriage and family relationships. Many times, if one is able to judge the whole person, and not just focus on one disturbing feature, a solid relationship of empathy and help can be created.

[ז] **נִתַּאי** הָאַרְבֵּלִי אוֹמֵר: הַרְחֵק מִשָּׁכֵן רָע, וְאַל תִּתְחַבֵּר לָרָשָׁע, וְאַל תִּתְיָאֵשׁ מִן הַפֻּרְעָנוּת.

נִתַּאי הָאַרְבֵּלִי
Nittai of Arbel

Mishnah 7 THE TOWN OF ARBEL IN THE GALILEE SECTION OF NORTHern Israel gained historical fame through its role in the war of the Jews against the Romans in 64 CE. The town is at the foot of a sheer cliff overlooking the Sea of Galilee. In the cliff are numerous caves, which the Jews employed as defensive positions from which to shower arrows, spears, and missiles upon the Roman legions below. The Romans eventually captured the top of the cliff, had their soldiers hang down from ropes to reach the mouths of the caves, and then throw in flaming brands to flush out the Jewish defenders, all of whom were then eventually captured or killed. In the time of Nittai, two centuries earlier, Arbel was but a small and relatively unknown village.

הַרְחֵק מִשָּׁכֵן רָע
Distance yourself from a bad neighbor

EVERY DAY, MURDERS AND OTHER FORMS OF MAYHEM OCCUR THROUGHout the world because of bad neighbors. A bad neighbor is such a misfortune that Jews pray every morning to be spared from such a plague. Such a person is usually a spiteful, selfish, insensitive person who is unwilling to make any accommodation for the needs and wishes of others. There are neighbors, however, who may be very fine and nice people personally, but whose negative behavior and hedonistic influence on others is very detrimental. They are no less bad neighbors. Jews were always concerned about the environment — physical, social, religious — that surrounded them. Being a minority, they always sought to insulate themselves from the majority culture — paganism, Christianity, Islam, secularism, etc. — that threatened to engulf them. As such, the Jews created their own ghettos long before any were forced upon them by their persecutors, and have maintained them long after the official restrictions regarding their abodes have lapsed. As a minority within a minority, Orthodox Jews follow Nittai's instruction strictly and regularly. It is a necessary method for survival and spiritual self-preservation.

It is obvious that no hermetic seal can keep the bad neighbors permanently and completely away. Therefore, Nittai's advice is to stay as far away as possible from such bad neighbors. When one looks to rent or buy an apartment or house, one's prime concern should be to check out the neighbors. The co-op apartment building system, prevalent in New York and other areas, which requires the current residents' approval of potential new neighbors, is a good idea; but the new neighbor should be wise enough to check out the checker-outers as well. Rambam states that if one finds

7. Nittai of Arbel says: Distance yourself from a bad neighbor; do not associate with a wicked person; and do not despair of retribution.

---

oneself in an environment of bad neighbors, then one should be willing to "flee to the desert" to avoid this plague. In our current world, the media — newspapers, magazines, television, radio, etc. — are also our "neighbors," and dealing with them requires great and sophisticated judgment. At least as far as these are concerned, we have the option of deciding which to invite into our homes and make into our neighbors, and which not. A balanced approach, which is the Torah's way in all of life's issues, applies to all neighbors, both human and mechanical.

וְאַל תִּתְחַבֵּר לָרָשָׁע
Do not associate with a wicked person

NOT TO ASSOCIATE WITH EVIL PEOPLE IS AN ADMONITION THAT FLOWS almost automatically from Nittai's first statement about avoiding bad neighbors. It is really an expansion of the idea, for it includes in its purview of warning not only one's home environment, but one's business, professional, and communal contacts as well. The Sages of the Mishnah saw evil as being such a pervasive danger that joining evildoers, even for ostensibly positive purposes, was frowned upon.

וְאַל תִּתְיָאֵשׁ מִן הַפֻּרְעָנוּת
And do not despair of retribution

NITTAI LIVED AT A TIME OF GROWING GRECO/ROMAN DOMINATION OVER the world, including the Land of Israel. The Jewish people seemed puny in the face of the established Greek and rising Roman powers. The Jewish world itself was badly split between the Perushim, who defended the traditional Torah way of life, and the Sadducees, Hellenists and Essenes who represented different and radical departures from tradition. These deviant groups, especially the Sadducees, had power and influence; and in times of trouble they offered "new" solutions that appeared attractive to many Jews who were frightened by the cultural and political changes that surrounded them. Overwhelming troubles and seemingly insoluble problems sap one's confidence and faith. The tendency to give up under such circumstances is natural and understandable. Yet, tenacity is the main quality of Jewish survival. Therefore, the words of Nittai, recited at a particular moment of crisis in Jewish history, have resonated throughout the ages. The strength of the Jew is that he never gives up — not his faith, not his hopes, not his destiny. The past century is a testament to this quality of the Jewish people. We remember the Holocaust, and our hearts mourn because of it and its six million victims. But we were not defeated by it. We Jews are never allowed to give up on our future. It is a famous aphorism that states: *ye'ush* — giving up — is *shelo mi'daas,* not judicious or intelligently acceptable.

[ח] **יְהוּדָה** בֶּן טַבַּאי וְשִׁמְעוֹן בֶּן שָׁטַח קִבְּלוּ מֵהֶם. יְהוּדָה בֶּן טַבַּאי אוֹמֵר: אַל תַּעַשׂ עַצְמְךָ כְּעוֹרְכֵי הַדַּיָּנִין; וּכְשֶׁיִּהְיוּ בַּעֲלֵי הַדִּין עוֹמְדִים לְפָנֶיךָ, יִהְיוּ בְעֵינֶיךָ כִּרְשָׁעִים; וּכְשֶׁנִּפְטָרִים מִלְּפָנֶיךָ,

---

Eventual retribution is also part of Jewish belief. There really are no free lunches in this world, especially regarding wicked and evil behavior. As it has been said correctly, "The wheels of history grind very slowly, but they grind exceedingly fine." Though the mechanisms of Divine retribution are seldom visible or even dimly apparent to mortal humans, they are omnipresent — an idea that we will meet again in our study of Avos. One therefore should never despair about the seeming absence of Divine justice. Justice will be done. This fundamental belief of Judaism is also a matter of personal faith and optimism, the two survival ingredients of Jewish life throughout the ages.

יְהוּדָה בֶּן טַבַּאי וְשִׁמְעוֹן בֶּן שָׁטַח ***Yehudah ben Tabbai and Shimon ben Shatach***

Mishnah 8 IN EACH OF THE PAIRS OF LEADERS CITED ABOVE, THE first was the *Nasi* (the main political and religious leader of the Sanhedrin and the Jews residing in Israel) and the second the *Av Beis Din* (the head of the court). This pair, however, is the subject of debate in the Talmud. Perhaps the confusion can be attributed to the fact that these sages lived in one of the most turbulent times of the already always turbulent Second Temple Era. The Hasmonean Yannai, who was the brother-in-law of Shimon ben Shatach, persecuted the rabbis unmercifully, killing many and driving others into Egyptian exile. Yehudah ben Tabbai and Shimon ben Shatach were among those exiled to Alexandria. After Yannai reconciled himself with Shimon, the sage returned to Jerusalem and, after the king's death, became a leader in the government of his sister, Alexander's widow, Queen Shlomzion. Shimon sent a message to Yehudah to return to Jerusalem as well. It is not clear from the Talmudic sources whether Yehudah actually did return to Jerusalem and resume his post of leadership there.

Be that as it may, it was the steadfastness of this rabbinic leadership pair that preserved the tradition of Torah and eventually forced Yannai, on his deathbed, to agree that the Perushim were not the real threat to the existence of the Jewish state and his dynasty. Rather, he ruefully said, in a most memorable phrase, the threat to Jewish society lay "with the charlatans and hypocrites who behave as did the evil Zimri (the Jewish prince who publicly committed an immoral act), yet demand to be rewarded as if they were the pious Pinchas," who slew Zimri and thereby saved the nation from a plague (see *Numbers* 25:6-15).

8. Yehudah ben Tabbai and Shimon ben Shatach received the tradition from them.

Yehudah ben Tabbai says: [When serving as a judge] do not act as a lawyer; when the litigants stand before you, consider them both as guilty; but when they are dismissed from

---

אַל תַּעַשׂ עַצְמְךָ כְּעוֹרְכֵי הַדַּיָּנִין
[When serving as a judge] do not act as a lawyer

YEHUDAH BEN TABBAI DEALS HERE WITH THE NECESSITY FOR OBJECTIVITY and professionalism on the part of judges; they are judges and not lawyers for the litigants. (Being a member of the bar myself, I will refrain from making any remarks about lawyers and their tactics.) The task of a lawyer is to represent his client as ably and tenaciously as possible, within the legal limits of the judicial system. The task of a judge is far different. It is to do what is right, just, and equitable, again within the confines of the prevailing legal system. Judges should be passionate advocates, but only for justice and truth, not for either of the parties. They are therefore not to be intimidated by the rich and powerful, nor are they to become overly compassionate for the poor and weak. They must remain objective, cool-headed and fair to a fault. Only if judges maintain objectivity and dispassionate control over the proceedings, will the general public have confidence in the legal system. True, a judge is allowed to point out matters of fact and general knowledge to a litigant who obviously has overlooked them — *Open your mouth on behalf of the mute* (*Proverbs* 31:8) — but that is a far cry from actively supporting one of the litigants. To do so would be a form of judicial corruption.

וּכְשֶׁיִּהְיוּ בַּעֲלֵי הַדִּין עוֹמְדִים לְפָנֶיךָ, יִהְיוּ בְעֵינֶיךָ כִּרְשָׁעִים
When the litigants stand before you, consider them both as guilty

RARELY ARE JUDICIAL CASES COMPLETELY BLACK-AND-WHITE, CUT AND dried, obviously right or obviously wrong. Most legal cases contain great areas of fuzziness and grayness. Therefore, Yehudah ben Tabbai's advice to consider both parties potentially wrong is an example of hardheaded rabbinic recognition of the foibles of humans. The litigants are to be considered equally capable of wrongdoing, equally capable of cupidity, greed and falsehood. Considering the parties to be equally innocent is romantic and appealing; interpreting their actions as being morally equivalent, and attributing to them only goodness of intentions may be politically correct, but it is naive and does not reflect the real world. Above all else, the judge must be realistic, and see the litigants as imperfect humans who could not settle the dispute between themselves. In the overwhelming majority of instances, their very recourse to a court of law is in itself testimony to their human imperfection and faults. Yehudah ben Tabbai saw humans and their situations clearly, painfully, and realistically, as befits the great judge that he was and the great example for us that he remains. His advice still is as valid today as it ever was.

יִהְיוּ בְעֵינֶיךָ כְּזַכָּאִין, כְּשֶׁקִּבְּלוּ עֲלֵיהֶם אֶת הַדִּין.

[ט] **שִׁמְעוֹן** בֶּן שָׁטַח אוֹמֵר: הֱוֵי מַרְבֶּה לַחֲקוֹר אֶת הָעֵדִים; וֶהֱוֵי זָהִיר בִּדְבָרֶיךָ, שֶׁמָּא מִתּוֹכָם יִלְמְדוּ לְשַׁקֵּר.

וּכְשֶׁנִּפְטָרִים מִלְּפָנֶיךָ, יִהְיוּ בְעֵינֶיךָ כְּזַכָּאִין
But when they are dismissed from you, consider them both as innocent

WHEN THE CASE IS OVER, IT IS OVER; BUT ONLY IF THE PARTIES TO THE dispute accept and implement the court's decision. When they do so, they may then be judged as righteous people, who put the rule of Torah and the respect for God and society above their own personal feelings and pockets.

The tendency of a losing party to appeal every decision to a different court or a different set of rabbis is a very pernicious and dangerous one. It destroys the harmony of society, it cheapens the respect and reputation of rabbis and judges, it lends itself to subtle, if not blatant corruption, and it causes continuing disputes and ill feeling in the community.

❦ ❦ ❦

The loser is a winner

I was once a member of a panel of rabbinic judges that had to render a decision on a complicated financial transaction involving a very large sum of money. The litigants fought the matter tenaciously, almost ruthlessly. The case took almost a year to try. When the decision was finally rendered, it was for a judgment amounting to millions of dollars, and we judges expected an emotional outburst from the litigants. Instead, they both heard the decision and reacted calmly. The next day, instead of appealing to a different court of rabbis or even to a secular court of law, the loser went out and bought a life insurance policy in the amount of the judgment against him, and named the other party as the beneficiary, so that if he died before paying the judgment, the decision of the court nevertheless would be upheld. That loser was really the greatest winner I have ever seen in all my years of participation in rabbinic court matters. His behavior exemplifies what Yehudah ben Tabbai meant when he said that once the court's decision has been rendered, and the litigants have accepted the decision upon themselves, they should now be viewed as innocent.

❦ ❦ ❦

שִׁמְעוֹן בֶּן שָׁטַח
Shimon ben Shatach

Mishnah 9 SHIMON BEN SHATACH WAS THE LEADER OF THE PERUSHIM, the preservers and guardians of traditional Jewish life, and through his determined efforts, the supremacy of the Oral Law and Torah comportment in Jewish life was re-established. Although he was the brother-in-law of the Sadducee King Yannai, the king persecuted him along with the other leaders of the Perushim, and prevented the people from

you, consider them both as innocent, provided they have accepted the judgment.

9. Shimon ben Shatach says: Interrogate the witnesses extensively; be cautious with your words, lest they learn from them to lie.

---

freely practicing traditional Judaism. But when Shimon came to power under the reign of his sister, Queen Shlomzion, he was able to restore the proper Torah balance to Jewish life. He strengthened the terms of the *kesubah*, the Jewish marriage contract, granting the wife more rights and helping to prevent divorces on frivolous grounds; and he established compulsory childhood education, with the schools and teachers necessary to service the students. During his reign with his sister, there was unparalleled prosperity in Israel. For all of these reasons, he is remembered in Jewish history as one of the positive pivotal figures of Jewish life in Second Temple times.

❦ ❦ ❦

The Talmud tells us that Shimon ben Shatach once purchased a donkey from a local Arab. Upon examining the animal's saddlebag, he discovered a precious stone hidden inside. He immediately searched for the Arab who had sold him the animal and returned the valuable stone to him. The Arab exclaimed, "Blessed be the God of Shimon ben Shatach!" He instinctively realized that Shimon ben Shatach's character was formed by the Torah of God that he, as leader of the Perushim, represented. The simple Arab understood that true leadership requires practicing a moral code that transcends expediency and current correctness. And he recognized that Shimon represented the efficacy of that moral code.

❦ ❦ ❦

הֱוֵי מַרְבֶּה לַחֲקוֹר אֶת הָעֵדִים
Interrogate the witnesses extensively

A JUDGE MUST BE SUSPICIOUS OF EVERYONE. WITNESSES CAN BE MISTAKEN and sometimes even corrupt. The Talmud provides instances that permit a judge to disregard even uncontradicted testimony of witnesses, if he discerns it to be false, because the ultimate task of the judge is to render a verdict that is true and fair, and not merely one that meets the legal niceties. Nevertheless, the judge's right to ignore the witnesses is one that must be severely limited, for otherwise the whole system of Jewish law is compromised. Therefore, Shimon's admonition to closely interrogate the witnesses is well understood. In a Jewish court, the judges, not lawyers, examine the witnesses. By concentrating on serious examination of the witnesses and not merely perfunctorily accepting their words, the judge will gain a sense of the witnesses' rectitude and the integrity of their testimony.

❦ ❦ ❦

[י] שְׁמַעְיָה וְאַבְטַלְיוֹן קִבְּלוּ מֵהֶם.

A practical application

This idea is true in life generally; we often jump to conclusions and make snap judgments. Even when the weight of evidence seems to point in one direction regarding life's important decisions, it is clear that important matters require analysis, patience and a sense of correct intuition. Thousands of people fall prey to confidence men and pie-in-the-sky schemes every day. Matters must be judged rationally and examined closely. Numerous times per week I receive e-mail requests for my bank account number so that someone (he's always in Africa) can transfer hundreds of millions of dollars into my account and generously share the loot with me. I am told tens of people every day do actually send these crooks their private banking information and then are scammed out of their money. The facts and circumstances of any given choice in real life must be examined closely. Their statements must coincide with known reality and not with wishful thinking.

❧ ❧ ❧

וֶהֱוֵי זָהִיר בִּדְבָרֶיךָ
Be cautious with your words

ALL LAWYERS AND JUDGES KNOW ABOUT THE TECHNIQUE OF LEADING A witness in order to create the testimony and impression desired. The witness thereby loses his independence and becomes a mere tool — willingly or unwillingly — in the hands of others. No doubt, justice may suffer damage through such a system. In fact, the integrity of the witness system must be compromised by judges who coach witnesses, however subtly, to say what they wish to hear. The authority of the judge is always intimidating to those who appear before him. As such, the judge should be aware that even slight nuances in his facial expressions, word phrasing, and general demeanor may influence the testimony of witnesses. The cause of truth will not be served by such influence.

This warning against leading witnesses in their testimony applies to other areas of life as well. Parents, teachers, school principals, rabbis, corporate executives, government and political leaders, almost all who are seen as being in a position of authority, subtly influence the information they receive from those in their charge. A parent who is unprepared to hear disappointing news from a child will create a situation wherein the child will constantly lie to gain approval. The inflexible, discipline-at-all-costs teacher or principal will rarely if ever hear truth from students. The world is full of sycophants, but encouraging yes-men is counter-productive. Blessed is the person who is sufficiently open and generous of spirit to allow others to tell him the truth unafraid and unabashed. Being constantly careful with one's words and expressions can create such a blessed situation.

10. Shemayah and Avtalyon received the tradition from them.

שְׁמַעְיָה וְאַבְטַלְיוֹן
Shemayah and Avtalyon

Mishnah 10 THESE TWO GREAT JEWS WERE DESCENDANTS OF CONverts. The Talmud traces their ancestry as far back as the Assyrian emperor, Sancherev, who conquered the Northern Kingdom of Israel and laid siege to Jerusalem during the time of the prophet Isaiah and the reign of the righteous King Hezekiah. Ironically, from this unsavory lineage came two great men who advanced the cause of Torah and tradition among the people of Israel. After the death of Queen Shlomzion, her two sons Hyrcanos and Aristobolus fought over succession to the Hasmonean throne. The Sadducees regained power and the Jewish people were subjected to an ongoing political power struggle and were severely demoralized by the cynicism and corruption it brought. Shemayah and Avtalyon stood above the fray. They labored to imbue the nation with a love of Torah and an adherence to tradition and the Jewish vision that would transcend the bitterness, ignominy and destruction of the political power struggle. They saw past the politics of the moment and focused on creating an eternal people that would survive all historical events by its loyalty to the Torah and God of Israel.

Consistent with this purposeful and studied withdrawal from political life are the statements of both sages. There is no longer the political involvement that marked the reign of their mentor, Shimon ben Shatach. Instead, we find wise words of caution as to the seductions of power, the potential corruption of government, and the suffocation that comes from dependence upon others for financial support. The task of building the Jewish people from the inside, of giving it the strength to withstand the political upheavals that are about to overwhelm it, becomes the order of the day for Shemayah and Avtalyon.

Shemayah's mentor, Shimon ben Shatach, had been able to wield effective political power during the reign of Queen Shlomzion. Then, the central political authority and the leading halachic authorities worked in tandem, and the wise exercise of power was accomplished. In the midst of the anarchy of the queen's sons' civil war, however, and the malevolent presence of Rome hovering on the horizon, Shemayah advises withdrawal from the field of political power. In such violent circumstances, measured and fair use of power is a dream and almost never a reality. The rabbis always advised that when the voices of Torah are not obeyed or even heard in society, it is best for the followers of Torah to exercise withdrawal from the fray, and to build spirit and faith from the inside, in order to ensure the preservation of Torah and the people of Israel.

שְׁמַעְיָה אוֹמֵר: אֱהַב אֶת הַמְּלָאכָה, וּשְׂנָא אֶת הָרַבָּנוּת, וְאַל תִּתְוַדַּע לָרָשׁוּת.

[יא] **אַבְטַלְיוֹן** אוֹמֵר: חֲכָמִים, הִזָּהֲרוּ בְּדִבְרֵיכֶם,

---

שְׁמַעְיָה אוֹמֵר: אֱהַב אֶת הַמְּלָאכָה ***Shemayah says: Love work***

THE THREE PRINCIPLES EXPRESSED BY SHEMAYAH ARE MEANT TO BUILD the self-worth and independence of the individual. The admonition to love work is to allow one to appreciate the achievement of financial independence. One should love work, for it offers the opportunity to be independent of the gifts of others. The rabbis of Avos subscribed wholeheartedly to the wisdom of Solomon who stated, *One who despises gifts will live (Proverbs* 15:27). In our prayers of thanks after eating, we beseech the Lord to allow us never to need the gifts of humans, nor even to borrow from fellow Jews.

Unfortunately, there is a trend in society to denigrate work as somehow being degrading. Devoting oneself exclusively to Torah study is understandably a profound career, and in comparison other endeavors pale in significance. But when circumstances dictate that study can no longer be one's sole occupation, work in other fields is by no means a fault. Productive, gainful work should be a source of pride for the one who practices it.

וּשְׂנָא אֶת הָרַבָּנוּת ***Despise lordliness***

POWER OVER OTHERS IS A DEADLY ELIXIR. IF NOT EXERCISED PROPERLY, it can influence one to govern one's subjects in a way that will waver between coercive slavery and loose anarchy. Of course, leaders must exercise power, and without some sort of hierarchy of authority and responsibility, any societal structure will falter. Nevertheless, one who is empowered must realize that he or she must take all measures to avoid becoming power-hungry. The appetite for power must be despised. The best example of this is our teacher Moses, who was able to wield power effectively and fairly because of his extreme humility. "Would that all the people of God be prophets [and leaders]!" was his mantra. Thus, only those who truly recoil at the thought of wielding authority over others are the ones able to wield that power most fairly and justly.

וְאַל תִּתְוַדַּע לָרָשׁוּת ***And do not become overly familiar with the government***

KEEPING A LOW PROFILE IN REGARD TO THE GOVERNMENT IS AN ANCIENT Jewish practice, even when the government is Jewish, and certainly when it is non-Jewish and often biased and bigoted against its Jewish residents. By its very nature, government is less than fair; it is bureaucratic, intrusive, and expensive. In contrast, individual enterprise and initiative, self-reliance and avoidance of dependence upon others, should be the hallmarks of Jewish life. Thus, unnecessary contact with government is not wise or productive. Although Judaism is never in favor of anarchy, it certainly is

Shemayah says: Love work; despise lordliness; and do not become overly familiar with the government.

11. Avtalyon says: Scholars, be cautious with your words,

---

not a fan of big government.

Shemayah's statement can also be seen as a warning against provoking the government and unnecessarily disregarding its norms and rules. It is a call for modesty, self-effacement and caution in public affairs and in relations with the authorities. We live in a time of professional "activists." Shemayah prefers a much more modest, low-key, but more steady and consistent, approach. In this, he sees the way to true personal freedom and the preservation of Torah values in society, no matter which government is currently in power.

אַבְטַלְיוֹן אוֹמֵר
Avtalyon says

Mishnah 11 AVTALYON ALLUDES TO AN INCIDENT THAT CREATED great problems in the Jewish society of his time and of later generations as well. As mentioned above, the ongoing civil war in Israel, the ascendancy of the Sadducees, and their persecution of the great teachers of Torah, had forced many of the scholars to flee Judea. Many fled to Egypt, while others found refuge in Babylonia. Because of this, many students of Torah had been unable to find proper teachers or educational institutions and, moreover, were forced to flee to places of "bad waters," a euphemism for the foreign influences and accompanying difficulties inherent in adjusting to a new environment and strange society.

Every immigrant generation in Jewish history has had difficulty imparting Torah to its children and students. The revival of Torah always occurs two generations later, when the Jews are already settled and at home in their new country. This historical truth is borne out by the early Jewish experiences in Spain, France, Poland, and certainly in North America and the modern return to the Land of Israel. The dislocation of emigration is always inimical to Torah study and Jewish life and stability.

חֲכָמִים, הִזָּהֲרוּ בְּדִבְרֵיכֶם
Scholars, be cautious with your words

AVTALYON SPEAKS OF EXILE, THE CONCEPT THAT IS MENTIONED IN THE Torah regarding unintentional murder. The killer is exiled to a city of refuge, even though his action was purely unintentional. Well, teachers, too, can be figuratively guilty of accidental murder. Not teaching clearly, ambiguity of thoughts and words, not understanding the student and his or her needs, misrepresenting Torah values and tradition, emphasis on form and not on content, are also forms of murder. It is not for naught that the rabbis of old characterized Torah teachings as *dinei nefashos*, matters of life and death. Students who "drink the waters" of teachers who are ill-equipped by reason

שֶׁמָּא תָחוּבוּ חוֹבַת גָּלוּת וְתִגְלוּ לִמְקוֹם מַיִם הָרָעִים, וְיִשְׁתּוּ הַתַּלְמִידִים הַבָּאִים אַחֲרֵיכֶם וְיָמוּתוּ, וְנִמְצָא שֵׁם שָׁמַיִם מִתְחַלֵּל.

[יב] **הִלֵּל** וְשַׁמַּאי קִבְּלוּ מֵהֶם.

---

of temperament, lack of knowledge, poor character, lack of professionalism, or extremist views are ill served and are condemned, albeit unintentionally, to various types of spiritual death.

❦ ❦ ❦

Kosher education

As head of the Orthodox Union Kashrus Division, I had a conversation with a leading rosh yeshivah, who wondered how I accepted the responsibility of feeding the Jewish people. I replied that every decision in the OU regarding matters of kashrus was based upon firm halachic precedents. However, echoing a comment of Rabbi Yisrael of Salant, I asked him, did he not realize that being a rosh yeshivah was a far more responsible position, for errors of judgment or behavior in dealing with students have no halachic precedents or technical fall-back positions to rely upon for correction. (The Lord punished me for my impertinence, for after my stint at the OU, I headed a yeshivah for twenty years, and I then had ample opportunity to see the bitter correctness of my words.) There is no room for accidents or negligence in education.

❦ ❦ ❦

וְנִמְצָא שֵׁם שָׁמַיִם מִתְחַלֵּל
And consequently the Name of Heaven will be desecrated

THE CARDINAL SIN IN JUDAISM IS THE DESECRATION OF GOD'S NAME. People who have received an intensive Jewish education and then behave badly, and are held up to public scorn and disdain, thereby desecrate God's Name. Ill-taught students with skewed visions of Torah and Judaism create the breeding ground for such desecration. All forms of exile contribute to the danger of this sin becoming actualized. Therefore, the warning of Avtalyon has to be seen not only in the specific instances of exile that he delineates, but in the broadest understanding of the demands of Torah and Jewish life. "Be cautious with your words!" — avoid the trauma of exile — is the first line of defense against the desecration of God's Name.

הִלֵּל וְשַׁמַּאי
Hillel and Shammai

Mishnah 12 IN THE YEAR 30 BCE, THE ROMAN GRIP ON THE LAND OF Israel intensified, and King Herod ruled most of Judea on behalf of his Roman patrons. Herod was a wily, cunning, unscrupulous, violent, and thoroughly evil person. He murdered his own children, forced his wife into suicide, and ruled through terror and indiscriminate violence. He attempted to gain the favor of the Jews by massive construction projects,

for you may incur the penalty of exile and be banished to a place of evil waters [heresy]. The disciples who follow you there may drink and die, and consequently the Name of Heaven will be desecrated.

12. Hillel and Shammai received the tradition from them.

---

whose remnants still dot the landscape of Israel. His most ambitious work was the magnificent and opulent reconstruction of the Second Temple in Jerusalem. In spite of all these efforts, the Jewish population despised him. The legitimacy of his Jewishness was generally contested, stemming as it did from his Idumean descent and questionable conversion to Judaism during the early Hasmonean period.

In stark contrast to this pathological murderer and evildoer, two of the greatest spiritual leaders of Judaism — Hillel and Shammai — came to the forefront of Torah leadership at this time. They founded great schools of Torah learning that for centuries survived them — *Beis Hillel* and *Beis Shammai* — the Houses of Hillel and Shammai. Hillel and Shammai themselves disputed over only three matters of Jewish law. However, the schools they founded would dispute over more than three hundred during the next few centuries. Hillel and Shammai were the last of the *Zugos*, the Pairs of leaders who headed religious life in the Land of Israel at that time. Throughout the ages, many tens of thousands of Jews chose to name their children Hillel or Shammai. There are few, if any, Jews who ever named their sons Herod. Names that are preserved in Jewish families over the generations accurately reflect the vote of history upon the original personages who bore those names.

Here in our first encounter with Hillel in Avos we are already aware of his personality and view of life. "Be a student of Aaron!" Every person needs heroes, role models after whom to pattern his life. Platitudes and high-sounding phrases rarely inspire. People — living, breathing people — are much more capable of inspiring others. Therefore, Hillel gives us an example of the type of person we should emulate: Aaron. We should all want to be Aaron. A tall order, but at least we know what we are aiming for in our lives. Once we have fixed the picture of Aaron in our minds, we can then better examine his traits and instructions.

We will meet Hillel many more times in our journey through Avos. His wisdom and concise aphorisms occupy a special place in the Jewish soul and mind. We are all his students and disciples, for his view of Judaism and Jewish life has shaped Jewish thought and attitudes from the very time he first appeared on the scene. The truth of the matter is that we should all try to be like Hillel.

הִלֵּל אוֹמֵר: הֱוֵי מִתַּלְמִידָיו שֶׁל אַהֲרֹן, אוֹהֵב שָׁלוֹם וְרוֹדֵף שָׁלוֹם, אוֹהֵב אֶת הַבְּרִיּוֹת וּמְקָרְבָן לַתּוֹרָה.

[יג] **הוּא הָיָה אוֹמֵר:** נְגִיד שְׁמָא אֲבַד שְׁמֵהּ, וּדְלָא מוֹסִיף יָסֵף,

---

אוֹהֵב שָׁלוֹם וְרוֹדֵף שָׁלוֹם
Loving peace and pursuing peace

TO LOVE PEACE IS A DECEPTIVELY SIMPLE SOUNDING GOAL, BUT MERELY praising it will not bring it about. Hillel teaches that one must be proactive regarding peace. One must actively and diligently pursue it, not merely love it as an abstract goal. The Jewish people has not known peace for so many centuries, and the goal of peace and security has proven itself to be so especially elusive in recent times, that there are many who have despaired of it as ever being a reality for us or for the world. But Hillel bids us never to give up on the hope for and benefits of peace. Everyone can contribute to the cause. One who loves peace does not cause strife in families and communities. One who loves peace is always careful about spoken words and certainly about deeds that are potentially divisive.

Greater than a *lover* of peace, however, is the person who *pursues* peace. He attempts to heal rifts that have already occurred. Aaron was dedicated to bringing an end to quarrels. He would visit each party to a dispute and, never discussing blame or guilt, would explain that the other party wanted reconciliation. He thus lowered the flame of hard feelings and made such reconciliation truly possible. The Sages (*Shabbos* 127a) counted bringing peace between humans as one of the deeds that bring reward both in this world and in the hereafter. Strength and force may be necessary at times for Israel to survive in a hostile world, but the true goal of the Jewish people should always be peace and harmony among all. The prophet Zechariah (4:6) enjoins: *Not through army and not through strength, but through My spirit, said HASHEM.* Hillel's idea is not new; Jewish prophecy is immersed in the idea of peace and fairness. Rather he reinforces and strengthens one of the basic goals of all Jewish and human life — the pursuit of peace and harmony in personal, familial, and communal life. But how is this goal to be achieved? In his next words, Hillel provides us with his plan.

וּמְקָרְבָן לַתּוֹרָה
And bringing them closer to the Torah

BRINGING PEOPLE CLOSER TO TORAH IS A FACET OF THE GENERAL OBLIgation of *kiddush Hashem*, sanctifying God's Name in the world. Again, Hillel's method is to do so by example, rather than by other means that may superficially appear more forceful. Torah is an attraction, and should not be pictured as an enormous burden. People have to be "brought closer" to Torah. It is a gradual process. Overnight transformations are dramatic, but are often short-lived. A person of Hillel's character traits and moral behavior, of his concern for

Hillel says: Be among the disciples of Aaron, loving peace and pursuing peace, loving people and bringing them closer to the Torah.

13. He used to say: He who seeks renown loses his renown; he who does not increase [his Torah learning] decreases

---

all human beings, of his refusal to succumb to anger and frustration — such a person attracts people to come closer to Torah. As the High Priest, Aaron was a very visible public figure and was always on stage, so to speak. By using Aaron as his example of bringing people closer to Torah, Hillel informs us that we Jews are always on stage. We have the power to bring the world closer to Torah through our behavior. We can also have an opposite effect, driving people further from Torah. The choice is always ours.

נְגִיד שְׁמָא אֲבַד שְׁמֵהּ
He who seeks renown loses his renown

Mishnah 13 HILLEL WOULD SAY THAT THE PURSUIT OF HONOR OFTEN has the opposite result from the one intended. In line with his personal life-credo of self-effacement and modesty, Hillel teaches that by actively attempting to improve one's standing in the community, one risks losing one's original standing.

The early *Tannaim,* quoted in this first chapter of Avos, from Shimon HaTzaddik to the reign of Hillel and Shammai, bore no official titles before their names, not even "rabbi." They all went to great lengths to withstand the temptation of arrogance that accompanies high public office. In more recent times, whoever was called up to the Torah in the Kelm Talmud Torah, the great Lithuanian *mussar* yeshivah, was called up only by his given name. No titles were allowed for people striving for true humility. Hillel was the champion of humility, the successor to Ezra, and even Moses, in combining great leadership skills with true humility. His modesty and kindness — contrasted with King Herod's vanity, paranoia, and cruelty — placed the king in a most unfavorable light. Hillel, by being Hillel, effectively destroyed Herod's hold on the Jewish people.

Humility is not meekness or weakness. Because it is based on the realization of self-worth and self-identity, it is in fact the strongest of all possible character traits. But it is also based on the realization of human foibles and of how puny we are in the Creator's universe. Maimonides describes humility and the control of anger as the only two traits that should be pursued to the extreme. Hillel personified both.

וּדְלָא מוֹסִיף יָסֵף
He who does not increase [his Torah learning] decreases it

IT IS A WELL-KNOWN AXIOM IN COMMERCE THAT A BUSINESS THAT DOES not grow automatically recedes. That is true in spiritual life and Torah studies as well. The rabbis of the Talmud stated the matter in their usual pithy style: "If you forsake it (Torah) for one day, it will forsake you for two days." Only by constant growth and maturity in Torah and spirit can one reinforce the holy

וּדְלָא יַלִּיף קְטָלָא חַיָּב, וּדְאִשְׁתַּמַּשׁ בְּתָגָא חֲלָף.

[יד] **הוּא הָיָה אוֹמֵר:** אִם אֵין אֲנִי לִי, מִי לִי?

---

gains already achieved. Many a brilliant student has eventually fallen by the wayside because he was content with previous accomplishments. When I was a lawyer, the firm's senior partner told me that an empty desktop is the sign of going out of business. One must always have a new case, a new project, a new goal on one's desk. The only way to consolidate past achievements is to build on them. The rabbis taught us that a Jew must always ask: "When will my achievements approach those of my forefathers?" Pushing up and ahead is the challenge that confronts us at all stages of our life. Adding is the only way to avoid the pain of subtracting.

וּדְלָא יַלִּיף קְטָלָא חַיָּב ***He who refuses to teach [Torah] deserves death***

THE ROOT OF THE "JEWISH PROBLEM" IS IGNORANCE. IGNORANCE *ABOUT* Jews and ignorance *by* Jews. Large sections of the non-Jewish world, mostly out of ignorance — although there are substantial pockets of malice as well — believe horrendous things about Jews and Judaism. The blood libel of the Middle Ages has survived down to our time. Ignorance of the true facts *about* Jews and Judaism creates an environment that allows anti-Jewish feeling to thrive and be socially acceptable.

Just as true, the problems of assimilation and alienation within the Jewish world can be traced in the main to the abysmal ignorance of so many Jews regarding their own heritage and tradition. The failure to study, the lack of knowledge about the Torah and our tradition, dramatically increase the danger to the survival of Jews, physical and spiritual. Ignorance of the law is never an excuse in any court of justice in the world. It is not an acceptable excuse in the Jewish world either. Gentle, patient, tolerant Hillel makes the point succinctly and boldly. Ignorance, in Jewish life, is a matter of life and death. Therefore, one who has the ability to share his knowledge but chooses not to do so, commits a serious offense against Jewish survival.

❦ ❦ ❦

Hillel himself exemplifies great personal sacrifice for Torah study. The Talmud relates that he was a woodsman who spent half his meager daily earnings to pay the admittance fee to the Torah lectures of Shemayah and Avtalyon. One wintry day, not having enough money for the fee, he climbed to the roof of the study hall and lay on top of the skylight in order to hear the words of Torah being taught. It snowed, but Hillel would not budge. The rabbis in the study hall, noting that it was somehow darker than usual, looked up at the skylight and saw the outline of a half-frozen person; it was Hillel, covered with snow. They brought him down into the study hall and revived him. His future greatness was established that day due to the sense of sacrifice he exhibited in

it; he who refuses to teach [Torah] deserves death; and he who exploits the crown [of Torah] will fade away.

14. He used to say: If I am not for myself, who will be for me?

---

order to study Torah. Gaining Torah knowledge is an effort. But it is a lifesaving effort. Hillel used the same effort to teach his vast treasure of Torah knowledge.

❦ ❦ ❦

וּדְאִשְׁתַּמֵּשׁ בְּתָגָא חֳלָף
And he who exploits the crown [of Torah] will fade away

THE CROWN OF ROYALTY SYMBOLIZES TORAH. ABUSE OR MISUSE OF THAT crown eventually leads to its loss. Hillel forbids using Torah status for personal monetary gain, undeserved personal honor, or for other perks and special treatment. It will only diminish the honor of the person and, even worse, the honor of Torah itself in the public eye. I will have much more to say on this delicate subject in Chapter Four. Suffice it to say that exploitation of Torah for individual prominence, monetary fortune, or social achievement is considered to be supremely arrogant. It is also counterproductive to the true interests of the person himself, and places the Torah in a most unfavorable public light. The Torah is incompatible with arrogance. Eventually it departs from those who exhibit such arrogance. The great men of Torah wear its royal crown lightly.

אִם אֵין אֲנִי לִי, מִי לִי?
If I am not for myself, who will be for me

Mishnah 14 THIS STATEMENT BY HILLEL IS PROBABLY THE BEST known of his profound aphorisms. A person's primary duty is to oneself, one's personal welfare, and one's family. This is as true in spiritual life as in physical life. In essence, we alone are both the first and last lines of defense for ourselves in this world. Unfortunately, some parents rely totally on caregivers and schools to raise their children, on their spiritual leaders to somehow guarantee their own Torah growth and maturity, on others to bring them financial success. The Torah demands maximum effort on our part, before we can expect Divine aid. Heaven helps those who help themselves.

The original successors of Shemayah and Avtalyon were the B'nei Beseira, the "Sons of Beseira." One year, the day before Pesach was on the Sabbath and a question arose regarding the proper procedure for the Pesach offering. The B'nei Beseira did not know the law, but Hillel did. Recognizing that Hillel was more qualified than they, the B'nei Beseira stepped aside and appointed him as the new *Nasi*. When he later discussed the change of power with them, Hillel emphasized that their failure was caused by their not having "served Shemayah and Avtalyon, the two great men of the previous generation." The degree of their personal sacrifice for Torah accomplishment was somehow deemed insufficient to qualify them as the leaders of Israel. They were not sufficiently "for me."

וּכְשֶׁאֲנִי לְעַצְמִי, מָה אֲנִי? וְאִם לֹא עַכְשָׁו, אֵימָתָי?

[טו] שַׁמַּאי אוֹמֵר: עֲשֵׂה תוֹרָתְךָ קֶבַע, אֱמֹר

❦ ❦ ❦

The prerequisite

My great teacher and mentor, Rabbi Chaim Kreiswirth, told me that there was a great and recognized Torah scholar (whose name I will not mention) who did not show much scholastic promise in his early years. He nevertheless devoted himself to the study of Torah with great devotion and almost superhuman diligence. Finally, he somehow "broke through" and achieved great heights of Torah scholarship and universal acceptance. Rabbi Kreiswirth told me that only after this scholar had exerted himself to the utmost, did Heaven intercede and aid him in his studies. We expect much from Heaven and pray constantly for what is in essence a "free lunch." Heaven expects much from us as well. We must be for ourselves before we can expect others to be for us. The personal sacrifice Hillel demonstrated on the study hall roof exemplifies this lesson.

❦ ❦ ❦

וּכְשֶׁאֲנִי לְעַצְמִי, מָה אֲנִי?
And if I am for myself, what am I?

TORAH IS ALWAYS A MATTER OF BALANCE, OF MODERATION, OF DISCOVERing the golden mean in all areas of life (except, as mentioned above, in the areas of humility and controlling anger). I must be for myself, for otherwise no one will be for me; but I am not allowed to be for myself exclusively. The Torah imposes responsibilities to others. Family, friends, work and career, communal organizations, the Jewish people generally, in fact humanity as a whole, are all parts of my concern. Closing oneself off from the legitimate concerns and needs of others is not sanctioned by the Torah's value system. Thus the task in life is to arrive at a formula that adequately balances "I must be for myself" with "I must not be only for myself."

This formula will influence how we spend our time and money, and how and where we expend our talents and efforts. Eating dinner nightly with the family, helping the children with their homework, attending the synagogue meetings or the organizational fund-raising dinners, all conflict with "being for myself." Yet such matters have their place in our lives and should not be totally ignored. Finding the proper place to draw this line and constantly fine-tuning it is the stuff of life. Hillel's words emphasize the delicate nature of our balance scale of life. It may very well be that in doing for others we will discover that we have really done a great deal for ourselves.

וְאִם לֹא עַכְשָׁו, אֵימָתָי?
And if not now, when?

PROCRASTINATION IS THE ENEMY OF HUMAN ACCOMPLISHMENT, AN IDEA we will meet many times in Avos. One of the traits in Rabbi Pinchas ben Yair's famous outline of achieving holiness is *zerizus*, alacrity, enthusiasm, and

And if I am for myself, what am I? And if not now, when?

15. Shammai says: Make your Torah [study] a fixed practice;

---

industry in performing deeds in life. *Now* is the time to do things; later is never the same. The noteworthy aphorism of Rabbi Avraham ibn Ezra states, "The past is gone, the future has not yet arrived, and the present is as fleeting as the blink of an eye." Therefore, if not now, then when?

Common wisdom states that if one wants a task accomplished, it should be assigned to a busy person. A busy person does things now, not tomorrow. The habit of procrastination is foreign to Jewish thought. The masters of *mussar* compiled a list of things that could be learned from a baby. Foremost on that list was "always be busy." We undoubtedly need time for ourselves, for rest and leisure and unwinding. But delaying and procrastinating are harmful traits if practiced regularly. *Now* is usually the most appropriate time for completing tasks and beginning new projects.

שַׁמַּאי
Shammai

Mishnah 15 THE GREAT SHAMMAI IS A COMPLETELY DIFFERENT PERsonality from his compatriot Hillel. The Talmud describes how he would not have tolerance or patience for those he considered fools or insincere, especially if they were proposing to convert to Judaism. He was a superb teacher and scholar, a charismatic leader who inspired great self-sacrifice in his followers and promoted a study method that prized intellectual sharpness, brilliance of thought, and constant creativity.

Although in the vast majority of halachic matters, the Talmud gives preference to the rulings of *Beis Hillel*, the Academy of Hillel, *Beis Shammai* prevail in many cases, especially in instances when "they laid down their lives" for the correctness and implementation of their decisions. Tenacity of purpose, intellectual acuity, and uncompromising honesty (which many times can be misinterpreted by others as unfriendliness) were the personal hallmarks of Shammai, and they are the traits he transmitted to his students and followers, the House of Shammai.

עֲשֵׂה תוֹרָתְךָ קֶבַע
Make your Torah [study] a fixed practice

HERE AGAIN, THE ISSUE OF PRIORITIES IN LIFE IS RAISED. WHAT IS TO BE *keva*, steady, regular, permanent practice, and what is to be *arai*, occasional, temporary, subject to change or omission? The main priority in the life of a Jew must be the Torah — its study, its value system, its lifetyle, its domination of Jewish life and thought. If it is treated as a side matter and not as the centerpiece of Jewish existence, it becomes weak and eventually loses its influence and effect upon us. Daily times for Torah study, the application of Torah values in the home and the marketplace, the respect for its absolutes

מְעַט וַעֲשֵׂה הַרְבֵּה, וֶהֱוֵי מְקַבֵּל אֶת כָּל הָאָדָם בְּסֵבֶר פָּנִים יָפוֹת.

[טז] רַבָּן גַּמְלִיאֵל הָיָה אוֹמֵר: עֲשֵׂה לְךָ רַב,

---

in judging morality, the centrality of a Torah way of life in raising children, are all part of Shammai's definition of *keva.*

The Talmud tells us that Shammai brought his grandson, even as an infant, into his *succah.* The key to a life of achievement and worth is the ability to identify what should be central in a person's life and what is peripheral. People flounder if they have no anchor of direction and purpose. The word *keva* denotes a permanence of place. Shammai uses it to impart a permanence of direction and goal in life.

אֱמֹר מְעַט וַעֲשֵׂה הַרְבֵּה
Say little and do much

SHAMMAI WOULD NOT HAVE BEEN A SUCCESSFUL POLITICIAN IN TODAY'S world. "Say little and do much" is precious wisdom, but, unfortunately, it is usually honored only in the breach. Theodore Roosevelt caught the gist of this message when he famously advised America to "speak softly and carry a big stick." Promise little, never boast, speak softly but do great things and have very high goals for one's self, is the advice of Shammai. We will find in studying this work that using words sparingly is a constant recommendation of the rabbis whose teachings comprise Avos. Extravagant promises, demagogic slogans and loose tongues always unleash false and unrealizable expectations that inevitably lead to disappointment, frustration and even violence. Shammai is the spiritual father, though not the actual author, of the well-known phrase, "actions speak louder than words." The impression of Shammai as being taciturn is not a criticism of this great man. Rather, it is a description of the personal fulfillment of his own advice to say little while doing much.

וֶהֱוֵי מְקַבֵּל אֶת כָּל הָאָדָם בְּסֵבֶר פָּנִים יָפוֹת
And receive everyone with a cheerful face

GREETING ALL HUMAN BEINGS IN A FRIENDLY FASHION LUBRICATES THE wheels of social interaction in our world. Rabbi Yisrael Salanter, the 19th-century founder of the *Mussar* movement of ethical behavior, once was snubbed by another rabbi. The rabbi's companion apologized for the unfriendly demeanor, explaining that the gentleman was greatly troubled by a personal problem that had just arisen. Rabbi Yisrael gently responded, "Why must I be the victim of his personal problems?" The Chazon Ish, the great sage of Bnei Brak, put it this way: One's heart is a private domain, and one's face is a public domain.

The Talmud relates to us that the great rabbis of Israel always greeted other people first, and in a friendly fashion, whether they were Jewish or not.

say little and do much; and receive everyone with a cheerful face.

16. Rabban Gamliel used to say: Accept a teacher upon your-

Needless to say, to pass by someone who greets you, without responding in a friendly manner, is not only boorish behavior, it is against Torah principles.

In the popular mind, Shammai is considered to have been harsh and unfriendly. His teaching in this mishnah — which is expressed as a primary leitmotif of his life — shows clearly how wrong this charge is. His apparent sternness of character was not indicative of his personality, rather it was a principled effort to preserve the Torah way of life among his fellow Jews, in a very difficult time and environment. In any event, we are all bidden to be the disciples of our father Abraham, and to be friendly, courteous and hospitable to all people we meet on our road of life. Shammai's statement reinforces this cardinal principle of Judaism.

רַבָּן גַּמְלִיאֵל ***Rabban Gamliel***

Mishnah 16 THERE ARE THREE RABBAN GAMLIELS IN THIS ERA. THE one in our mishnah is Rabban Gamliel the Elder, the grandson of Hillel and the *Nasi* (prince, head) of the Sanhedrin. He consolidated the dynasty of Jewish leadership that his grandfather founded. A man of strong leadership qualities and great scholarship, who did not share the role of leadership with another partner, he is described as the counterforce to the dissolution of the Jewish state that surrounded him. He lived at the beginning of the Common Era, at the time when Jewish society splintered into many differing groups, some of them even criminal and violent in nature. He tried to hold the nucleus of Jewish life together, while the centrifugal forces of Rome, of Herod and his successors, the Jewish Zealots, the Sadducees, and the bandit Sicarii (dagger-holders) all pulled away. These groups, warring with the rabbis and the Perushim and among themselves, occasioned the comment of the Talmud that it was baseless hatred between the different Jewish factions that led to the destruction of the Second Temple.

עֲשֵׂה לְךָ רַב ***Accept a teacher upon yourself***

ACCEPT A MENTOR, A TEACHER, A GUIDE, AND YOU WILL BE SPARED FROM doubts over what course you should follow. Many of the ideas inherent in this statement have already been discussed in the comments to mishnah 6, above, but Rabban Gamliel adds a nuance. Although the simple context of his counsel instructs us to make use of a mentor to help resolve doubts in matters of halachah, the deeper meaning of Rabban Gamliel's words carries over to all avenues of life. Everyone always needs someone. And if one can have that someone not only as a friend, but also as a guide and an inspiration, a pathfinder and wise person, even a hero, then one is most fortunate.

וְהִסְתַּלֵּק מִן הַסָּפֵק, וְאַל תַּרְבֶּה לְעַשֵּׂר אֻמָּדוֹת.

[יז] **שִׁמְעוֹן** בְּנוֹ אוֹמֵר: כָּל יָמַי גָּדַלְתִּי בֵּין הַחֲכָמִים, וְלֹא מָצָאתִי לְגוּף טוֹב אֶלָּא שְׁתִיקָה. וְלֹא הַמִּדְרָשׁ הוּא הָעִקָּר, אֶלָּא הַמַּעֲשֶׂה.

The basis of the chain of Jewish tradition is formed by each link connecting to such a mentor and master. The word used in yeshivos for a teacher of Torah is *rebbi*. Literally, that word means *my master*. It implies that one has found a guide for life and its problems, someone to rely on and to respect and obey. To this very day, more than three millennia after his death, Moshe is called *Rabbeinu*, our teacher and mentor and hero. The Chassidic world, the yeshivah society, the environment of our schools and synagogues, are all based on finding a mentor for ourselves. When successful, such a search helps minimize doubtful situations in our lives.

No person is perfect and no one is infallible. The Torah purposely emphasizes the mistakes (certainly minor, by our standards) of Moses, to impress upon us the inevitability of some human error, especially for those who assume leadership or instructional roles. For this very reason, Rabban Gamliel states that one must "make" a master, a mentor, for one's self. As stated earlier in this chapter, anyone looking for the perfect hero, for the unblemished mentor, is doomed to disappointment. Therefore, one must "make" into one's *rebbi* the best person or teacher one can find, even when aware of that person's shortcomings. One should never ascribe perfection or infallibility to another human being. By doing so, one crosses the line of Jewish thought and tradition. It is wholly possible that my *rebbi* may be wrong in his predictions and his advice. He is not infallible. But he is a superior person who is giving me his best appraisal of the issue concerned, based on his knowledge, experience, and spiritual intuition. I cannot ask for more than that from any human being. As in marriage, most of the problems that exist between congregants and their rabbis, students and their teachers, children and their parents, stem from unreasonable expectations. The *rebbi*/rabbi must aim to be an angel of God. The people who deal with him should focus on his greatness, talent, scholarship, and fear of God, even though he is only human.

וְאַל תַּרְבֶּה לְעַשֵּׂר אֻמָּדוֹת ***And do not give excess tithes by estimating [instead of measuring]***

RABBAN GAMLIEL IS APPARENTLY REFERRING TO THE HALACHIC RULE that the various tithes ordained by the Torah require exactitude of amounts, and he advises us that estimating the amount to be given can cause serious halachic problems regarding the food from which the tithes are taken. This exactitude is not only needed to avoid shortchanging the tithe, but also to avoid giving more than necessary.

self, and remove yourself from uncertainty; and do not give excess tithes by estimating [instead of measuring].

17. Shimon his son says: All my days I have been raised among the Sages, and I found nothing better for the body than silence; not study, but practice is the main thing;

Estimating was once considered sufficient when the "new math" was in vogue in the 1960's and 1970's; but it is not advisable when balancing a checkbook or in dealing with atomic formulas. In life too, being exact is a necessary trait at times. Looseness with numbers, with time, with commitments, is always troublesome and even dangerous. Estimating and guessing at solutions to life's problems is rarely productive. True, one should never be a prisoner to exactitude (I shall resist telling any German/Swiss punctuality stories), but one should never disregard the trait completely. Again, the Torah rule of balance comes into practical play. Certainly in halachic matters, guesswork and estimation should never be employed. If one has a *rav* /*rebbi*/ rabbi/adviser, then the need to estimate things can be greatly reduced.

שִׁמְעוֹן בְּנוֹ
Shimon his son

Mishnah 17 SHIMON, THE SON OF RABBAN GAMLIEL THE ELDER AND the great-grandson of Hillel, led the Jews just prior to the destruction of the Second Temple. At a time of great noise in the Jewish world, he repeated the wise aphorism that silence is truly golden. He was privileged to have been raised in the house of his father, the great *Nasi* of Israel, and thus saw all the wise men of the previous generation congregated in his father's house. The great attribute he derived from that experience was the value of silence, of not saying the extra sentence, the unnecessary word. He mentions that this attribute is most beneficial, not only to the spirit of the person but to the *guf*, the person's body. Measured speech is a health-giving trait. It lowers one's blood pressure, wards off anger and frustration, and allows for a sense of serenity even in the midst of the turbulence of difficult times.

An additional thought is that while being raised in his formative years in the company of wise men, Shimon never heard them emphasizing the *guf*, the body. They did not dwell upon praises of men's physiques or earthy matters. Shimon never heard discussions of hedonism and desire from the wise men of Israel. He heard only worthy and serious discussions about important matters of life and Torah. Thus he was spared the inanity of the ordinary conversations of many people. And he was eternally grateful for that favor.

וְלֹא הַמִּדְרָשׁ הוּא הָעִקָּר, אֶלָּא הַמַּעֲשֶׂה
Not study, but practice is the main thing

THIS STATEMENT BY THE GREAT-GRANDSON OF HILLEL IS IN ESSENCE a reiteration of one of Shammai's ideas, recorded above in mishnah 14, to say little and do much. A person is ultimately judged not by his knowledge and intellectual prowess but by his deeds, his actions and behavior. In fact,

וְכָל הַמַּרְבֶּה דְבָרִים מֵבִיא חֵטְא.

[יח] רַבָּן שִׁמְעוֹן בֶּן גַּמְלִיאֵל אוֹמֵר: עַל שְׁלֹשָׁה דְבָרִים הָעוֹלָם קַיָּם — עַל הַדִּין וְעַל הָאֱמֶת וְעַל הַשָּׁלוֹם, שֶׁנֶּאֱמַר: „אֱמֶת וּמִשְׁפַּט שָׁלוֹם שִׁפְטוּ בְּשַׁעֲרֵיכֶם.״

---

the more knowledge one possesses, the more one is obligated to scale greater heights of action and behavior. There are many people who were "A" students in school yet somehow turned out to be dismal failures in life. Similarly, there are many who are knowledgeable in Jewish studies, but practice no Judaism. The challenge of Torah is to live like a Jew, not merely to possess the scholarship to reveal what color cloak Rashi wore.

Studying Talmud is a fascinating intellectual exercise, but it must be translated into moral and ethical behavior in the home, the marketplace, and the community. Otherwise, instead of being the elixir of life, the knowledge of Judaism becomes a detriment — a poison, in the words of the Talmud itself — to the owner of that knowledge. A boastful scholar once told the great Rabbi Menachem Mendel of Kotzk, "Rebbi, I have gone through half the Talmud!" The Kotzker Rebbe answered, "But how much of the Talmud has gone through you?" It is not only what you know that counts; what ultimately decides your worth in life is what you do with your knowledge.

וְכָל הַמַּרְבֶּה דְבָרִים מֵבִיא חֵטְא
The one who talks excessively brings on sin

IT IS USUALLY THE EXTRA WORD THAT GETS US INTO TROUBLE. TRIAL lawyers prepare their witnesses to answer only the specific question posed to them, and not to volunteer any extra information. In speech, as in most areas of life, too much is a detriment. A great public speech of 20 minutes is destroyed when it is made into a 30-minute oration. The rabbis phrased it thusly: כָּל הַמּוֹסִיף גּוֹרֵעַ, *All who add too much really subtract*. This is especially true in private, personal speech. Once stated, the words can never be retracted. They remain etched in our beings long after the incident or conversational basis is forgotten.

In mishnah 9 and again in mishnah 11 above, the rabbis warned of the dangers of uninhibited speech. Over thirty Scriptural and Rabbinic prohibitions can be transgresses through *lashon hara*, "bad" speech, such as slander, lies, gossip, etc. But there are other incalculable damages inherent in loose speech. Saying little contributes to being thought a wise man, said King Solomon. A fool prattles on, no matter what. I remember that a young man, a student of mine, began courting a certain girl, but was undecided as to whether to proceed further in the matter. As he discussed the issue with me,

the one who talks excessively brings on sin.

18. Rabban Shimon ben Gamliel says: The world endures on three things — justice, truth, and peace, as it is said: *You shall adjudicate the verdict of truth and peace at your gates* (*Zechariah* 8:16).

I asked what his hesitations were. He answered, "Rebbi, she is very quiet and soft-spoken. She doesn't talk much." I responded, "Grab her! Don't let her get away!" One can never be faulted for what was not said. Additional and unnecessary words always lead to sad complications.

רַבָּן שִׁמְעוֹן בֶּן גַּמְלִיאֵל ***Rabban Shimon ben Gamliel***

Mishnah 18 IN CONTRAST TO THE ABOVE MISHNAH, HERE THE GREAT sage is not introduced as Shimon, his [Rabban Gamliel's] son, but with the title of *Rabban*. Some explain that the previous mishnah was authored before his accession to power, whereas this mishnah was taught by him when he was already the *Nasi,* the Prince of Israel.

עַל שְׁלֹשָׁה דְבָרִים הָעוֹלָם קַיָּם ***The world endures on three things***

THIS MISHNAH IS THE BOOKEND, SO TO SPEAK, TO THE FIRST CHAPTER OF Avos. The second mishnah of the chapter dealt with the three pillars upon which the world has rested since creation — Torah Study, Godly Service, and Human Kindness; this mishnah teaches that although the world's creation was based on those three pillars, society cannot continue to survive unless those pillars are buttressed by Justice, Truth, and Peace. In essence, therefore, this mishnah reveals the attitudes and values that are the underpinnings of the behavior patterns taught in mishnah 2.

עַל הַדִּין ***Justice***

WITHOUT A SYSTEM OF JUSTICE, SO-CALLED PIETY BECOMES LAWLESS, violent and sinks into anarchy, but justice can be achieved only on the basis of law and a system that will decide and enforce just decisions. Thus, study and knowledge of Torah is essential for justice to function in Jewish society. The ignorant rarely can be just. Without Torah knowledge and rules, no Jewish society can really reach its goal of being a just society.

וְעַל הָאֱמֶת ***Truth***

GODLY SERVICE (MISHNAH 2) REQUIRES THE PRINCIPLE OF TRUTH. TRUTH is often vicious and painful; it is the only value not susceptible to compromise. Something that is 99 percent true is still tainted by one percent of falsehood; hence it is not true. In order to have influence in society, however, truth will have to be softened somehow, and that will be the task of peace, which I will shortly discuss. Nevertheless, in some areas of life truth must reign supreme. To be effective, Godly service — prayer and performance of *mitzvos* (commandments) — requires the striving for absolute truth and

❦ ❦ ❦

רַבִּי חֲנַנְיָא בֶּן עֲקַשְׁיָא אוֹמֵר: רָצָה הַקָּדוֹשׁ בָּרוּךְ הוּא לְזַכּוֹת אֶת יִשְׂרָאֵל, לְפִיכָךְ הִרְבָּה לָהֶם תּוֹרָה וּמִצְוֹת, שֶׁנֶּאֱמַר: „יהוה חָפֵץ לְמַעַן צִדְקוֹ, יַגְדִּיל תּוֹרָה וְיַאְדִּיר."

---

sincerity. That is what the Talmud means when it says, רַחֲמָנָא לִיבָּא בָּעֵי, *God wants the heart*. When praying — talking to Him, so to speak — there is no room for hypocrisy, false compliments, or exaggerations. Only the real truth will suffice. In performing *mitzvos*, sincerity is essential. Although the Talmud suggests that מִצְווֹת אֵינָן צְרִיכוֹת כַּוָּנָה, the performance of a commandment is valid even without totally concentrated intent, it is obvious that true and full Godly service requires intent, direction, and true sincerity. The rabbis have taught us that God's seal, so to speak, is truth. At least in dealing with the Almighty, we should try to make truth our seal as well.

But in relationships between people, truth many times destroys more than it heals. No one enjoys being told that his tie is truly hideous or that her dress is the wrong color for her complexion. Saying hard truths all the time to everyone under all circumstances creates enemies, bitterness, and eventually hatreds. We know that even the Torah advises tact in telling humans about certain things. The Lord Himself omitted telling Abraham that Sarah thought he was too old to be able to father a child. So, for the sake of peace, truth must be tempered, controlled, judiciously employed. Peace is an overriding factor in all of our lives. We need it at home, in the workplace, in society and among nations and different groups.

❧ ❧ ❧

Rabbi Chanania ben Akashia says: The Holy One, Blessed is He, wished to confer merit upon Israel; therefore He gave them Torah and *mitzvos* in abundance, as it is said: *HASHEM desired, for the sake of its [Israel's] righteousness, that the Torah be made great and glorious* (*Isaiah* 42:21).

וְעַל הַשָּׁלוֹם
Peace

PEACE WHICH IS MEANT TO CREATE HARMONY AND A SENSE OF ONENESS with others, is represented by proactive behavior — by *gemillus chassadim* (mishnah 2), acts of charity and kindness towards others. One of God's names is *Shalom*, Peace. The conclusion to all the sixty-three volumes of the Mishnah is the statement that the Lord found no other vessel that can contain blessings for human beings other than peace. In a great sense, all of the wisdom in Avos is directed toward only one goal — the attainment of peace, internal and external, spiritual and physical. In a society that is just in its relationships between people and strives to be true in its relationship with God, peace becomes an attainable objective.

It is interesting that the statement of Rabban Shimon ben Gamliel in this mishnah is based upon his advice in the previous mishnah, about how careful one must be with words. Loose talk and unnecessary words undermine the concepts of justice, truth, and peace. Silence is peaceful and soothing. Passionate and provocative speech can destroy any semblance of justice, truth, or peace. Ill-used words are the province and weapons of demagogues. Therefore, wise men are often silent.

פרק שני
CHAPTER TWO

כָּל יִשְׂרָאֵל יֵשׁ לָהֶם חֵלֶק לָעוֹלָם הַבָּא, שֶׁנֶּאֱמַר: ,,וְעַמֵּךְ כֻּלָּם צַדִּיקִים, לְעוֹלָם יִירְשׁוּ אָרֶץ, נֵצֶר מַטָּעַי, מַעֲשֵׂה יָדַי לְהִתְפָּאֵר.״

All Israel has a share in the World to Come, as it is said: *And your people are all righteous; they shall inherit the land forever; a branch of My plantings, My handiwork, in which to take pride* (Isaiah 60:21).

Chapter Two

Mishnah 1 THIS TITLE, WHICH MEANS *MY MASTER AND TEACHER*, IS the name bestowed by the Jewish people on Rabbi Yehudah HaNasi, [the "Prince"], who is also known as *Rabbeinu HaKadosh, our holy teacher and master*. The rabbis ascribed this latter title to him because of his great modesty and probity in all human and Godly affairs. They used the euphemism that "he never placed his hand below his waist" to describe his holy conduct. As the Prince, he was also the temporal leader of the nation and was a close personal friend of his great admirer, the Roman emperor Antoninus Pius.

רַבִּי
Rebbi

❦ ❦ ❦

Unholy "holiness"

Rabbi Meir Shapiro, the great Polish rabbi and Torah educator in the period between the two World Wars of the 20th century, was noted for his quick and incisive wit. He was the founder, builder, and rosh yeshivah of Yeshivah Chachmei Lublin, one of the outstanding pre-World War II Torah institutions in the world, and he traveled extensively to raise funds to erect its majestic building, which still stands. Rabbi Shapiro remarked that on his fund-raising forays he met many "holy" people who would not put their hand below their waist to reach into their pockets.

❦ ❦ ❦

What singles out Rabbi Yehudah HaNasi for particular honor and note in Jewish history is that he recognized the need to assemble and redact the teachings and rulings of the Oral Law in order that they not be forgotten, due to the ravages of persecution and exile. He had the courage to implement his decision to publish the corpus of the laws, which is known as the Mishnah. The core of the Mishnah is the collection of wisdom and Torah law details of the Oral Teaching — *Torah Sheb'al Peh* — given to Moses on Sinai.

The Oral Teaching, or Law, truly represents Judaism. Jewish continuity has been guaranteed by Israel's continual understanding of and building upon the Oral Law over the millennia. Though it has continually been attacked by groups of Jews — Sadducees, Karaites, German Reform, etc. — over the ages, it has successfully weathered such attacks while its detractors eventually disappeared from the Jewish scene, even though the process of extinction may have taken centuries. There is a lesson in this for our times as well.

The Oral Law, as the name implies, was meant to be transmitted orally, generation to generation, teacher to student, parent to child. Originally it was never meant to be a written book, for putting words on paper or parchment automatically freezes the subject and makes it less vital, flexible and creative.

1. Rebbi says: Which is the proper path that a person

Futhermore, the electricity of the teacher-student relationship cannot be captured on paper. Thus the rule was that the Written Torah was not to be taught orally, while the Oral Law was not to be written as a book or text for study.

This rule prevailed without exception during the time of the First Temple. The Second Temple was completed in 349 BCE (3412) but the difficulties in maintaining such a rule intensified. Because of the constant political turmoil, wars, and violence that marked that most difficult period, many of the rabbis began to keep private notes of the Oral Law and the decisions regarding its interpretation and application to new situations. These became notebooks, beginning with the one called Mishnah Rishonah (First Mishnah, dating back to the times of the *Zugos*, 3rd century BCE) until those of Rabbi Akiva and Rabbi Meir, of the 2nd century CE, two generations just preceding Rebbi.

Finally, Rabbi Yehudah HaNasi edited, reformulated, expanded, and organized those notebooks and the remaining oral teachings to produce the work called the Mishnah, in the form we have it today. He accomplished this massive task toward the end of the 2nd century CE. The Babylonian Talmud, the massive discussion of and commentary to the Mishnah, was completed in the 5th and 6th centuries CE. The Talmud remains the basis for all Torah scholarship to this day.

❦ ❦ ❦

Rebbi was a temporal leader of Jewish society as well. A fabulously wealthy person, he himself led a simple, almost ascetic life, which is why he is known simply as *Rabbeinu HaKadosh,* our holy teacher and master. He had influential friends in the hierarchy of Roman government and society and is recorded as being an adviser and confidant of the Roman emperor himself. His devotion to rebuilding Jewish society after the failure of the Bar Kochba rebellion and the persecutions of Jews and Judaism by Hadrian earlier in the 2nd century CE earned him a place in the eternal memory of the people of Israel. He is one of the great personages and heroes of all Jewish history.

אֵיזוֹ הִיא דֶרֶךְ יְשָׁרָה
Which is the proper path

REBBI POSES FOR US ONE OF THE BASIC QUESTIONS OF LIFE: WHAT IS THE right path in life? What is good living? What are the parameters that define successful living? How can a human being judge the correctness of his goals and achievements in life? Rebbi advises us to measure our lives by the standard of whether our deeds bring glory to the Name of God and win the approval of the hearts of our fellow human beings. Can we be proud of our behavior? The approval of God and also of one's fellow human beings is the true source of legitimate human pride and glory.

הָאָדָם? כָּל שֶׁהִיא תִפְאֶרֶת לְעֹשֶׂהָ וְתִפְאֶרֶת לוֹ מִן הָאָדָם. וֶהֱוֵי זָהִיר בְּמִצְוָה קַלָּה כְּבַחֲמוּרָה, שֶׁאֵין אַתָּה יוֹדֵעַ מַתַּן שְׂכָרָן שֶׁל מִצְוֹת. וֶהֱוֵי מְחַשֵּׁב הֶפְסֵד מִצְוָה כְּנֶגֶד שְׂכָרָהּ, וּשְׂכַר עֲבֵרָה כְּנֶגֶד הֶפְסֵדָהּ. הִסְתַּכֵּל

The sainted Rabbi Yisrael Meir HaKohen Kagan, known as the Chafetz Chaim, stated that before saying or doing anything, a person should ask himself, "What benefit will I have spiritually or physically from the words I am about to speak or the action I wish to perform?" Using such an approach, one is far less prone to be guilty of foolish or forbidden words or behavior. Rebbi's advice is reminiscent of the Biblical injunction, *And you shall be vindicated from Hashem and from Israel* (*Numbers* 32:22). One of my teachers paraphrased the matter thusly: "Behave in a manner in which both your grandparents and grandchildren will be proud of you."

וֶהֱוֵי זָהִיר בְּמִצְוָה קַלָּה כְּבַחֲמוּרָה
Be as scrupulous in performing a "minor" mitzvah as in a "major" one

REBBI NOW ADVANCES IDEAS THAT WILL HELP US FIND OUR "RIGHT PATH" in life. One should not differentiate in the observance of God's commandments. There are *mitzvos* that appear to be simple and easy, that do not require great mental concentration, physical effort, or monetary sacrifice. There are *mitzvos* that are downright enjoyable, such as eating the Shabbos meal or drinking wine on the holidays, while other *mitzvos,* such as giving charity, studying Torah, and fasting on Yom Kippur certainly require physical and mental sacrifice, if not even anguish. Yet, we have no right to differentiate between one *mitzvah* and another. The rule of the rabbis is: "If a *mitzvah* presents itself before you, do it immediately, without delay."

True, elsewhere the Mishnah and Talmud offer a scale of priority regarding the performance of *mitzvos* and their inherent rewards. There are certain *mitzvos* for whose performance the Torah itself mentions long life as a reward, and there are *mitzvos* for whose performance the Talmud promises partial reward in this world and complete reward in the World to Come. Yet, none of this contradicts the words of Rebbi. His intent is to caution against "saving" oneself for later, perhaps grander, *mitzvos.* He is telling us: Don't save yourself for the "great things." They may never arrive for you. Do not judge *mitzvos* in terms of lightness and severity, of their potential rewards and benefits. Many times in life, it is the small thing that makes the great difference. The almost offhand smile and kind word to a stranger or child, the small coins easily given to the poor, the care and devotion involved in kindling the Shabbos lights, have changed the life of many a beneficiary and performer of these acts. They intimately affect the life of a person, many times in a fashion that is initially hard to discern.

A *mitzvah* in hand is worth far more than a potential "greater" *mitzvah* that

should choose for himself? Whatever [path] is a credit to himself and earns him the esteem of fellow men. Be as scrupulous in performing a "minor" *mitzvah* as in a "major" one, for you never know the reward given for the [respective] *mitzvos.* Calculate the cost of a *mitzvah* against its reward, and the reward of a sin against its cost. Consider

---

may never come. I can testify from my efforts at fund-raising for synagogues and yeshivos that people often promise to help build the roof when one is asking them for help to lay the foundation. One can never know if the foundation is perhaps more important than the roof. Or, one is sometimes told: "Try me when you have something really special that needs money." It is difficult for finite humans to judge what is "really special" in the eyes of the infinite Lord.

שֶׁאֵין אַתָּה יוֹדֵעַ
For you never know

I HAD A YESHIVAH STUDENT IN ISRAEL WHO CAME FROM A COMPLETELY non-observant background. When he had told his family that after graduating college he intended to spend a year or two in Israel studying in a yeshivah, his parents refused to support his decision, financially or emotionally. However, his grandmother, although also completely non-observant and assimilated, roundly defended his decision and volunteered to pay for the trip and the tuition. She explained to her grandson that many years earlier she had had an encounter with an Orthodox, European-born rabbi, in which the rabbi went out of his way to make her feel comfortable and not embarrass her, despite her less than halachically acceptable dress and mode of speaking. She told her grandson: "If you grow to be like that rabbi, I will be more than happy and proud."

I am certain that the rabbi paid no special attention to that incident when it occurred. He was surely unaware at the time of the impact of his behavior, not feeling it to be out of the ordinary. In retrospect, however, that "light" mitzvah ultimately allowed that woman to have a family that would not be estranged from Torah and Judaism, and the Torah studied by this young student undoubtedly accrues to the credit of that rabbi, now no longer alive. One never truly knows the effects and reward of *mitzvos* and good deeds.

וֶהֱוֵי מְחַשֵּׁב הֶפְסֵד מִצְוָה כְּנֶגֶד שְׂכָרָהּ
Calculate the cost of a mitzvah against its reward

THE WORD מְחַשֵּׁב IS A VERB THAT LITERALLY MEANS *TO THINK, TO RECKON, to calculate.* (In modern Hebrew it is also used as a noun, meaning a computer, a machine which is undoubtedly a great tool for knowledge and communication, but still cannot think.) Rebbi bids us not to let our decisions be impulsive ones. Shop for the ingredients of life with a prepared list, and that list should be the Torah's commandments and values. (When I was the director of *kashrus* for the Orthodox Union, an officer of a leading supermarket chain told me only half in jest that he would love to invent a device that could destroy the shopping lists

בִּשְׁלֹשָׁה דְבָרִים, וְאֵין אַתָּה בָא לִידֵי עֲבֵרָה; דַּע מַה לְּמַעְלָה מִמְּךָ – עַיִן רוֹאָה, וְאֹזֶן שׁוֹמַעַת, וְכָל מַעֲשֶׂיךָ בְּסֵפֶר נִכְתָּבִים.

[ב] **רַבָּן** גַּמְלִיאֵל בְּנוֹ שֶׁל רַבִּי יְהוּדָה הַנָּשִׂיא אוֹמֵר: יָפֶה תַלְמוּד תּוֹרָה עִם דֶּרֶךְ אֶרֶץ,

---

of husbands, so that they would resort to their innate nature of buying impulsively.)

Impulsive decisions, dictated by the passion and desire of the moment, are usually disastrous in the long run. Calculate the perceived pleasure and long-term benefit of performing a good deed against its cost; and calculate the loss of a such a holy opportunity against the short-term saving and restful inaction of not performing the commandment. In effect, Rebbi bids us to live life with a calculator in hand, with a definite shopping list of goals and priorities to which we must constantly refer. Good and bad, short-term advantage versus long-term cost, instant gratification against patient sacrifice, are the everyday crosscurrents that Rebbi deals with. IBM was on to a good thing decades ago when it placed a sign that said "Think" on the desks of its employees. Most self-caused problems in life stem from thoughtlessness and carelessness.

הִסְתַּכֵּל בִּשְׁלֹשָׁה דְבָרִים
Consider three things

ORDINARY PEOPLE ARE MUCH MORE CIRCUMSPECT IN THEIR BEHAVIOR if they know they are being photographed, much more careful in their speech if they know the room is bugged, and much more careful of their image if they are aware that a book is being written about them. It is only when one is certain that the photograph, the audio recording, the book, will never see the light of day that caution and good sense are thrown to the winds. In our modern world of hidden security cameras, voice-activated recording machines, and infrared surveillance equipment, Rebbi's description of the seeing eye, the listening ear and the documented event is readily understood and appreciated.

Rebbi informs us that God has a "camcorder," that the video of our behavior, the tape cassette of our words, the record of our lives written in indelible ink will all be produced at our time of judgment to prove merit or guilt. In the prayers of the Days of Awe, we state: וְחוֹתָם יַד כָּל אָדָם בּוֹ, every person's own signature appears on the document delineating the verdict decreed for him. The events of life and our behavior in reaction to them do not pass unknown. They are recorded meticulously and accurately by our Creator. Therefore, we are bidden to be holy and clean, upright and moral, for we are always on camera and no throwaway words or actions are allowed. Rebbi's

three things, and you will not come into the grip of sin: Know what is above you — a watchful Eye, an attentive Ear, and all your deeds are recorded in a Book.

2. Rabban Gamliel, the son of Rabbi Yehudah HaNasi, says: Torah study is good together with an occupation,

---

simple and understandable imagery harmonizes perfectly with his preceding message, to deliberate carefully before embarking upon any deed, and it serves as a practical aid in helping us to constantly choose the right and straight path in life.

רַבָּן גַּמְלִיאֵל בְּנוֹ שֶׁל רַבִּי יְהוּדָה הַנָּשִׂיא
Rabban Gamliel, the son of Rabbi Yehudah HaNasi

Mishnah 2 THIS SON OF REBBI IS THE THIRD OF THE RABBAN GAMliels who appear in the mishnah. He is almost always identified clearly in the Talmud as "Rabban Gamliel, the son of Rebbi." (The first Rabban Gamliel is usually referred to as Rabban Gamliel HaZaken, *the elder*. The second Rabban Gamliel is known by historians as Rabban Gamliel of Yavneh, although the Talmud usually refers to him simply as Rabban Gamliel, without any modifiers to his name.)

Rabban Gamliel, son of Rebbi, was at the head of the transition generation of scholars, the students of Rebbi who served as the bridging generation between the last of the *Tannaim* (the rabbis of the Mishnah) and the first of the *Amoraim* (the rabbis of the Talmud). Just before his death, Rebbi appointed his oldest son, Gamliel, as his successor as the *Nasi,* the temporal leader of the Jewish community. To the position of the head of the yeshivah (which Rebbi has also held), Rebbi appointed Gamliel's younger brother, Shimon. To further diffuse the power base, Rebbi appointed Rabbi Chanina ben Chama to "sit first," i.e., to be the actual leading scholar in the yeshivah. Evidently Rebbi felt that all three positions were too great a concentration of power for one individual, at least for any individual that he knew of in the next generation. In any event, during the reign of this third Rabban Gamliel, the center of Jewish life slowly but inexorably began to shift to the scholars and yeshivos of Babylonia, and away from the Land of Israel.

יָפֶה תַּלְמוּד תּוֹרָה עִם דֶּרֶךְ אֶרֶץ
Torah study is good together with an occupation

THE PHRASE *DERECH ERETZ* LITERALLY MEANS "THE WAY OF THE WORLD," a phrase that covers a wide area in Jewish thought and life. It encompasses courtesy and manners, consideration for others, and a civil and respectful attitude toward government and society. It also deals with the necessity of being employed and industrious, earning a living for oneself and family, and contributing to the society that forms an integral part of the world and the way it runs. It is this latter idea of *derech eretz* that Rabban Gamliel emphasizes by saying that the effort required for both tasks — studying Torah and working to

שֶׁיְּגִיעַת שְׁנֵיהֶם מַשְׁכַּחַת עָוֹן. וְכָל תּוֹרָה שֶׁאֵין עִמָּהּ מְלָאכָה, סוֹפָהּ בְּטֵלָה וְגוֹרֶרֶת עָוֹן. וְכָל הָעוֹסְקִים עִם הַצִּבּוּר, יִהְיוּ עוֹסְקִים עִמָּהֶם לְשֵׁם שָׁמַיִם, שֶׁזְּכוּת אֲבוֹתָם מְסַיַּעְתָּם, וְצִדְקָתָם עוֹמֶדֶת לָעַד. וְאַתֶּם, מַעֲלֶה אֲנִי עֲלֵיכֶם שָׂכָר הַרְבֵּה, כְּאִלּוּ עֲשִׂיתֶם.

---

earn a living — will weaken any desire or opportunity for sinfulness. Excessive leisure time, coupled with shirking responsibility for the welfare of one's family and a willingness to be dependant upon the generosity of others, increases the likelihood of sinful behavior in one's lifestyle. Rabban Gamliel clearly warns that Torah study without work will in the end be unworthy of itself. It will reach a point of diminishing returns. It will be unable to sustain itself. According to his statement, productive work in itself guarantees the maintenance of true Torah study and spiritual accomplishment among the masses of Israel.

The question of full-time Torah study without any type of employment or work, and the resultant dependence upon others, will be discussed at length in a commentary on a later mishnah. Suffice it to say that there are different opinions regarding the implementation of such a program on a mass basis. I will not inject my own view into the matter and let the great men of the Mishnah and those who commented upon their words speak for themselves.

In the 19th century, Rabbi Samson Raphael Hirsch, the great leader of German Neo-Orthodoxy, co-opted the words of Rabban Gamliel, *Torah im derech eretz*, as the banner of his view of Jewish life in the modern era. By *derech eretz,* he meant not only gainful employment — though he strongly emphasized that — but professional training and higher education and general knowledge. Rabbi Hirsch's ideology was a source of controversy in his own lifetime and remains so one hundred fifty years later. Although the leaders of Eastern European Jewry admired Rabbi Hirsch personally and were impressed by his accomplishments in revitalizing traditional Jewish life in Frankfurt and Germany, they did not adopt his policy.

In his own commentary on Avos, Rabbi Hirsch defines Rabban Gamliel's *derech eretz* as "everything that life encompasses, everything that mankind attempts in order to bring to fruition one's existence, one's goals, one's relationship to others in this world, by the exploitation and use of all of the possibilities and causes that exist in society. Therefore, this term — *derech eretz* — includes the means by which humans make a livelihood, one's national citizenship, the courtesy, sensitivity, rectitude, customs and manners of the milieu in which one lives and all of the forms — cultural, personal, general and national — of society generally."

2/2

for exertion of them both makes sin forgotten. All Torah study that is not joined with work will cease in the end, and lead to sin. All who exert themselves for the community should do so for the sake of Heaven, for then the merit of their ancestors will assist them, and their righteousness will endure forever. And you, I will bestow upon you as great a reward, as though you had achieved what you wished.

וְכָל הָעוֹסְקִים עִם הַצִּבּוּר, יִהְיוּ עוֹסְקִים עִמָּהֶם לְשֵׁם שָׁמַיִם
All who exert themselves for the community should do so for the sake of Heaven

WORKING FOR THE PUBLIC'S BENEFIT CAN BE MADDENINGLY FRUSTRATING. One should therefore be steeled to the likelihood of significant disappointments in people and projects, and of being misunderstood and unappreciated. Such is the lot of those who work for the general good, and it seems that it has always been so. Therefore, anyone who undertakes the difficult but imperative task of public office or service on behalf of the Jewish people should do so *l'sheim Shamayim*, for purely altruistic and Heavenly motives. Then one will not be crushed by the negative reactions of others to one's valid and necessary attempts to improve and order the Jewish society, synagogue, or group that one undertakes to serve.

Acting for the sake of Heaven, without personal or ulterior motives, is a positive virtue in itself, irrespective of how it steels us to the difficulties inherent in public service. For by acting *l'sheim Shamayim*, one guarantees Heavenly aid and the mobilization of the merit of pious ancestors to the cause at hand. The achievement of *l'sheim Shamayim* is a difficult task, however. Arrogance often masquerades behind the mask of selflessness. Both Rabbi Yisrael of Salant and Rabbi Simcha Bunim of P'shis'cha put it very pithily: "One must make certain that one's *l'sheim Shamayim* is also *l'sheim Shamayim.*"

People who work for the public good are prone to feelings of self-pity and self-righteousness. Since public work is nearly always under-appreciated and many times not even known to the public, such frustration and self-justification is understandable. Nevertheless, the key to maintaining mental health while engaging in public service is to avoid such attitudes and strive for the achievement of productive public service that is truly *l'sheim Shamayim*.

מַעֲלֶה אֲנִי עֲלֵיכֶם שָׂכָר הַרְבֵּה
I will bestow upon you as great a reward . . .

THOSE WHO STRIVE TO WORK FOR THE PUBLIC *L'SHEIM SHAMAYIM* MUST realize that the Lord will provide great reward for their efforts, even if those efforts are not initially blessed with the success they envisioned and hoped for. Even though the world always assesses success or failure based on the mighty "bottom line" of results, there is in Judaism the concept of an "A" for effort. Since complete success in public agendas and service is well nigh impossible — who can satisfy everyone at all times? — sincere effort must be taken into

[ג] **הֱווּ** זְהִירִין בָּרָשׁוּת, שֶׁאֵין מְקָרְבִין לוֹ לְאָדָם אֶלָּא לְצֹרֶךְ עַצְמָן; נִרְאִין כְּאוֹהֲבִין בִּשְׁעַת הֲנָאָתָן, וְאֵין עוֹמְדִין לוֹ לְאָדָם בִּשְׁעַת דָּחְקוֹ.

[ד] **הוּא הָיָה אוֹמֵר:** עֲשֵׂה רְצוֹנוֹ כִּרְצוֹנֶךָ, כְּדֵי שֶׁיַּעֲשֶׂה רְצוֹנְךָ

---

account when assessing that service. Many, if not most, times, the success of one generation is built upon the efforts of a previous one, so it is premature to judge the success of ideas and plans by immediate results. Many a discarded idea or plan has become a later centerpiece of accomplishment. Therefore, the only thing that can truly be measured during the course of an undertaking is the degree of one's effort. Accomplishment, however, can only be assessed much later; but when it comes, even generations later, it always redounds to the credit of the predecessors who labored honestly for the public good.

Rabban Gamliel's teaching implies a good piece of managerial advice. There is a tendency among leaders to micromanage everything. It is difficult to let go, to delegate authority to others, when one feels that one can do the task at hand, no matter how minor, much better than anyone else. To counteract that tendency, the mishnah teaches that one deserves credit for success even when it was accomplished by others, through his request, direction, or instruction — or even through his inspiration. Moreover, the Sages stated (*Bava Basra* 9a): גָּדוֹל הַמְּעַשֶּׂה יוֹתֵר מִן הָעוֹשֶׂה, *one who inspires and activates someone else to do good is greater than the doer himself.* The true public servant seeks the help of others. He or she is inclusive and not power hungry. He or she brings others into leadership and responsibility, delegates authority and shares vision and wisdom. Therefore, such a person merits reward for the actions of those others whom he or she has inspired and led. It is more than a vicarious sense of accomplishment; it is as though the person who inspired or instructed accomplished the task on his or her own.

הֱווּ זְהִירִין בָּרָשׁוּת
Beware of rulers

Mishnah 3 THE TRADITIONAL JEWISH VIEW OF GOVERNMENT IS THAT its rules and laws are to be obeyed, but its promises and motives are not necessarily to be trusted. In the utopian world of human dreams, government is unnecessary since everyone behaves nobly, legally, and kindly. In the real world, however, where perfect human behavior is usually absent, government is a necessity. One is reminded of Winston Churchill's quip that "democracy is a terrible form of government, but it is far

3. Beware of rulers, for they befriend someone only for their own benefit; they act friendly when it benefits them, but do not stand by someone in his time of need.

4. He used to say: Treat His will as if it were your own will, so that He will treat your will as if it were

---

better than any other form created till now." Though all governments posture as servants of the people, governments are made up of people, and people have weaknesses that belie their claimed true altruism.

Rabban Gamliel, like his father Rebbi before him, was much involved with the Roman authorities governing the Land of Israel. From his experience, he concluded that the policy of government is basically one of self-interest. If the people in power need you, they will be all sweetness and light, to enlist your aid or vote, but one should never take that attitude to be sincere or permanent. When the election is over or when the emergency passes, the very same government officials can very well be quite indifferent to you and your plight. Therefore, uncritical trust in the rulers and in their policies and behavior is naive. Rabban Gamliel's language indicates that his evaluation was not restricted to a particular form of government or specific ruler, but was a general commentary on the inherent nature of government and power. Especially for Jews living under regimes that were basically intolerant of them, this advice of Rabban Gamliel was particularly cogent.

עֲשֵׂה רְצוֹנוֹ כִּרְצוֹנְךָ ***Treat His will as if it were your own will***

Mishnah 4 RABBAN GAMLIEL RESTATES THE BASIC JEWISH GUIDE FOR living, that one should try to make his will and goals coincide with those of God, as expressed in the Torah and Jewish tradition. The question that should always be uppermost in our minds is, "What does God think about this. Is my will identical with the standards of God's Torah?"

❦ ❦ ❦

The ultimate question

I am reminded of an incident that deeply affected me. I was once in the office of the late and great Rabbi Alexander Rosenberg, the founding rabbinic administrator of the Orthodox Union Kashrus Division. A Holocaust survivor was in the office attempting to obtain immediate OU approval for a product of his (Rabbi Rosenberg had enormous empathy with such people, many of whom took unfair advantage of his compassion). The man wanted to bypass the normal procedure of applications, inspections, rabbinic and lay commissions' approval and contract signing, which sometimes took months, and he was in a hurry. Unabashedly, he offered Rabbi Rosenberg a five percent interest in the profits of this product as a reward for expediting OU approval on the spot. Rabbi Rosenberg remained silent, his eyes

כִּרְצוֹנוֹ. בַּטֵּל רְצוֹנְךָ מִפְּנֵי רְצוֹנוֹ, כְּדֵי שֶׁיְּבַטֵּל רְצוֹן אֲחֵרִים מִפְּנֵי רְצוֹנֶךָ.

[ה] **הִלֵּל אוֹמֵר:** אַל תִּפְרוֹשׁ מִן הַצִּבּוּר, וְאַל תַּאֲמִין בְּעַצְמְךָ עַד יוֹם מוֹתְךָ,

---

half-closed. The man persisted and upped the ante to seven and one half percent. Rabbi Rosenberg continued his silence. Completely misinterpreting Rabbi Rosenberg's silence as a bargaining position, the man proposed 10 percent as a final offer. Rabbi Rosenberg opened his eyes fully and gazed directly at the man and asked him: "Un vas zagt Gott dertzu? And what would God say about such a transaction?"

❦ ❦ ❦

The main question in life is, "What would God say about this?" Our will should follow His will. Our behavior should be in consonance with His standards. That is the fulfillment of a true Jewish life.

בַּטֵּל רְצוֹנְךָ מִפְּנֵי רְצוֹנוֹ
Nullify your will before His will

THIS IS THE FLIP SIDE OF RABBAN GAMLIEL'S PREVIOUS IDEA. IT IS DIFFICULT to subjugate one's will and desires to those of the Creator; few of us are great enough to eliminate or sublimate all of our inner urgings, fantasies and base desires completely. But we can deny fulfillment to those inner weaknesses and failings. We can "cancel" our will before the will of the Eternal. And in effect, this is the major struggle of life — the war within each of us between good and bad, nobility and baseness, right and wrong. This war is decided by behavior and action — by canceling our own will and desires, in order to serve the Creator and live in line with His Torah and moral standards.

Moreover, if one is able to so sublimate his will and not insist on always having his way, he will discover that others will treat him in the same fashion and be willing to forego insistence on their will against his interests. The rabbis of the Talmud emphasized that in most areas of human life, others react to us in the fashion that we initially treat them. *As a face reflects itself in water, so is the heart of one man to another.* That verse from *Proverbs* (27:19) is the basis for this viewpoint of the great rabbis. Therefore, by bending our will before that of the Creator, we will create a situation where we will see that others are willing to bend, in order to accommodate us.

אַל תִּפְרוֹשׁ מִן הַצִּבּוּר
Do not separate yourself from the community

Mishnah 5 ONCE AGAIN WE MEET THE WISDOM AND INSIGHTS OF THE great Hillel. There are many rationalizations for going it alone. Being merely one part of the whole is a challenging exercise. There are always differing opinions, difficult personalities, and great heartache in

His will. Nullify your will before His will, so that He will nullify the will of others in the face of your will.

5. Hillel says: Do not separate yourself from the community; do not believe in yourself until the day you die;

---

belonging to a community. The normalization of the standards of piety and observance, the necessity of personal compromise for the public good, the incessant minor frictions that are present in a public community, all interfere with our sense of self and personal worth. There is a normal tendency to say, "Stop the world, I want to get off." Comes the great Hillel, the man who is personally proven to be beyond anger or arrogance, and proclaims the necessity of always remaining part of a community. For only by obtaining the reactions of others can one accurately assess one's moral standing and true worth. The community helps mitigate one's tendency toward self-righteousness, selfishness, and narrow vision. The community is one's support group in social and spiritual life.

There has always been a tendency in Jewish life to break away and divide socially and even religiously. Jews tend to be strong individualists, each of whom prefers doing things his own particular way. Many a Jewish community, synagogue, and organization has fragmented in our history, many on matters of nuance, interpretation of custom, and even personal pique. However, there have been noteworthy and understandable splits on matters of conscience, interpretation of halachah (Jewish law) and other major issues.

וְאַל תַּאֲמִין בְּעַצְמְךָ עַד יוֹם מוֹתְךָ
Do not believe in yourself until the day you die

SELF-CONFIDENCE IS NECESSARY FOR PRODUCTIVE HUMAN LIFE, BUT arrogant belief in one's infallibility and invulnerability is enormously dangerous. These words of Hillel are a follow-up to his previous statement regarding separation from the community. Hillel warns of the dangers of going it alone, of thinking that we know better than others, of being smugly self-righteous. Never say, "It can't happen to me!"

The Talmud records that a great *Kohen Gadol* (High Priest) of Israel served for decades in the Temple, yet at the end of his life succumbed to the temptation of the Sadducees and deserted Jewish tradition. Even great men are capable of great errors. Judaism teaches us to drive defensively, not only on the road, but also in all avenues of behavior. We are all subject to sinful temptations, lapses of judgment, foolish behavior and grievous errors. Hillel teaches us to believe in ourselves, but only with balance and caution. Utter and complete reliance on one's wisdom and rectitude gives birth to the curse of bad leadership and irresponsible personal and national behavior. Someone once said, "It's what you learn after you know it all that counts."

❧ ❧ ❧

It can happen to you

I have often thought that this idea of "defensive driving" is alluded to, at least homiletically, in the Talmud's discussions of three unusual cases described in the Torah. These cases are עִיר הַנִּדַּחַת*, a Jewish city whose inhabitants became idol worshipers;* בֵּן סוֹרֵר וּמוֹרֶה*, a rebellious son who is guilty of robbery and gluttony; and* נִגְעֵי בָתִּים*, plagues that infest the walls of houses. Because of the many complex and unusual stipulations needed to create the halachic status of these cases, the Talmud states an opinion that these three cases are purely theoretical and can never occur in the real world. Nevertheless, the Talmud quotes another sage who declares that each of these cases did actually occur, and that he was witness to physical evidence to that effect. Apparently, these two opinions are irreconcilable. However, it may be that the Talmud cites the dissenting opinion to suggest that the one who says "It can't happen to me, not to my house, not to my child, not to my community," is the sort of person who is most likely to have to bear actual witness to the destruction that one was so confident would never touch one's self. Defensive driving, spiritually and physically speaking, can ward off accidents and tragedies.*

❧ ❧ ❧

וְאַל תָּדִין אֶת חֲבֵרְךָ עַד שֶׁתַּגִּיעַ לִמְקוֹמוֹ
Do not judge your fellow until you have reached his place

THE SIMPLE TRUTH OF HILLEL'S STATEMENT HAS ECHOES IN ALMOST all human societies. The Native American Indians said: "Judge not the other warrior until you have walked in his moccasins." One should never be quick to judge others, for no one can ever truly put himself in someone else's exact circumstances. Who knows how I would have behaved in his place and time? The Talmud records that King Menashe of Judah, a notorious idolater and evildoer, appeared in a dream to a scholar of Talmudic times and interpreted for him a difficult passage regarding Jewish law and halachah. Astounded by Menashe's Torah erudition, the scholar asked him: "If you are so knowledgeable of Torah, how could you have worshiped idols?" To which Menashe replied: "Had you lived in my time and society, you would have lifted the hem of your robe to rush even faster to idols' temples!"

Hindsight claims to provide perfect vision, but it does not and cannot take into account the milieu and circumstances, the atmosphere and attitudes of a particular time long past. Thus, our judgment of past events and personalities is always skewed. The same is true of our judgment of current events and people. For even here our knowledge is incomplete and faulty,

2/5 do not judge your fellow until you have reached his place;

---

for we cannot place ourselves exactly in the other person's position. Therefore, judgment of others should always be tempered and cautious, if not completely withheld.

This idea is in complete consonance with Hillel's previous statement that one should always question one's own actions. Since I cannot be sure of myself, it is hardly in place for me to be certain when judging others. In my years in the rabbinate and in heading a yeshivah, one of the more painful but most necessary lessons life has taught me is to refrain from being judgmental of others. Don't jump to conclusions about people based on appearances and first impressions. In general, successful personal relations almost always require an unbiased and tolerant attitude toward others. Naturally, if a person proves to be untrustworthy, violent, dangerous, and so on, only a fool would refrain from avoiding further contact with such a person. The Torah never encourages folly. But initially giving someone the benefit of the doubt, until facts prove otherwise, is the golden mean in life that Hillel advocates.

❦ ❦ ❦

I would be remiss if I did not include here the more sardonic comment of Rabbi Menachem HaMeiri, the 14th-century Provencal Torah scholar and prolific commentator on the Bible and Talmud. In the name of his teachers, Meiri explains the advice to refrain from judging someone "until you reach his place" as follows: Often, someone who comes to a new community where he is unknown puts on airs of external holiness and piety in order to make an impression. Do not judge that stranger on his apparently pious external behavior and appearance, but rather judge him in "his place," i.e., how he behaves at home, in his former community, with his family and friends, when he is alone and no one is watching except Heaven itself. Meiri comments, "Many people who are in truth boorish and low, when coming to a strange community, publicly exhibit false piety and represent themselves hypocritically as holy people when they are not."

Meiri had little patience with such fraudulent piety, which unfortunately appears in all generations and communities. In his commentary to the Talmud (*Sotah* 20b), he rails against this type of false holiness with the following statement: "They cover themselves with large *taleisim* (prayer shawls) and with long *tzitzis* (the fringes that are set in the four corners of the tallis) that hang down so that they can be noticed in public, but their hearts are very distant from the Lord. Concerning them I apply the verse וַיָּצִיצוּ כָּל פֹּעֲלֵי אָוֶן, *And all evildoers blossom*" (*Psalms* 92:8). Meiri is using a play on words. The Hebrew word for blossom, וַיָּצִיצוּ, sounds like the word *tzitzis*, the fringes that customarily are worn in such a way that they can be seen. Thus

וְאַל תֹּאמַר דָּבָר שֶׁאִי אֶפְשַׁר לִשְׁמוֹעַ, שֶׁסּוֹפוֹ לְהִשָּׁמַע. וְאַל תֹּאמַר לִכְשֶׁאֶפְנֶה אֶשְׁנֶה, שֶׁמָּא לֹא תִפָּנֶה.

[ו] הוּא הָיָה אוֹמֵר: אֵין בּוּר יְרֵא חֵטְא,

Meiri renders it as if to say that evildoers make a hypocritical show of their *tzitzis,* to appear to be pious and God-fearing. Meiri has only contempt for such behavior. So should we all.

❦ ❦ ❦

וְאַל תֹּאמַר דָּבָר שֶׁאִי אֶפְשַׁר לִשְׁמוֹעַ, שֶׁסּוֹפוֹ לְהִשָּׁמַע
Do not say something that is not possible to be heard, for in the end it will be heard

ONE SHOULD NEVER EXPECT ONE'S PRIVATELY UTTERED WORDS TO remain unknown to others. Many a person has suffered or been caused irreparable harm because of injudicious remarks that he thought would never become public knowledge. King Solomon in Ecclesiastes/*Koheles* (10:20) warned that "the birds of heaven transmit the [human] voice." In our modern age of hidden personal recording devices and "bugged" premises, it is obvious that one must fear that one's private remarks will be overheard in one fashion or another. But Hillel has a far deeper purpose than offering advice on how to protect one's secrets. Following his counsel, one will refrain from making any remarks he would later regret were they to be revealed to the public.

If one says something in private because he would be ashamed or chagrined if it would be known by the public, then one is certainly wiser in not saying it at all. It is another warning against hypocrisy and falseness. The laws of *lashon hara* — negative speech — apply to private, even to intimate, conversations. The sense of shame that governs public revelations of wicked or foolish words applies to words spoken in private, as well.

Another interpretation of not saying "something that is not possible to be heard, for in the end it will be heard," is that one should never be afraid to express one's opinion on important issues — family, communal, educational, and so on — merely because one is convinced that this opinion will not be immediately accepted by others. Jewish and world history are replete with minority opinions that eventually became majority opinions. Throughout the Mishnah and Talmud, the minority opinion of an individual scholar is always faithfully recorded, and many times, the law is eventually decided in favor of that minority opinion. Do not be convinced that it is futile to present your view, because it won't "be heard." The end may well be that, in time, it "will be heard" and adopted. This interpretation blends well with Hillel's earlier statement that one must not separate oneself from the community. Merely do not say something that is impossible to be heard, for in the end it will be heard; and do not say, "When I am free I will study," for perhaps you will not become free.

6. He used to say: A boor cannot be fearful of sin;

---

because your community does not adopt your view immediately, do not give up on pressing your point. Eventually, if your opinion has true merit, it "will be heard." But, if you are no longer part of the community, no one will respect your ideas, and then they most certainly "will not be heard."

וְאַל תֹּאמַר לִכְשֶׁאֶפְנֶה אֶשְׁנֶה
And do not say "When I am free I will study"

PROCRASTINATION IS THE ENEMY OF ALL HUMAN ACCOMPLISHMENT, spiritual or material. The Yiddish joke is that the procrastinators of the world created an organization for themselves, but they haven't gotten around to calling a meeting yet. All of us are at least honorary members of the procrastinator's organization. This book itself, having taken three times as long to write as originally planned, is a monument to the ails of procrastination. Since time is irreplaceable, wasting it is the ultimate destructive habit. It is the uncertainty of life, its length and circumstances, that lends urgency to this warning. The Sages taught (*Koheles Rabbah* 1:34) that "no person dies having fulfilled even half his desires in life." This refers not only to physical, monetary, and other earthly goals, but to spiritual and intellectual goals as well. The time to study Torah, to read things of value, to grow in spirit and soul, is now. Hillel warns us of the "when I retire" syndrome. His warning affirms the statement of his colleague, Shammai, to make one's study of Torah a daily, fixed, and regular occurrence. Today is here and now and real. Tomorrow is always distant and uncertain.

אֵין בּוּר יְרֵא חֵטְא
A boor cannot be fearful of sin

Mishnah 6 A *BOOR* IN HEBREW IS THE SAME BOOR IN ENGLISH AS WELL. He is someone who is so ill-mannered, uncouth, and insensitive to others, so ignorant of Torah norms and values, as to be completely unaware that he is in fact a boor. A sinner usually knows he is sinner. A boor never realizes he is a boor. Such a person can never be truly afraid of sin, since he is oblivious to societal norms and the discipline of correct behavior, the violations of which cause sin. I think that it is this boor that Ramban (Rabbi Moshe ben Nachman of 13th-century Spain) had in mind when he coined the famous phrase that a person can be a נָבָל בִּרְשׁוּת הַתּוֹרָה, an obnoxious person who yet sees himself as behaving within the literal parameters of Torah law. To truly live up to Torah standards in life requires sensitivity of mind and character, and a magical blend of simplicity and sophistication. The boor, who unfortunately possesses none of these qualities, will have a well-nigh impossible task in achieving fear of wrongdoing and sin.

וְלֹא עַם הָאָרֶץ חָסִיד, וְלֹא הַבַּיְשָׁן לָמֵד, וְלֹא הַקַּפְּדָן מְלַמֵּד, וְלֹא כָל הַמַּרְבֶּה בִסְחוֹרָה מַחְכִּים, וּבִמְקוֹם שֶׁאֵין

וְלֹא עַם הָאָרֶץ חָסִיד
An unlearned person cannot be scrupulously pious

SOMEONE IGNORANT OF TORAH LAW AND JEWISH TRADITION IS NOT A good candidate for piety. One cannot be a true Sabbath observer without at least minimal knowledge of the laws of the Sabbath. Judaism is a religion that demands not only faith, but knowledge and study as well. The study and knowledge of Torah reigns supreme in Jewish life — above all else, a Jew must not be ignorant of Judaism, its tenets, beliefs, and scholarship. The truly pious Jew *knows* the Lord through the study and understanding of His Torah. It is the combination of faith and knowledge, of the heart and the mind, of obeying and understanding, that creates the pious personality within the Jewish community. Ignorance, like boorishness, stands in the way of any meaningful Jewish life, let alone piety.

In fact, ignorance breeds false and sham piety, which is worse than no piety at all. The Chasam Sofer, Rabbi Moses Sofer/Schreiber of 19th-century Pressburg (Bratislava today), Slovakia, stated that the punishment of all those who falsely act pious is that they eventually come to believe they are really pious. And that is truly a most bitter punishment, for ignorance also leads to hubris and arrogance. The pious Hillel is the perfect source for this important lesson, since he risked and sacrificed much in his youth in order to study Torah. His growth in Torah was so phenomenal that he was recruited to become leader of the nation, and his piety kept pace with his scholarship. It was fitting, therefore, that Hillel became the prime example of both scholarship and piety in the century preceding the destruction of the Second Temple.

וְלֹא הַבַּיְשָׁן לָמֵד
A bashful person cannot learn

CURIOSITY, INQUISITIVENESS, A PROBING MIND, AND THE GIFT OF ANALYSIS are all hallmarks of true scholarship. Every idea and lesson should be subject to the student's critical review. Study of Talmud, and Torah study generally, is always in a give and take, question and answer, debate and counter-debate style. The shy and reticent student, who accepts what is taught but is never bold enough to challenge it, to think on his own, to debate the matter with his or her teacher, will not really achieve educational growth and maturity. Judaism respects modesty as a great virtue, but it should never be allowed to stifle one's creativity and search for knowledge and the truth. Such reticence is a liability instead of an asset.

וְלֹא הַקַּפְּדָן מְלַמֵּד
And a quick, impatient person cannot teach

HILLEL CONTINUES HIS ADVICE ON EDUCATION BY STATING *V'LO HAKAPDAN melameid,* the impatient, tyrannical, perfectionist person is not qualified to teach. Teaching requires infinite patience and compassion. Students need to be nurtured, encouraged, flattered, developed, and inspired. The classroom should be a place of respect, not terror. The Talmud tells us of Rav Preida, an

an unlearned person cannot be scrupulously pious; a bashful person cannot learn, and a quick, impatient person cannot teach; anyone excessively occupied in business cannot become a scholar; and in a place where there are no

---

exemplary teacher, who repeated his lesson four hundred times until it was at last clear to his student. In school, as in life, honey captures more flies than does vinegar.

Not only will a tyrannical, impatient teacher stunt intellectual growth, he will likely also create student hostility to the subject matter. In the case of teaching Torah, this often means creating a hostility to Judaism itself — and this is a catastrophe. Unfortunately, I knew great teachers of Talmud who were tyrants in their classrooms. Many of their students came to adore them and admire their intellectual prowess, but there were other students who fell by the wayside, victims of a sharp tongue and an impatient attitude. A teacher must be held accountable for student failures and not only credited for successes. It is most logical, therefore, that someone whose manner causes students to dislike their studies should not teach.

❦ ❦ ❦

A boomerang

What often stifles students is having a pedantic martinet for a teacher. The worst course I ever sat through in law school was taught by a brilliant professor, an expert in his field. But he was a cruel and vindictive teacher, who cut up his students for their allegedly "stupid" questions and comments. After the first month of the course, no one ever again volunteered a comment, no one asked a question, and all were in dread of being called upon to review a case. Although almost all of us received a decent final mark and knew the subject material well, we had a terrible taste in our mouths regarding that subject, and few if any of us had any interest in specializing in that particular field of law in our professional careers.

❦ ❦ ❦

וְלֹא כָל הַמַּרְבֶּה בִסְחוֹרָה מַחְכִּים

Anyone excessively occupied in business cannot become a scholar

THE SIMPLE EXPLANATION OF THIS STATEMENT IS THAT IMMERSION IN commerce does not guarantee further Torah wisdom and certainly does not elevate one's spiritual level. Wisdom and spirit come from Torah study and practice. Thus we are returned to the constant theme repeated throughout Avos that one must make Torah study a fixed, regular, and integral part of one's daily schedule. Commerce, business, money, and finance are addictive. Commerce should be only a tool to earn a livelihood, but it can easily become an end in itself. The Torah, as I have repeatedly pointed out, demands balance. Earning a livelihood is necessary, but if it becomes one's primary interest in life, then one forsakes the attainment of wisdom and spiritual growth.

אֲנָשִׁים, הִשְׁתַּדֵּל לִהְיוֹת אִישׁ.

[ז] **אַף** הוּא רָאָה גֻּלְגֹּלֶת אַחַת שֶׁצָּפָה עַל פְּנֵי הַמָּיִם. אָמַר לָהּ: „עַל דַּאֲטֵפְתְּ אַטְפוּךְ, וְסוֹף מְטַיְּפָיִךְ יְטוּפוּן.״

[ח] **הוּא** הָיָה אוֹמֵר: מַרְבֶּה בָשָׂר, מַרְבֶּה רִמָּה;

The problem is always to determine when enough is enough. Current wisdom is that one can never be wealthy enough or thin enough. But that is terribly wrong. King Solomon, who was rich enough, ruefully records in *Ecclesiastes* (5:12), *I have seen that wealth creates evil for its owner*. The wise person, who has interests in life besides wealth, particularly interests in spiritual and intellectual Torah goals, will sense when enough is truly enough. (As far as being thin enough, I will discuss that sensitive topic in my comments on the eighth mishnah of this chapter.)

ובמקום שֶׁאֵין אֲנָשִׁים, הִשְׁתַּדֵּל לִהְיוֹת אִישׁ

And in a place where there are no leaders, strive to be a leader

HILLEL KNOWS THAT IN MANY SITUATIONS THERE IS SCANT LEADERSHIP and few good people to set a proper tone for society. In such instances, the tendency is to give up, to bow to the tyranny of the majority. But Judaism allows for no excuses and rationalizations. It has no room for self-pity and false self-justification. It does not compromise its ideals and goals. Jews have therefore been able to survive as a small, persecuted, hated minority, and yet prosper and be greatly influential in world affairs and civilizations. When there were no others to help rise to the challenges of paganism, hedonism, cruelty, and injustice, we nevertheless persevered in our struggle against these evils.

Judaism believes that a few good people can save humankind in spite of the many bad people. As we noted in Chapter One, Sodom was destroyed not because of its hordes of evildoers, but because it lacked ten good people in its midst. Our task, therefore, is to be a good person, no matter how lonely such a policy may be. If there are no others, then the responsibility upon us to be "the leader" is even greater. Complacency, defeatism, depression, inaction, and passive acceptance of evil people and ideas, are all foreign to Judaism.

Mishnah 7 WHEN READING HILLEL'S EXALTED WORDS OF GENTLENESS and kindness in the previous *mishnayos,* one may be tempted to think of him as unrealistic in his demands for rectitude and goodness in human life. This is far from the case. Hillel is not a dreamer with rose-colored glasses, living in a utopian, academic, tenured ivory tower. This

leaders, strive to be a leader.

7. Hillel also saw a skull floating on the surface of the water. Speaking to the skull, he observed: "Since you drowned others, you were also drowned, but we can rest assured that eventually those that unjustly drowned you will themselves be drowned."

8. He used to say: The more flesh, the more worms; the

---

mishnah tells us that he was equally aware of the violence and cruelty in human society, that he is grounded in this unpleasant, messy and dangerous world we all live in.

אַף הוּא רָאָה גֻּלְגֹּלֶת אַחַת שֶׁצָּפָה עַל פְּנֵי הַמָּיִם
Hillel also saw a skull floating on the surface of the water

HILLEL SEES SKULLS FLOATING ON THE SURFACE OF THE WATERS OF human behavior and society. He knows that sometimes there is no "nice way" to confront evil. Hillel, therefore, issues this stirring call for faith in eventual judgment and fairness. If human efforts to prevent and punish murder are thwarted, and the killers seem to "get away with it," we should never despair of ultimate retribution and justice. A chain of violence will always create a chain of retribution. It may take generations and acute insight to see God's judgment at work, but such judgment is always forthcoming. Those who drown innocent people are eventually drowned themselves, or are punished in some other appropriate way. In Chapter One we referred to the often quoted aphorism, "The wheels of history grind very slowly, but they grind exceedingly fine." We would hope that they begin to grind a little faster.

הוּא הָיָה אוֹמֵר
He used to say

Mishnah 8 THIS CONCLUDING MISHNAH OF HILLEL'S SAYINGS CONtrasts the downside of life's alleged pleasures with the eternal upside of Torah and spiritual endeavors. It is noteworthy that Hillel speaks not of *forbidden* activities, but of technically permitted behavior that is nevertheless wrong, and that brings great harm in its wake.

מַרְבֶּה בָשָׂר, מַרְבֶּה רִמָּה
The more flesh, the more worms

MUCH FOOD — UNCONTROLLED GLUTTONY — LEADS TO MAGGOTS AND the grave. Not only will more food produce more for the scavengers to consume once the body decomposes, bad eating habits themselves often bring a person to an untimely and early grave. The Torah stresses moderation in life and habits; excesses should always be avoided. Anything that is "too much" is usually not "too good." Thus Hillel's list of things that are "too much" and not "too good" gives us a sober and wise view of life and its pleasures and obligations.

מַרְבֶּה נְכָסִים, מַרְבֶּה דְאָגָה; מַרְבֶּה נָשִׁים, מַרְבֶּה כְשָׁפִים;
מַרְבֶּה שְׁפָחוֹת, מַרְבֶּה זִמָּה; מַרְבֶּה עֲבָדִים, מַרְבֶּה גָזֵל.
מַרְבֶּה תוֹרָה, מַרְבֶּה חַיִּים; מַרְבֶּה יְשִׁיבָה, מַרְבֶּה חָכְמָה;

מַרְבֶּה נְכָסִים, מַרְבֶּה דְאָגָה
The more possessions, the more worry

WEALTH AND PROPERTY INHERENTLY COME WITH PROBLEMS AND DIFFICULTIES. The tyranny of money often skews one's view of the world. Families are often torn apart over distribution of wealth and property, even when there is more than enough for everyone. The one thing about money is that people are rarely satisfied, and worries, tribulations, frustrations, and aggravation are as much the lot of the wealthy as of the poor. In fact, Hillel proposes that the more wealth one has, the more worrisome life may be for that person. The ability to handle money well financially, emotionally, spiritually, socially and legally is a great gift — as great a gift as the ability to amass great wealth itself. Personally, I have long ago stopped responding to grand sweepstakes, fabulous lotteries, unbelievable offers that promise, nay, guarantee, to make me wealthy. I wouldn't mind having more money. I am just afraid of the consequences of having "too much."

מַרְבֶּה נָשִׁים, מַרְבֶּה כְשָׁפִים
The more wives, the more witchcraft

JUDAISM HAS ALWAYS CHAMPIONED MONOGAMY AS THE IDEAL FORM OF marriage. Although there are cases of polygamy in the Bible, they do not represent the mainstream behavior of Jews, especially after the Torah was granted to Israel on Sinai. The now thousand-year-old חֵרֶם דְּרַבֵּינוּ גֵּרְשׁוֹם, *ban of Rabbeinu Gershom,* confirmed this ancient tradition and ended any possibility of polygamy in Ashkenazic Jewish lifestyle. Even among Sephardic Jews, who were not bound by Rabbeinu Gershom's decree, polygamous marriages were not the norm and existed usually only in extenuating circumstances. In our time, all sections of the Jewish people have rejected polygamy. In ancient times, the rivalry among jealous wives often led to witchcraft to get the upper hand over others in the household and gain the husband's affections.

מַרְבֶּה שְׁפָחוֹת, מַרְבֶּה זִמָּה
The more maidservants, the more lewdness

HAVING MAIDSERVANTS AROUND THE HOUSE ALSO POSES PROBLEMS. Especially in the ancient world of slavery, women servants were often seriously mistreated. Even in more modern times, such as during the Victorian Era in England and 19th-century America, employers were notorious for exploiting their female servants. The very vulnerability of such servants, due to their low economic and social status, guaranteed the prevalence of such problems. Such behavior helped reinforce the disdain of slavery among Jews, even though the Torah permitted it, albeit with strict restrictions. Slaves were invariably guilty of theft and promiscuity — a general loss of respect for property and people. The Talmud characterized slave mentality as that in

2/8 more possessions, the more worry; the more wives, the more witchcraft; the more maidservants, the more lewdness; the more manservants, the more thievery. [However,] the more Torah, the more life; the more study, the more wisdom;

---

which one is uncaring of self, of others, of social and spiritual norms and goals. No wonder the rabbis ruefully commented (*Kiddushin* 20a) that "one who acquires a slave for oneself has in reality acquired a master over one's self." Slavery damaged not only the slave, it also crippled the master.

There were always exceptions to this rule, however. The prime example of an idyllic master-servant relationship was that of Rabban Gamliel and his indentured servant, Tavi, for whom Rabban Gamliel even observed mourning/*shivah*. Generally speaking, however, it was frowned upon to have slaves and maidservants living in a Jewish home. The basic warning of "driving defensively," so often repeated in Avos, governs here as well. Hillel's warning is a splash of reality in the face of those who may seem to think they are somehow unaffected by basic human nature and drives.

❦ ❦ ❦

Having completed his list of the side effects of permissible but poor behavior, Hillel now gives a list of conduct that is not only desirable itself, but also brings with it infinite benefit.

מַרְבֶּה תוֹרָה, מַרְבֶּה חַיִּים ***[However,] the more Torah, the more life***

THIS "INCREASE IN LIFE" REFERS NOT NECESSARILY TO LONGEVITY, rather Hillel teaches that Torah increases the *quality* of one's days on earth. It allows a greater appreciation of life, of family, of the beauty of the world, and of the wonders of God's creation. It allows one to deal not only with the joys and triumphs of human existence, but also with its vicissitudes, tragedies, and disappointments. It provides balance, focus and perspective in an otherwise bewildering and often frightening world. Therefore Hillel uses the word מַרְבֶּה, literally: *increases*. Torah "increases" life by making us aware of life's importance and value, in terms of both time and behavior. It increases our sense of self, of our potential and importance, of our uniqueness and individual worth. Death and defeat are always tragic, but they are unavoidable. The greatest tragedy in human experience, however, is a lifetime squandered, which *is* avoidable. The preventive of such a tragedy is to increase Torah in one's life.

מַרְבֶּה יְשִׁיבָה, מַרְבֶּה חָכְמָה ***The more study, the more wisdom***

THERE IS NO SUBSTITUTE FOR DILIGENCE IN STUDYING TORAH. GENIUSES and people with great minds and memories do not always develop into true scholars unless they also acquire good study habits and diligent devotion to their studies. My *rebbi* in Chicago constantly told us budding geniuses that "the Lord counts the hours of study more than the pages turned." In the

מַרְבֶּה עֵצָה, מַרְבֶּה תְבוּנָה; מַרְבֶּה צְדָקָה, מַרְבֶּה שָׁלוֹם. קָנָה שֵׁם טוֹב, קָנָה לְעַצְמוֹ; קָנָה לוֹ דִּבְרֵי תוֹרָה, קָנָה לוֹ חַיֵּי הָעוֹלָם הַבָּא.

Jewish world, *bitul Torah* — wasting time away from Torah studies — is considered a major defect. It is reputed that the Gaon of Vilna, Rabbi Eliyahu Kramer, as part of his Yom Kippur repentance, took stock of each moment throughout the year, and expressed remorse for every moment he could not account for. None of us are the Gaon's caliber, but we all realize that we do not become wise by time wasted or ill spent.

A further idea included in the concept of *the more study, the more wisdom* is that mentioned in the first mishnah of Avos, that one should increase the number of students and yeshivos. The way to increase knowledge and wisdom is to increase the numbers that actually participate in Torah study. This results in increased scholarship not only for the students, but for the teachers as well, for students make their teacher wiser. The interaction of student and teacher, which is the basis of traditional Jewish scholarship, sharpens the intellect of both. This is beautifully expressed by Rabbi Chanina in the Talmud (*Taanis* 7a): "Much have I learned from my teachers; more have I learned from my colleagues; but from my students I have learned the most"; this remains the basis of Jewish educational practice to this day. It follows, then, that the more students an instructor has, the more he gains in his own wisdom.

Increasing the number of students also heightens the element of competition among them, which is an important goad to Torah study: קִנְאַת סוֹפְרִים תַּרְבֶּה חָכְמָה, *competition among scholars increases wisdom*. Even though the proliferation of yeshivos and Torah schools has always been criticized as inefficient for economic and other reasons, the truth is that in terms of scholarship and Torah creativity, the more the merrier.

מַרְבֶּה עֵצָה, מַרְבֶּה תְבוּנָה
The more counsel, the more understanding

SEEKING ADVICE IS THE KEY TO UNDERSTANDING THE NATURE OF problems and difficulties, whether they are in scholarship, personal life, or communal affairs. The counsel of the wise and experienced should be sought and treasured. This advice of Hillel is the forerunner to that of his grandson, Rabban Gamliel, as quoted in the previous chapter (1:16), that one should accept upon oneself a master instructor. Jewish life stresses the trait of accepting advice from the wise. Even though we treasure our personal freedom and emotional autonomy, rare is the person who does not at one time or another require counsel and sage advice from others. True understanding usually requires some outside input, especially from recognized authorities, given with wisdom and compassion.

2/8

the more counsel, the more understanding; the more charity, the more peace. One who has gained a good reputation has gained it for his own benefit; one who has gained himself Torah knowledge has gained himself the life of the World to Come.

מַרְבֶּה צְדָקָה, מַרְבֶּה שָׁלוֹם
The more charity, the more peace

PEACE — WITH ONESELF AND WITH OTHERS — IS AN ULTIMATE GOOD OF Jewish life. The very last mishnah of the Talmud teaches that the Lord found no vessel to contain and hold life's blessings except peace. I know someone who always brings a large, empty box to bar mitzvah celebrations, to make it easier for the young boy to take home his gifts. Without the box, the gifts would easily be dropped and might even get lost. Well, peace is that large box that holds all the other gifts of life. Without it, much else is lost and discarded. And peace, like health — the other supreme container of the gifts of life — requires care, effort and spiritual merit in order to be pursued successfully.

Hillel explains that *tzedakah* — charity and righteousness — increases the chance for the attainment of peace. I feel that Hillel refers not only to the giving of *tzedakah* of money — important and holy as that may be. He also means the charitableness of attitude. The absence of judgmental thinking and behavior, the refusal to demonize those with whom one disagrees, the tolerance of others who differ with one — all combine to create the type of *tzedakah* that enhances peace. Righteousness and charity are character traits and not just check-signing exercises. They go to the depth of the human personality and soul. They increase our sensitivity to others and thereby create a climate for greater peace and harmony — with one's own self, as well as with others.

קָנָה שֵׁם טוֹב
One who has gained a good reputation

A "GOOD NAME" IS ONE OF LIFE'S GREAT ACCOMPLISHMENTS AND treasures. Yet it is a private accomplishment, one that cannot be shared with others, and cannot even be passed on to children and descendants. A good name has a limited life span, usually only the life of the person who earned it, but Torah is the stuff of eternity; when one acquires Torah one acquires immortality. Nevertheless, we will read later that the crown of a good name is apparently greater than the crown of Torah (4:13). I have often thought about this apparent contradiction. I think now that Hillel is telling us here that even though the crown of a good name may be the greatest of all crowns, that is true only while its possessor still lives. The crown of Torah, however, lives on eternally, for Torah is never limited to one person or to one scholar alone. One's study of Torah and contribution to its scholarship lives on, even if time eventually dims the memory of one's good name. Here Hillel deals not with "greatness," but with eternity.

[ט] **רַבָּן** יוֹחָנָן בֶּן זַכַּאי קִבֵּל מֵהִלֵּל וּמִשַּׁמַּאי. הוּא הָיָה אוֹמֵר: אִם לָמַדְתָּ תּוֹרָה הַרְבֵּה, אַל תַּחֲזִיק טוֹבָה לְעַצְמְךָ, כִּי לְכָךְ נוֹצָרְתָּ.

[י] **חֲמִשָּׁה** תַלְמִידִים הָיוּ לוֹ לְרַבָּן יוֹחָנָן בֶּן זַכַּאי, וְאֵלּוּ הֵן: רַבִּי אֱלִיעֶזֶר בֶּן הֻרְקְנוֹס, רַבִּי יְהוֹשֻׁעַ בֶּן חֲנַנְיָא, רַבִּי יוֹסֵי הַכֹּהֵן, רַבִּי שִׁמְעוֹן בֶּן נְתַנְאֵל, וְרַבִּי אֶלְעָזָר בֶּן עֲרָךְ.

רַבָּן יוֹחָנָן בֶּן זַכַּאי
Rabban Yochanan ben Zakkai

Mishnah 9 THE TALMUD INFORMS US THAT THE GREAT HILLEL RAISED eighty main disciples, and the least of them was Rabban Yochanan ben Zakkai! But nevertheless, he was the main conduit for the traditions of Hillel and Shammai to later generations. This "least" disciple was the savior of the Jewish people in the generation of the Roman conquest of Jerusalem and the destruction of the Second Temple by Titus. Rabban Yochanan chose to rebuild Israel through Torah and the further development of Jewish life, in accordance with the Oral Law and its values and teachings. Together with the *Nasi*, Rabban Gamliel II of Yavneh, Rabban Yochanan reinstituted the Sanhedrin and established Yavneh and its academy of Torah scholars as the center of Jewish law and authority. Thus he created the mechanism for Jewish survival that would serve Israel in its long and dark exile. His genius in establishing a spiritual "government" for the Jews to replace their lost national independence was the decisive factor in the survival of Judaism itself.

In his personal life, Rabban Yochanan was a teacher, scholar, businessman and a person of charisma and inspiration. He lived in the small town of Bror Chayil, traveling to Yavneh, the dwelling place of Rabban Gamliel, as the occasion demanded. Even though Rabban Gamliel was the *Nasi*, the official head of the Sanhedrin and of the Yavneh academy, Yavneh is always associated in Jewish memory with the vision and courage of Rabban Yochanan ben Zakkai.

אִם לָמַדְתָּ תּוֹרָה הַרְבֵּה, אַל תַּחֲזִיק טוֹבָה לְעַצְמְךָ
If you have studied much Torah, do not take credit for yourself

SELF-PRIDE IS AN OBVIOUS ASSET AND NECESSITY IN LIFE, BUT SELF-congratulation and adulation is not. In fact, it is a destructive and harmful influence that leads to frustration with others and the world generally. The job of Jewish scholars is to study and teach Torah as well as possible. Therefore, if one does become a recognized scholar of Torah, one should feel the self-satisfaction of accomplishment, but nothing more. No arrogance, no self-congratulations, no lording it over others, כִּי לְכָךְ נוֹצָרְתָּ, *because that is what you were created to do*. God gave you a good mind, the ability and opportu-

9. Rabban Yochanan ben Zakkai received the tradition from Hillel and Shammai. He used to say: If you have studied much Torah, do not take credit for yourself, because that is what you were created to do.

10. Rabban Yochanan ben Zakkai had five [primary] disciples. They were: Rabbi Eliezer ben Hyrkanos, Rabbi Yehoshua ben Chanania, Rabbi Yose the Kohen, Rabbi Shimon ben Nesanel, and Rabbi Elazar ben Arach.

---

nity to study, and the never-ending joy and challenge of Torah study. You are just doing your job. One should be thankful for an employer who allows one to do one's job in an efficient and productive manner. The Creator has favored us with His Torah. Our job is to study it, live it, and preserve it.

❦ ❦ ❦

Doing the job

When I was a young rabbi starting out in my career as a public speaker, I was often crestfallen by the lack of enthusiastic accolades from my congregants at the end of my brilliant sermons. But after a number of years, I began to realize that they were paying me to deliver scintillating sermons regularly and consistently. That was part of my job. So, I came to appreciate the fact that as long as they did not sleep (at least not snore) through the sermon and did not complain unduly after its completion, I was doing well. In fact, I realized that one of the highest achievements in life is simply doing one's job well.

❦ ❦ ❦

חֲמִשָּׁה תַלְמִידִים
Five [primary] disciples

Mishnah 10 THESE FIVE STUDENTS ARE MENTIONED AS A GROUP IN A number of places in the Talmud and Midrash. As long as their teacher was alive, they stayed with him in his village of Bror Chayil, journeying to Yavneh, where Rabban Gamliel II reigned, only when Rabban Yochanan himself went there to take part in the deliberations of the Sanhedrin. After his death, the five joined Rabban Gamliel II as the leaders of Israel after Rabban Yochanan's death. Four of them — Rabbis Eliezer ben Hyrkanos, Yehoshua ben Chanania, Yose the Kohen, and Shimon ben Nesanel — settled in Yavneh.

Eventually there was friction between them and Rabban Gamliel II. Rabbi Eliezer ben Hyrkanos was a strong proponent of the school of Shammai and refused to submit to the halachic rule of the majority. As such, many disputes regarding his rulings arose and in spite of his great scholarship, supernatural abilities and role as a master teacher (he was the main mentor of Rabbi Akiva among others), he was eventually banned from public life and ostracized by the rabbis of Yavneh. Rabbi Yehoshua ben Chanania was the main catalyst in a rebellion against the rule of Rabban Gamliel II that resulted in the latter's

[יא] **הוּא** הָיָה מוֹנֶה שִׁבְחָן: (רַבִּי) אֱלִיעֶזֶר בֶּן הֻרְקְנוֹס, בּוֹר סוּד שֶׁאֵינוֹ מְאַבֵּד טִפָּה; (רַבִּי) יְהוֹשֻׁעַ בֶּן חֲנַנְיָא, אַשְׁרֵי יוֹלַדְתּוֹ; (רַבִּי) יוֹסֵי הַכֹּהֵן, חָסִיד; (רַבִּי) שִׁמְעוֹן בֶּן נְתַנְאֵל, יְרֵא חֵטְא; וְ(רַבִּי) אֶלְעָזָר בֶּן עֲרָךְ, כְּמַעְיָן הַמִּתְגַּבֵּר.

[יב] **הוּא** הָיָה אוֹמֵר: אִם יִהְיוּ כָּל חַכְמֵי יִשְׂרָאֵל

---

temporary demotion from his position as leader of the nation. It seems that as long as Rabban Yochanan ben Zakkai lived, his disciples did not assert themselves publicly in controversial matters of halachah and/or public policy. However, after the death of Rabban Yochanan, they felt responsible to take a leading role in public matters and this often led to divisions.

Rabban Yochanan's fifth disciple was Rabbi Elazar ben Arach. It seems from *mishnayos* 12-14 that Rabban Yochanan regarded him as the greatest of his generation. He was destined for tragedy, however, for he did not accompany his colleagues to Yavneh, the seat of Torah learning, but instead, at the urging of his wife, moved to Diomseys, a seaside resort town in Syria. There, he deteriorated physically and even mentally, to the point that he was unable even to read verses of the Torah accurately. The rabbis drew a lesson from his tragic end: No matter how great one is, one should never "retire" from study and/or distance oneself from the main study hall of Torah and its resident scholars. An often-repeated piece of advice in Avos is to live in a community of Torah learning and respect for its scholarship. This is as true in one's later years as it is during the formative years of youth and early maturity.

הוּא הָיָה מוֹנֶה שִׁבְחָן
He used to enumerate their praises

Mishnah 11 RABBAN YOCHANAN HIGHLIGHTS THE INDIVIDUALITY OF his five disciples. *Rabbi Eliezer ben Hyrkanos* has instant recall of everything he has learned.

Rabbi Yehoshua ben Chanania brings joy to the mother who brought him into the world. Among the five disciples, Rabbi Yehoshua emerges as the leading activist in public matters. He took a major role in excluding the newly formed and rapidly growing Christian community from the social and religious life of the Jewish people.

Rabbi Yose the Kohen is a *chassid*, a pious man who breaks down the barriers between man and the Creator and between man and one's fellow human beings. The linguistic definition of *chassid* is one who can extend oneself, to break the chains that bind us to our earthliness and selfishness. Rabbi Yose is a leader, a scholar, a wise man, a diplomat, personally humble, yet a person of principle and greatness. He is also a blacksmith, monetarily

11. He used to enumerate their praises: (Rabbi) Eliezer ben Hyrkanos is [like] a cemented cistern that loses not a drop; (Rabbi) Yehoshua ben Chanania, praiseworthy is she who bore him; (Rabbi) Yose the Kohen is a scrupulously pious person; (Rabbi) Shimon ben Nesanel fears sin; (and Rabbi) Elazar ben Arach is like a spring flowing stronger and stronger.

12. He used to say: If all of the sages of Israel were on

---

poor while being spiritually wealthy. Together with Rabbi Eliezer and Rabban Gamliel II, Rabbi Yose visited Rome, where they helped create a strong Jewish community and won concessions from the Romans to rebuild Jewish life in conquered and despoiled Judea. The character and demeanor of these great rabbis of Israel so impressed many of the Romans that there was a wave of conversions to Judaism by prominent Romans.

Rabbi Shimon ben Nesanel, a member of the priestly family and a son-in-law of Rabban Gamliel I, is described as being "fearful of sin." This phrase usually denotes someone who is cautious in nature and pious and punctilious in observance of halachah. It is the description of the ultimate defensive driver in life, one who avoids temptation and risks.

Rabbi Elazar ben Arach is continuously creative and innovative.

What is clear from this mishnah is that these five disciples were each very unique people, different one from another. It is also clear that Rabban Yochanan encouraged these differences, recognizing the individual talents and personal natures of each. The great teacher is not a cookie cutter who produces identical people. Rather, the greater the teacher, the more diverse and all encompassing will be his own personality, so that each student will be attracted to the facets of that personality that most appeal to his own persona and nature. Thus, the great teacher will inspire a wide variety of students, students with differing views and talents, public roles and accomplishments. The Torah, within the parameters of halachah, encourages individuality and opposes the dreaded hand of oppressive conformity. Rabban Yochanan's identification of the different and positive individual strengths and talents of his five main students should serve as an example for every teacher and mentor of Torah in all times and places. We should rejoice in the diversity of our students (and our children as well) and not attempt to stifle their individuality and personal uniqueness.

הוּא הָיָה אוֹמֵר
He used to say

Mishnah 12 A CONSTANT DEBATE IN THE TALMUD CONCERNS THE ISSUE of which is superior, *sinai* (wide-ranging, thorough, retentive knowledge) or *okeir harim* (innovative, inventive, original thought). This

בְּכַף מֹאזְנַיִם, וֶאֱלִיעֶזֶר בֶּן הֻרְקְנוֹס בְּכַף שְׁנִיָּה, מַכְרִיעַ אֶת כֻּלָּם. אַבָּא שָׁאוּל אוֹמֵר מִשְּׁמוֹ: אִם יִהְיוּ כָּל חַכְמֵי יִשְׂרָאֵל בְּכַף מֹאזְנַיִם, וְ(רַבִּי) אֱלִיעֶזֶר בֶּן הֻרְקְנוֹס אַף עִמָּהֶם, וְ(רַבִּי) אֶלְעָזָר בֶּן עֲרָךְ בְּכַף שְׁנִיָּה, מַכְרִיעַ אֶת כֻּלָּם.

[יג] **אָמַר** לָהֶם: צְאוּ וּרְאוּ אֵיזוֹ הִיא דֶּרֶךְ טוֹבָה שֶׁיִּדְבַּק בָּהּ הָאָדָם. רַבִּי אֱלִיעֶזֶר אוֹמֵר: עַיִן טוֹבָה. רַבִּי יְהוֹשֻׁעַ אוֹמֵר: חָבֵר טוֹב. רַבִּי יוֹסֵי

---

debate is played out in the two opinions recorded here, as to whether Rabbi Eliezer (the *sinai*) or Rabbi Elazar ben Arach (the *okeir harim*) is the greater Torah scholar. The eventual conclusion of the Talmud seems to indicate that the one indispensable ingredient for Torah achievement is knowledge of the Torah. The greater the fund of knowledge, the more a scholar can understand, apply to new situations and grow into greatness. In the aphorism of the Sages, "Everyone depends on the owner of the wheat," for without wheat there is no bread. Without knowledge there is no Torah greatness.

We tend to be blinded by brilliance and great minds, and are willing to overlook the faults of the genius, while demanding that the more plodding always toe the line. But as with the fable of the tortoise and the hare, the genius does not always prevail. In my own experience as a teacher, I have often been amazed by how my students eventually turned out. Many times, the sure winners somehow became losers, while those I thought were average at best became successful leaders, scholars, and role models for others. The wisdom of Solomon (*Ecclesiastes* 9:11) that "the race is not always to the swift" is borne out by life's events.

צְאוּ וּרְאוּ
Go out and discern

Mishnah 13 RABBAN YOCHANAN WAS WELL AWARE OF THE ENORMOUS difference between the atmosphere and theories of the study hall and the rough and tumble of everyday life. As mentioned above, he was a businessman; in fact he spent forty years of his long life engaged in commerce. As such, he understood the pressures and challenges of the world, and how dangerous to one's soul life's events can be, if one does not have a firm value system. Therefore, he encouraged his students to go out in the world and view the events of life as they really occur and then to decide which path, which character trait, which value, to pursue above all others, in order to be spiritually successful. Being five different individuals, as explained

one pan of a balance scale, and Eliezer ben Hyrkanos were on the other, he would outweigh them all. Abba Shaul said in [Rabban Yochanan's] name: If all the sages of Israel with even (Rabbi) Eliezer ben Hyrkanos among them, were on one pan of the balance scale, and (Rabbi) Elazar ben Arach were on the other, he would outweigh them all.

13. He [Rabban Yochanan ben Zakkai] said to them [the five disciples]: Go out and discern which is the proper path to which a man should cling. Rabbi Eliezer says: A good eye. Rabbi Yehoshua says: A good friend. Rabbi Yose

---

above, they returned to him with five different, though in reality quite similar, responses to his challenge.

All the advice of the rabbis in this mishnah is based on the presupposition of a Torah-observant lifestyle. On top of that commitment to Torah observance, they advise that one should also have a good eye, be a good neighbor, a good friend, a far-sighted and responsible human being, and a person with a good heart. A bad person, however, can abuse Torah observance. In its simplest form, punctilious adherence to halachah does not necessarily guarantee that one will be a good person. The well-known comment of Nachmanides that a person can be a *naval* — an obscene reprehensible human being — even within the confines of Torah observance, is very well known. In order to save oneself from the trap of being a *naval,* the rabbis here in this mishnah advanced these ideas of character and life traits that a person should follow in order to help him achieve nobility and holiness. When combined with the adoption of a Torah-observant lifestyle and traditional Jewish values, these traits, especially the achievement of a good heart — the trait lauded by Rabban Yochanan — then create a Jewish personality that is worthy of study, admiration and emulation.

עַיִן טוֹבָה
A good eye

IN ITS MOST OBVIOUS SENSE, A *GOOD EYE* MEANS TO BE TOLERANT AND to be happy when someone else succeeds. It also means having a realistic eye. Fanciful do-gooders who close their eye to the dangers involved in their pet projects do not have a *good* eye, but rather a *blind* eye. True, we are bidden to look at all people and situations favorably and optimistically. We are required to give others the benefit of the doubt and not be harshly judgmental and suspicious of others. Nevertheless, having said this, we should not be foolish and wildly impractical simply because we wish that good should prevail. It is the good eye that is practical, reasonable, and sensible that can encompass the other traits mentioned by Rabbi Eliezer's colleagues.

אוֹמֵר: שָׁכֵן טוֹב. רַבִּי שִׁמְעוֹן אוֹמֵר: הָרוֹאֶה אֶת הַנּוֹלָד. רַבִּי אֶלְעָזָר אוֹמֵר: לֵב טוֹב. אָמַר לָהֶם: רוֹאֶה אֲנִי אֶת דִּבְרֵי אֶלְעָזָר בֶּן עֲרָךְ מִדִּבְרֵיכֶם, שֶׁבִּכְלַל דְּבָרָיו דִּבְרֵיכֶם.

[יד] **אָמַר** לָהֶם: צְאוּ וּרְאוּ אֵיזוֹ הִיא דֶּרֶךְ רָעָה שֶׁיִּתְרַחֵק מִמֶּנָּה הָאָדָם. רַבִּי אֱלִיעֶזֶר

In a sense, all of the positive traits mentioned in this mishnah are really cumulative, one being built upon the successful attainment of the previously mentioned trait. It is therefore clear to us why Rabban Yochanan himself was able to state that Rabbi Elazar's advocacy of the trait of a good heart was the most inclusive of all of the traits mentioned, since it included and was itself based upon all of the other traits mentioned, while the other rabbis' recommendations were based only on some of them.

חָבֵר טוֹב
A good friend

A GOOD FRIEND IS SOMEONE WHO REMAINS A GOOD FRIEND EVEN WHEN aware of your imperfections. In the Bible we read of Yehudah's good friend the Adulami who remained his friend and confidant, even after Yehudah acted improperly. Good friends are rare in life. One who has such a friend should truly appreciate such a blessing.

שָׁכֵן טוֹב
A good neighbor

BEING A GOOD NEIGHBOR, A GOOD FRIEND, HAVING A GOOD EYE ON THE world, seeing well the consequences of one's behavior — all are admirable goals and paths in life. Yet, being a good neighbor or a good friend can many times be dependent on who one's neighbor is or what group of people one is associated with.

❦ ❦ ❦

When I was a young newlywed in Chicago, my wife and I erected a succah in the backyard of our newly purchased and heavily mortgaged home. My non-observant Jewish neighbor, who was undoubtedly convinced that our mere presence on the block was ruining the neighborhood, complained about us to the Building Department for erecting a "structure" without a permit. Much to the dismay of the neighbor, I dutifully obtained the permit. Many months later, I asked him why he was so hostile when he had never even said a word to us. I expected that he would quote Robert Frost's cynical statement that "Goods fences make good neighbors." But he just gave me a dirty look — a bad eye — and never spoke to me in all the years that we lived side by side. I found it awfully difficult to be a good neighbor, though I certainly never caused him any trouble or harm. It seems that one needs receptive neighbors to

says: A good neighbor. Rabbi Shimon says: One who considers the outcome [of a deed]. R' Elazar says: A good heart. He said to them: I prefer the words of Elazar ben Arach to your words, for your words are included in his words.

14. He said to them: Go out and discern which is the evil path from which a man should distance himself. Rabbi Eliezer

---

completely fulfill the path in life of being a good neighbor.

❦ ❦ ❦

לֵב טוֹב
A good heart

THE TERM "A GOOD HEART" HAS BEEN SEVERELY OVERWORKED — AND abused — in modern Jewish life. Generations of well-intentioned Jews were raised to believe that a "good Jewish heart" was sufficient to insure Jewish survival, both individually and communally. Sadly, reality has proven that a "good Jewish heart" is not nearly enough. A good heart is the source of compassion, empathy, and tolerance. It is the ability to encompass other human beings in one's "family" and emotions.

❦ ❦ ❦

A great person, especially a great teacher, is a multifaceted personality. Contrary to "one size fits all" biographies that are sometimes popularized in the Jewish world, no great person is one-dimensional. It is not surprising, therefore, that each of his five students saw in Rabban Yochanan ben Zakkai different character traits that each of them then adopted for himself as his own best pathway in life. One saw him as a good neighbor and another saw him as a good friend and so forth. Rabban Yochanan apparently saw himself essentially as a good heart and thus chose that description to encapsulate all of the other attributes that his students saw in him. Yet, Rabban Yochanan encouraged each of his students to test their individual opinions in the marketplace of life itself. "Go out and see" was what the master teacher told his disciples. Individual personality and differing life circumstances often lead loyal students of one great teacher to differing opinions and attitudes on basic questions of living and improving within the framework of Torah goodness.

צְאוּ וּרְאוּ אֵיזוֹ הִיא דֶּרֶךְ רָעָה
Go out and discern which is the evil path

Mishnah 14 THE PATHS OF LIFE THAT LEAD TO EVIL BEHAVIOR MAY be varied, but they all have one common ancestor — a supreme degree of selfishness, and callousness toward the physical condition of others. This is an echo of Rabban Yochanan's great teacher, Hillel, who said, "If I am only for myself, then of what value am I?" It is Abraham, the good friend and neighbor with the kind eye and the open tent, who is the progenitor of Israel and the founder of our faith. Thus, it is no coincidence that all the evil ways described in this mishnah deal with human interpersonal relationships. A

אוֹמֵר: עַיִן רָעָה. רַבִּי יְהוֹשֻׁעַ אוֹמֵר: חָבֵר רָע. רַבִּי יוֹסֵי אוֹמֵר: שָׁכֵן רָע. רַבִּי שִׁמְעוֹן אוֹמֵר: הַלֹּוֶה וְאֵינוֹ מְשַׁלֵּם. אֶחָד הַלֹּוֶה מִן הָאָדָם כְּלֹוֶה מִן הַמָּקוֹם, שֶׁנֶּאֱמַר: „לֹוֶה רָשָׁע וְלֹא יְשַׁלֵּם, וְצַדִּיק חוֹנֵן וְנוֹתֵן.״ רַבִּי אֶלְעָזָר אוֹמֵר: לֵב רָע. אָמַר לָהֶם: רוֹאֶה אֲנִי אֶת דִּבְרֵי אֶלְעָזָר בֶּן עֲרָךְ מִדִּבְרֵיכֶם, שֶׁבִּכְלַל דְּבָרָיו דִּבְרֵיכֶם.

[טו] **הֵם** אָמְרוּ שְׁלֹשָׁה דְבָרִים. רַבִּי אֱלִיעֶזֶר אוֹמֵר: יְהִי כְבוֹד חֲבֵרְךָ חָבִיב עָלֶיךָ כְּשֶׁלָּךְ,

---

bad neighbor, a friend who is a bad influence, someone who borrows and never repays (basically, a taker and never a giver), someone who has a bad eye (blind to reality, jealous of others, a misanthropic pessimist), and someone who has an evil heart — these are the ones who foster evil in the world. The rapacious society of Sodom, the hypocrisy and wickedness of Bilaam, are built upon these evil character traits. And again, Rabban Yochanan informs us that it is the bad heart that feeds all the other woes described in the mishnah.

לֵב רָע
A bad heart

A BAD HEART SPIRITUALLY, LIKE A WEAK HEART PHYSICALLY, IS SUBJECT to treatment and improvement. A good Jewish heart needs regular exercise and training. Aside from the constant necessity to observe halachah and tradition, giving charity daily, visiting the sick, comforting the bereaved, paying attention to the widow and aiding the orphan, honoring and caring for aged parents, feeling concerned about the fate of others, are all part of the exercise regimen to create a healthy Jewish heart. The prophet Yechezkel (36:26) promised that the Lord would eventually remove our hearts of stone and replace them with hearts of yielding flesh. The Lord is the great surgeon Who performs the transformation of our hearts. However, the maintenance and rehabilitation necessary for the good heart to function properly is left to us to accomplish.

❦ ❦ ❦

One final personal word regarding this mishnah. In my years as a lawyer and then as a rabbi, I discovered that nothing ever poisoned a relationship within a family or among close friends as much as not repaying a monetary debt. The rabbis of the Talmud warned against borrowing money when the borrower knows he will probably not be able to repay the loan. A bad experience with a borrower is likely to firmly lock the door of that lender to other borrowers who are reliable and truthful.

The rabbis steadfastly believed in the words of Proverbs/Mishlei (22:7) that

says: An evil eye. Rabbi Yehoshua says: An evil friend. Rabbi Yose says: A wicked neighbor. Rabbi Shimon says: One who borrows and does not repay; one who borrows from man is like one who borrows from the Omnipresent, as it says: *The wicked one borrows and does not pay, while the Righteous One is gracious and gives* (*Psalms* 37:21). Rabbi Elazar says: A bad heart. He [Rabban Yochanan ben Zakkai] said to them: I prefer the words of Elazar ben Arach to your words, for your words are included in his words.

15. They each said three things. Rabbi Eliezer says: Let your fellow's honor be as dear to you as your own,

---

"a borrower becomes a slave to the lender." The relationship between people is automatically skewed by borrowing money. Thus, an unnatural relationship is always created when an individual lends money to someone. In order to prevent that relationship from deterioration, the Torah set strict guidelines as to the methods a creditor may use to collect the debt. Dunning the debtor for repayment is forbidden. However, the Torah obviously demanded that the borrower live up to his end of the bargain as well. Defaulting on a loan is not only a monetary indiscretion. It is just as much a spiritual blemish on one's soul. Sometimes extenuating circumstances make a borrower unable to make payment, but such exceptions are rare and in no way change the rule and attitude enunciated here. Money, like life itself, is ultimately being borrowed from our Creator. We are duty bound to use it and return it in an honorable and worthwhile fashion.

❦ ❦ ❦

הֵם אָמְרוּ
They each said

Mishnah 15 EACH OF RABBAN YOCHANAN'S ILLUSTRIOUS DISCIPLES contributed three maxims regarding productive human life. In a sense, their maxims may be used to illuminate their previously stated opinions regarding the unique core value, both positive and negative, of life.

יְהִי כְבוֹד חֲבֵרְךָ חָבִיב עָלֶיךָ כְּשֶׁלָּךְ
Let your fellow's honor be as dear to you as your own

THE GREAT RABBI ELIEZER BEN HYRKANOS, WHO POSITED THE IDEA OF A good eye as the central characteristic of a good life, now expands on this idea. A "good eye" entails a respect for the feelings, self-respect, and honor of one's fellow. How many children have been scarred for life by the insults or cutting remarks — even of the "it's for your own good" kind — of a parent, teacher, or any other authority figures. Everyone is entitled to be treated with decency, courtesy, and respect. In my opinion, Rabbi Eliezer's statement may represent his own rueful comment on the censure and ban that was placed upon him by

וְאַל תְּהִי נוֹחַ לִכְעוֹס; וְשׁוּב יוֹם אֶחָד לִפְנֵי מִיתָתְךָ; וֶהֱוֵי מִתְחַמֵּם כְּנֶגֶד אוּרָן שֶׁל חֲכָמִים, וֶהֱוֵי זָהִיר בְּגַחַלְתָּן שֶׁלֹּא תִכָּוֶה – שֶׁנְּשִׁיכָתָן נְשִׁיכַת שׁוּעָל, וַעֲקִיצָתָן עֲקִיצַת עַקְרָב, וּלְחִישָׁתָן לְחִישַׁת שָׂרָף, וְכָל דִּבְרֵיהֶם כְּגַחֲלֵי אֵשׁ.

---

the majority of his colleagues when he refused their demand to abandon his support of the rulings of the House of Shammai. Although he accepted the ban and lived out his life in enforced isolation from his colleagues, he may have felt that they had not treated him with enough sensitivity on that sad occasion.

❦ ❦ ❦

Poor eyesight/ good eye

I had a great teacher in the Chicago yeshivah who was one of the kindest, gentlest, most considerate teachers I ever had. He was teaching Talmud to a class of thirty American teenagers who had a rambunctious side to them. When he wanted to speak to one of us about our academic, attendance, or personal failings, he never did so in front of another student. Rather, he took us into the clothes closet of the classroom, where he cajoled us to be better Jews. Once we came to know and appreciate this wonderful man, none of us wanted to be subjected to his gentle and most respectful "closet treatment." The shame of disappointing our holy teacher was too great to bear — so we began to behave ourselves. After a while, good behavior became a part of our makeup. Honey always catches more flies than does vinegar. Our beloved teacher had very poor eyesight, but he certainly possessed a good eye.

❦ ❦ ❦

A good eye also has a calming effect upon a person. One who possesses such a good eye sees less in the world and in the behavior of others to be angry about. As is obvious from even a cursory examination of Avos, its great authors were of the opinion that uncontrolled anger is the worst of traits and the precursor to major sin. Quick to anger is quick to sin. Not only is it harmful to lash out in anger, it is equally harmful to be angry even if one never gives it physical expression. There is a great deal of difference between anger and tension. Tension can be relieved, anger is a constant state of being. Tension is unavoidable, anger can be avoided through training, self-discipline and the acquisition of a good eye. Tension can sometimes be transformed into a positive goad for achievements in life. Anger always harms the angry person as well as his victims.

2/15

and do not anger easily; repent one day before your death; warm yourself by the fire of the sages, but beware of their glowing coal lest you be burnt — for their bite is the bite of a fox, their sting is the sting of a scorpion, their hiss is the hiss of a serpent, and all their words are like fiery coals.

וְשׁוּב יוֹם אֶחָד לִפְנֵי מִיתָתְךָ
Repent one day before your death

A GOOD EYE CERTAINLY INCLUDES RESPECT TOWARD ONESELF. THE concept of *teshuvah* — repentance and improvement — is central in this view, for to despair about oneself is tantamount to committing evil. Despair about one's spiritual and moral state is the ultimate evil eye. But *teshuvah* should not be reserved for Yom Kippur alone. Every day is a good day for review, assessment, and improvement. And *teshuvah* is possible only while one is still alive. Since the day of our departure from this world is almost always hidden from us, we should therefore constantly be engaged in this exercise of introspection and self-improvement.

The graph of life's achievements, like all graphs, has jagged lines of ascent and descent on it. My stockbroker friends tell me that one should never despair in a bear market — eventually it will turn bullish again. Maybe they are right, though financial histories tell us that there have been a lot of satiated bears around over the years. But though the graph of human life requires effort and tenacity, direction and work, *teshuvah* guarantees that one's life graph will turn upwards. *Teshuvah* is not a free lunch, but it does allow for great and eternal gain. In Jewish thought, *teshuvah* is pretty much synonymous with life itself.

וֶהֱוֵי זָהִיר בְּגַחַלְתָּן שֶׁלֹּא תִכָּוֶה
But beware of their glowing coal lest you be burnt

RABBI ELIEZER'S COMPARISON OF THE RESULT OF THE DISPLEASURE OF the great Torah scholars of Israel to fox bites, scorpion stings, and burning coals reflects his own personal experience.

Each of these three painful examples illustrates a different level of suffering and each of them can be fatal. Jewish history testifies to the lethal results of disregarding the words, decisions, and ordinances of the great rabbinical scholars of Israel. As mentioned above, Rabbi Eliezer was isolated from his rabbinic colleagues because of his refusal to follow the will of the majority regarding halachic decisions. He felt the bite, the sting, the burn of their opposition to him and paid the penalty for not accepting the Torah-prescribed rule of the majority.

The Talmud records Rabbi Eliezer's prowess as a miracle worker, who apparently had heavenly approval for his view of the halachah. None of that mattered, though, in the earthly court of the rabbis, where the halachah was actually decided. "It is not in heaven!" the rabbis said of the right to decide the halachah, and so it is not.

[טז] **רַבִּי** יְהוֹשֻׁעַ אוֹמֵר: עַיִן הָרָע, וְיֵצֶר הָרָע, וְשִׂנְאַת הַבְּרִיּוֹת מוֹצִיאִין אֶת הָאָדָם מִן הָעוֹלָם.

[יז] **רַבִּי** יוֹסֵי אוֹמֵר: יְהִי מָמוֹן חֲבֵרְךָ חָבִיב עָלֶיךָ כְּשֶׁלָּךְ; וְהַתְקֵן עַצְמְךָ לִלְמוֹד תּוֹרָה,

---

Fire is meant to warm and be productive and not to injure and maim, but one must be careful when dealing with fire. So too must one be careful when relating to Torah scholars. Their opinions matter and their criticisms and advice should be taken seriously. One should warm oneself at the fire of their knowledge and goodness, but one should not become overly familiar and fail to treat them with proper respect. The eternal coal of Torah from which all Jewish fire springs is in their keep. They guard it zealously and uncompromisingly, and thus these scholars and their fire should be treated with great respect and caution.

רַבִּי יְהוֹשֻׁעַ אוֹמֵר
Rabbi Yehoshua says

Mishnah 16 THE ENGLISH EXPRESSION "OUT OF THIS WORLD" USUALLY has a positive connotation; not so its Hebrew equivalent. Taking someone "out of this world" in the Hebrew idiom means doom and destruction. It implies the loss of the right to be considered a worthy member of a holy and civilized society. The "evil friend" that Rabbi Yehoshua warned against in mishnah 14 is here defined. It is a person with a bad eye toward others, a hedonistic instinct that seeks only self-gratification, and the tendency to actually hate other human beings. Such a person is certainly bad news for all those who find themselves in his vicinity or under his influence.

Here, Rabbi Yehoshua adopts Rabbi Eliezer's understanding of a bad eye and how destructive it can be. Yet, a bad eye alone doesn't make for an evil friend. That dubious accomplishment must also include a selfish pursuit of one's own pleasure at all costs and the hatred and demonization of any others with whom one many disagree, or of those who somehow appear to stand in the way of the pleasure so ardently pursued by an evil friend. Hatred of others is corrosive poison to one's own soul. Self-righteous proclaimers of their own version of truth, who justify and encourage hatred of others who do not quite agree with them or live up to their standards of faith, observance and lifestyle are in essence evil friends. They harm their own cause much more than they aid it. But they harm the general Jewish cause, the cause of Torah, even more grievously. Evil friends are truly "out of this world." The greater problem is that they drag others with them "out of this world."

16. Rabbi Yehoshua says: An evil eye, the evil inclination, and hatred of other people remove a person from the world.

17. Rabbi Yose says: Let your fellow's money be as dear to you as your own; apply yourself to study Torah,

---

יְהִי מָמוֹן חֲבֵרְךָ חָבִיב עָלֶיךָ כְּשֶׁלָּךְ
Let your fellow's money be as dear to you as your own

Mishnah 17 OTHER PEOPLE'S MONEY IS SPENT EASILY, IF NOT EVEN wantonly. One of the first rules taught in law school is that one is forbidden to mention to the jury that the defendant is insured. A violation of this principle during the actual trial will result in an automatic mistrial and a severe rebuke from the presiding judge. The reason for this is simple. Juries feel no compunction in awarding large, often unjustified sums of money to plaintiffs, if they know that rich insurance companies will pay the bill. The same tendency applies when awards are made against governmental entities and agencies. That kind of money — insurance money, government money, other people's money — is easily spent. But consideration for others' property is the essence of being a good neighbor. Thus, Rabbi Yose reinforces his previous assessment of good and bad with this most practical example — how one deals with other people's property. When your neighbor's property is as dear to you as your own, then you are well on the way to being a good neighbor. Money, property, and material things constitute a terrible test in life. The rabbis of the Talmud knew that most people fail that test. Everyone needs help in passing that test. Seeing others' money and property as being equal to yours is an enormous boost toward doing so.

וְהַתְקֵן עַצְמְךָ לִלְמוֹד תּוֹרָה
Apply yourself to study Torah

TORAH IS THE INHERITANCE OF THE ENTIRE JEWISH PEOPLE, BUT IT DOES not guarantee that any particular individual will be its guardian or receive its knowledge and insight. Nothing is automatic; everything must be earned. All Jews have great ancestors, but that does not guarantee that later generations will also be outstanding Torah scholars. To our great misfortune, many Jews stem from families of great Torah accomplishment, but are themselves ignorant of their Jewish heritage. Even the greatest of Jews have had unfortunate experiences with their descendants. A grandson of Moshe himself served as a pagan priest! (see *Judges* 8:30 and *Bava Basra* 109b). There may be a predisposition within families for Torah greatness — the Talmud teaches us that the Torah attempts to return to where it feels comfortably at home — but there is no assurance. People often treat spiritual attainment and serenity as if they were buying a lottery ticket, but Torah attainment is not a matter of good luck. One must prepare oneself for Torah greatness and knowledge.

שֶׁאֵינָהּ יְרֻשָּׁה לָךְ; וְכָל מַעֲשֶׂיךָ יִהְיוּ לְשֵׁם שָׁמָיִם.

[יח] **רַבִּי** שִׁמְעוֹן אוֹמֵר: הֱוֵי זָהִיר בִּקְרִיאַת שְׁמַע וּבִתְפִלָּה; וּכְשֶׁאַתָּה מִתְפַּלֵּל, אַל תַּעַשׂ תְּפִלָּתְךָ קֶבַע, אֶלָּא רַחֲמִים וְתַחֲנוּנִים לִפְנֵי הַמָּקוֹם, שֶׁנֶּאֱמַר: „כִּי חַנּוּן וְרַחוּם הוּא אֶרֶךְ אַפַּיִם וְרַב חֶסֶד וְנִחָם עַל הָרָעָה"; וְאַל תְּהִי רָשָׁע בִּפְנֵי עַצְמֶךָ.

וְכָל מַעֲשֶׂיךָ יִהְיוּ לְשֵׁם שָׁמָיִם
And let all your deeds be for the sake of Heaven

THERE ARE MANY THINGS THAT PEOPLE CONVINCE THEMSELVES THEY are doing "for the sake of heaven." The ironic comment of Rabbi Yisrael Lipkin of Salant and Rabbi Bunim of P'shis'cha — "Make sure that your 'sake of heaven' is for the sake of heaven" — is once again certainly in order. Because we are all affected by inner drives and considerations, and many times we are unaware of our true motivations in any given matter, the warning to do things for the sake of Heaven applies constantly. We should always ask ourselves: "Why am I doing this, saying this, acting this way?" Our entire lives, all that we do, the profound and the mundane, the physical and the spiritual — all should be harnessed for the sake of Heaven. It is this idea of the "sake of Heaven" that improves our lives and justifies our efforts in all of the varied and many fields of our endeavors.

❧ ❧ ❧

There is an important caveat to the "sake of Heaven" rule. Wrong behavior, even for the sake of Heaven, remains wrong behavior. Right is not accomplished by employing wrong means. A pseudo-zealot who arrogates to himself the knowledge of God's mind, so to speak, is able to justify cruelty to others, a lack of tolerance for differing viewpoints, and spiteful behavior, by claiming to do so in the name of Heaven. But boorishness, zealotry, and demonization of others are not justified by merely adding the phrase "for the sake of Heaven" to one's wrongful behavior. That is what Rabbi Yisrael of Salant and Rabbi Bunim of P'shis'cha truly meant by stating that the "sake of Heaven" must also be "for the sake of Heaven."

הֱוֵי זָהִיר בִּקְרִיאַת שְׁמַע וּבִתְפִלָּה
Be meticulous in reading the Shema and in prayer

Mishnah 18 CARE IN PRAYING IS ESSENTIAL FOR MEANINGFUL SPIRITUAL growth and service. The two main parts of Jewish prayer are the recitation of the *Shema* (the "Hear O Israel," which is recited twice daily) and the *Amidah* (the "Eighteen Blessings" prayer recited thrice daily). One should attempt to always pray — especially when reciting the *Shema* and the *Amidah* — with dignity, concentration, and freshness. This is a formidable task due to the fact that we recite these prayers daily. Their

for it is not yours by inheritance; and let all your deeds be for the sake of Heaven.

18. Rabbi Shimon says: Be meticulous in reading the *Shema* and in prayer; when you pray, do not make your prayer a set routine, rather [an entreaty for] mercy and a supplication before the Omnipresent, as it is said: *For He is gracious and compassionate, slow to anger, abounding in kindness, and relentful of punishment* (*Joel* 2:13); and do not judge yourself to be a wicked person.

---

recitation can easily become a matter of rote and habit, mumbled almost absentmindedly. Concentration for even a short period of time is not easily achieved. It requires will and training. The great Rabbi of Kotzk, Rabbi Menachem Mendel Morgenstern, was once asked by a Polish nobleman: "Wherein lies your greatness, that thousands of Jews respect you so?" The Rabbi answered: "I am able to concentrate on a given subject of Torah knowledge for a number of hours consecutively!" Therefore, the realization that one stands before God in prayer, seeking mercy and favor, is essential for achieving at least minimum concentration in prayer.

❦ ❦ ❦

Freshness is another matter entirely. The great men of the *Mussar* movement demanded of themselves a new and creative thought every day while engaged in prayer. My father-in-law, Rabbi Leizer Levin, of blessed memory, kept a notebook/diary in which he wrote the new thoughts in his daily prayers. As I perused the notebook/diary after his passing, I was struck by the fact that he took the occurrences of the day, the people he met, the situations he faced, the mundane stuff of living, and transformed them into the basis of his conversation with God that day. Life is fresh every day, with no two days being the same. Therefore, it is not unreasonable to ask that our prayer also somehow have a sense of daily freshness, which will create a relationship to our Creator that allows for creative and meaningful prayer on a regular, daily, ongoing basis.

וְאַל תְּהִי רָשָׁע בִּפְנֵי עַצְמֶךָ
And do not judge yourself to be a wicked person

WE SEE HERE AGAIN THE GREAT SENSE OF BALANCED THOUGHT AND living that is a framework for all of Avos. The Torah demands a sense of introspection and constant self-appraisal from us. Yet, the Torah is not about to allow us to fall into depression regarding ourselves and our accomplishments, or lack thereof. A person should never give up on himself or herself and on the possibility of improvement and spiritual advancement. Declaring oneself as beyond salvation is in itself a sin of major magnitude. It is also a

[יט] **רַבִּי** אֶלְעָזָר אוֹמֵר: הֱוֵי שָׁקוּד לִלְמוֹד תּוֹרָה, וְדַע מַה שֶּׁתָּשִׁיב לְאֶפִּיקוֹרוֹס; וְדַע לִפְנֵי מִי אַתָּה עָמֵל; וְנֶאֱמָן הוּא בַּעַל מְלַאכְתְּךָ,

---

cop-out. It allows one the luxury of not having to attempt to improve, to grow, to change and to repent. It is also a self-fulfilling prophecy. If I say I am no good, then eventually I am no good. Such an attitude eventually condones and justifies evil behavior and is utterly destructive to the individual and to his society.

❦ ❦ ❦

Decades ago, I was flying in the United States in the midst of a slowdown by the air traffic controllers who were operating "by the book." My plane spent almost three hours on the tarmac until it was allowed to take off. To keep the natives from becoming mutinous, the flight attendants served free liquor to all passengers who requested it. Finally, they ran out of liquor. The chief flight attendant held up the last small bottle of bourbon and asked who wanted it. Many hands flashed up. She then made a Solomonic decision and gave it to a gentleman who was already quite drunk. She explained: "He is soused already, so what's the difference!" People who feel that they are beyond improvement and redemption sink into doing ever worse things because they say to themselves, "What's the difference, I am lost anyway." As long as we are alive, it is never too late to change, improve, atone. Giving up on oneself is an act of folly that leads to further disaster. Saying that one is drunk is no excuse for further drinking. Often, being "hard on oneself" is a way of being soft and easy on oneself. It is the ultimate cop-out.

❦ ❦ ❦

הֱוֵי שָׁקוּד לִלְמוֹד תּוֹרָה
Be diligent in the study of Torah

Mishnah 19 THOUGH HE ADVOCATED A GOOD HEART ABOVE ALL else, Rabbi Elazar is well aware that a good heart, good intentions, alone will not be sufficient to weather the tests of life. One must be devoted to acquiring Torah knowledge and be diligent and persistent in pursuit of this goal. For it is only *Torah* knowledge that can refute the naysayers and doubters that appear in every generation of Jewish existence. The assaults on the authenticity of the Bible, the so-called "scholarly" denials of the truths of Biblical and Jewish history, the wildly inaccurate distortions of Torah law and tradition, are all apparently reasonable, on their surface. They are basically flawed, however, because they are in the main based on abysmal ignorance of the Oral Law and Talmudic tradition and on very questionable interpretations of archaeological finds and non-finds. For those who are well versed in Torah — in fact, for those who are truly intellectually honest and who do not arrive at the matter with a preconceived agenda —

19. Rabbi Elazar says: Be diligent in the study of Torah, and know what to answer a heretic; know before Whom you toil; and [know that] your Employer can be relied upon

---

this pseudo-scholarship will not raise doubts as to their faith. Thus, diligence in Torah study grants one the knowledge and the ability to answer the nonbelievers. Perhaps even more importantly, it gives one the ability to answer one's own doubts and questions.

וְדַע מַה שֶׁתָּשִׁיב לְאֶפִּיקוֹרוֹס
And know what to answer a heretic

THE SCOFFER AND NONBELIEVER SHOULD NOT BE IGNORED; HE OR SHE must be answered and refuted. The problems raised by the outside world have to be confronted, dealt with, and solved; and qualified people should be trained to carry out this mission. Torah knowledge is the best armor for the never-ending struggle to justify and explain traditional Jewish life and values. Judaism has always been able to contest opposing beliefs and value systems and emerge whole and vital. There is no reason to doubt its continuing ability to do so in all present and future contests of ideas and values. Rabbi Elazar's instruction to "know" what to answer to the nonbeliever is the best guarantee of the triumph of faith and tradition in the Jewish world.

It is true that most people are not skilled debaters and will not be qualified to represent the Torah in a battle of ideas; indeed, Judaism traditionally has not gone out to argue its case in the public arena. But Rabbi Elazar urges that students must be prepared to "know" how to respond to the problems raised by those who lack belief in the Torah.

וְדַע לִפְנֵי מִי אַתָּה עָמֵל
Know before Whom you toil

GOD IS CENTRAL TO THE BIBLICAL NARRATIVE, TO JEWISH LAW AND LIFE, and to the psyche of every believing Jew. Tragically, the main agenda of many modern-day nonbelievers — "scholars" and secular Jews — is to remove God from the picture and disclaim any authenticity for Jewish tradition and Biblical narrative. But this leaves one not only without faith, but also eventually without hope and purpose.

One of the great dangers facing those who are engaged in Jewish public service, whether as professionals or volunteers, is the cynicism and disappointment that many of them may come to feel due to the lack of appreciation or sometimes unjustified outright hostility toward them by some sections of the public that they serve. People working in the Jewish public world — religious, social, administrative — should not expect grand expressions of gratitude for their efforts. They must realize that they are not working for other human beings, for boards, presidents, administrators, etc., even if those are the ones who sign their paychecks. We really work for our Creator. Such an attitude will ease the psychological pain of ingratitude. It will also enhance our efforts and redouble our commitment to serve Torah and Israel,

שֶׁיְּשַׁלֶּם לְךָ שְׂכַר פְּעֻלָּתֶךָ.

[כ] **רַבִּי** טַרְפוֹן אוֹמֵר: הַיּוֹם קָצֵר, וְהַמְּלָאכָה מְרֻבָּה, וְהַפּוֹעֲלִים עֲצֵלִים, וְהַשָּׂכָר הַרְבֵּה,

---

for we then realize that we are truly working for an appreciative Employer, so to speak. The quality of our labor will also improve, for we will not wish to be guilty of shoddy workmanship when toiling for the ultimate Perfectionist.

שֶׁיְּשַׁלֶּם לְךָ שְׂכַר פְּעֻלָּתֶךָ ***To pay you the wage of your labor***

EVEN AT THE CONCLUSION OF OUR LABORS AND ACCOMPLISHMENTS IN the real world of everyday living, we are not always guaranteed that we will receive the agreed upon payment for our efforts. All of us remember times when the check somehow did not clear the bank or a promised remuneration or profit never appeared. Being cheated out of one's just compensation is a sad fact of life in the world of commerce and labor. Failed pension funds, unscrupulous financial advisers, embezzled bank deposits, crooked corporate heads, dishonest bookkeepers and accountants, are all part of our human experience. So, having a reliable employer who can be counted on to pay and reward fully and graciously is a great boon. In line with the previous statement that we are all essentially working for the Lord, we should be grateful that we have such an Employer Who will undoubtedly meet all obligations and dispense all payments faithfully. This knowledge should therefore also aid us in our devotion to the service of God and the commitment to His values and commandments. We rest assured that we will be paid for our deeds and efforts.

רַבִּי טַרְפוֹן ***Rabbi Tarfon***

Mishnah 20 LIKE HIS COLLEAGUE RABBI AKIVA, RABBI TARFON WAS descended from converts and was one of the leaders of Israel before the Bar Kochba rebellion (135 CE). He lived in the city of Lod and died in approximately 130 CE. The name Tarfon is a form of the Greco/Roman name Tryphon. He was a person of wealth and stature who studiously avoided personal honor or gain. He even regretted an instance when he used his name and position to save himself from death at the hands of a Jew who mistook him for a vicious thief! He stated that "I should have offered him ransom money and obtained my release in that fashion rather than using the crown of Torah to free myself." His scholarship and sterling character, combined with his piety and sense of devotion to Torah and Israel, made him one of the heroes of the period of the Mishnah.

הַיּוֹם קָצֵר ***The day is short***

THE DAY IS TRULY SHORT. LIFE FLIES BY. WHO DOES NOT REMEMBER holding one's first child in one's arms as though it were only yesterday — yet it is forty years later? Where did the time go? When we are very young, time

to pay you the wage of your labor.

20. Rabbi Tarfon says: The day is short, the task is abundant, the workers are lazy, the wage is great,

---

drags on. When will I be old enough to drive a car, to leave home for higher education, to seriously search for a mate? But as we grow older, life advances in the fast-forward mode. Because we realize the shortness of life, we have a special responsibility to make the most of our time and opportunities. The Gaon of Vilna, Rabbi Eliyahu Kramer, slept very little — only about two hours a day during his mature years. He commented that there would be plenty of time to rest and sleep after life ends. Our very mortality drives human creativity and the advances that mark the story of civilization. Knowledge of the shortness of the day haunts our entire life. Rabbi Tarfon's concept echoes the words of Hillel, who cautions that one should never postpone the study of Torah until the future, for one does not know when that future will end. It is the shortness, the uncertainty of life itself, that fuels much human behavior, for better or worse.

וְהַמְּלָאכָה מְרֻבָּה ***The task is abundant***

THE WORK IS CERTAINLY GREAT AND MANIFOLD. MOST PROJECTS ARE LEFT uncompleted by the end of our sojourn on earth. If this is true regarding the physical world, it is certainly true regarding our spiritual goals. There is always more to study and to know, more good deeds to be done, and more help to be proffered to others. Judaism provides a never-ending list of challenges, demands, and hopes. It provides no easy respites nor does it give long vacations. Being Jewish is being productive, so Rabbi Tarfon's next words regarding the workers being lazy are a warning against lulling ourselves into a state of non-productivity.

וְהַפּוֹעֲלִים עֲצֵלִים ***The workers are lazy***

IT IS HUMAN NATURE TO TAKE IT EASY, BUT LAZINESS MUST BE FOUGHT and discarded. The story of my dear friend, Rabbi Emanuel Feldman, resonates constantly in all of our ears and psyches. A newly observant Jew who suddenly discovered the time constraints of morning prayer exclaimed, "Does that mean I can never sleep late on Sunday morning again?"

וְהַשָּׂכָר הַרְבֵּה ***The wage is great***

PEOPLE RESPOND TO AN OPPORTUNITY FOR GREAT GAIN. NO ONE WILLINGLY invests $10,000 in an investment that will allow him a profit of only $100, but if there is an opportunity to receive $100,000 for the $10,000 investment, there will be many interested investors. Judaism promises great rewards for those who invest in it, rewards that are available in this world and the next. It holds the promise of meaningful life, of serenity of spirit, and quality of character. It provides for family continuity and generations proud and united

וּבַעַל הַבַּיִת דּוֹחֵק.

[כא] **הוּא** הָיָה אוֹמֵר: לֹא עָלֶיךָ הַמְּלָאכָה לִגְמוֹר, וְלֹא אַתָּה בֶן חוֹרִין לְהִבָּטֵל מִמֶּנָּה. אִם לָמַדְתָּ תּוֹרָה הַרְבֵּה, נוֹתְנִים לְךָ שָׂכָר הַרְבֵּה; וְנֶאֱמָן הוּא בַּעַל מְלַאכְתְּךָ, שֶׁיְּשַׁלֶּם לְךָ שְׂכַר פְּעֻלָּתֶךָ. וְדַע

---

with one another. Jewish life transcends the mundane world of our everyday existence and provides a connection with the eternal and valuable. But the profit must be earned; it is not a windfall or a winning lottery ticket. We will read in Avos, לְפוּם צַעֲרָא אַגְרָא, *the return is in proportion to the investment.* One cannot realize the $100,000 return without first investing the $10,000. But the rock-solid Guarantor of the investment and the opportunity for great reward have sustained Jews and Jewish life throughout history.

וּבַעַל הַבַּיִת דּוֹחֵק
And the Master of the house is insistent

THE LORD IS NOTHING IF NOT DEMANDING OF US. JEWISH LIFE COVERS every facet of human behavior. Our diet, daily and weekly time schedule, education, business practices, speech and interaction with other human beings, all are governed by Torah standards and Godly demands. And God — our Employer for life — is insistent and uncompromising in the regimen that He has prescribed for His people, Israel. He pushes us ahead in life, sometimes with a gentle nudge and other times with a stronger momentum. But He is always interested in us and makes us aware of the shortness of time and the mountain of work yet ahead of us. There is so much to accomplish in life! This inner feeling of urgency that exists within us, which is in itself the basis of human creativity and humanity, is a reflection of the soul that the Lord has planted within us. It is the message of the Employer that demands a concerted effort. Therefore He pushes us to greater heights and more intensive productivity. This was Rabbi Tarfon's message, and it shows how an ordinary "Tryphon" can eventually turn himself into a Rabbi Tarfon.

לֹא עָלֶיךָ הַמְּלָאכָה לִגְמוֹר
You are not required to complete the task

Mishnah 21 THE TALMUD TELLS OF A VERY OLD MAN PLANTING A FRUIT tree sapling that would not bear fruit for many years. He did so because he had come into a world of fruit trees that had been planted for his benefit by his predecessors, so he, too, planted for future generations. Even if he would not live to see the benefit of his labors, he felt enjoined to begin the project that would benefit others. It is not incumbent upon us humans to see successful completion of every project that we are engaged in.

and the Master of the house is insistent.

21. He [R' Tarfon] used to say: You are not required to complete the task, yet you are not free to withdraw from it. If you have studied much Torah, they give you great reward; and [know that] your Employer can be relied upon to pay you the wage of your labor, but be aware that

---

It is incumbent upon us to work toward the successful completion of such projects.

When I was young lawyer just beginning my first job, the senior partner of the firm told me: "Your desk should always be neat but never empty. An empty desk means that we are out of business!" One should always have projects and goals. Jewish tradition remarked that if one was in the middle of a good and beneficial project for Torah, for Israel, for other human beings, then Heaven would allow the person to live in order to continue the task at hand. Therefore, upon completion of one project, or even while working on it, one should immediately begin work on the next project. That way, we are always in the middle of doing positive things and Heaven will reckon with that fact in granting us long life.

One should never minimize one's abilities or opportunities. To say, "Who am I to undertake such a task?" is false and dangerous modesty. We have to at least propose while the Lord will dispose. The great Rebbe of Kotzk, Rabbi Menachem Mendel Morgenstern, would say: "All Jews have two pockets. In one pocket, there is a scrap of paper that says, 'I am but dust and ashes.' In the other pocket there is a scrap of paper that says, 'The whole world was created only for me.' The task of Jewish life is to put your hand in the right pocket at the right time!" The problem is that often when we are asked to assume positions of responsibility, our response is, "Who am I to undertake such an important task?" And when one is demanding honors and position that perhaps are not one's due, one maintains loudly and forcefully that "the whole world was created for me!" Successful living teaches us to be modest in our demands and committed in our efforts, to put our hand in the right pocket at the right time.

אִם לָמַדְתָּ תּוֹרָה הַרְבֵּה ***If you have studied much Torah***

THERE IS GREAT REWARD FOR TORAH STUDY. SUCH STUDY HAS ALWAYS been an end in itself in Jewish life. It is a supreme value all unto itself, aside from any of its practical purposes. No wonder Rabbi Tarfon assures us that the reward for such study is inestimable, and even if the immediate reward in this world is not apparent, one should realize that the main reward is in the World to Come, in the afterlife. Torah study is not merely an educational exercise. It is a spiritual experience and as such its fitting reward is in the

ב/כא

שֶׁמַּתַּן שְׂכָרָן שֶׁל צַדִּיקִים לֶעָתִיד לָבֹא.

❦ ❦ ❦

רַבִּי חֲנַנְיָא בֶּן עֲקַשְׁיָא אוֹמֵר: רָצָה הַקָּדוֹשׁ בָּרוּךְ הוּא לְזַכּוֹת אֶת יִשְׂרָאֵל, לְפִיכָךְ הִרְבָּה לָהֶם תּוֹרָה וּמִצְוֹת, שֶׁנֶּאֱמַר: „יהוה חָפֵץ לְמַעַן צִדְקוֹ, יַגְדִּיל תּוֹרָה וְיַאְדִּיר.״

---

world of immortal souls. Since that reward is hidden from our view while we are in this world, Rabbi Tarfon reiterates the necessity for faith and trust in the Almighty, Who is the Guarantor of that ultimate reward.

Ultimately all of the wisdom of Avos is grounded in the necessity of faith in God. That God can be relied upon is the essential message of the tractate

2/21 the reward of the righteous will be given in the World to Come.

❦ ❦ ❦

Rabbi Chanania ben Akashia says: The Holy One, Blessed is He, wished to confer merit upon Israel; therefore He gave them Torah and *mitzvos* in abundance, as it is said: *HASHEM desired, for the sake of its [Israel's] righteousness, that the Torah be made great and glorious* (*Isaiah* 42:21).

---

and of all Jewish belief and life. Though Jewish history is replete with pain, the survival of the Jewish people over the millennia is eloquent testimony to the truths expressed by Rabbi Tarfon in this mishnah. The Employer is most demanding and his work is most taxing, but He is also absolutely reliable.

פרק שלישי
CHAPTER THREE

כָּל יִשְׂרָאֵל יֵשׁ לָהֶם חֵלֶק לָעוֹלָם הַבָּא, שֶׁנֶּאֱמַר: „וְעַמֵּךְ כֻּלָּם צַדִּיקִים, לְעוֹלָם יִירְשׁוּ אָרֶץ, נֵצֶר מַטָּעַי, מַעֲשֵׂה יָדַי לְהִתְפָּאֵר.״

All Israel has a share in the World to Come, as it is said: *And your people are all righteous; they shall inherit the land forever; a branch of My plantings, My handiwork, in which to take pride* (Isaiah 60:21).

[א] **עֲקַבְיָא** בֶּן מַהֲלַלְאֵל אוֹמֵר: הִסְתַּכֵּל בִּשְׁלֹשָׁה דְבָרִים וְאֵין אַתָּה בָא לִידֵי עֲבֵרָה: דַּע מֵאַיִן בָּאתָ, וּלְאָן אַתָּה הוֹלֵךְ, וְלִפְנֵי מִי אַתָּה עָתִיד לִתֵּן דִּין וְחֶשְׁבּוֹן. מֵאַיִן בָּאתָ? מִטִּפָּה סְרוּחָה. וּלְאָן אַתָּה הוֹלֵךְ? לִמְקוֹם עָפָר, רִמָּה וְתוֹלֵעָה.

Chapter Three

עֲקַבְיָא בֶּן מַהֲלַלְאֵל ***Akavia ben Mahalalel***

Mishnah 1 VERY LITTLE IS KNOWN ABOUT THIS *TANNA*, WHOSE name is probably an inverted form of *Akiva*. He was a colleague and contemporary of Rabban Gamliel I and of Rabban Yochanan ben Zakkai, and this is one of the few references to him in Mishnah or Talmud.

He was a man of great strength, integrity, and principle, as is seen from his halachic views and personal conduct in *Eduyos* 5:5-7. There we are told that he disagreed with his peers regarding four matters of ritual purity, and did not bow to the majority opinion. He based his steadfastness on the fact that he "heard them expounded from the great and the many [of the past generation]." However, out of deference to the majority, he never ruled against them in actual practice.

Before his death, he instructed his son to follow the majority ruling in these matters, since his son "heard them only from an individual (Akavia himself)" and not from "the great and the many." He also told his son: "I will not give you any special recommendation to my great rabbinic colleagues. Your behavior and actions will either bring you close to them or distance you from them." These incidents reveal his unusual blend of strong character, balanced vision, and sense of public responsibility.

הִסְתַּכֵּל בִּשְׁלֹשָׁה דְבָרִים ***Consider [lit. stare at] three things***

GIVEN THE CHARACTER AND UNMITIGATED TRUTHFULNESS OF AKAVIA, AS described above, it is no surprise that his words of ethics and guidance would be very stark and direct. The word הִסְתַּכֵּל means *to stare*, to look at closely and with focus, to look intently, to analyze, to see well, to understand and appreciate. Most of us are reluctant to look life — let alone death — straight in the eye. But without being truly honest and realistic with ourselves regarding life and death, we are unable to give meaningful purpose to our years. The parameters for measuring successful living are just not present without such a hard look at the reality of our mortality. And Akavia urges us to consider that mortality, and thus to view the human condition, from three viewpoints.

1. Akavia ben Mahalalel says: Consider three things and you will not come into the grip of sin: Know whence you came, whither you go, and before Whom you will give justification and reckoning. "Whence you came?" — from a putrid drop; "whither you go?" — to a place of dust, worms, and mag-

---

***וְאֵין אַתָּה בָא לִידֵי עֲבֵרָה* And you will not come into the grip [lit. the hands] of sin**

AKAVIA PERSONIFIES SIN AS HAVING HANDS. IT GRIPS A PERSON AND holds on to him or her. The Jewish view of sin is that it is never passive. It is always active, looking for customers, alluring and attractive. The Rabbis of the Talmud stated that once one falls into the clutches of a sin a number of times, one no longer believes that the act is a sin. Therefore, the importance of avoiding the first transgression is paramount in Jewish life and thought. Sin is a pit that it is not easy to escape. One should therefore step carefully in life and avoid the open pit that always lies just under one's feet. The three viewpoints of life that Akavia describes in this mishnah provide the framework for escaping from the grip of sin.

***דַּע מֵאַיִן בָּאתָ* Know whence you came**

THIS IS AKAVIA'S FIRST VIEWPOINT, AND HE GIVES THE ANSWER VERY frankly by dealing with our biological origin: מִטִּפָּה סְרוּחָה, *from a putrid drop.* We are created from an act of desire and passion that momentarily erases all other emotions and thoughts from those that brought us into this world. That is a humbling insight into our origins. We are brought into the world by an act that can be immoral or holy, depending on the quality and aspirations of the people involved. In essence, this is the lesson for our entire life. Our life can be one of purpose and accomplishment, spiritual growth, and goodness to others. It can be holy and noble. Or it can be one of selfishness and evil, of violence and harm.

Consideration of where we come from makes us realize that we have enormous choices in life. A decaying drop somehow created life. Was that drop wasted or was it productive? Only we can create the answer to that question. Every human being provides the answer by the way he or she lives his or her life.

***וּלְאָן אַתָּה הוֹלֵךְ* Whither you go**

THE SECOND VIEWPOINT OF JUDGING LIFE AND OUR PURPOSE IN LIVING is raised by the question: "Where are we going?" Here also, Akavia deals with the question starkly: *You go to a place of dust, worms, and maggots*. He does not mince words in his portrayal of the grave and the decay of our physical remains. The realization of our mortality haunts our entire life, and it allows us the freedom to control it while we are alive. One choice is summed up in the ancient phrase, "eat, drink, and be merry, for tomorrow we die." This nihilistic and hedonistic view of life has had countless adherents over the millennia. All

וְלִפְנֵי מִי אַתָּה עָתִיד לִתֵּן דִּין וְחֶשְׁבּוֹן? לִפְנֵי מֶלֶךְ מַלְכֵי הַמְּלָכִים, הַקָּדוֹשׁ בָּרוּךְ הוּא.

[ב] **רַבִּי חֲנִינָא** סְגַן הַכֹּהֲנִים אוֹמֵר: הֱוֵי מִתְפַּלֵּל בִּשְׁלוֹמָהּ שֶׁל מַלְכוּת, שֶׁאִלְמָלֵא מוֹרָאָהּ, אִישׁ אֶת רֵעֵהוּ חַיִּים בְּלָעוֹ.

---

in all, it typifies a wasted life, an essential hopelessness and depression regarding the human condition, simply because realization of our mortality makes it futile to strive for more than temporal pleasures. A second choice is to use the time granted to us to invest in things that will outlive us — in family and generations, in acts of permanence and goodness, in scholarship and human benefit. In other words, our very mortality forces us to become immortal.

In truth, only the sense of potential immortality that lies within us allows us to live a life of purpose and even of happiness, while at the same time we realize how truly mortal and very fragile we are. So, we must always know where we are going.

וְלִפְנֵי מִי אַתָּה עָתִיד לִתֵּן דִּין וְחֶשְׁבּוֹן
And before Whom you will give justification and account

AKAVIA'S THIRD ASPECT OF VIEWING LIFE IS IN KNOWING BEFORE WHOM we will give an accounting for our lives. Accountability is the centerpiece of all Jewish thought and behavior. There is no "free lunch." All behavior and actions are brought into account, and the Judge Who weighs human behavior is incorruptible and all-knowing. Therefore, all human behavior should be measured, responsible and, as mentioned, fully accountable. When life is viewed this way, all human behavior becomes important and meaningful.

Many times we think that what we do does not really matter, but the concept of Godly judgment for all of our actions lends a sense of importance, urgency and responsibility to all of human life. Such an approach almost automatically makes for meaningful and productive living and a better society. The combination of Akavia's three viewpoints provides the full Jewish insight on life and human behavior.

❦ ❦ ❦

I was once invited to a meeting with a major company here in Jerusalem. The head of the company called me and said he was sending a taxi to pick me up. When I entered the taxi, the driver asked me, "Where are we going?" I told him, "I don't know." Quite upset, the driver shouted, "How can you get into a cab and not know where you are going?" I explained that the company sent the cab and that I didn't know the address. I told the driver to wait and went upstairs to my apartment and called the company. I went back

gots; "and before Whom will you give justification and account?" — before the King Who reigns over kings, the Holy One, Blessed is He.

2. Rabbi Chanina, the Deputy Kohen Gadol, says: Pray for the welfare of the government, because if people did not fear it, a person would swallow his fellow alive.

---

to the cab and gave the driver the address. The company is located in a brand new area of Jerusalem and its street did not appear on the driver's street map. He was fit to be tied, ranting at me as he contacted his dispatcher to get instructions. He missed the street a few times (there were no street signs posted as yet in the new neighborhood), muttering at me all the way that it was somehow all my fault. At last we finally arrived. Since the company had sent the cab for me, I left home without taking money to pay the fare. Well, that put the taxi driver over the top. "How dare you get into my cab without money?!" he roared at me. I finally got the company man down to pay the cab bill and escaped from the cab and its driver, who was still loudly complaining that I somehow ruined his afternoon.

I thought about this ordinary incident and realized that it was a miniature drama of Akavia's words. "Where are you going?" asked the cab driver. And I did not know. Neither did I have the ability to pay the bill at the end of the trip, when the account was due. The example of the cab trip was more humorous than truly serious. But as far as Akavia's words are concerned, the situation is truly serious and the lesson should be taken to heart and mind.

❦ ❦ ❦

רַבִּי חֲנִינָא סְגַן הַכֹּהֲנִים
Rabbi Chanina, the Deputy Kohen Gadol

Mishnah 2 RABBI CHANINA WAS A COLLEAGUE OF AKAVIA BEN MAHA-lalel and lived in the generation of the destruction of the Second Temple. He was one of the great Torah scholars who accompanied Rabban Yochanan ben Zakkai to Yavneh. As the Deputy High Priest, he was a source of knowledge for later generations regarding the Temple, its procedures and the laws of purity that were relevant then in everyday life. He recorded the pain of the Jewish people, who were suffering under the yoke of confiscatory Roman taxes and cruel rule after the destruction of the Temple.

הֱוֵי מִתְפַּלֵּל בִּשְׁלוֹמָהּ שֶׁל מַלְכוּת
Pray for the welfare of the government

RABBI CHANINA'S BACKGROUND MAKES HIS STATEMENT REGARDING the necessity to pray for the stability of the ruling government ever more poignant. His exhortation applied to the rule of King Agrippa II, the Roman puppet who ruled over Judea before and during the time of the destruction of the Second Temple, and Rabbi Chanina spoke also of the time thereafter, of complete Roman rule over the country. We can well imagine that there

[ג] **רַבִּי חֲנִינָא** בֶּן תְּרַדְיוֹן אוֹמֵר: שְׁנַיִם שֶׁיּוֹשְׁבִין וְאֵין בֵּינֵיהֶם דִּבְרֵי תוֹרָה, הֲרֵי זֶה מוֹשַׁב לֵצִים, שֶׁנֶּאֱמַר: ,,וּבְמוֹשַׁב לֵצִים לֹא יָשָׁב.״

---

was great bitterness against the Romans among the Jews who survived the cruel four-year rebellion against Rome that ended in defeat in 70 CE. Yet, Rabbi Chanina encouraged a more positive attitude toward government. Without its stabilizing effect on society, he insisted, anarchy would reign and "a person would swallow his fellow alive."

In its long history of exile and dispersion, the Jewish people often faced a major dilemma regarding its loyalty to the government of its host country. In the vast majority of times and countries, Jews followed the edict of the prophet Jeremiah, to "pray for the welfare of the country where they dwelt." In fact, they did more than that. Jews were patriots wherever they lived. They helped develop the country's economy, social structure, and well-being. Even in societies that shunned and discriminated against them, Jews remained overwhelmingly loyal to the government that ruled them. Russian Jews tended to side with the Czar against Napoleon, though Napoleon apparently held out the hope and promise of a better future for them and their descendants.

However, as the oppressive anti-Semitism of 19th- and 20th-century Russia increasingly progressed, the Jewish position became more ambivalent. The openly anti-Jewish government of the Czars, with its officially inspired pogroms and anti-Jewish laws, hardly inspired enthusiasm or support among the Jews of Russia and Poland. These cruelties turned a minority of young Jews into hardened revolutionaries, determined to bring down the Czar and his evil autocracy. German Jews, the most loyal and staunch patriots of the 19th and early-20th centuries, were thrown into despair and confusion by Hitler's rise to power. How could one in good conscience pray for the welfare of the Nazi government? Or for Stalin's murderous regime? There was no escape from such Hobbesian choices. Even then, Jews feared anarchy more than they did discrimination and insult.

As Rabbi Chanina pointed out, the main task of government is to prevent chaos and anarchy. Being a minority and a defenseless one at that, Jews knew that they would always be victimized in times of anarchy, violent revolution and weak government.

Throughout history, those countries that have dealt fairly with Jews have been rewarded with a talented, loyal, and creative community, whose contributions to the general society have never been insignificant. It seems obvious that Rabbi Chanina presupposed some sort of mutuality in the relationship between the general government of a country and its treatment of Jews, and the obligation of Jews to "pray for the welfare of the government." Yet, all of this is true only if Jews have some rights and the ability to live their lives as Jews.

3. Rabbi Chanina ben Tradyon says: If two sit together and there are no words of Torah between them, it is a session of scorners, as it is said: *In the session of scorners he does not sit*

The words of Rabbi Chanina have a bittersweet quality to them in the light of the many centuries of the Jewish story that have followed after him.

רַבִּי חֲנִינָא בֶּן תְּרַדְיוֹן
Rabbi Chanina ben Tradyon

Mishnah 3 RABBI CHANINA WAS ONE OF THE MARTYRS TORTURED TO death by the Romans in the aftermath of Bar Kochba's failed rebellion in the 2nd century CE. He was burned alive (c. 140 CE) while wrapped in a holy Torah scroll. The Romans placed wet sponges near his heart so that he would suffer longer. Rabbi Chanina's executioner asked if he would be Divinely rewarded for removing the sponges, and the righteous sage promised him eternal reward. The Roman did so and leaped into the flames. He was himself consumed in the roaring blaze and a voice proclaimed that Rabbi Chanina and his executioner had been admitted to Heaven's eternal rewards.

The Talmud relates that Rabbi Chanina assured his heartbroken and horrified students who were witnessing his execution that Heaven would exact revenge for the desecration of the Torah scroll and that his death would therefore also be avenged. In describing his final vision on earth, Rabbi Chanina said, "Only the parchment of the Torah scroll burns in the Roman fire, but the holy letters fly in the air." Thus, he became the prototype for Jewish martyrdom throughout the long centuries of persecution, culminating in the Holocaust and the continuing Arab terror against Israel. His two final assurances — that the Lord will eventually avenge every Jewish death and that only the body of the Jew, the parchment of the Torah scroll, is destroyed, but the Jewish spirit, the scroll's holy letters live on, floating in the air we breathe — remain the basis for Jewish survival against cruel and implacable foes.

Rabbi Chanina was the father of Beruriah, the famous wife of Rabbi Meir. Another daughter was saved from forced service in a Roman brothel by Rabbi Meir's miraculous intervention. Stories about Rabbi Chanina, Rabbi Meir and their family abound in the Talmud and Midrash, testifying to their influence in the Jewish world.

שְׁנַיִם שֶׁיּוֹשְׁבִין וְאֵין בֵּינֵיהֶם דִּבְרֵי תוֹרָה, הֲרֵי זֶה מוֹשַׁב לֵצִים
If two sit together and there are no words of Torah between them, it is a session of scorners

AS BEFITS RABBI CHANINA, WHO LITERALLY LIVED AND DIED WITH THE Torah, his statement in this mishnah regarding Torah study and its primacy and constancy is entirely understandable. Without Torah, the world becomes a place of mockers, scoffers, jesters, and spiritual emptiness. Two people who engage in nothing but frivolous conversation and do not share words of importance and spiritual import damage themselves and eventually society at large. The same two people who discuss Torah with one another create a bond between themselves that includes the presence of the Creator, so to speak.

אֲבָל שְׁנַיִם שֶׁיּוֹשְׁבִין וְיֵשׁ בֵּינֵיהֶם דִּבְרֵי תוֹרָה, שְׁכִינָה שְׁרוּיָה בֵינֵיהֶם, שֶׁנֶּאֱמַר: „אָז נִדְבְּרוּ יִרְאֵי יהוה אִישׁ אֶל רֵעֵהוּ, וַיַּקְשֵׁב יהוה וַיִּשְׁמָע, וַיִּכָּתֵב סֵפֶר זִכָּרוֹן לְפָנָיו, לְיִרְאֵי יהוה וּלְחשְׁבֵי שְׁמוֹ.״ אֵין לִי אֶלָּא שְׁנַיִם; מִנַּיִן שֶׁאֲפִילוּ אֶחָד שֶׁיּוֹשֵׁב וְעוֹסֵק בַּתּוֹרָה, שֶׁהַקָּדוֹשׁ בָּרוּךְ הוּא קוֹבֵעַ לוֹ שָׂכָר? שֶׁנֶּאֱמַר: „יֵשֵׁב בָּדָד וְיִדֹּם, כִּי נָטַל עָלָיו.״

[ד] **רַבִּי** שִׁמְעוֹן אוֹמֵר: שְׁלֹשָׁה שֶׁאָכְלוּ עַל שֻׁלְחָן אֶחָד וְלֹא אָמְרוּ עָלָיו דִּבְרֵי תוֹרָה, כְּאִלּוּ

Such a relationship transcends ordinary expressions of courtesy, conversation, and friendship.

The mishnah does not mean to imply that ordinary, necessary conversation is automatically defined as being frivolous. Many conversations that are vital to one's welfare do not directly deal with Torah, and are perfectly natural and acceptable. The mishnah refers to those that are deliberately nonsensical, or those that interrupt the study of Torah itself and those that border on forbidden or immoral speech. It is not hard to appreciate that Rabbi Chanina, who lived and taught Torah in such a difficult time in the annals of Jewish survival, would have little patience with idle chatter and cynical attitudes. He, who knew he was liable to be killed by the Romans because of his loyalty to Torah and its studies, understandably had little patience with those who fritter away the opportunity to benefit from Torah words, thoughts, and attitudes, and instead engage in vain and foolish talk.

שֶׁאֲפִילוּ אֶחָד שֶׁיּוֹשֵׁב וְעוֹסֵק בַּתּוֹרָה
If even one person sits and occupies himself with Torah

RABBI CHANINA ALSO VALUES INDIVIDUAL STUDY OF TORAH. ONE SHOULD never be discouraged simply because of being the only one doing the right thing at a particular moment. Some of the greatest works in Torah scholarship have been fashioned in loneliness and under severe conditions of hardship. The 12th-century *Commentary to the Mishnah* of Rabbi Moshe ben Maimon was written mainly while in hiding from the Almohad persecutors of the Jews. In the past century, Rabbi Yechezkel Abramsky, in Siberian Gulag exile, formulated *Chazon Yechezkel*, his great commentary on *Tosefta,* in frigid labor camp loneliness. The Lord is with those who study Torah in such loneliness, just as He is with those that study it in the great study halls filled with hundreds and thousands of participating students.

(*Psalms* 1:1). But if two sit together and words of Torah are between them, the Divine Presence rests between them, as it is said: *Then those who fear HASHEM spoke to one another, and HASHEM listened and heard, and a book of remembrance was written before Him for those who fear HASHEM and give thought to His Name* (*Malachi* 3:16). From this verse we would know this only about two people; how do we know that if even one person sits and occupies himself with Torah, the Holy One, Blessed is He, determines a reward for him? For it is said: *Let one sit in solitude and be still, for he will have received [a reward] for it* (*Lamentations* 3:28).

4. Rabbi Shimon says: If three have eaten at the same table and have not spoken words of Torah there, it is as if

---

רַבִּי שִׁמְעוֹן
Rabbi Shimon

Mishnah 4 THIS GREAT DISCIPLE OF RABBI AKIVA IS THE RABBI SHIMON ben Yochai who appears numerous times in the Mishnah and Talmud. A fierce opponent of the Roman rulers of the Land of Israel and their culture, he spent many years as a fugitive from the Roman police who wanted to execute him, as they had done to his mentor, Rabbi Akiva. Rabbi Shimon and his son Rabbi Elazar spent twelve years hiding in a cave in the Galil, sustained only by the fruit of a nearby carob tree and a miraculous stream of water. Under such conditions, Rabbi Shimon developed into such a holy person that when it was safe for him to leave the cave and return to human society, he could not tolerate the sight of ordinary human beings engaged in their everyday work and lives. His gaze upon them was so critically fearsome that Heaven warned him that if he persisted in viewing ordinary life in such a manner he should better "return to the cave" — which he did for another year, during which he mellowed to a significant degree. Nevertheless, Rabbi Shimon's holiness of attitude remained essentially uncompromising.

שְׁלשָׁה שֶׁאָכְלוּ עַל שֻׁלְחָן אֶחָד וְלֹא אָמְרוּ עָלָיו דִּבְרֵי תוֹרָה
If three have eaten at the same table and have not spoken words of Torah there

GIVEN RABBI SHIMON'S LIFE EXPERIENCE AND HOLY OUTLOOK, AND AS A logical continuation of the previous mishnah of Rabbi Chanina ben Tradyon, Rabbi Shimon speaks of Torah study not only as an intellectual imperative, but as a necessity even in the ordinary course of life — even while eating at one's table. He says that Jews eating at a table without discussing words of Torah have defiled their table. The words that Rabbi Shimon chooses to describe such a table without Torah are very graphic; "it is as if they have eaten of offerings to dead idols." He likens it to the prophecy of Isaiah: a table devoid of Torah words, is *full of vomit and filth, without the Omnipresent*; it is a table of

אָכְלוּ מִזִּבְחֵי מֵתִים, שֶׁנֶּאֱמַר: „כִּי כָּל שֻׁלְחָנוֹת מָלְאוּ קִיא צוֹאָה, בְּלִי מָקוֹם"; אֲבָל שְׁלֹשָׁה שֶׁאָכְלוּ עַל שֻׁלְחָן אֶחָד וְאָמְרוּ עָלָיו דִּבְרֵי תוֹרָה, כְּאִלּוּ אָכְלוּ מִשֻּׁלְחָנוֹ שֶׁל מָקוֹם, שֶׁנֶּאֱמַר: „וַיְדַבֵּר אֵלַי, זֶה הַשֻּׁלְחָן אֲשֶׁר לִפְנֵי יהוה."

[ה] **רַבִּי חֲנִינָא** בֶּן חֲכִינַאי אוֹמֵר: הַנֵּעוֹר בַּלַּיְלָה, וְהַמְהַלֵּךְ בַּדֶּרֶךְ יְחִידִי, וּמְפַנֶּה לִבּוֹ לְבַטָּלָה – הֲרֵי זֶה מִתְחַיֵּב בְּנַפְשׁוֹ.

---

idolatry, of spiritual worthlessness, of animal appetite without higher purpose. However, even such a degraded table can be elevated into *the table that is before Hashem* by words of Torah, goodness, and spiritual and social value.

The example of a Jew's table as being a holy place is taken from the Temple in Jerusalem. There the priests of Israel ate their share of the offerings on "God's Table," as it were, in purity and holy dedication. Jews have always striven to keep the noble attitudes of the Temple alive in their personal behavior, even though the physical Temple does not yet exist again. In the words of the Talmud (*Berachos* 55a): "As long as the Temple stood in Jerusalem, its Altar brought forth forgiveness for Israel. Now that the Temple no longer stands there, it is the table of the person that brings forth forgiveness for him."

In Jewish life, a table is no mere piece of furniture. Rather, it speaks of Sabbaths and holidays, family gatherings and life-cycle occasions, Torah study and children's schoolwork, Purim baskets and the great Passover Seder. It is the focal piece of furniture, the center of all family life, the silent witness to our words and deeds and attitudes. We have the ability to make it "the table that is before Hashem." Engaging in Torah conversation and study at the otherwise ordinary and mundane mealtime enhances the spirituality and serenity that can exist in one's home and everyday living.

Certain meals in Jewish life are elevated to the status of being a *seudas mitzvah*, a meal that is sanctified by being obligatory under Jewish law and custom. Such meals — bar mitzvah, circumcision, redemption of the first-born, completion of a tractate of the Talmud, etc. — are marked by a formal address of Torah thoughts and knowledge. In fact, many commentators stress that it is the public discussion of Torah at the meal that elevates it to become a *seudas mitzvah*! This is but a further reiteration of Rabbi Shimon's

they have eaten of offerings to dead idols, as it is said: *For all tables are full of vomit and filth, without the Omnipresent* (*Isaiah* 28:8). But if three have eaten at the same table and have spoken words of Torah there, it is as if they have eaten from the table of the Omnipresent, as it is said: *And he said to me, "This is the table that is before HASHEM"* (*Ezekiel* 41:22).

5. Rabbi Chanina ben Chachinai says: One who stays awake at night or who travels alone on the road, and turns his heart to idleness — indeed, he bears guilt for his soul.

---

insight that a meal at which words of Torah are spoken creates a holy table and a connection to God. The physical act of eating is transformed into a spiritual activity. In a very real sense, therefore, following Rabbi Shimon's dictum will elevate every meal to the status of being a *seudas mitzvah*. There can be no greater achievement in life than transforming the ordinary and mundane — eating — into the holy and spiritually noble.

רַבִּי חֲנִינָא בֶּן חֲכִינַאי
Rabbi Chanina ben Chachinai

Mishnah 5 RABBI CHANINA BEN CHACHINAI WAS MARTYRED BY THE Romans when they tried to destroy the Jewish faith after the abortive revolt of Bar Kochba, in the 2nd century CE. By then the Romans realized that the source of all Jewish vitality, nationalistic fervor, and tenacity came from the study of Torah and from its scholars. Accordingly, Rome embarked on a campaign to eradicate the teachers and scholars of Torah, hoping thereby to end the "Jewish problem" once and for all. This campaign of persecution created an even more tenacious determination among the Jews to replace the martyred scholars with new teachers of Torah, no matter what the personal risk, for only through the survival of Torah study could survival of the Jewish people be guaranteed. In light of this background of the times, we can perhaps better understand Rabbi Chanina's mishnah.

Basically, Rabbi Chanina speaks out against wasting time (בִּטּוּל זְמַן), the most precious and irreplaceable item in life. According to this interpretation, the phrase וּמְפַנֶּה לִבּוֹ לְבַטָּלָה, *and turns his heart to idleness*, modifies the first two phrases in the sentence, which speak of staying up late at night and taking solitary walks. Those hours when one is free — such as late at night and when one is alone — should be used for the study of Torah and spiritual meditation. One who fritters away those precious times for idleness and frivolity places heavy obstacles against ever advancing his spiritual life. The Talmud teaches

[ו] **רַבִּי** נְחוּנְיָא בֶּן הַקָּנָה אוֹמֵר: כָּל הַמְקַבֵּל עָלָיו עֹל תּוֹרָה, מַעֲבִירִין מִמֶּנּוּ עֹל מַלְכוּת וְעֹל דֶּרֶךְ אֶרֶץ; וְכָל הַפּוֹרֵק מִמֶּנּוּ עֹל תּוֹרָה, נוֹתְנִין עָלָיו עֹל מַלְכוּת וְעֹל דֶּרֶךְ אֶרֶץ.

[ז] **רַבִּי** חֲלַפְתָּא בֶּן דּוֹסָא אִישׁ כְּפַר חֲנַנְיָא אוֹמֵר:

---

that night was created for Torah study; solitude and silence are tools for introspection and self-improvement. But they can also be squandered in creating fantasies and reveries that can lead to danger and sin. In a generation when the light of Torah was threatened with extinction by the Roman despots, when thousands of Torah scholars were hunted down by the Roman police, there was no excuse for idleness and wasted time on the part of the Jewish people as a whole. Rabbi Chanina's words emphasize that vital message of Jewish survival.

רַבִּי נְחוּנְיָא בֶּן הַקָּנָה ***Rabbi Nechunia ben Hakanah***

Mishnah 6 RABBI NECHUNIA WAS A SURVIVOR OF THE SECOND TEMple destruction and an eyewitness to the horrors that befell Israel at that time.

כָּל הַמְקַבֵּל עָלָיו עֹל תּוֹרָה ***If someone takes upon himself the yoke of Torah***

RABBI NECHUNIA REFLECTS ON THE CHOICES ONE FACES IN LIFE. ALL OF us carry yokes, one way or another, but, unbeknownst to many, we do have a choice as to which burdens to bear. Carrying the yoke of Torah lightens the load of the other yokes — those of the government, the turbulence of national life, and the burdens of daily life and of making a living. Torah places events in perspective and organizes our priorities, so that so-called "important" matters gradually recede in significance. People who live a life of spirit and nobility, and not merely one of the flesh and accumulation of wealth, have a different outlook on life and therefore measure their success by loftier standards.

People who value nothing except their material needs, their financial enterprises, their drive to "get ahead," carry a heavy burden indeed. When I was a lawyer and an entrepreneur, I never could take a vacation. The law office and the business I operated in my spare time owned me more than I owned them. My children ruefully pointed out to me that only their friends who were children of rabbis and teachers took long summer vacations and interesting trips. When I changed vocations and became a rabbi, I proved to them that their childish observation was right. The yoke of Torah is not a light one. But on balance, it is far lighter than many of the other alternative yokes in life that some of us somehow choose to bear.

6. Rabbi Nechunia ben Hakanah says: If someone takes upon himself the yoke of Torah — the yoke of government and the yoke of worldly responsibilities are removed from him. But if someone throws off the yoke of Torah from himself — the yoke of government and the yoke of worldly responsibilities are placed upon him.

7. Rabbi Chalafta ben Dosa of Kfar Chanania says: If

מַעֲבִירִין מִמֶּנּוּ עֹל מַלְכוּת וְעֹל דֶּרֶךְ אֶרֶץ
The yoke of government and the yoke of worldly responsibilities are removed from him

THROUGHOUT HISTORY, JEWISH COMMUNITIES SOUGHT TO REMOVE THE yokes of government and finances from the backs of Torah scholars. They were excused from paying communal taxes, their businesses were favored, and they were exempted from compulsory community service. Thus, Rabbi Nechunia's words became a practical reality in Jewish life — one who accepted the yoke of full-time Torah study and leadership was protected by a grateful and respectful Jewish community itself from having to bear the yokes of government and economic responsibility. This practice still exists in many Jewish communities throughout the world today.

One additional insight into Rabbi Nechunia's words may be added. As mentioned above, he witnessed the destruction of the Second Temple and the end of Jewish national sovereignty in the Land of Israel. Surveying the bleakness of the scene, he taught that the destroyed yoke of independent Jewish government and national life must now be exchanged for the yoke of Torah. Jewish survival through millennia of exile would now be based only on the nation's acceptance of the yoke of Torah, and then the Jew would survive and sometimes prosper even without the benefits of independent government and financial security. In the seeming obliqueness of Rabbi Nechunia's message, he communicated the secret of permanent survival to his Jewish brothers and sisters. Though foreign societies and cultures would now be almost universally hostile to the Jews, the presence of Torah in the midst of Israel would somehow compensate for all these troubles and guarantee the continuity of Israel throughout the ages.

רַבִּי חֲלַפְתָּא בֶּן דוֹסָא
Rabbi Chalafta ben Dosa

Mishnah 7 RABBI CHALAFTA IS ALSO KNOWN IN THE MISHNAH AND Talmud as Abba Chalafta, a title of respect and affection. He was of the third generation (c. 110-140 CE) of *Tannaim*, the scholars of the Mishnah. He headed a great yeshivah in Tzippori and was involved in the tumultuous process of the deposing of Rabban Gamliel of Yavneh and his temporary replacement by Rabbi Elazar ben Azariah. He also witnessed Rome's attempts to destroy the scholars and faith of Judaism, though he apparently died before the emperor Hadrian began the great wave of persecution after the crushing of the Bar Kochba revolt.

עֲשָׂרָה שֶׁיּוֹשְׁבִין וְעוֹסְקִין בַּתּוֹרָה, שְׁכִינָה שְׁרוּיָה בֵינֵיהֶם, שֶׁנֶּאֱמַר: „אֱלֹהִים נִצָּב בַּעֲדַת אֵל.” וּמִנַּיִן אֲפִילוּ חֲמִשָּׁה? שֶׁנֶּאֱמַר: „וַאֲגֻדָּתוֹ עַל אֶרֶץ יְסָדָהּ.” וּמִנַּיִן אֲפִילוּ שְׁלֹשָׁה? שֶׁנֶּאֱמַר: „בְּקֶרֶב אֱלֹהִים יִשְׁפֹּט.” וּמִנַּיִן אֲפִילוּ שְׁנַיִם? שֶׁנֶּאֱמַר: „אָז נִדְבְּרוּ יִרְאֵי יהוה אִישׁ אֶל רֵעֵהוּ וַיַּקְשֵׁב יהוה וַיִּשְׁמָע.” וּמִנַּיִן אֲפִילוּ אֶחָד? שֶׁנֶּאֱמַר: „בְּכָל הַמָּקוֹם אֲשֶׁר אַזְכִּיר אֶת שְׁמִי, אָבוֹא אֵלֶיךָ וּבֵרַכְתִּיךָ.”

[ח] **רַבִּי** אֶלְעָזָר אִישׁ בַּרְתּוֹתָא אוֹמֵר: תֶּן לוֹ מִשֶּׁלּוֹ, שֶׁאַתָּה וְשֶׁלְּךָ שֶׁלּוֹ; וְכֵן בְּדָוִד

עֲשָׂרָה שֶׁיּוֹשְׁבִין וְעוֹסְקִין בַּתּוֹרָה
If ten people sit together and engage in Torah study

IN THIS MISHNAH, RABBI CHALAFTA FOLLOWS THE PATTERN AND IDEAS of Rabbi Chanina ben Tradyon in the third mishnah of this chapter. The presence of God, so to speak, is apparent wherever Jews study Torah. Even an isolated Jew, studying in solitude and hiding, without books and intellectual companions, can be assured that the Lord is with him.

In Rabbi Chalafta's generation, when the scholars of Israel had to scatter and go into hiding to avoid the Romans, he provided reassurance as to the value of Torah study even in such lonely circumstances where not ten, not five, not three, not even two Jews could come together safely for such Torah study. God's promise that *In every place where I cause My Name to be mentioned* [in Torah study], *I will come to you and bless you* (*Exodus* 20:21) is eternally valid and trustworthy. It is the basis of Jewish scholarship and a principle of Jewish faith itself. As mentioned above, therefore, Jews should not be discouraged when they are few and their Torah scholars are scattered, lonely and isolated.

It has been said that in prayer, man speaks to God, but in Torah study, God speaks to man. As such, anyone who studies Torah is never truly alone, for God's presence, so to speak, is always there in the pages being studied. In this insight lies the secret of the tenacity of the Jew to study Torah no matter the hardships.

Sadly, there have always been Jews who heaped scorn upon Torah scholars. In the words of the Talmud, the scoffers mocked the great rabbis, saying, "What good are the scholars to us?" This cry of ridicule, heard even today in parts of the Jewish world, is a vestige of the poison planted

ten people sit together and engage in Torah study, the Divine Presence is present among them, as it is said: *God stands in the assembly of God* (*Psalms* 82:1). How do we know this [is true] even of five? For it is said: *He has established His bundle upon earth* (*Amos* 9:6). How do we know this [is true] even of three? For it is said: *In the midst of judges He shall judge* (*Psalms* 82:1). How do we know this [is true] even of two? For it is said: *Then those who fear HASHEM spoke to one another, and HASHEM listened and heard* (*Malachi* 3:16). How do we know this [is true] even of one? For it is said: *In every place where I cause My Name to be mentioned, I will come to you and bless you* (*Exodus* 20:21).

8. Rabbi Elazar of Bartosa says: Give Him what is His, for you and your possessions are His. And so has David

---

in Jewish society by the "enlightened ones" of 18th- and 19th-century Germany and Eastern Europe. Despite such critics, it is the presence of Torah scholars that enables the conversation between the Jewish people and its Creator to continue and resonate in Jewish and world society. Their contribution to Jewish survival, continuity and vitality is inestimable, even if they number only ten, only five, only three, only two — or even only one.

תֵּן לוֹ מִשֶּׁלּוֹ, שֶׁאַתָּה וְשֶׁלְּךָ שֶׁלּוֹ

Give Him from what is His, for you and your possessions are His

Mishnah 8 RABBI ELAZAR WAS A COLLEAGUE OF RABBI CHALAFTA. His teaching reflects a basic truism of Judaism's faith and *weltanschauung*. Namely, that all we have as human beings is given to us in trust by our Creator. Our families, our homes, our wealth, our talents, our breath of life itself, are all entrusted to us by God, Who expects us to use these gifts for positive purposes. We, so to speak, are His "investment portfolio managers." God expects to make a "profit" on our endeavors, to make it worth His enormous investment in each of us. Whatever we have should always be harnessed for positive projects that benefit God and humans.

If we realize that our attributes and assets are deposited with us only temporarily and are not inherently ours, we will have a better perspective on life and our participation in society and community; in other words, we are bidden to "return to the Lord what is really His." This realization makes it much easier and more natural to do good deeds, give charity, care for others, and work for the communal good.

הוּא אוֹמֵר: „כִּי מִמְּךָ הַכֹּל, וּמִיָּדְךָ נָתַנּוּ לָךְ.״

[ט] **רַבִּי** יַעֲקֹב אוֹמֵר: הַמְּהַלֵּךְ בַּדֶּרֶךְ וְשׁוֹנֶה, וּמַפְסִיק מִמִּשְׁנָתוֹ, וְאוֹמֵר: „מַה נָּאֶה אִילָן זֶה! וּמַה נָּאֶה נִיר זֶה!״ – מַעֲלֶה עָלָיו הַכָּתוּב כְּאִלּוּ מִתְחַיֵּב בְּנַפְשׁוֹ.

[י] **רַבִּי** דוֹסְתָּאִי בַּר יַנַּאי מִשּׁוּם רַבִּי מֵאִיר אוֹמֵר:

כִּי מִמְּךָ הַכֹּל, וּמִיָּדְךָ נָתַנּוּ לָךְ ***For everything is from You, and from Your own hand we have given to You***

RABBI ELAZAR USES KING DAVID'S WORDS AS THE MOST FITTING EXAMPLE for this lesson of life and truth. David is a multifaceted and multi-talented person. He is king and scholar, judge and builder, the greatest ruler king (outside of Moses) that the Jewish people ever knew. He has charisma and leadership qualities. He is strong and courageous, unafraid and self-confident, a mighty warrior. He is also a poet, an author, "the sweet singer of Israel." Such a man would be expected to have a certain amount of pride in himself, his achievements and talents. And we would all understand and forgive such an attitude. Nevertheless, it is King David himself who prays: *For everything is from You, and from Your hand we have given to You* (*I Chronicles* 29:14). This is echoed by the prophet Haggai (2:8), *Mine is the silver and Mine is the gold — the word of HASHEM, Master of Legions.*

This example of King David gives life to the stirring words of the prophet Jeremiah (9:22-3): *Thus says HASHEM: Let not the wise man glorify himself with his wisdom, and let not the strong glorify himself with his strength, let not the rich man glorify himself with his wealth . For only with this may one glorify himself — contemplating and knowing Me, for I am HASHEM Who does kindness, justice, and righteousness in the land, for in this is My desire — the word of HASHEM.* In our popular slang vernacular we would say that the Lord wants us to "get it." The greatest mistakes in life are caused when we "just don't get it." Appreciating that all of our talents and lives and material assets are from God and still belong to Him is the beginning of the process of "getting it."

רַבִּי יַעֲקֹב ***Rabbi Yaakov***

Mishnah 9 THIS MISHNAH IS THE PRODUCT OF RABBI YAAKOV BEN Korshai, a member of the Sanhedrin of Rabban Shimon ben Gamliel II, in the fourth generation (c. 140-170 CE) of the scholars of the Mishnah. This was the generation after Rabbi Akiva and the other martyrs, who were killed by Hadrian's decrees. The Roman hand was still heavy against the scholars of Torah and this difficult period was also marked by prolonged dissension among the great rabbis of the time. Rabbi Meir and Rabbi Nathan attempted to have Rabban Shimon ben Gamliel II removed

said: *For everything is from You, and from Your hand we have given to You* (*I Chronicles* 29:14).

9. Rabbi Yaakov says: One who walks on the road while reviewing his Torah lesson, but interrupts his review and exclaims: "How beautiful is this tree! How beautiful is this plowed furrow!" — Scripture considers it as if he bears guilt for his soul.

10. Rabbi Dostai bar Yannai says in the name of Rabbi Meir:

---

from his position as *Nasi,* the temporal and spiritual head of the remaining Jews in the Land of Israel. Rabbi Yaakov supported the *Nasi* and was active in thwarting the attempts of the opposition to remove him. Rabbi Yaakov was also one of the teachers of the great Rabbi Yehudah HaNasi, the redactor of the Mishnah.

הַמְהַלֵּךְ בַּדֶּרֶךְ וְשׁוֹנֶה, וּמַפְסִיק מִמִּשְׁנָתוֹ
One who walks on the road while reviewing his Torah lesson, but interrupts his review

RABBI YAAKOV'S LESSON RESEMBLES THAT OF RABBI CHANINA BEN Chachinai in mishnah 5 of this chapter. Both speak about idleness, dawdling, stopping to smell the flowers while the world is burning.

Judaism lauds balance as opposed to an emphasis on one area of life to the exclusion of all others. The exception to this rule is the study and observance of Torah. Nature's truest beauty is found not only in trees, mountains and spectacular waterfalls. It is to be found in the soul and heart of human beings, in their compassionate behavior, soaring faith, tenacious optimism and limitless goodness. Admiration of nature's beauty, being an environmentalist or a "green," does not by itself guarantee nobility of character and/or purity of behavior.

True, Judaism preaches a strong appreciation for the beauties and wonders of nature, but the time and place for that appreciation has limits. If it takes precedent over the study of Torah, over the spiritual development of individuals and Jewish society, then those expressions of admiration for the beauty of nature reverse the true priorities of Jewish living. They are out of place and eventually harmful.

רַבִּי דוֹסְתָּאִי בַּר יַנַּאי
Rabbi Dostai bar Yannai

Mishnah 10 VERY LITTLE IS KNOWN ABOUT RABBI DOSTAI. IF HIS father was the *Tanna,* Rabbi Yannai, then he was a member of the generation that arose immediately after Rabbi Yehudah HaNasi and he lived c. 200-225 CE. Rabbi Yannai himself was a disciple of Rabbi Meir and later of Rabbi Yehudah HaNasi. Rabbi Yannai was one of those who gathered material for the *beraisos,* which were Tannaitic teachings not included in Rabbi Yehudah HaNasi's Mishnah, but which the Talmud considers to be legally

כָּל הַשּׁוֹכֵחַ דָּבָר אֶחָד מִמִּשְׁנָתוֹ, מַעֲלֶה עָלָיו הַכָּתוּב כְּאִלּוּ מִתְחַיֵּב בְּנַפְשׁוֹ, שֶׁנֶּאֱמַר: „רַק הִשָּׁמֶר לְךָ, וּשְׁמֹר נַפְשְׁךָ מְאֹד, פֶּן תִּשְׁכַּח אֶת הַדְּבָרִים אֲשֶׁר רָאוּ עֵינֶיךָ.״ יָכוֹל אֲפִילוּ תָּקְפָה עָלָיו מִשְׁנָתוֹ? תַּלְמוּד לוֹמַר: „וּפֶן יָסוּרוּ מִלְּבָבְךָ כֹּל יְמֵי חַיֶּיךָ״; הָא אֵינוֹ מִתְחַיֵּב בְּנַפְשׁוֹ עַד שֶׁיֵּשֵׁב וִיסִירֵם מִלִּבּוֹ.

[יא] **רַבִּי** חֲנִינָא בֶּן דּוֹסָא אוֹמֵר: כֹּל שֶׁיִּרְאַת

---

authoritative. If this chain of genealogy is correct, then Rabbi Dostai's quoting of Rabbi Meir, his father's teacher, is perfectly understandable.

כָּל הַשּׁוֹכֵחַ . . . כְּאִלּוּ מִתְחַיֵּב בְּנַפְשׁוֹ, *Whoever forgets . . . as if he bears guilt for his soul*

THIS MISHNAH DEALS WITH MEMORY AND ITS NEMESIS, FORGETTING. Forgetting is a heavenly gift. If we were unable to forget life's moments of pain and embarrassment, the times of failure and grief, if our conscious will did not sublimate them into the dark regions of our subconscious mind, then we would be unable to live in any sort of normal fashion. Thus the Sages speak of forgetting as a gift from Heaven, but like all such gifts, humans can use it for the good, or they can abuse it.

❦ ❦ ❦

Abuse of the gift

The Maggid of Dubno, Rabbi Yaakov Krantz, typically illustrates this idea with a parable. Once someone borrowed a great deal of money to invest in a new enterprise. His business failed and he was unable to meet his creditors' demands for repayment of the loans. Desperate for relief from the incessant hounding of his creditors, he turned to a good friend for advice as to how to cope with his situation. The friend, who had also lent him money, advised him to pretend that he was insane and the creditors would soon stop bothering him, realizing that they had no chance to collect from a crazy man. The beleaguered debtor took this advice and began behaving like a lunatic, speaking nonsense, drooling and rolling on the floor. The word got out that he had gone mad and creditors stopped knocking at his door. This respite allowed him to concentrate on restoring his business fortunes and to stand on his feet again.

His friend and adviser now came to the debtor to ask for his payment. The man immediately began to roll on the floor and pretend to be insane. The adviser shouted at him: "Don't use that trick on me! I am the one who gave you this advice!"

So too, said the Maggid of Dubno, God is the One Who gave us the ability

Whoever forgets anything of his Torah learning, Scripture considers it as if he bears guilt for his soul, as it says: *But beware and guard your soul exceedingly, lest you forget the things your eyes have seen* (*Deuteronomy* 4:9). Does this apply even if [he forgot because] his studies were too difficult for him? [This is not so, for] Scripture says: *And lest they be removed from your heart all the days of your life* (ibid.); thus, one bears no guilt for his soul unless he sits [idly] and [through lack of concentration and review] removes them from his consciousness.

11. Rabbi Chanina ben Dosa says: Anyone whose fear of

---

to forget – how dare man use that ability to forget God? The power to forget must be used sparingly and properly; to forget one's obligations to God and man is an abuse of that gift.

❦ ❦ ❦

The Torah specifically warns Israel never to forget the revelation at Sinai. That moment in history is the basis of Judaism and all Jewish life. To forget it, to deny it, is to destroy all of Judaism and eventually Jewish society. One is also forbidden to purposely forget the words and ideas of Torah that one has learned. Natural forgetting is understandable and excusable, and, as the mishnah continues, one is not blamed if his learning was too difficult for him. But to purposely forget who we are, why we are, and what we should strive for is lethal to Jewish continuity and survival, both personal and national.

The Baal Shem Tov is reputed to have said that "exile is forgetting." The outstanding quality of the Jewish people is its ability to remember. The major disease of the Jewish world today is amnesia. That alone explains self-hatred, assimilation, ignorance, and the falsification of Jewish attitudes and values. The attempt by sections of Jewry to blot out the past in favor of the brave new world of all the "isms" of the last centuries has ended in abysmal failure and tragedy. Millions of Jews have fallen into national oblivion. Our task is to restore Jewish memory. When that happens, all Jews will face a brighter day and a more meaningful existence.

רַבִּי חֲנִינָא בֶּן דּוֹסָא
Rabbi Chanina ben Dosa

Mishnah 11 RABBI CHANINA WAS RENOWNED AS ONE OF THE HOLIEST men of his era. His father, Rabbi Dosa ben Hyrkanos, also a famous and righteous scholar, said, "The whole world is sustained in the merit of Chanina my son, but he himself requires only a small measure of carob fruit from Friday to Friday" (*Taanis* 10a).

חֶטְאוֹ קוֹדֶמֶת לְחָכְמָתוֹ, חָכְמָתוֹ מִתְקַיֶּמֶת; וְכֹל שֶׁחָכְמָתוֹ קוֹדֶמֶת לְיִרְאַת חֶטְאוֹ, אֵין חָכְמָתוֹ מִתְקַיֶּמֶת.

[יב] **הוּא** הָיָה אוֹמֵר: כֹּל שֶׁמַּעֲשָׂיו מְרֻבִּין מֵחָכְמָתוֹ, חָכְמָתוֹ מִתְקַיֶּמֶת; וְכֹל שֶׁחָכְמָתוֹ מְרֻבָּה מִמַּעֲשָׂיו, אֵין חָכְמָתוֹ מִתְקַיֶּמֶת.

Power of the individual

That the merit of an individual or a few people is great enough to support multitudes is a familiar concept in Jewish thought. The best known example is that of "the thirty-six righteous people" in every generation, in whose merit the world exists. (As I have often mentioned, if one thinks that he or she is one of those thirty-six, rest assured that he or she is not.) This entire chapter of Avos concentrates on the importance of the individual, even in the universal scheme of things. This has been emphasized previously in this chapter (such as mishnahs 3 and 7).

Self-improvement counts not only for the individual but for all mankind, as well. Consequently, Judaism and Jews (as of 2000, only 0.4% of the world's population!) have been disproportionately influential and central in human civilization and advancement. In the medical world, the research of one doctor, Jonas Salk for example, benefits millions. In the world of theoretical physics, the creative genius of an Einstein changes society and improves everyone's life. In financial matters, the creativity of the Rothschilds revolutionized finance and banking. In the realm of the spirit, as well, one person — such as the Chafetz Chaim — can change the world.

But in spiritual matters, there is an additional element. As we have seen above, even the growth of a single person can cause the Divine spirit to rest upon him — and when that happens the entire world is elevated. Rabbi Chanina was such a person. He may not have been a charismatic leader or teacher, but in his quiet, private way, he sustained an entire world.

כָּל שֶׁיִּרְאַת חֶטְאוֹ קוֹדֶמֶת לְחָכְמָתוֹ, חָכְמָתוֹ מִתְקַיֶּמֶת
Anyone whose fear of sin takes priority over his wisdom — his wisdom will endure

SPIRITUALITY, THE ACHIEVEMENT OF HOLINESS, IS NOT COMPRISED OF intellect or creative talent alone. Many of the greatest intellectuals, musicians and artists in history have been rotten or cruel people. The value of their intellectual and creative accomplishments was negated by their personal deportment and behavior. Hardly any Jew with a feeling for his people can listen to Wagnerian music without shuddering, as he remembers its association with the barbarism of Nazism and the Holocaust. Rabbi Chanina's statement, therefore, is all the more trenchant: the products of wisdom,

sin takes priority over his wisdom — his wisdom will endure; but anyone whose wisdom takes priority over his fear of sin, his wisdom will not endure.

12. He used to say: Anyone whose good deeds exceed his wisdom, his wisdom will endure; but anyone whose wisdom exceeds his good deeds, his wisdom will not endure.

---

knowledge, and creativity cannot endure unless they are based on a sense of morality — on fear and avoidance of evil and sin. Only if built upon a moral foundation do wisdom and talent bear the stamp of eternity.

An extreme but most telling example of this idea is the refusal of the world's medical community to use the medical research that Nazi doctors conducted on their hapless "patients" to determine the human body's limits of suffering, pain and privation. Such research is morally stained. Without moral restraints in society, wisdom, knowledge, research, creativity and artistic endeavor can carry with them the seeds of depravity and danger.

הוּא הָיָה אוֹמֵר
He [Rabbi Chanina ben Dosa] used to say

Mishnah 12 THIS TEACHING OF RABBI CHANINA FLOWS FROM HIS lesson in the previous mishnah. There he emphasized that wisdom must be based on a moral code and a fear of Heaven; here he adds another dimension. Theoretical wisdom and accumulated knowledge are enormously important assets, but if they are not translated into actual practice, they eventually prove temporary and barren. A great rule mentioned in Avos is that acquiring knowledge is not the fundamental basis of Judaism. Rather the goal of Jewish life is human behavior. As I have pointed out before, many a great intellectual has been an awful person. The great rabbi of the Talmud, Rava, stated that "the goal of wisdom is repentance and good deeds, so that a person shall not study Torah and Mishnah and yet kick away his father and teacher" (*Berachos* 17a).

כֹּל שֶׁמַּעֲשָׂיו מְרֻבִּין מֵחָכְמָתוֹ, חָכְמָתוֹ מִתְקַיֶּמֶת
Anyone whose good deeds exceed his wisdom, his wisdom will endure

A FAVORITE WEAKNESS OF INTELLECTUALS IS TO PROVE THEMSELVES RIGHT at the expense of previous scholars, and sometimes even at the expense of society at large. It is true that one is always entitled to disagree with other opinions — but one has no right to arrogantly and contemptuously "kick away" elders, teachers, traditions, and past verities. Reasoned discussion is allowed and encouraged in Jewish life. Outright rebellion and rejection of the past, at least in terms of Jewish history, leads to divisiveness and eventually to ignorance of Torah and alienation from Jewish values and society. Judaism always judged people more on what they did in life than on their intellectual attainments. Certainly pious pronouncements without similar deeds have no value.

[יג] **הוּא** הָיָה אוֹמֵר: כֹּל שֶׁרְוּחַ הַבְּרִיּוֹת נוֹחָה הֵימֶנּוּ, רְוּחַ הַמָּקוֹם נוֹחָה הֵימֶנּוּ; וְכֹל שֶׁאֵין רְוּחַ הַבְּרִיּוֹת נוֹחָה הֵימֶנּוּ, אֵין רְוּחַ הַמָּקוֹם נוֹחָה הֵימֶנּוּ.

[יד] **רַבִּי** דוֹסָא בֶּן הָרְכִּינַס אוֹמֵר: שֵׁנָה שֶׁל שַׁחֲרִית, וְיַיִן שֶׁל צָהֳרַיִם, וְשִׂיחַת הַיְלָדִים, וִישִׁיבַת בָּתֵּי כְנֵסִיּוֹת שֶׁל עַמֵּי הָאָרֶץ – מוֹצִיאִין אֶת הָאָדָם מִן הָעוֹלָם.

If fear of sin must precede wisdom, as Rabbi Chanina taught in mishnah 11, then one's behavior must reflect a moral caliber that surpasses mere intellectual knowledge. One of the axioms of Jewish thought is that "A person is shaped by his actions" (*Sefer HaChinuch*). One who gives money to the poor and to worthy causes becomes a charitable person. It shapes our character and opens our hand. No philanthropist was ever created by pontificating about the holiness of giving.

כֹּל שֶׁרְוּחַ הַבְּרִיּוֹת נוֹחָה הֵימֶנּוּ, רְוּחַ הַמָּקוֹם נוֹחָה הֵימֶנּוּ

If the spirit of one's fellows is pleased with him, the spirit of the Omnipresent is pleased with him

Mishnah 13 RABBI CHANINA COMPLETES HIS THREE-MISHNAH CYCLE of moral advice. If actual behavior is the measure of a person's worth, as he stated above, then what is the criterion for judging such behavior? Rabbi Chanina advises us to look at someone's reputation. If people generally do not have a good opinion of his behavior, he teaches, it is unlikely that in Heaven they will have a better opinion of him. The story is told about a chassid who was summoned by his *rebbe*. The *rebbe* said: "I have heard that people say you are dishonest in your commercial dealings." The chassid heatedly denied the charge, saying, "*Rebbe*, that is not true!" To which the *rebbe* responded in amazement: "It should be true!? Is it not bad enough that people say this? It should be true, yet?"

Good reputations are hard to acquire and easy to lose. A person's most precious asset is his or her good name, as the rabbis declared, "the crown of a good name surpasses all other crowns" (*Avos* 4:17). It is interesting that Rabbi Chanina, a well-known wonder-worker who was intimately familiar with the ways of Heaven, should say that God's judgment, so to speak, is heavily influenced by human opinion and reputation. This is perfectly understandable, however, for if Heaven favored someone who had a terrible personal reputation among other people, such favor and its rewards would play itself on earth as a *chillul Hashem*, a desecration of God's Name and holiness. The rabbis of the

13. He used to say: If the spirit of one's fellows is pleased with him, the spirit of the Omnipresent is pleased with him; but if the spirit of one's fellows is not pleased with him, the spirit of the Omnipresent is not pleased with him.

14. Rabbi Dosa ben Harkinas says: Late morning sleep, midday wine, children's chatter, and sitting at gatherings of the ignorant — remove a man from the world.

Talmud always were attuned to the public mood and opinions. "See what the people say" is one of their favorite aphorisms.

There have been prophets and martyrs in Jewish history who were unpopular in their lifetimes, but eventually become heroes, but none of them suffered from a bad reputation for ethics or morality and the like. Their warnings and chastisements displeased society, but no one ever accused them of personal corruption, loose morals, or disregard for the welfare of others. Because their personal probity was acknowledged and respected even while their views were unpopular, many of them came to be regarded as heroes after their deaths. Character, not only opinions and causes, is the part of society's opinion that Heaven factors into its judgment.

רַבִּי דוֹסָא בֶּן הָרְכִּינַס
Rabbi Dosa ben Harkinas

Mishnah 14 RABBI DOSA, A STUDENT/COLLEAGUE OF RABBAN Yochanan ben Zakkai, witnessed the destruction of the Second Temple. His combination of wealth and scholarship established him as a person of influence and prestige. Living in that era of great turmoil and stress in the Jewish world, he was appalled by people who were unable to rise to the challenges of the time. In this mishnah he warns against the attitudes and behavior that cause people to plunge to oblivion.

שֵׁנָה שֶׁל שַׁחֲרִית
Late morning sleep . . .

SLEEPING LATE IN THE MORNING, INDULGING IN AFTERNOON WINE FESTS (apparently, afternoon "happy hours" is not a modern invention), taking part in silly and childish conversations, wasting one's precious time with unlettered and vulgar people, all are inappropriate responses to times of challenge. In Rabbi Dosa's time, the Jewish world lay in tatters. It needed revival and renewal. Idle behavior and self-indulgent attitudes would only seal the then apparent doom of the Jewish people. This is what Rabbi Dosa warned about when he predicted that such behavior and attitudes would "remove a person from the world."

In modern times, after the Holocaust and World War II, when the Jewish world again lay despairing and bleeding, the Jewish people was rebuilt in Israel and the Diaspora by driven people. I knew some of them personally. None of them ever slept late or frittered away their time and talents in frivolous conversation, meaningless banter or unbecoming behavior. They were all

[טו] **רַבִּי** אֶלְעָזָר הַמּוֹדָעִי אוֹמֵר: הַמְחַלֵּל אֶת הַקָּדָשִׁים, וְהַמְבַזֶּה אֶת הַמּוֹעֲדוֹת, וְהַמַּלְבִּין פְּנֵי חֲבֵרוֹ בָּרַבִּים, וְהַמֵּפֵר בְּרִיתוֹ שֶׁל

---

haunted by the disaster they had witnessed and experienced, and were determined to make Torah and Israel rise from the ashes of destruction and flourish again. They had no time to waste, for the holy task that they had undertaken was of enormous proportions and eternal worth.

❦ ❦ ❦

In a telling anecdote, Rabbi Emanuel Feldman describes a conversation with a Jew who was slowly returning to Jewish observance and learning. As Rabbi Feldman described the concept of specific times of prayer and the requirement to recite the Shema and Amidah prayers before a certain time in the morning, the man's eyes widened. He exclaimed: "Does that mean that I won't ever be able to sleep late on a Sunday morning again?" Rabbi Feldman answered: "You got it!" The shocked Jew responded that he was never so aware as now that an alarm clock was an essential appliance in a Jewish home.

❦ ❦ ❦

Wise use of time, avoidance of bad company, and disciplined behavior are the pillars of healthy Jewish society. Without these guidelines, we are easily susceptible to being "driven out of this world." And out of this world means out of the eternal world as well.

רַבִּי אֶלְעָזָר הַמּוֹדָעִי
Rabbi Elazar the Moda'ite

Mishnah 15 A RELATIVE OF BAR KOCHBA, RABBI ELAZAR SUPPORTED and participated in his aborted rebellion against Rome (135-139 CE). As the tides of war began turning against him, Bar Kochba searched for scapegoats to blame for his impending defeat. A Samaritan member of Bar Kochba's troops falsely accused Rabbi Elazar of treason, and in a fit of anger and frustration, Bar Kochba executed the great sage of Israel. This brutal and unjustified act turned popular support away from Bar Kochba and his rebelliion ended in defeat and tragedy.

There were many Jews who wanted to surrender not only to Roman arms, but to Roman pagan culture and values as well. These assimilationist Jews undermined the rabbis of the Mishnah in their attempt to rebuild Jewish religious life in the Land of Israel after the destruction of the Second Temple. The renegades were aided and abetted in their struggle against the rabbis by the nascent Christian religion that had as yet not completely separated itself from the midst of Jewish society. In this mishnah, Rabbi Elazar alludes to the underlying tensions that gripped the Jewish society of his time, and specifies practices of the assimilationists that cut them off from the Jewish people.

15. Rabbi Elazar the Moda'ite says: One who profanes things that are sacred, who despises the festivals, who humiliates his fellow in public, who voids the covenant of

---

הַמְחַלֵּל אֶת הַקֳּדָשִׁים ***One who profanes things that are sacred***

THESE WERE THE MAIN POINTS OF BATTLE AGAINST TORAH LIFE IN RABBI Elazar the Moda'ite's time: profaning of everything sacred in Judaism by mockery, secularization and pseudo-scholarship — "profaning things that are sacred"; rejection of the Jewish calendar and the holy days — "the despising of the festivals"; the abrogation of circumcision as the covenant of Israel — "voiding the covenant of Abraham"; and distorting the ideas of Jewish law and halachah — "revealing a face of Torah that is not in accordance with halachah."

These issues were all in contention during the Mishnaic era. In fact, from the times of the Hasmoneans onward, the issue of circumcision was debated fiercely in Jewish society. Many assimilated Jews even went so far as to undergo painful cosmetic surgery to remove the appearance of being circumcised, thus "voiding the covenant of Abraham." Based on their false interpretation of Scripture, the Sadducees changed the calendar in order to have the festival of Shavuos always fall on a Sunday; the Christians substituted Sunday for Shabbos as the day of rest.

The opponents of tradition scoffed at the rabbis and the eternal values of Judaism. Some opponents of Torah may have been well-intentioned and even scholarly. They may also have been nice people personally, possessed of good deeds and a good heart. Nevertheless, the harm they caused to the survival of Judaism and the Jewish people was so significant that they lost their share of eternity because of the consequences of their behavior and false beliefs.

History is always a harsh judge, even of those who have good intentions and sincerely believe in the causes they advocate. Fighting against Jewish tradition and denigrating Torah scholars have always been a certain course for eventual personal loss and Jewish oblivion. Rabbi Elazar's words resound down the corridor of Jewish history and society till our day.

וְהַמַּלְבִּין פְּנֵי חֲבֵרוֹ בָּרַבִּים ***One who humiliates his fellow in public***

SPECIAL MENTION MUST BE MADE OF RABBI ELAZAR'S ADMONITION NOT to shame people publicly. The Talmud views such behavior harshly, even comparing it to murder! We all know from personal experience the hurt of being shamed in a classroom, at a social gathering, or in our profession or workplace. People in positions of authority and power, especially teachers, parents, and administrators and managers should be extremely sensitive to the terrible effects that shaming others publicly can cause.

I had a teacher in my yeshivah days who was a great disciplinarian. He never raised his voice, was of extremely noble and gentle character, and never reprimanded or corrected a student publicly. If a student gave a wrong answer to a question, he gently rearranged the student's answer — "this is what you

אַבְרָהָם אָבִינוּ, וְהַמְגַלֶּה פָנִים בַּתּוֹרָה שֶׁלֹּא כַהֲלָכָה, אַף עַל פִּי שֶׁיֵּשׁ בְּיָדוֹ תּוֹרָה וּמַעֲשִׂים טוֹבִים — אֵין לוֹ חֵלֶק לָעוֹלָם הַבָּא.

[טז] **רַבִּי** יִשְׁמָעֵאל אוֹמֵר: הֱוֵי קַל לְרֹאשׁ, וְנוֹחַ לְתִשְׁחֹרֶת, וֶהֱוֵי מְקַבֵּל אֶת כָּל הָאָדָם בְּשִׂמְחָה.

---

really meant to say" — to make it the correct response. And if he had to criticize, he always did it privately and lovingly. There were never any discipline problems in his classroom.

The mishnah employs the words "to whiten one's face" as the metaphor for embarrassing others. Causing the blood to be drained from someone's face in embarrassment is truly akin to shedding his blood. The rabbis of the Talmud rightly compared shaming someone to killing him. Even in debate with the Sadducees and the Christians, when tempers flared and Jewish truths had to be protected and defended, Rabbi Elazar warned against the embarrassment of others. The way of the Torah is always the way of pleasantness. Insulting wall posters, personal attacks against those who may not conform to current political correctness, and abusive language and behavior directed against people with different views are not acceptable forms of behavior for people who purport to be loyal to the Torah.

רַבִּי יִשְׁמָעֵאל ***Rabbi Yishmael***

Mishnah 16 HE WAS THE GRANDSON OF RABBI YISHMAEL, A HIGH Priest at the end of the Second Temple Era, who was one of the Ten Martyrs murdered by the Romans. The Rabbi Yishmael of our mishnah was a colleague of Rabbi Akiva and a great scholar. His categorization of the Oral Law's Thirteen Principles of exegesis of the Written Torah remained the accepted basis of Talmudic interpretation. He was a prisoner of Rome as a child, apparently destined for slavery, and was redeemed from captivity through the efforts of Rabbi Yehoshua ben Chanania. The original Yishmael was Abraham's first son by Hagar, who was banished because he turned to violent and sinful behavior. The use of this name in Jewish families, therefore, especially in the families of High Priests and rabbinic scholars of the Mishnah, strikes us today as strange and disconcerting. However, in Biblical and Second Temple times, the name was common among Jews, in accordance with the tradition that Yishmael repented toward the end of his life, and was a righteous person at the time of his death. He was the ancestor of the Arab nation, and with the rise of Islam in the 7th century CE, the name Yishmael was no longer used by Jewish families.

our forefather Abraham, or who reveals a face of Torah that is not in accordance with halachah — though he may have Torah and good deeds, he has no share in the World to Come.

16. Rabbi Yishmael says: Be yielding to a superior, pleasant to the young, and receive every person cheerfully.

הֱוֵי קַל לְרֹאשׁ
Be yielding to a superior

RABBI YISHMAEL'S ADVICE TO BE FLEXIBLE AND YIELDING IN DEALING with superior governmental authority was based on the realities of Rome's dominance over the Land of Israel and the Jewish people. The two great rebellions against Rome (in 66 and 135 CE) had brought disaster on Israel. The rabbis of the Mishnah were in the main great realists. Throughout the long night of the Jewish Exile, Jews bent their heads and attempted to survive and continue their observance of the Torah in the face of implacable hatred and persecution. Though this attitude may hardly qualify for dramatic heroism, especially by modern standards, in the long run it was a successful mechanism for the continuity of the Jewish people and Jewish life. The situation would naturally change under circumstances of Jewish statehood and power, and in many liberal democracies, but Rabbi Yishmael was dealing with a world where the physical might of the Jewish people had been shattered twice within a century by the overwhelming power of Rome. Hence, his most practical advice was the wisest course of Jewish behavior. Indeed, his counsel was valid for nearly all the centuries of dispersion and in the overwhelming majority of our host countries.

וְנוֹחַ לְתִשְׁחֹרֶת
Pleasant to the young

RABBI YISHMAEL ALSO ADVISED BEING LENIENT WITH THE YOUNG. THERE is a fine line between leniency and a lack of discipline; children and youths need standards and a framework for their young lives. Nevertheless, rules should be imposed gently and leniently, albeit with an underlying and omnipresent degree of firmness and definition. A household that is governed too rigidly invites rebellion and disaffection. The Lord Himself, so to speak, treats us leniently, as He says, *When Israel was a youth I loved him* (*Hosea* 11:1). Youth needs space and patience and a loving and lenient environment in which to grow and mature. In many instances it must be given the benefit of the doubt. How to balance this attitude of leniency with the necessity for rules and goals is the ultimate test of the art of parenting, teaching, administering. It may well be the most difficult task in life.

וֶהֱוֵי מְקַבֵּל אֶת כָּל הָאָדָם בְּשִׂמְחָה
And receive every person cheerfully

RABBI YISHMAEL ECHOES THE WORDS OF SHAMMAI IN CHAPTER 1 (1:15), that receiving others with a smile, a happy countenance and a cheerful disposition is a necessity for a happy life and for positive social influence. No one loves a grouch.

[יז] **רַבִּי** עֲקִיבָא אוֹמֵר: שְׂחוֹק וְקַלּוּת רֹאשׁ מַרְגִּילִין אֶת הָאָדָם לְעֶרְוָה. מַסּוֹרֶת סְיָג לַתּוֹרָה; מַעְשְׂרוֹת סְיָג לָעֹשֶׁר; נְדָרִים סְיָג לַפְּרִישׁוּת;

I once arranged for a congregant of mine to visit the study of a great scholar. This congregant was struggling with issues of faith and personal problems, and I felt that the visit would be of enormous help to him. Although the scholar was wise and articulate, he did not exude warmth. The visit turned out to be a disaster, for it had the exact opposite effect upon my congregant than the one I had intended. Soon after, the man resigned from the congregation and drifted away from participation in active Jewish life. I have often wondered whether the scholar even remembers the visit, let alone is aware of the damage done by his lack of hospitality. People are delicate beings. Greeting them with a smile and a good word goes a long way in this world in advancing the cause of righteous behavior.

רַבִּי עֲקִיבָא
Rabbi Akiva

Mishnah 17 RABBI AKIVA BEN YOSEF IS ONE OF THE GREATEST PERsonages in Jewish history. Beginning his Torah studies at the age of 40, thanks to the urging of his noble wife Rachel, he rose after twenty-six years of diligent study to be the preeminent Torah scholar of his generation. In his long lifetime, he represented Judaism and the cause of his people to the Romans on many diplomatic missions. Believing in Bar Kochba as a potential messiah, he encouraged the armed rebellion against Rome that ended in Jewish defeat in 139 CE. Rabbi Akiva himself was tortured to death by the Romans in Caesarea; by tradition his burial place is in Tiberias. He had tens of thousands of students, and his five main disciples rebuilt the Jewish and Torah world after his death in the spirit of his life and teachings.

There is a difference of scholarly opinion as to whether Akiva is a Hebrew name (if so the last letter of the name would be the Hebrew letter *hei*), or non-Hebrew name (and if so the last letter of the name would be an *aleph*). In any event, *Akiva* has remained a very popular name for Jewish boys throughout the centuries.

שְׂחוֹק וְקַלּוּת רֹאשׁ מַרְגִּילִין אֶת הָאָדָם לְעֶרְוָה
Mockery and levity accustom a man to immorality

THE WORLD IS A SERIOUS PLACE TO LIVE IN, AND WHILE HUMOR IS AN important component of a balanced personality, the abandonment of one's self to levity and irresponsibility breeds immoral behavior. Rabbi Akiva emphasizes that it "accustoms" one to sinful behavior. It accommodates and rationalizes wrongdoing. Eventually, it mocks rules and disciplines. When one becomes accustomed to sin, it is infinitely more difficult to crawl out of the pit of sin. Usually, levity turns into mockery and thus precludes even the attempt to turn

17. Rabbi Akiva says: Mockery and levity accustom a man to immorality. The transmitted Oral Torah is a protective fence around the Torah; tithes are a protective fence for wealth; vows are a protective fence for abstinence;

---

away from evil and immorality.

מְסוֹרֶת סְיָג לַתּוֹרָה ***The transmitted Oral Torah is a protective fence around the Torah***

RABBI AKIVA ESTABLISHES BOUNDARIES IN LIFE THAT SHOULD NEVER BE crossed. The understanding and interpretation of Torah is regulated by the boundary of tradition. We would not even be able to read or understand the words of the Torah, unpunctuated as they are, were it not for the Masoretic tradition that punctuates each and every word and sentence of the written Torah. More importantly, only the Oral Torah enables us to understand the true meaning of the verses. Among the classic demonstrations of this truth is that the Torah speaks of such commandments as kosher slaughter and *tefillin,* but without the Oral Torah there is no way to know how to slaughter or what *tefillin* are. Similarly, it is the Oral Torah that defines "an eye for an eye" as referring not to the literal blinding of the assailant, but to payment of the monetary damages caused by the assault.

Rabbi Akiva teaches a deeper lesson. as we saw in the first mishnah of this tractate, the Divine revelation of the Torah that occurred at Sinai has been preserved throughout the ages by the Oral Tradition that was given to Moses and that has been passed on throughout the centuries. Ignoring, falsifying or abandoning that tradition eventually creates a false Torah and an ersatz Judaism. Without the boundary and limitation of tradition, the Torah loses its holiness and eternity.

מַעְשְׂרוֹת סְיָג לָעֹשֶׁר ***Tithes are a protective fence for wealth***

TITHING TO CHARITY IS AN EFFECTIVE BRAKE UPON THE ARROGANCE THAT comes with wealth. Only by giving a set portion of one's money to charity does one develop a proper appreciation of God's gift of wealth. Without the boundary of tithing and giving, wealth can be an all-consuming monster that destroys families and communities, not to speak of the wealthy person himself or herself. According to the Talmud, Rabbi Akiva was himself an extremely wealthy person. This advice, therefore, is not a pious platitude, but rather an expression of hard-earned experience.

נְדָרִים סְיָג לַפְּרִישׁוּת ***Vows are a protective fence for abstinence***

VOWS ARE A BOUNDARY TO HELP ONE ABSTAIN FROM UNWANTED behavior. It allows one to separate oneself from sin and dangerous temptations. It reinforces self-control and inhibition. Although Judaism generally frowns on vows and warns against the danger of unfulfilled ones, there are times when a vow is in order, even necessary, to help one over the hurdle of temptation and sin. This is the type of vow that Rabbi Akiva commends as a boundary.

סְיָג לַחָכְמָה שְׁתִיקָה.

[יח] **הוּא** הָיָה אוֹמֵר: חָבִיב אָדָם שֶׁנִּבְרָא בְצֶלֶם; חִבָּה יְתֵרָה נוֹדַעַת לוֹ שֶׁנִּבְרָא בְּצֶלֶם, שֶׁנֶּאֱמַר: „כִּי בְּצֶלֶם אֱלֹהִים עָשָׂה אֶת הָאָדָם." חֲבִיבִין יִשְׂרָאֵל, שֶׁנִּקְרְאוּ בָנִים לַמָּקוֹם; חִבָּה יְתֵרָה נוֹדַעַת לָהֶם שֶׁנִּקְרְאוּ בָנִים לַמָּקוֹם, שֶׁנֶּאֱמַר: „בָּנִים אַתֶּם לַיהוה אֱלֹהֵיכֶם." חֲבִיבִין יִשְׂרָאֵל, שֶׁנִּתַּן לָהֶם כְּלִי חֶמְדָּה;

סְיָג לַחָכְמָה שְׁתִיקָה ***A protective fence for wisdom is silence***

FINALLY, RABBI AKIVA REITERATES THE LESSON MENTIONED MANY TIMES in Avos that silence is the ultimate boundary for wisdom. A wise person not only knows what to say, but perhaps even more importantly, he knows what not to say. Solomon's wisdom teaches us that there is a time for silence. Generally, Jewish wisdom subscribes to the maxim that the less said the better. The silence of the wise man guarantees the retention of wisdom.

Mishnah 18

חָבִיב אָדָם שֶׁנִּבְרָא בְצֶלֶם ***Beloved is man, for he was created in God's image***

RABBI AKIVA MAINTAINS THAT THE EXISTENCE OF HUMAN beings on this planet is in itself an expression of God's love for His creatures and His Creation. Just as a parent loves a child because every child is a piece of him or her, and resembles its parent genetically, so too is God attached, so to speak, to each and every human being, for all human beings are formed "in the image of God" (*Genesis* 1:26). But it is not enough to love a child; the child must know that its parents love it, otherwise that love may pass unrecognized and unappreciated, and the child will fail to gain the full benefits of the affection and concern of its parents. In fact all love — between spouses, siblings, generations in a family, friends and people — requires appreciation and expression.

Emotionally frozen people, who are unable to receive or give love, lack this essential quality of being able to communicate their deeply held feelings. The Lord, Who is the paradigm for all positive conduct, informed humans of His love for them, by saying in the Torah: *Let us make man in Our likeness, in Our image* (ibid.). Human beings can receive no greater compliment than to be told that they are created in God's image.

חֲבִיבִין יִשְׂרָאֵל, שֶׁנִּקְרְאוּ בָנִים לַמָּקוֹם ***Beloved are the people of Israel, for they are described as children of the Omnipresent***

OVER AND ABOVE GOD'S LOVE FOR AND RELATIONSHIP WITH ALL HUMAN beings, there is a special relationship and bond with the people of Israel. He has chosen to act out His Divine role in history and human events through this relationship with the Jewish people. The entire Biblical narrative from

a [protective] fence for wisdom is silence.

18. He [R' Akiva] used to say: Beloved is man, for he was created in [God's] image; it is indicative of a greater love that it was made known to him that he was created in [God's] image, as it is said: *For in the image of God He made man* (*Genesis* 9:6). Beloved are the people of Israel, for they are described as children of the Omnipresent; it is indicative of a greater love that it was made known to them that they are described as children of the Omnipresent, as it is said: *You are children of HASHEM, your God* (*Deuteronomy* 14:1). Beloved are the people of Israel, for a most cherished vessel was given to them;

Abraham through Ezra and all of Jewish history testify to this relationship between God and Israel. Often, Israel's sinful behavior has caused this relationship to be difficult and stormy. Many times, if not most, Jewish history has comprised unfathomable, inexplicable patterns and occurrences. The Lord remains mysterious and inscrutable to us, but our relationship has never been severed by either party to it.

The prophet Malachi stated (3:6): אֲנִי ה׳ לֹא שָׁנִיתִי וְאַתֶּם בְּנֵי יַעֲקֹב לֹא כְלִיתֶם, *I, HASHEM have not changed, and you, the children of Jacob, you have not perished.* Thus Israel and its God, Who is also the God of all creatures, march lockstep through the entire story of human civilization. By calling us "His children," God has informed us of His special love for us; a parent always remains a parent. No matter what a child does, the relationship of parent to child never really changes. This can cause much tension and anguish, but the blunt reality of the bond remains unchanged. Only by looking at the Jewish experience in these terms does any sort of rational understanding of our story become possible. That God informs us of this parent-child relationship thus becomes a further act of love on His part.

שֶׁנִּתַּן לָהֶם כְּלִי חֶמְדָּה ***For a most cherished vessel was given to them***

GOD'S ULTIMATE EXPRESSION OF LOVE TOWARD ISRAEL WAS IN GRANTING us His Torah, which this mishnah describes as "a most cherished vessel." The Midrash speaks of the Torah as the source and tool for the creation of the world. Without Torah, the world is purposeless and unnecessary. An 18th-century rabbinic scholar raised the possibility that there may be other forms of life existing elsewhere in our universe, and he wondered whether their Torah was similar to ours. He took it for granted that such life would have a Torah, for it never entered the mind of a rabbinic Jew that the Lord would create intelligent life anywhere in the universe without giving it a moral standard and

חִבָּה יְתֵרָה נוֹדַעַת לָהֶם, שֶׁנִּתַּן לָהֶם כְּלִי חֶמְדָּה, שֶׁנֶּאֱמַר: „כִּי לֶקַח טוֹב נָתַתִּי לָכֶם, תּוֹרָתִי אַל תַּעֲזֹבוּ.״

[יט] **הַכֹּל** צָפוּי, וְהָרְשׁוּת נְתוּנָה. וּבְטוּב הָעוֹלָם נָדוֹן, וְהַכֹּל לְפִי רוֹב הַמַּעֲשֶׂה.

[כ] **הוּא** הָיָה אוֹמֵר: הַכֹּל נָתוּן בָּעֵרָבוֹן, וּמְצוּדָה

---

an appreciation of God — of a Torah.

In the indispensability of the Torah lies the secret of its desirability. In the words of our evening prayer service: "For [Torah] is our life and the length of our days." It is the ultimate gift, therefore, and the highest expression of God's love for us. As King Solomon expressed it (*Proverbs* 4:2): *For I have given you a good acquisition, do not forsake My Torah.* God gave us a valuable gift, a wonderful investment, in which to fully participate and reap its benefits. He exhorted us to guard it and treasure it, because it is His most desirable possession. It is akin to a grandmother giving a generations-old family heirloom to her newly married granddaughter — her inestimable joy if the gift is treasured and appreciated more than the expensive and stylish baubles, and her anguished disappointment if it is not. So too, the Lord is gratified when we appreciate His loving gift to us.

הַכֹּל צָפוּי, וְהָרְשׁוּת נְתוּנָה
Everything is foreseen, yet freedom of choice is given

Mishnah 19 HERE RABBI AKIVA DEALS WITH THE PHILOSOPHICAL enigma of how free choice can exist for humans when the omniscient God knows in advance what we are going to do, and we are therefore coerced into doing what He knows in advance. Judaism maintains that somehow God's foreknowledge of events and behavior in no way influences man's freedom of choice and action. Maimonides stated that God's system of logic, so to speak, is not subject to the limitations of our logical rules of thought and therefore the entire issue is a moot one. The finite can never understand or truly appreciate the Infinite. So therefore, although beyond man's ken, everything is foreseen by God, but man retains all of his options and behavior choices. And so be it.

וּבְטוּב הָעוֹלָם נָדוֹן
The world is judged with goodness

GOD JUDGES ALWAYS ON THE SIDE OF GOOD. THE RABBIS MAINTAINED THAT everything the Lord does is really for ultimate human good and benefit. The power of good is held to be five hundred times more powerful than the power of evil (*Tosefta, Sotah* 3:4). God always pushes for good and judges with mercy and kindness. Even the smallest act of goodness can be sufficient to tip

it is indicative of a greater love that it was made known to them that they were given a cherished utensil, as it is said: *For I have given you a good teaching; do not forsake My Torah* (*Proverbs* 4:2).

19. Everything is foreseen, yet freedom of choice is given. The world is judged with goodness, and everything depends on the abundance of good deeds.

20. He used to say: Everything is given on collateral, and a net

---

the Heavenly scales of justice in our favor. It is this idea that lies at the heart of the principle of the Torah's criminal jurisprudence, which maintains that the court must exhaust every possibility to acquit a defendant before passing judgment.

Although we should imitate our Creator and also judge others for good, we should not do so naively. The most important consideration is human behavior, what actually was done. There may be mitigating circumstances for certain acts — and these should be regarded sympathetically — but the conduct itself remains the focal point of the issue and the judgment.

Humans are judged according to the preponderance of their deeds. The more good we do here on earth, the more likely we are to obtain a favorable hearing and decision from the heavenly court. God records every one of our deeds. It is our task to make that count turn out to be for good.

הַכֹּל נָתוּן בָּעֵרָבוֹן
Everything is given on collateral

Mishnah 20 RABBI AKIVA RETURNS TO THE PARADOX OF FREE WILL versus God's predetermination and His active guidance of human events. Everything is allowed to man and every potential opportunity awaits his choice. The Lord grants us material wealth, inordinate talents, life itself, and the ability to create and destroy. All these gifts, however, are given on a leash. We hold them in trust, so to speak, for they are not really ours. The test of life is how good a trustee we are. Whether we abuse or vindicate the Lord's trust is the main determining factor in assessing the success of one's life. People feel that what they have — family, material wealth, talents, accomplishments, etc. — is truly theirs. But the reality of our mortality belies that. We are but temporary guardians, and no more than that.

The realization that we are God's surrogates allows us to be more charitable and compassionate, for after all, what we "give away" is not really ours. All trial lawyers know that one is not allowed to disclose to the jury that the defendant is insured against the liability of the potential judgment, because the tendency of humans is to be far freer with other people's money than with their own wealth — especially if it comes from insurance companies,

פְּרוּסָה עַל כָּל הַחַיִּים. הֶחָנוּת פְּתוּחָה, וְהַחֶנְוָנִי מַקִּיף, וְהַפִּנְקָס פָּתוּחַ, וְהַיָּד כּוֹתֶבֶת, וְכָל הָרוֹצֶה לִלְווֹת יָבֹא וְיִלְוֶה. וְהַגַּבָּאִים מַחֲזִירִין תָּדִיר בְּכָל יוֹם וְנִפְרָעִין מִן הָאָדָם, מִדַּעְתּוֹ וְשֶׁלֹּא מִדַּעְתּוֹ, וְיֵשׁ לָהֶם עַל מַה שֶּׁיִּסְמֹכוּ. וְהַדִּין דִּין אֱמֶת, וְהַכֹּל מְתֻקָּן לִסְעוּדָה.

[כא] **רַבִּי** אֶלְעָזָר בֶּן עֲזַרְיָה אוֹמֵר: אִם אֵין תּוֹרָה,

---

the government, or a corporation's "deep pockets." Once a person realizes that "his" wealth is not his, but that he is the executor of God's trust fund, the tendency toward generosity increases.

וּמְצוּדָה פְּרוּסָה עַל כָּל הַחַיִּים
And a net is spread over all the living

THOUGH WE CAN MAKE CHOICES, ALL OF OUR FREEDOMS ARE IN FACT limited. We are caught in a great net that the Lord has spread over human existence and all forms of life; "like fish that are caught in the great net." Rabbi Akiva's metaphor of a net, especially modern fishing nets, is extremely apt. During my years as Kashruth Administrator of the Orthodox Union, I had many opportunities to observe the fishing industry. The nets used by the fishing trawlers are literally miles in length. Thousands and thousands of fish are ensnared in them every time they are cast and spread. Yet, because the nets are so huge, the fish swim in them freely, unaware that they have been trapped. That metaphor applies to human life as well. We swim unfettered in whatever direction we wish to go, and we fail to realize that we are caught up in the gigantic net of God's will and plan. Eventually there are limits to our freedoms, and accountability for our behavior and actions.

הֶחָנוּת פְּתוּחָה, וְהַחֶנְוָנִי מַקִּיף
The shop is open; the Merchant extends credit

RABBI AKIVA LIKENS PEOPLE'S PURSUIT OF THIS WORLD'S EASILY AVAILABLE pleasures to a business that is always open and to customers whose unlimited credit leaves them vulnerable to pay for their indiscreet purchases. This metaphor is so apt, and especially well understood and appreciated in our world of mass credit buying and deficit financing thinking. The store is always open; God's world is the original seven-days-a-week, 24-hours-a-day shopping mall. The storekeeper will always extend credit and accept "plastic" in payment. But the account book is open and every transaction is meticulously recorded.

❦ ❦ ❦

The American financial guru and Nobel Laureate, Milton Friedman, was invited to address the Israeli Knesset and give advice about stimulating the

is spread over all the living. The shop is open; the Merchant extends credit; the ledger is open; the hand writes; and whoever wishes to borrow, let him come and borrow. The collectors make their rounds constantly, every day, and collect payment from the person, whether he realizes it or not. They have proof to rely upon; the judgment is a truthful judgment; and everything is prepared for the [final festive] banquet.

21. Rabbi Elazar ben Azariah says: If there is no Torah,

---

eternally ailing Israeli economy. The then-chairman of the Finance Committee of the Knesset, Rabbi Menachem Porush, introduced the distinguished guest by saying that Hillel was able to summarize the whole Torah in one sentence, but that he did not expect Friedman to match that feat in his discussion of economics. Friedman rose and said: "I do not wish to publicly disagree with the distinguished Chairman, but I am able to summarize all economic theory in one sentence: There is no free lunch!"

❦ ❦ ❦

In life, too, there is no free lunch. Eventually all accounts are balanced and all bills will have to be paid. Everyone is allowed credit and the ability to borrow. But everyone is liable for judgment and collection, and every day the collectors — sickness, frustration, disappointment, financial worry, family problems, world events, etc. — circulate to redeem the debts. And these collections, so to speak, occur *whether one realizes it or not.* Everything that occurs to us in life is ultimately fair, because God's justice is absolute and correct. Therefore, the "collectors" are always justified in their methods of collection.

מְתֻקָּן לִסְעוּדָה
Prepared for the [final festive] banquet

THE "BANQUET" IS A METAPHOR FOR THE REWARDS OF THE WORLD TO Come and the eternal grace extended to our soul, the ultimate prize for being a loyal, honest, clever and faithful trustee of God's gift.

רַבִּי אֶלְעָזָר בֶּן עֲזַרְיָה
Rabbi Elazar ben Azariah

Mishnah 21 THE GREAT RABBI ELAZAR BEN AZARIAH SUCCEEDED Rabban Gamliel of Yavneh as the *Nasi,* when the latter was temporarily deposed by the Rabbis. Upon the restoration of Rabban Gamliel to his position as *Nasi,* Rabbi Elazar remained as a somewhat co-equal to him. Rabbi Elazar was a man of wealth and personal charisma. In his statement in the Talmud, repeated and popularized in the Pesach Haggadah, he testifies that he looked aged even in his early years, as a result of his assumption of the public duties of Jewish leadership.

אֵין דֶּרֶךְ אֶרֶץ; אִם אֵין דֶּרֶךְ אֶרֶץ, אֵין תּוֹרָה. אִם אֵין חָכְמָה, אֵין יִרְאָה; אִם אֵין יִרְאָה, אֵין חָכְמָה. אִם אֵין דַּעַת, אֵין בִּינָה; אִם אֵין בִּינָה, אֵין דַּעַת. אִם אֵין קֶמַח, אֵין תּוֹרָה; אִם אֵין תּוֹרָה, אֵין קֶמַח.

[כב] **הוּא** הָיָה אוֹמֵר: כֹּל שֶׁחָכְמָתוֹ מְרֻבָּה מִמַּעֲשָׂיו, לְמָה הוּא דוֹמֶה? לְאִילָן שֶׁעֲנָפָיו מְרֻבִּין

אִם אֵין תּוֹרָה, אֵין דֶּרֶךְ אֶרֶץ ***If there is no Torah, there is no worldly occupation***

THIS STATEMENT REITERATES THE COMMON THEME FOUND THROUGHOUT Avos of the necessity of balance in life, and of the centrality of this path of balance and moderation in Jewish thought and practice. The ways of the world without Torah are cheap, tawdry and profane. Wisdom and worldly knowledge, intellect and education, without being regulated by the Lord's will and fear of Heaven, are dangerous and oftentimes destructive. Torah without the ways of the world — a broad vision, livelihood, and a well-developed moral character — is sterile and in danger of not enduring.

אִם אֵין חָכְמָה, אֵין יִרְאָה ***If there is no wisdom, there is no fear of God***

FEAR OF HEAVEN WITHOUT THE LEAVENING OF WORLDLY WISDOM AND interaction with people and their problems leads to fanaticism and distortion of Judaism. Without knowledge there cannot be creativity and understanding. Without creativity and understanding, intellectual curiosity and innovation, knowledge alone is of little avail to humankind. But wisdom in the hands of immoral people without fear of God can be terribly dangerous and destructive, as history testifies to all too eloquently.

אִם אֵין דַּעַת, אֵין בִּינָה ***If there is no knowledge, there is no understanding***

"KNOWLEDGE" IN THIS CONTEXT CONSISTS OF CONCLUSIONS BASED ON realistic observation and honest inquiry, When one has such a fund of knowledge, one can then deduce other facts and further expand the boundaries of one's knowledge. But if one cannot utilize the power of deduction, then one will never reach the level of true understanding.

אִם אֵין קֶמַח, אֵין תּוֹרָה ***If there is no flour, there is no Torah***

WITHOUT "FLOUR" — ENOUGH MATERIAL NECESSITIES TO PHYSICALLY sustain oneself — Torah will not be able to survive, not in an individual, a family or Israel generally. Although wealth is a difficult challenge to moral and religious life, in the long run, poverty is not an asset for Torah study. Much of the breakdown of Torah life and observance in Eastern European Jewry in the 19th and 20th centuries can be traced to the abject poverty of the Jewish community there. Many people came to reject Torah life because they equated it with grinding poverty; in the long run, poverty cannot be sold as an

there is no worldly occupation; if there is no worldly occupation, there is no Torah. If there is no wisdom, there is no fear of God; if there is no fear of God, there is no wisdom. If there is no knowledge, there is no understanding; if there is no understanding, there is no knowledge. If there is no flour, there is no Torah; if there is no Torah, there is no flour.

22. He [R' Elazar ben Azariah] used to say: Anyone whose wisdom exceeds his good deeds, to what is he likened? — to a tree whose branches are numerous

---

acceptable way of life, if other choices are available as well. But if the sole purpose in life is "flour" — financial success and wealth — and Torah is not the dominant part of an individual's lifestyle and goals, then life is in essence squandered. Rabbi Elazar's dictum of balance lies at the heart of all Jewish thought and attitude.

כֹּל שֶׁחָכְמָתוֹ מְרֻבָּה מִמַּעֲשָׂיו
Anyone whose wisdom exceeds his good deeds

Mishnah 22 RABBI ELAZAR COMPARES WISDOM TO THE BRANCHES AND foliage of a tree, and good deeds to the tree's roots. Anyone whose wisdom exceeds the good deeds of his everyday behavior is like a luxuriant tree with a shallow root system. Attractive as it seems at first glance, the tree will not be able to survive a powerful wind; it will be uprooted and die.

When I was a rabbi in Miami Beach, I was witness to great, tall, majestic royal palm trees being blown over by hurricanes — because of their unbending trunks and shallow roots — while less glamorous coconut palms bowed before the wind and, when the storm was over, resumed their original position.

Wisdom is foliage; beauty is fruit. But moral behavior, Torah observance, and good deeds are roots, solidity, commitment. Just as one cannot build skyscrapers on flimsy foundations, many an intelligent and gifted person has failed to achieve his or her potential because their conduct fell short of their intellect.

A wonderful parable illustrates Rabbi Elazar's lesson. When the cold weather arrives in autumn, the leaves fall one by one from the trees. Each falling leaf bemoans the fate of the poor tree, which will be left bare and alone to face the cold and wind of the harsh winter. But the leaf does not realize that the tree will stay alive because of its deep roots. It will survive the winter and, in the spring, it will sprout new leaves, becoming verdant and green again. But the falling leaf is dead forever. This is the meaning of עֵץ חַיִּים הוּא לַמַּחֲזִיקִים בָּהּ, *It* [the Torah] *is a tree of life for those that grasp it* (*Proverbs* 3:18). The tree of Torah gives life to its leaves as long as they are attached to it. It is common in Jewish life, especially in organizational life, to devote major efforts to the

וְשָׁרָשָׁיו מוּעָטִין, וְהָרְוּחַ בָּאָה וְעוֹקַרְתּוֹ וְהוֹפַכְתּוֹ עַל פָּנָיו, שֶׁנֶּאֱמַר: „וְהָיָה כְּעַרְעָר בָּעֲרָבָה, וְלֹא יִרְאֶה כִּי יָבוֹא טוֹב, וְשָׁכַן חֲרֵרִים בַּמִּדְבָּר, אֶרֶץ מְלֵחָה וְלֹא תֵשֵׁב." אֲבָל כֹּל שֶׁמַּעֲשָׂיו מְרֻבִּין מֵחָכְמָתוֹ, לְמָה הוּא דוֹמֶה? לְאִילָן שֶׁעֲנָפָיו מוּעָטִין וְשָׁרָשָׁיו מְרֻבִּין, שֶׁאֲפִילוּ כָּל הָרוּחוֹת שֶׁבָּעוֹלָם בָּאוֹת וְנוֹשְׁבוֹת בּוֹ, אֵין מְזִיזִין אוֹתוֹ מִמְּקוֹמוֹ, שֶׁנֶּאֱמַר: „וְהָיָה כְּעֵץ שָׁתוּל עַל מַיִם, וְעַל יוּבַל יְשַׁלַּח שָׁרָשָׁיו, וְלֹא יִרְאֶה כִּי יָבֹא חֹם, וְהָיָה עָלֵהוּ רַעֲנָן, וּבִשְׁנַת בַּצֹּרֶת לֹא יִדְאָג, וְלֹא יָמִישׁ מֵעֲשׂוֹת פֶּרִי."

[כג] **רַבִּי** אֱלְעָזָר בֶּן חִסְמָא אוֹמֵר: קִנִּין וּפִתְחֵי נִדָּה הֵן הֵן גּוּפֵי הֲלָכוֹת; תְּקוּפוֹת

"tree" and neglect its "leaves." Every Jew's task must be to maintain his attachment to the tree. This can be done only by remaining loyal to Torah, mitzvah observance, and acts of compassion. Then, both the tree and its leaves will live on for eternity.

רַבִּי אֶלְעָזָר בֶּן חִסְמָא
Rabbi Elazar ben Chisma

Mishnah 23 RABBI ELAZAR WAS ONE OF THE YOUNGER DISCIPLES OF Rabbi Akiva. There are various explanations of the name *Chisma.* Some say Rabbi Elazar's father was named *Chisma*, and others are of the opinion that *Chisma* was the name of the town of his origin.

The Jerusalem Talmud relates that before Rabbi Elazar became a noted Torah scholar, he once visited a Jewish community and was asked to lead the prayer services. He was unable to do so properly and left the synagogue in embarrassment. He then met Rabbi Akiva and told him about the incident, whereupon Rabbi Akiva invited Rabbi Elazar to become his student, which he then proceeded to do. When he became an accomplished Torah scholar, he returned to the synagogue where he had been shamed and led the services admirably. The people remembered his previous humiliation and said that Rabbi Elazar was now "*chisma*," which can be translated sharp, honed, strong. And that appellation stuck to him.

The version of the Jerusalem Talmud does not necessarily contradict the other opinions. Those townspeople may have emphasized the use of

but whose roots are few; then the wind comes and uproots it and turns it upside down, as it is said: *And he shall be like an isolated tree in an arid land and shall not see when good comes; he shall dwell on parched soil in the wilderness, on a salted and uninhabited land* (*Jeremiah* 17:6). But one whose good deeds exceed his wisdom, to what is he likened? — to a tree whose branches are few but whose roots are numerous; even if all the winds in the world were to come and blow against it, they could not budge it from its place, as it says: *And he shall be like a tree planted by waters, spreading its roots toward the stream, and it shall not notice the heat's arrival, and its foliage shall be fresh; in the year of drought it shall not worry, nor shall it cease from yielding fruit* (ibid. v. 8).

23. Rabbi Elazar ben Chisma says: The laws of bird offerings and the laws regarding the beginning of menstrual periods — these are essential laws; astronomy

---

Chisma, his original name, and added a new dimension to it by playing on its other connotation of renewed strength.

Rabbi Elazar was known as a man of great intellect and knowledge, who specialized in mathematics and science. Hyperbolically, the Talmud states, "that he was able even to estimate how many drops of water are in the oceans!" This background may provide some insight into the otherwise cryptic nature of his words in this mishnah.

קִנִּין וּפִתְחֵי נִדָּה הֵן הֵן גּוּפֵי הֲלָכוֹת
The laws of bird offerings and the laws regarding the beginning of menstrual periods — these are essential laws

THE LAWS OF *KINNIM* — NESTS OF BIRDS THAT WERE USED FOR TEMPLE offerings — are enormously complicated and difficult. There is an entire volume in the Mishnah devoted to this topic and it contains portions that almost defy understanding. In the event that one or more birds — previously sanctified for one type of offering, or on behalf of one person — became mixed up with birds assigned for another offering or sacrifice, the question arises how to decide the halachic permissibility of how the unidentified birds may be used. All sorts of statistical probabilities enter into deciding the halachah in these matters. Such laws of *kinnim* were vital to the purification process of women after childbirth, of people cured from the skin disease of *tzaraas*, and other instances where bird offerings were required by Torah law. Rabbi Elazar, who was skilled in mathematical probability computation, wished to emphasize the importance of all ritual laws in the Torah, even those that, like

ג/כג וְגִמַטְרִיָּאוֹת – פַּרְפְּרָאוֹת לַחָכְמָה.

❦ ❦ ❦

רַבִּי חֲנַנְיָא בֶּן עֲקַשְׁיָא אוֹמֵר: רָצָה הַקָּדוֹשׁ בָּרוּךְ הוּא לְזַכּוֹת אֶת יִשְׂרָאֵל, לְפִיכָךְ הִרְבָּה לָהֶם תּוֹרָה וּמִצְוֹת, שֶׁנֶּאֱמַר: „יהוה חָפֵץ לְמַעַן צִדְקוֹ, יַגְדִּיל תּוֹרָה וְיַאְדִּיר."

---

kinnim, are esoteric and complex. Thus he teaches that these laws are part of the basic structure of Jewish life — Torah and halachah — and are not to be ignored, belittled, or treated as purely ancillary knowledge.

So too does Rabbi Elazar advance the laws of *niddah* as an example of the essential laws of the Torah. These laws govern Jewish family life and marital relations. They are basic to the concept of purity in Jewish family life. In Temple times, they also governed the status of purity regarding entry into the Temple precincts and other matters of ritual purity relating to sacred foods and artifacts. The laws of *niddah* are also quite complicated and require intense study and knowledge. Even today, questions and problems that arise in this area often require the judgment of expert rabbinic scholars for response and solution. Mathematical calculations, anatomy and biology, too, are involved in resolving such questions. It is obvious that whereas the laws of *kinnim* play no practical role in everyday Jewish life today, the laws of *niddah* are vital to all Jewish homes and families. Because of their complexity and importance, these laws are the heart and essence of Torah life and study itself.

3/23 and mathematics are like seasonings to wisdom.

❦ ❦ ❦

Rabbi Chanania ben Akashia says: The Holy One, Blessed is He, wished to confer merit upon Israel; therefore He gave them Torah and *mitzvos* in abundance, as it is said: *HASHEM desired, for the sake of its [Israel's] righteousness, that the Torah be made great and glorious* (*Isaiah* 42:21).

תְּקוּפוֹת וְגִמַּטְרִיָּאוֹת — פַּרְפְּרָאוֹת לַחָכְמָה

Astronomy and mathematics are like seasonings to wisdom

THESE ARE OTHER MATTERS IN JEWISH TRADITION THAT ARE ESOTERIC, complex, and require some mathematical skills. *Tekufos* refers to the reckoning of the calendar and seasons. The word *gematriyot* generally refers to the ability to find Torah insights by means of the numerical values of Hebrew letters and words, but it may very well be that Rabbi Elazar uses the word *gematriyos* in its original Greek origin as an exact mathematical science. Although such mathematic skills are necessary for the laws of *kinnim* and *niddah,* Rabbi Elazar says that *tekufos* and *gematriyos* should be viewed as the "appetizer" or "dessert" of the meal, and not as the main course. They are aids, skills that are valuable in the study of Torah and halachah, but they are not of their essence.

Throughout the ages, Jewish scholars have been proficient in matters of astronomy and mathematics, but they viewed such proficiency not as an end in itself but as a tool for the correct understanding of Torah and the traditions of Sinai. One of the early rules of life that parents should teach children is that one should not subsist on appetizers and desserts alone. They help make a meal enjoyable and tasty, but they are no substitute for the main course. So too, worldly knowledge should be used for a greater understanding of Torah and for the promotion of spirituality and human peace and harmony, but not as an end in itself.

פרק רביעי
CHAPTER FOUR

כָּל יִשְׂרָאֵל יֵשׁ לָהֶם חֵלֶק לָעוֹלָם הַבָּא, שֶׁנֶּאֱמַר: „וְעַמֵּךְ כֻּלָּם צַדִּיקִים, לְעוֹלָם יִירְשׁוּ אָרֶץ, נֵצֶר מַטָּעַי, מַעֲשֵׂה יָדַי לְהִתְפָּאֵר.״

All Israel has a share in the World to Come, as it is said: *And your people are all righteous; they shall inherit the land forever; a branch of My plantings, My handiwork, in which to take pride* (Isaiah 60:21).

[א] **בֶּן זוֹמָא** אוֹמֵר: אֵיזֶהוּ חָכָם? הַלּוֹמֵד מִכָּל אָדָם שֶׁנֶּאֱמַר: „מִכָּל מְלַמְּדַי הִשְׂכַּלְתִּי." אֵיזֶהוּ גִבּוֹר? הַכּוֹבֵשׁ אֶת יִצְרוֹ, שֶׁנֶּאֱמַר: „טוֹב אֶרֶךְ אַפַּיִם מִגִּבּוֹר, וּמֹשֵׁל בְּרוּחוֹ מִלֹּכֵד עִיר." אֵיזֶהוּ עָשִׁיר?

Chapter Four

בֶּן זוֹמָא ***Ben Zoma***

Mishnah 1 SHIMON BEN ZOMA, A COLLEAGUE OF RABBI AKIVA AND A member of the Sanhedrin, lived during the terrible times of the Bar Kochba uprising and the subsequent persecution of the rabbis by the Romans. He was known as a person of great scholarship and of general erudition, and he is mentioned in Talmud Yerushalmi as being one of the four members of the Sanhedrin who "knew seventy languages." He attempted "to peer into" the mysterious Heavenly spiritual realms, and he was severely harmed by the experience.

אֵיזֶהוּ חָכָם? ***Who is wise?***

HOW IS WISDOM TO BE MANAGED OR MEASURED? WISDOM IS CERTAINLY not book knowledge alone. Many a so-called scholar has been proven a fool by life's events. The Rabbinic writings include many definitions of wisdom and wise people. Among them are a sense of foresight, the ability to remain silent, and requisite devotion to teachers and elders. Ben Zoma adds another dimension to wisdom — the ability to observe life and learn from everyone and from all of life's events. A wise person does not put down anyone, is not prejudiced by a person's status or class in society. The Talmud is replete with stories of great rabbis being taught and even bested by simple shepherds and tradesmen. This is in line with the admonition in mishnah 3 of this chapter that every human being has "his time and place," his value and worth. A wise person applies that truth to life, learning from everyone who passes through his life.

❦ ❦ ❦

The baker's lesson

The story is told that at a gathering of Chassidic masters, each of the participants related tales of the erudition and miracle-working of their respective fathers. The Ostrovtzer Rebbe came from a much more humble background, his father having been a simple baker. When his turn came to speak, the other rebbes were prepared to excuse him from speaking, sensing that there could be nothing of value to be learned from a baker. But the Ostrovtzer Rebbe proudly said: "My father taught me a great lesson about the service of God and man. He always said that when you want to bake good bread, you have to make the oven extremely hot with a great flame! From him I learned

1. Ben Zoma says: Who is wise? He who learns from every person, as it is said: *From all my teachers I grew wise* (*Psalms* 119:99). Who is strong? He who subdues his personal inclination, as it is said: *He who is slow to anger is better than a strong man, and a master of his passions is better than a conqueror of a city* (*Proverbs* 16:32). Who is rich?

---

that God also has to be served with a great flame and enormous fervor. He also taught me that fresh black bread is better than a stale challah." Everyone can teach others something of value about life. The wise man pays attention to others and is ready to learn from them, no matter who they are.

❧ ❧ ❧

אֵיזֶהוּ גִבּוֹר?
Who is strong?

THE ULTIMATE STRONG PERSON IS SOMEONE WHO CAN OVERCOME HIMSELF. To quote a great fictional "general": "We have met the enemy and he is us!" Judaism is a religion of self-discipline and long-term perspective. Even the conqueror of cities and nations can prove to be a weakling when called upon to overcome his craven desires. Temptations abound in life. Terrible decisions resulting in tragic consequences often stem from the inability to forgo temporary pleasure, material gain, or imagined honor. Thus, true strength lies in inner fortitude, the ability to say no to oneself as well as to others, and in the realization that life's great struggle is often against one's own weaknesses and imperfections. Strength, therefore, is not so much a measure of muscles. It is a measure of self-discipline, restraint and conscience.

אֵיזֶהוּ עָשִׁיר?
Who is rich?

THE TRULY WEALTHY PERSON IS SOMEONE WHO FINDS SATISFACTION in what he already has. The pursuit of more knows no bounds. The rabbis (*Koheles Rabbah* 1:34) long ago cautioned that "one who 100 *zuz* (or dollars or euros) desires to have 200." That is true no matter how many zeroes follow the one hundred. Satisfaction in what one has in life — be it material possessions, family, position or social status — brings a sense of happiness in this world and contributes to one's share in the World to Come.

There is a bitter Jewish joke about the man who invited all of his friends to visit his brand new mansion. As everyone was oohing and aahing about the opulence of the house, the host was heard to remark: "This is nothing. Wait till see you the *next* house I am going to build!" The unchecked pursuit of unnecessary wealth is harmful for it becomes an end in itself, unrelated to what pleasures those items can bring to the person.

Ben Zoma speaks of happiness in the World to Come. I have often felt that the greatest punishment that one can suffer in the eternal world is to witness what problems his wealth caused after his death. How many families have been destroyed by squabbles over the parents' estate! In my rabbinic

הַשָּׂמֵחַ בְּחֶלְקוֹ, שֶׁנֶּאֱמַר: „יְגִיעַ כַּפֶּיךָ כִּי תֹאכֵל אַשְׁרֶיךָ וְטוֹב לָךְ.״ „אַשְׁרֶיךָ״ – בָּעוֹלָם הַזֶּה, „וְטוֹב לָךְ״ – לָעוֹלָם הַבָּא. אֵיזֶהוּ מְכֻבָּד? הַמְּכַבֵּד אֶת הַבְּרִיּוֹת, שֶׁנֶּאֱמַר: „כִּי מְכַבְּדַי אֲכַבֵּד, וּבֹזַי יֵקָלּוּ.״

[ב] **בֶּן עַזַּאי** אוֹמֵר: הֱוֵי רָץ לְמִצְוָה קַלָּה,

---

career, I saw many instances when relatives, siblings, and whole families engaged in legal battles over the wealth of their parents or relatives. There is no greater pain for a parent than for such legal battles to take place. A wealthy man once told me that he was going to sue his father's estate because he felt that he was being shortchanged in the distribution of the assets, and he was ready to spend hundreds of thousands of dollars in legal costs. I gently recommended to him that perhaps he should donate that amount of money to a worthy charity in memory of his father. He looked at me in amazement and said: "Rabbi, you just don't understand!" He was right, I did not and still do not understand. The unabated pursuit of wealth is akin to drinking saltwater, never satisfying or slaking the thirst. I do not preach poverty as an absolute virtue. Great and good things can be accomplished with wealth. But one must be satisfied with what one has, and not succumb to the insatiable drive for more. Only then can wealth, fame and position bring with them a modicum of true satisfaction.

❦ ❦ ❦

The wealth of a child

My 3-year-old grandson was being harassed by his 6-year-old brother to do something that he did not want to do. The 6-year-old attempted to bribe him, saying, "I will give you a penny if you do this for me." To which the precocious 3-year-old (all of my grandchildren, as I am certain, all of your grandchildren as well, are precocious) responded, "I already have a penny. Why do I need another one?" Well, I am fairly certain that my little grandchild will outgrow this holy innocence and strive to have another penny at some point in his lifetime. But the point that he made as a small child – "Why do I need another one?" – is a lesson that I pray remains with him for all time. Everyone should always ask, "Do I really need this?" before plunging on in the never-ending pursuit of material gain.

❦ ❦ ❦

אֵיזֶהוּ מְכֻבָּד?
Who is honored?

THE PURSUIT OF HONOR, LIKE THE PURSUIT OF WEALTH, CAN BECOME addictive. People who seek honor and fame often attempt to do so at the expense of others, somehow feeling that by lowering others, they enhance their own worth and position in the eyes of the public. The truth is otherwise.

He who is happy with his lot, as it is said: *When you eat of the labor of your hands, you are praiseworthy and all is well with you* (*Psalms* 128:2). *You are praiseworthy* — in this world; *and all is well with you* — in the World to Come. Who is honored? He who honors others, as it is said: *I will give honor to those who who honor Me, and those who dishonor Me will be dishonored by Me* (*I Samuel* 2:30).

2. Ben Azzai says: Run to [perform even] a "minor" *mitzvah,*

One cannot be truly honored unless one can give respect to others, as well. By honoring deserving human beings, one honors the Creator Who fashioned them. Thus, the Lord informs us, *I will give honor to those who honor Me (by honoring My creatures), and those who dishonor Me (by refusing to honor My creatures) will in turn be dishonored by Me* (*I Samuel* 2:30). By understanding that conferring honor upon others is a form of honoring God, one can do so without hesitation, recrimination, or jealousy. In fact, the one doing so becomes the true honoree, for God guarantees that He will extend His glory to him.

בֶּן עַזַּאי
Ben Azzai

Mishnah 2 SHIMON BEN AZZAI WAS A COLLEAGUE OF BEN ZOMA AND Rabbi Akiva. Like Ben Zoma, Ben Azzai "peered into the heavenly realm" and did not escape completely unscathed. In fact, of the four great rabbis, Elisha ben Avuyah, Ben Zoma, Ben Azzai and Rabbi Akiva, who "peered into the heavenly realm," only Rabbi Akiva emerged from the experience unscathed in faith, mind, and body. Ben Azzai never married, claiming that his soul desired only Torah and that marriage would interfere with his studies. Though he was a great scholar, his colleagues never approved of his celibate existence.

הֱוֵי רָץ לְמִצְוָה קַלָּה
Run to [perform even] a "minor" mitzvah

ONE SHOULD BE ENTHUSIASTIC IN THE PERFORMANCE OF GOD'S COMmandments; even "easy" ones that do not require a great sacrifice of time, effort or money should be pursued with alacrity and dispatch. For as we learned earlier in Avos, one never knows the worth and reward of individual *mitzvos,* even of those that appear to be simple, or even "minor," for good deeds and *mitzvos* inevitably lead to other good deeds and *mitzvos.* A charitable person is pursued by many charities and a good person will find many good causes waiting for his help. In the famed Psalm 23, King David asked: *May only goodness and charity pursue me all the days of my life*. A person inevitably has many pursuers in life. Often they are unwanted pursuers — problems of health, finances, family, etc. So King David prayed

וּבוֹרֵחַ מִן הָעֲבֵרָה; שֶׁמִּצְוָה גוֹרֶרֶת מִצְוָה, וַעֲבֵרָה גוֹרֶרֶת עֲבֵרָה, שֶׁשְּׂכַר מִצְוָה מִצְוָה, וּשְׂכַר עֲבֵרָה עֲבֵרָה.

[ג] **הוּא** הָיָה אוֹמֵר: אַל תְּהִי בָז לְכָל אָדָם, וְאַל תְּהִי מַפְלִיג לְכָל דָּבָר, שֶׁאֵין לְךָ אָדָם שֶׁאֵין לוֹ שָׁעָה, וְאֵין לְךָ דָּבָר שֶׁאֵין לוֹ מָקוֹם.

---

that if he had to have pursuers, may they be opportunities to do good works and charity, for that type of pursuit is ultimately one's great reward in life.

Ben Azzai points out that the reward for a *mitzvah* is the opportunity that will surely follow of doing another *mitzvah.* Goodness is cumulative and one good act builds upon previous ones. Therefore the "easy" *mitzvah* may be the gateway to a lifetime of good deeds and noble behavior. It should therefore be pursued with great enthusiasm and joy.

In its negative sense, the same idea applies to committing *aveiros*, transgressions against Torah law and moral tradition. Sin inevitably leads to other sin, and usually to greater sin. One becomes hardened to the act being committed, so that it no longer weighs upon one's moral conscience. The Talmud teaches that once one becomes accustomed to doing a certain sin, one loses moral inhibition and the act becomes permissible in the transgressor's mind. No one wants to feel like an evildoer, so it is human nature to rationalize and justify one's actions. Therefore, one should flee from the possibility and circumstances of sinning, even if it be only a "light" sin. For again, one sin opens the gates to more sin, and new and continued opportunities for sinning in all avenues of life will constantly pursue the sinner.

Since there are no perfect people in the world (though the Talmud lists four people who died because of human mortality, and not because they ever sinned), all of us are mightily susceptible to err in all walks of life. Realizing this vulnerability, one should flee from the clutches of any and all sin to the extent possible, not allow oneself to be trapped in compromising situations, and avoid temptations at all costs. For the "reward" of sin — the temporary pleasure it may afford — will only lead to further sin and deeper angst. Thus the "reward" is identical with punishment — the opening of the floodgates that will corrupt a person's life.

The famous novel about the picture of Dorian Gray is an apt example of this idea. Gray was a decent person who began to act immorally. As he progressed in his downward fall, the features on his portrait began to change, becoming evil and malevolent. So it is in real life. Eventually the sin transforms us and makes us morally ugly and repulsive, and this is reflected in our countenance and personality. Eventually, the change will not be limited to a picture on the wall. Therefore, one should always be on guard against sin and be ready to flee and flee from sin; for one *mitzvah* leads to another *mitzvah,* and one sin leads to another sin; for the consequence of a *mitzvah* is a *mitzvah,* and the consequence of a sin is a sin.

3. He used to say: Do not be scornful of any person, and do not be disdainful of anything, for you have no person without his hour, and you have no thing without its place.

---

from it at all costs, never willingly allowing oneself to fall into its clutches.

אַל תְּהִי בָז לְכָל אָדָם
Do not be scornful of any person

Mishnah 3 NEVER SAY NEVER. DO NOT DISREGARD OR PURPOSELY denigrate any person, and never say that a worst case scenario cannot possibly occur. The nerd whom one derided in high school may turn out to be one's boss later in life. Thus, as a practical matter, leaving piety and morality aside, one should always show respect and sensitivity to other human beings, for one never knows when and how one will encounter that person again.

❦ ❦ ❦

Unexpected dividend

Rabbi Yechiel Munk once told me that he and his family were warned of their impending arrest by the Gestapo in Berlin by a Gestapo officer himself. It seems that Rabbi Munk's father had once done a great favor to the father of that officer and the German wanted to even the score. The Munks were therefore able to escape Berlin and eventually come to the United States. One should never disregard the plight of another person, for the situations of life often reunite people in far differing circumstances.

וְאֵין לְךָ דָּבָר שֶׁאֵין לוֹ מָקוֹם
And you have no thing without its place

EVERYTHING IN THE UNIVERSE HAS A PLACE AND A PURPOSE. AS SCIENCE progresses in its understanding of the natural world, it becomes clearer than ever that every molecule in existence has a reason for being and contributes its minute share to the life of the universe itself. Nothing is therefore to be abused, disregarded, or wantonly destroyed. This is in line with the Jewish prohibition of bal tashchis, the prohibition against the unnecessary destruction of animate and inanimate objects in our world.

❦ ❦ ❦

The great holy man, Rabbi Aryeh Levin of Jerusalem, was once walking in Jerusalem with Rabbi Avraham Yitzchak Kook, the Chief Rabbi of then Palestine. Deep in conversation with Rabbi Kook, Reb Aryeh absentmindedly plucked a leaf from a tree. Rabbi Kook gently admonished him, "Why did you not allow that leaf to live out its appointed time?"

❦ ❦ ❦

I hate to throw things away, but every so often I feel compelled to clean the

[ד] **רַבִּי** לְוִיטַס אִישׁ יַבְנֶה אוֹמֵר: מְאֹד מְאֹד הֱוֵי שְׁפַל רוּחַ, שֶׁתִּקְוַת אֱנוֹשׁ רִמָּה.

[ה] **רַבִּי** יוֹחָנָן בֶּן בְּרוֹקָא אוֹמֵר: כָּל הַמְחַלֵּל שֵׁם שָׁמַיִם בְּסֵתֶר, נִפְרָעִין מִמֶּנּוּ בְּגָלוּי. אֶחָד שׁוֹגֵג וְאֶחָד מֵזִיד בְּחִלּוּל הַשֵּׁם.

---

debris from my desk and study. So, I make a clean sweep of those items that I am sure I will never need again. Invariably, shortly afterwards, I find that I need a newspaper article or other item that I threw away. So, for another year or two, I again squirrel away everything that comes into my hands, until the urge to clean out comes upon me again. And so the cycle continues.

❦ ❦ ❦

Impossible?

One should never deem events to be impossible of occurrence. The story that best illustrates this is the meeting between Kaiser Wilhelm II and Theodor Herzl in then Palestine just before the turn of the 19th into the 20th century. The Kaiser pooh-poohed Herzl's suggestion of a Jewish state arising in the Holy Land. In order for such a state to arise, he said, all of the major European empires of the day — England, France, Germany, Czarist Russia, Hapsburg Austria-Hungary, Ottoman Turkey — would have to collapse and disappear. "And, Herr Herzl, you know that that is impossible." The Kaiser was a prophet, but not in a way that he ever imagined. Fifty years later all of those empires in truth had disappeared or lost their power, and a Jewish state did somehow arise in the Holy Land. The only thing certain about world events and life generally is its guaranteed uncertainty. Therefore, all people and objects must be viewed in the light of that uncertainty and treated accordingly.

❦ ❦ ❦

מְאֹד מְאֹד הֱוֵי שְׁפַל רוּחַ
Be exceedingly humble of spirit

Mishnah 4 THE GREATEST AID TO HUMILITY IS OUR VERY MORTALITY. The grave awaits us all. As such, all the accomplishments of life must be tempered by the knowledge of our temporary existence. The great Chassidic master, Reb Zusia of Anipoli, once when walking along a dirt road remarked: "O you dirt that I now walk upon. Now, I stride confidently upon you. But you and I both know that there will come a day when you will be on top of me." The great rabbis of the Mishnah were never despondent and depressed about the inevitability of life and death. But they were realistic, and realism about the fragility of the human condition contributes greatly to true humility and tempers unwarranted arrogance.

In the Middle Ages, Christian society was haunted by death. The great 14th-century clock tower in Prague, crowned by an image of the Angel of Death, is

4. Rabbi Levitas of Yavneh says: Be exceedingly humble of spirit, for the anticipated end of mortal man is worms.

5. Rabbi Yochanan ben Beroka says: Whoever desecrates the Name of Heaven in secret, they will exact punishment from him in public; unintentional and intentional, both are alike regarding desecration of the Name.

---

expressive of that fixation. In that world, life was short, brutal, and of little value. Modern Western civilization has gone to the other extreme, practically ignoring human mortality and hiding death from human sight altogether. The Jewish view of balance and reality remains the only intelligent and positive view of human mortality and productivity, coupled with the realization of the inevitability of death. The Torah bids us to choose life, and to live it fully, all the while knowing that we are mortal and temporary creatures.

רַבִּי יוֹחָנָן בֶּן בְּרוֹקָא *Rabbi Yochanan ben Beroka*

Mishnah 5 HE WAS A COLLEAGUE OF RABBI ELAZAR BEN CHISMA AND was active during the time of the great dispute between Rabbi Yehoshua ben Chanania and Rabban Gamliel of Yavneh. That dispute eventually led to the temporary removal of Rabban Gamliel as head of the Sanhedrin and *rosh yeshivah* at Yavneh and his replacement by Rabbi Elazar ben Azariah. After a short period of time, Rabban Gamliel reconciled with Rabbi Yehoshua and was restored to his office, albeit having to share some of the honor with Rabbi Elazar ben Azariah. It could very well be that this painful incident in the history of the great men of the Mishnah serves as the backdrop for these words of Rabbi Yochanan.

כָּל הַמְחַלֵּל שֵׁם שָׁמַיִם בְּסֵתֶר *Whoever desecrates the Name of Heaven in secret*

AT THE TOP OF THE LIST OF JEWISH HIGH CRIMES AND MISDEMEANORS is *chillul Hashem,* bringing disrepute to the Name of God and to Torah and the Jewish people through unseemly behavior. Even such behavior in private is also held to the standard of severe punishment. In fact, it is the private *chillul Hashem* that leads to hypocrisy and cynicism, for a person of genuine integrity will not do wrong merely because no one is looking. Such conduct is the main enemy of public trust and respect in religious leaders. *Chillul Hashem* permits no excuses or rationalizations. Its consequences on society are so harmful that they are almost impossible to remedy. Therefore Rabbi Yochanan warns us of the terrible consequences of being part of such a situation. Apologies and excuses are perhaps necessary for any healing process to ensue. But they will not erase the actual stain of *chillul Hashem.*

Chillul Hashem is a sin because of public perception, even if no actual law-breaking was involved. "What I did was perfectly legal" is not an acceptable excuse in the realm of *chillul Hashem.* A rabbi called in one of his congregants

[ו] **רַבִּי** יִשְׁמָעֵאל בַּר רַבִּי יוֹסֵי אוֹמֵר: הַלּוֹמֵד עַל מְנָת לְלַמֵּד, מַסְפִּיקִין בְּיָדוֹ לִלְמוֹד וּלְלַמֵּד; וְהַלּוֹמֵד עַל מְנָת לַעֲשׂוֹת, מַסְפִּיקִין בְּיָדוֹ לִלְמוֹד וּלְלַמֵּד, לִשְׁמוֹר וְלַעֲשׂוֹת.

---

for a heart-to-heart talk. The rabbi said: "Many people have complained to me that you are a thief, dishonest in your business dealings." The congregant indignantly replied: "Rabbi, it is not true!" To which the rabbi responded: "It should be true yet?!! Isn't it bad enough that people say it about you?"

Chillul Hashem is such a difficult issue because it is a matter of how others judge a certain person or act, even if that perception is not necessarily the actual fact of the matter. Also, it is very personal to the person being judged, varying from individual to individual. The great scholar, Rav (2nd-/3rd-century Babylonia), stated that if he did not pay his butcher bill in a timely fashion he would be guilty of *chillul Hashem*. The greater the person, the higher one's public status, the greater the risk of *chillul Hashem*. Therefore, every action and statement of religious leaders and other Jewish figures must be cautious and carefully considered, so that no blemish of *chillul Hashem* falls upon them.

From perusing most halachic sources, one reaches the conclusion that even *teshuvah*, full repentance, will not erase the sin of *chillul Hashem*. The damage is so great that it is apparently irreparable. However, in his classic work, *Shaarei Teshuvah* (Gates of Repentance), *Rabbeinu Yonah* of 13th-century Gerona, Spain writes that performing an act of *kiddush Hashem*, public sanctification of God's Name and cause, will ameliorate the effects of previous *chillul Hashem* behavior and thereby bring forgiveness. My great teacher, Rabbi Chaim Kreiswirth, used this idea many times when he spoke to those of his students who entered the rabbinate. He would tell us that a rabbi is always in danger of being the victim of others' skewed perceptions of him, and often of misinterpretation of his motives and actions by members of his community. This means that he is always walking on the edge of a potential *chillul Hashem*. The rabbi's best defense is always to engage in behavior that leads to *kiddush Hashem*.

Teaching, speaking, writing, raising money for charitable causes, visiting the sick, comforting the bereaved, listening to others' problems sympathetically, and being a moral guide and role model to the young people of the community are all acts that lead to *kiddush Hashem*. By pursuing such goals and tasks, by striving to create *kiddush Hashem*, the awful consequences of *chillul Hashem* may be avoided and even rectified. This is good advice not only for rabbis, but also for all Jews in all walks of life and under all circumstances.

6. Rabbi Yishmael bar Rabbi Yose says: One who studies Torah in order to teach is given the means to study and to teach; and one who studies Torah in order to practice is given the means to study and to teach, to observe and to practice.

רַבִּי יִשְׁמָעֵאל בַּר רַבִּי יוֹסֵי
Rabbi Yishmael bar Rabbi Yose

Mishnah 6 IT IS SURPRISING THAT A GREAT RABBI SHOULD BE NAMED Yishmael, the name of Abraham's son, whom the Patriarch had to send away because of his sinfulness, and who became the ancestor of the Arab nation. Another famous Yishmael was a *Kohen Gadol,* High Priest of Israel, at the end of the Second Temple Era, and he was one of the Ten Martyrs butchered by the Romans (see Mishnah 9 below). Perhaps use of this name was in recognition of the tradition that Yishmael had after all returned to God-fearing ways before his death. It could also be a reflection of the times that these great people lived in, when such names were for some reason given widely to Jewish children. Such is the situation in all of Jewish history; names appear in waves and many of them eventually fall out of use.

הַלּוֹמֵד עַל מְנָת לְלַמֵּד, מַסְפִּיקִין בְּיָדוֹ לִלְמוֹד וּלְלַמֵּד
One who studies Torah in order to teach is given the means to study and to teach

TO STUDY TORAH PURELY FOR ITS OWN SAKE IS A GREAT CONCEPT IN Jewish life. However, it is emphasized a number of times in Avos that it is even greater to study Torah in order to teach others and help in spreading Torah among the Jewish people. He who studies will perhaps be able to teach others, and from my personal experience, this is not always a guarantee of successful teaching; but he whose motive for learning is so that he will be able to benefit all of Israel through his knowledge, creativity, and actions, will be privileged to be successful, pious, and beneficial to the general spiritual and physical well being of Israel. This motivation also forces a sense of practicality into what might otherwise be rarefied towers of learning that have no connection with the Jewish community.

The rabbis of the Talmud counseled: פּוּק חֲזֵי מַה עַמָּא דְּבַר, *see what the people say.* Torah study that is unrelated to the needs and realities of the people of Israel eventually becomes sterile, and is counterproductive to the honor of Torah study itself. Many of the basic concepts and practices in Jewish life are found not so much in the basic codes of law as in the responsa (*she'eilos u'teshuvos*) of the great rabbis over the ages to actual human and societal problems placed before them. The highest rung on the ladder of Jewish respect was always reserved for the Torah scholar, but that scholar was urged to toil for the public good in order to retain his position of honor and respect. When *Torah Umesorah,* the Jewish Society for Day Schools, was created by the great leaders of American Orthodoxy in the 1940's, those great rabbis assured their young students that those who left the large urban centers of Torah life in order to educate Jewish children in the smaller Jewish commu-

[ז] **רַבִּי** צָדוֹק אוֹמֵר: אַל תִּפְרוֹשׁ מִן הַצִּבּוּר; וְאַל תַּעַשׂ עַצְמְךָ כְּעוֹרְכֵי הַדַּיָּנִין; וְאַל תַּעֲשֶׂהָ עֲטָרָה לְהִתְגַּדֶּל בָּהּ, וְלֹא קַרְדֹּם לַחְפָּר בָּהּ. וְכָךְ הָיָה הִלֵּל אוֹמֵר: וּדְאִשְׁתַּמֵּשׁ בְּתָגָא חֲלָף. הָא לָמַדְתָּ: כָּל הַנֶּהֱנֶה מִדִּבְרֵי תוֹרָה, נוֹטֵל חַיָּיו מִן הָעוֹלָם.

---

nities of America would be personally rewarded and blessed in raising Torah families. Sixty years later it became apparent to all how much that blessing was fulfilled.

רַבִּי צָדוֹק ***Rabbi Tzadok***

Mishnah 7 HE WAS A MEMBER OF THE GENERATION THAT WITNESSED and survived the destruction of the Second Temple. Due to the bitter struggles between sections of the Jewish population in Judea, Rabbi Tzadok forecast the inevitability of the destruction of the Temple. He engaged in penitential fasting for the last forty years that the Temple stood, thereby seriously undermining his health and damaging his digestive system. One of the three requests that Rabban Yochanan ben Zakkai made to Vespasian — and only three requests were allowed to him by that Roman general — was to give medical aid and attention to Rabbi Tzadok, so highly was he held in the eyes of the leaders of Israel.

אַל תִּפְרוֹשׁ מִן הַצִּבּוּר ***Do not separate yourself from the community***

THIS IS A REPETITION OF HILLEL'S ADMONITION IN CHAPTER 2:5. BECAUSE of the circumstances of his time, when many groups splintered away from the main body of Jewish life and each insisted on its own way and despised those who differed from them, Rabbi Tzadok's warning about not separating oneself from the general community is most aptly understood. The tendency to "break away" is always a danger in Jewish society. Sometimes it seems as if there is a death wish within the Jewish people to splinter into smaller and smaller groups and communities. Jewish history has shown us that such tendencies, though perhaps temporarily satisfying, eventually damage the Jewish people, including the "breakaways."

וְאַל תַּעַשׂ עַצְמְךָ כְּעוֹרְכֵי הַדַּיָּנִין ***[When serving as a judge] do not act as a lawyer***

THIS PHRASE APPEARED PREVIOUSLY IN CHAPTER 1:8, WHICH LEADS some commentators to contend that this maxim is really not part of Rabbi Tzadok's mishnah in this chapter. Without entering into the discussion between the scholars on this point, I would suggest that perhaps Rabbi Tzadok is using this phrase in a different way than it was used above. In Chapter One, the phrase was an admonition to judges as to how to conduct their court proceedings. Here, it may be a statement to the "breakaway" Jews to resist

7. Rabbi Tzadok says: Do not separate yourself from the community; [when serving as a judge] do not act as a lawyer; do not make the Torah a crown for self-glorification, nor a spade with which to dig. So too, Hillel used to say: And one who uses the crown [of Torah] for self-gratification shall fade away. From this you derive that whoever seeks personal benefit from the words of Torah removes his life from the world.

---

the temptation of self-justification of their divisive behavior by legalistic thinking and partisan interests — i.e., not to be a lawyer for themselves. Lawyers argue on behalf of their clients, even if this may sometimes not coincide with the general public good. Rabbi Tzadok demands from us a higher standard of attitude and behavior.

וְדִאִשְׁתַּמֵּשׁ בְּתָגָא חֲלָף ***And one who uses the crown [of Torah] for self-gratification shall fade away***

USING THE TORAH FOR PERSONAL GAIN IS AN ABUSE OF ITS HOLINESS and noble purpose. This is an extension of the concept of מְעִילָה, the prohibition against the use of holy articles and wealth of the Temple for private use. Appropriating the crown of Torah for one's own honor and advancement, not to mention financial gain, is a direct violation of the spirit of Torah, and a public debasement of its position in Jewish life and society. Rabbi Tzadok echoes the message of Hillel in 1:13. The surest way to lose the crown of Torah and forfeit one's own spiritual life as well is to abuse the Torah by using it for private purposes and personal gain.

Rabbi Tzadok decries the use of Torah as a "spade to dig with" for personal gain. Until the 14th century it was very unusual for anyone to be paid a salary to head a yeshivah or serve as a communal rabbi. The great Torah scholars taught and led without recompense, and earned their living through labor or commerce. They were honored by being patronized so that they could succeed more easily in their business or trade, but the idea of people living on the public dole or being paid for teaching Torah or for community leadership was foreign to Jewish life until the Middle Ages. (Those at the higher levels of education, however, and also primary-school teachers and private tutors, were always paid for their services.)

Not being paid for one's rabbinical services naturally gave the rabbi a degree of independence and public authority that was lost when he eventually became a hired employee, subservient to the powers-that-be of the community. The pressures, economic and social, of the exile, especially for the Ashkenazic community living under the oppression of Christian Europe, became so great that payment of salaries to rabbis and heads of yeshivos became necessary and publicly accepted. Since that time, with rare exceptions only,

[ח] **רַבִּי** יוֹסֵי אוֹמֵר: כָּל הַמְכַבֵּד אֶת הַתּוֹרָה, גּוּפוֹ מְכֻבָּד עַל הַבְּרִיּוֹת; וְכָל הַמְחַלֵּל אֶת הַתּוֹרָה, גּוּפוֹ מְחֻלָּל עַל הַבְּרִיּוֹת.

[ט] **רַבִּי** יִשְׁמָעֵאל בְּנוֹ אוֹמֵר: הַחוֹשֵׂךְ עַצְמוֹ מִן הַדִּין, פּוֹרֵק מִמֶּנּוּ אֵיבָה וְגָזֵל וּשְׁבוּעַת שָׁוְא.

---

all rabbis and heads of yeshivos in Ashkenazic Jewry were directly supported financially, for good or for better. Among the Sephardic communities, the tradition of rabbis and scholars supporting themselves without direct communal salaries continued until the 20th century. Many a great Sephardic Torah scholar was also a competent merchant or tradesperson.

In his commentary to Avos, the greatest Sephardi of them all, Rabbi Moshe ben Maimon, the Rambam, is sharply critical of people receiving payment for studying Torah. He writes: "The great men of the Talmud did not allow themselves to [accept payment for Torah study], and they thought that by so doing they would create in the eyes of the masses a *chillul Hashem*; that people would think that learning Torah is a job like any other means of employment by which people earn their livelihood, and thus Torah study would be degraded in the eyes of the masses; and therefore one who does engage in this practice insults the word of God." Rambam recommended to those who wished to help support Torah scholars that they provide the necessary financing to those scholars to allow them to engage in commerce and thus earn their own way in life.

Rambam's judgment was observed in practice for most of Jewish history. There were always individuals who were fully supported in their full-time Torah studies by their families or by individual philanthropists in their communities, many of whom made a "*Yissachar/Zevulun* arrangement" with the scholar. This arrangement provided for the *Zevulun* — the person supporting the scholar — to receive a share of the merit of the Torah being studied by the scholar — the *Yissachar*.

With the passage of time and changing economic conditions, as maintained above, it became necessary for communities to support their rabbis, judges, and teachers. In 19th-century Lithuania, in response to the need for scholars, teachers, and rabbis with superior Torah knowledge, there arose the idea of an institution — a *kollel* — that would support full-time students of Torah. In 1877, Rabbi Nosson Tzvi Finkel, the head of the Slabodka Yeshivah, founded a *kollel* of ten scholars in Slabodka. Two years later, the *kollel* was moved to nearby Kovna (Kaunas) under the guidance of Rabbi Yitzchak Elchanan Spector. Thereafter, it was known throughout the Jewish world as the Kovner Kollel. In 1886, the Netziv, Rabbi Naftali Tzvi Yehuda Berlin, the head of the

8. Rabbi Yose says: Whoever honors the Torah is himself honored by people; and whoever disgraces the Torah is himself disgraced by people.

9. Rabbi Yishmael [R' Yose bar Chalafta's] son says: One who withdraws from judgment removes from himself hatred, robbery, and [the responsibility for] an unnecessary oath,

---

famed Volozhin Yeshivah, founded a *kollel* for ten married scholars (the Brodsky Kollel, named after its financial patron).

Following World War II, there was a sense of urgency in attempting to rebuild the Torah world after the Holocaust, and even communities that had historically frowned on the *kollel* concept recognized that it was now necessary to provide stipends for full-time Torah scholars. *Kollelim* soon became the main source for teachers, rabbis, rabbinic judges, outreach professionals and *roshei yeshivah.* The success of the *kollel* idea was so pronounced that at the beginning of the 21st century, many thousands of married scholars were studying Torah full time, while being supported by outside sources. Thus the *kollel* movement represented a major change in the Jewish world, a distinct modification of the literal acceptance of Rabbi Tzadok's words in this mishnah.

כָּל הַמְכַבֵּד אֶת הַתּוֹרָה, גּוּפוֹ מְכֻבָּד עַל הַבְּרִיּוֹת
Whoever honors the Torah is himself honored by people

Mishnah 8 RABBI YOSE CONTINUES IN THE VEIN OF THE PREVIOUS mishnah. One who honors Torah and its scholars is worthy of being honored by others, while those who do not know how to give honor to others, especially to Torah ideals and scholars, are held in low esteem by their fellow human beings. And those who desecrate the honor of the Torah and its scholars and supporters will ultimately suffer dishonor at the hands and words of others. The Torah is jealous of its honor. As the blueprint for Creation itself and the *raison d'etre* of the Jewish people, it does not suffer insult and ridicule easily. All of Jewish history testifies to the truth of Rabbi Yose's words. The motto of Israel in all times and places has been תְּנוּ כָבוֹד לַתּוֹרָה, *give honor to the Torah,* by words, deeds and attitudes.

הַחוֹשֵׂךְ עַצְמוֹ מִן הַדִּין
One who withdraws from judgment

Mishnah 9 ONE OF THE WORRISOME FACETS OF GENERAL SOCIETY IN the beginning of the 21st century is its litigious nature. It seems as if everyone rushes to lawyers and courts at the slightest hint of a disagreement, especially over matters of money. This nature has spilled over into Jewish society as well. When I was young, my *rebbis* drummed into us the idea that pious Jews should avoid involving themselves in litigation, even in a *din Torah,* a rabbinic court trial. When I was in law school, we were taught Abraham Lincoln's motto: "A bad settlement is still better than a good lawsuit." But that view of life changed radically in the last half of the 20th century.

וְהַגַּס לִבּוֹ בְּהוֹרָאָה, שׁוֹטֶה רָשָׁע וְגַס רוּחַ.

[י] **הוּא** הָיָה אוֹמֵר: אַל תְּהִי דָן יְחִידִי, שֶׁאֵין דָּן יְחִידִי אֶלָּא אֶחָד. וְאַל תֹּאמַר: „קַבְּלוּ דַעְתִּי״! שֶׁהֵן רַשָּׁאִין וְלֹא אַתָּה.

Summonses to rabbinical courts now fly in the wind as often as raindrops. Rabbi Yishmael's warning is therefore doubly apt. Avoiding such litigation spares the parties from unnecessary hatreds and animosities. It minimizes physical, emotional, and mental aggravation, as well as other costs, both physical and monetary. It also removes the temptations of suborning perjury, encouraging false claims, lying, cheating, and eventually even stealing. It also prevents the necessity of taking oaths, thus eliminating the grave sin of taking a false oath, which shakes the very foundations of this world and its society.

The zeal of the parties in attempting to "win" at a *din Torah* often leads to cynicism and corruption in Jewish society. Many times in my rabbinic career when I attempted to prevent litigation and an unwarranted *din Torah* I was told: "Rabbi, it's not the money I'm after, it's the principle of the thing!" Unfortunately, I discovered that nine out of ten times it was the money after all. Money can drive people to do shameful things. Rabbi Yishmael warns us to refrain from litigation and thus avoid all of the terrible pitfalls of such litigation outlined here in this mishnah.

וְהַגַּס לִבּוֹ
But one who is too self-confident

RABBI YISHMAEL WARNS JUDGES IN RABBINIC COURTS AND SCHOLARS who undertake to decide questions of halachah. The status enjoyed by such a judge can lead him to hubris. He can become callous, haughty, arrogant. He can become a fool, potentially evil, and a pompous, self-aggrandizing person. Judges and rabbinic decisors wield great power and influence, and, therefore, only the truly humble should undertake those roles, for their humility will protect them from the temptations and delusions of grandeur that inevitably destroy people, even great people.

❦ ❦ ❦

Time for everyone

Rabbi Moshe Feinstein was the great American rabbinic decisor of the second half of the 20th century. He was a person of great humanity, simplicity, and humility. Once, a woman who was a neighbor of his burst into his apartment demanding to see the rabbi. Rabbi Feinstein's assistant, Rabbi Moshe Rivlin, prevented her from barging into the rabbi's office, explaining that she had not made an appointment, was not dressed properly, and that Rabbi Feinstein was busy answering correspondence. The woman nevertheless insisted loudly that she had to see "the rabbi." Hearing the commotion, Rabbi

but one who is too self-confident in issuing legal decisions is a fool, wicked, and arrogant of spirit.

10. He used to say: Do not act as a judge alone, for none judges alone except One; and do not say, "Accept my view," for they are permitted to, but not you.

Feinstein opened the door and motioned for her to come in. The woman stayed with Rabbi Feinstein for about 20 minutes and, even though the door was slightly ajar, Rabbi Rivlin could not determine the purpose of her visit. When she was leaving the apartment, she turned around and berated Rabbi Rivlin for preventing her from seeing "the rabbi." He apologized profusely and asked her why it was so important for her to see "the rabbi." She answered: "I am his neighbor. When I get a letter from my aunt in Israel, I bring it to the rabbi to read and translate it for me!" Many a person carrying Rabbi Feinstein's heavy burdens would not have had time for something so trivial. But Rabbi Feinstein had time for everyone, because he never saw himself as being "THE rabbi."

אַל תְּהִי דָן יְחִידִי
Do not act as a judge alone

Mishnah 10 IN THE VEIN OF HIS WARNING TO LITIGANTS AND JUDGES in the previous mishnah, Rabbi Yishmael now cautions against relying solely on one's own judgment. Only the Lord is entitled to judge alone, and even there the rabbis teach us that God somehow "consults" with His heavenly court of angels. One of the main lessons in life is that there always is another opinion. Listening to others is a way of clarifying one's own opinion and strengthening one's own logical approach. Even though an individual judge who is a מוּמְחֶה לָרַבִּים, a widely acknowledged legal expert, is allowed by Jewish law to judge cases on his own, the recommendation of the rabbis is to have a rabbinical court of three or more members in cases of litigation between two parties.

וְאַל תֹּאמַר: ,,קַבְּלוּ דַעְתִּי!״
And do not say, "Accept my view"

ONE SHOULD NEVER INSIST TO ONE'S FELLOW JUDGES, "YOU MUST ACCEPT my opinion!" The prerogative of whether to do so lies with the listener. No one is infallible, so even if one is completely convinced of the correctness of one's opinion — and rarely are humans 100 percent convinced of anything — one should not use coercion or bombast to force one's opinion on others. Rabbi Yishmael's views are not restricted to rabbinic judges and decisors. They apply to us all in our life encounters with others. The ability to hear out and consider other opinions, not to be judgmental about others, to be modest and yet steadfast in maintaining one's deeply held beliefs, and not to attempt to coerce others to accept one's opinions — all these together create a healthier and more peaceful society. Dreaded conformity forces eventual upheaval and disaffection, possibly resulting in violence and internal strife. Respect for the "other"

[יא] **רַבִּי** יוֹנָתָן אוֹמֵר: כָּל הַמְקַיֵּם אֶת הַתּוֹרָה מֵעֹנִי, סוֹפוֹ לְקַיְּמָהּ מֵעֹשֶׁר; וְכָל הַמְבַטֵּל אֶת הַתּוֹרָה מֵעֹשֶׁר, סוֹפוֹ לְבַטְּלָהּ מֵעֹנִי.

[יב] **רַבִּי** מֵאִיר אוֹמֵר: הֱוֵי מְמַעֵט בְּעֵסֶק, וַעֲסֹק בַּתּוֹרָה; וֶהֱוֵי שְׁפַל רוּחַ בִּפְנֵי כָל אָדָם;

---

as a human being is a fundamental part of the ways of pleasantness and peace that are the hallmarks of a Torah society.

כָּל הַמְקַיֵּם אֶת הַתּוֹרָה מֵעֹנִי
Whoever fulfills the Torah despite poverty

Mishnah 11 I HAVE ALWAYS THOUGHT THAT RABBI YONASAN IS NOT promising wealth to poor people who observe the Torah, nor is he foretelling poverty to wealthy people who do not observe the Torah. Our empiric view of life evidence confirms that observance of Torah in poverty does not automatically produce wealth, and *vice versa.* I believe that Rabbi Yonasan's message is far more subtle and meaningful than the realities of poverty and wealth. Loyalty to Torah must be unconditional. Even if one is in abject poverty, one must be able to disassociate oneself spiritually from financial difficulties. Such a person will be able to remain loyal to Torah values, observances, and lifestyle even when later faced with the temptations of wealth. But if one's attachment to Torah is only a societal one, influenced by one's environment and current financial situation, then when the society and financial fortunes change, the attachment to Torah can easily dissipate.

Many a Jew who was traditional in outlook and life view and religious practice while being poor, later became very distanced from the Torah by financial success and upward social mobility. One can almost say that this is the story of much of American Jewry's alienation from its Jewish roots and value system. The immigrant generation's attachment to Torah was mainly based on community, habit, and inertia, instead of deep commitment and loyalty. Therefore, when the American Jewish community became more and more affluent, the sad distancing of that community from Torah was inexorable. Torah cannot be dependent upon poverty or affluence. Those who do not find room for Torah in their lives when they are either too rich or too poor, will not find room for it when their financial condition changes.

רַבִּי מֵאִיר
Rabbi Meir

Mishnah 12 RABBI MEIR IS ONE OF THE CENTRAL FIGURES OF THE mishnah. When a mishnah is not attributed to an author, it is generally ascribed to Rabbi Meir [סְתָם מִשְׁנָה רַבִּי מֵאִיר]. He lived a turbulent, controversial, and difficult life. He was descended from converts from the family of the Roman emperor Nero, and, though he was one of the main

11. Rabbi Yonasan says: Whoever fulfills the Torah despite poverty will ultimately fulfill it in wealth; but whoever neglects the Torah because of wealth will ultimately neglect it in poverty.

12. Rabbi Meir says: Reduce your business activities and engage in Torah study. Be of humble spirit before every

---

disciples of Rabbi Akiva, he also studied under Elisha ben Avuyah. In fact, Rabbi Meir remained a disciple of Elisha ben Avuyah even after the latter's apostasy.

Rabbi Meir's wife, Beruriah, the daughter of the martyred Rabbi Chanina ben Teradyon, was a great scholar in her own right. Together they suffered the death of children and other difficulties. Rabbi Meir was forced by social and collegial circumstances to leave the Land of Israel and immigrate to present day Turkey, where he died. Before his death he asked to be buried near the Mediterranean Sea so that his bones would be washed by the same waters that reach the shores of the Land of Israel. In a later generation, Rabbi Yehudah HaNasi attributed much of his prowess in Torah studies to his "having seen Rabbi Meir from the back." Rabbi Yehudah HaNasi's final redaction of the Mishnah was based largely on Rabbi Meir's notes. Rabbi Meir was engaged in controversies for most of his public career. He was the greatest scholar of his generation, but his opinions were not followed by his colleagues who "were unable to plumb the depth and intricacies of his thoughts." One of his controversies led to his being banned from participating in the Sanhedrin and yeshivah of Rabban Shimon ben Gamliel II. Nevertheless, his colleagues said of Rabbi Meir that he was called Meir — meaning to illuminate — because he lit the lamp of Torah for the eyes of all Israel. He was a scribe, and in his Torah was written that the Lord dressed Adam and Eve — humankind — in כָּתְנוֹת אוֹר, *garments of "light,"* unlike the text of standard Torah scrolls, which read כָּתְנוֹת עוֹר, *garments of skin*.

הֱוֵי מְמַעֵט בְּעֵסֶק, וַעֲסֹק בַּתּוֹרָה ***Reduce your business activities and engage in Torah study***

BUSINESS, COMMERCE, PROFESSIONS — ALL CAN BECOME ADDICTIVE. IT is not only pursuit of money that drives people to become workaholics, but it is the joy of the chase that takes hold of them. Rabbi Meir's advice is to curtail one's work activities to the amount truly necessary for earning a livelihood. The time thus saved should be dedicated to Torah study and spiritual and charitable pursuits. The operative word in his statement is *reduce*. We can all safely do less in our daily lives and find time for Torah study. The famed Rabbi Yisrael Lipkin of Salant, the founder of the *Mussar* movement, which he developed in the latter half of the 19th century in Lithuania, was once asked by an opponent of *mussar,* "If one has 10 minutes of spare time from his work

וְאִם בָּטַלְתָּ מִן הַתּוֹרָה, יֶשׁ לְךָ בְּטֵלִים הַרְבֵּה כְּנֶגְדְּךָ; וְאִם עָמַלְתָּ בַּתּוֹרָה, יֶשׁ לוֹ שָׂכָר הַרְבֵּה לִתֶּן לָךְ.

[יג] **רַבִּי** אֱלִיעֶזֶר בֶּן יַעֲקֹב אוֹמֵר: הָעוֹשֶׂה מִצְוָה אַחַת קוֹנֶה לוֹ פְּרַקְלִיט אֶחָד; וְהָעוֹבֵר עֲבֵרָה אַחַת, קוֹנֶה לוֹ קַטֵּיגוֹר אֶחָד. תְּשׁוּבָה וּמַעֲשִׂים טוֹבִים כִּתְרִיס בִּפְנֵי הַפֻּרְעָנוּת.

---

during the day, should one spend that time studying Talmud or studying *mussar?*" Rabbi Yisrael answered: "One should study *mussar*, for then one will realize that more than 10 minutes can be made available for Torah study."

וֶהֱוֵי שְׁפַל רוּחַ בִּפְנֵי כָל אָדָם
Be of humble spirit before every person

SUCH AN ATTITUDE WILL ALSO ENGENDER A FEELING OF HUMILITY AND respect for other human beings. This theme of respect for others is a constant theme of Avos, spoken from the lips of many of the great men in this tractate. Perhaps Rabbi Meir was also making a veiled reference to his continued respect for his teacher Elisha ben Avuyah, in spite of Elisha's loss of faith.

❦ ❦ ❦

It has been mentioned above that one can learn something of value from everyone. In my years as a rabbi in Miami Beach there were professional beggars who came down from the cold North to winter in the balmy Miami sun. One of them was a regular at my synagogue. He was enormously aggressive and tenacious in his request for charity from the worshipers. In exasperation, someone once asked him: "Why should I help you?" The beggar replied: "Because I am better than you!" Indignant, the man retorted, "You schnorrer, how are you better than I?" The beggar responded, "I am a better beggar than you!"

❦ ❦ ❦

Only later in life when I became a *rosh yeshivah* responsible for major fundraising did I appreciate that beggar's talent and appreciate his persistence. Humility is always the great guarantee of spiritual accomplishment and greatness.

וְאִם בָּטַלְתָּ מִן הַתּוֹרָה
If you neglect the [study of] Torah

IF ONE HAS NO TIME FOR TORAH STUDY, THEN ONE WILL HAVE NO TIME for other important things either — family, holiday enjoyment, social compassion. An orderly person has time for everything and everyone. Regular study of Torah — a set time of the day and a set curriculum of study — creates an orderliness that will carry over to all other aspects of one's life. If one allows oneself to be distracted from Torah study, other distractions will come along to interfere with many other important things in life. Distraction begets distraction. The place to begin fighting them is in the realm of Torah study, for toiling in

person. If you neglect the [study of] Torah, you will have excuses to neglect it; but if you labor in the Torah, He has ample reward to give you.

13. Rabbi Eliezer ben Yaakov says: He who fulfills even a single *mitzvah* gains himself a single advocate, and he who commits even a single transgression gains himself a single accuser. Repentance and good deeds are like a shield against retribution.

Torah brings great reward, both in this world and the next. Torah study should always be viewed as a matter of Divine service, and the Lord has many types of reward for those who truly serve Him. Rashi's famous comment to *Leviticus* (26:3) — "that you shall toil in the study of the Torah" — reflects Rabbi Meir's teaching in this mishnah. As the rabbis put it in their famous dictum, לְפוּם צַעֲרָא אַגְרָא, *according to the toil is the reward.* If Rabbi Meir guarantees great reward, it follows that he is also demanding great toil and effort in Torah study.

רַבִּי אֱלִיעֶזֶר בֶּן יַעֲקֹב
Rabbi Eliezer ben Yaakov

Mishnah 13 THIS TANNA IS RABBI ELIEZER BEN YAAKOV II, A COLLEAGUE of Rabbi Meir and a disciple of Rabbi Akiva. The first Rabbi Eliezer ben Yaakov witnessed the destruction of the Temple, and was a contemporary of Rabban Yochanan ben Zakkai and a student of both Hillel and Shammai. It is regarding the first Rabbi Eliezer that the rabbis declared: מִשְׁנָתוֹ קַב וְנָקִי, his words in the Mishnah are few but they are pure (meaning that the halachah follows his opinion).He was the author of Tractate *Middos*, which deals with the physical measurements and layout of the Temple and its vessels, and is a reconstruction of the Temple based on his memory. The Rabbi Eliezer of this mishnah was one of the leaders in reconstituting the Sanhedrin and its attendant yeshivos in the Galilee after the failure of the Bar Kochba rebellion. He is not quoted extensively in the Mishnah.

הָעוֹשֶׂה מִצְוָה אַחַת קוֹנֶה לּוֹ פְּרַקְלִיט אֶחָד
He who fulfills even a single mitzvah gains himself a single advocate

GOOD DEEDS AND SINS ARE LIVING THINGS AND NOT JUST INANIMATE ACTS. A *mitzvah* performed correctly creates an angelic "defense attorney" for the day of judgment in the eternal world. And a sin conversely produces an accuser and prosecutor for that same moment. *Mitzvos* soothe one's being and soul while *aveiros* snarl and snap at their perpetrator. If one visualizes them as living defenders and attackers — and ultimately the decisors of one's eternal fate — this realization will have a profound influence on one's conduct. The person will search for the opportunity to do a *mitzvah* and avoid an *aveirah* at all costs. In any event, repentance and continued performance of good deeds are bulwarks of defense; they are shields and shutters that shut out earthly and heavenly spiritual disaster from one's life.

[יד] **רַבִּי** יוֹחָנָן הַסַּנְדְּלָר אוֹמֵר: כָּל כְּנֵסִיָּה שֶׁהִיא לְשֵׁם שָׁמַיִם, סוֹפָהּ לְהִתְקַיֵּם; וְשֶׁאֵינָהּ לְשֵׁם שָׁמַיִם, אֵין סוֹפָהּ לְהִתְקַיֵּם.

[טו] **רַבִּי** אֶלְעָזָר בֶּן שַׁמּוּעַ אוֹמֵר: יְהִי כְבוֹד תַּלְמִידְךָ חָבִיב עָלֶיךָ כְּשֶׁלָּךְ; וּכְבוֹד חֲבֵרְךָ כְּמוֹרָא רַבָּךְ; וּמוֹרָא רַבָּךְ כְּמוֹרָא שָׁמָיִם.

רַבִּי יוֹחָנָן הַסַּנְדְּלָר *Rabbi Yochanan HaSandlar*

Mishnah 14 RABBI YOCHANAN HASANDLAR WAS A DISCIPLE OF RABBI Akiva and later of Rabbi Yehudah ben Beseira II. He is called a *sandlar,* a shoemaker, but whether that was his actual trade or a title given to him for some unknown reason is a matter of scholarly debate.

כָּל כְּנֵסִיָּה שֶׁהִיא לְשֵׁם שָׁמַיִם *Every assembly that is dedicated to the sake of Heaven*

THIS LESSON REFERS TO GATHERINGS, CONFERENCES, AND CONVENTIONS called for specific purposes. If the goal that unites the participants is to advance the cause for the sake of Heaven, then the gathering will have lasting influence and benefit, and it is worthy of being remembered. If, however, it is a gathering of people interested primarily in their personal goals and achievements, and the "sake of Heaven" plays no role in its deliberations, then it contains within itself the seeds of its own irrelevance and limited value. There are many conferences and gatherings, even of people who are considered to be great and wise, that are of no lasting influence on society or even on the participants. The "sake of Heaven" is missing from the deliberations and the hearts of such participants, and their gatherings are doomed to be soon forgotten. The greatest punishment in life is to be considered irrelevant while alive and eventually to be forgotten.

רַבִּי אֶלְעָזָר בֶּן שַׁמּוּעַ *Rabbi Elazar ben Shamua*

Mishnah 15 RABBI ELAZAR BEN SHAMUA WAS ONE OF THE FIVE GREAT disciples of the martyred Rabbi Akiva who were later ordained by Rabbi Yehudah ben Bava, in order to continue the rabbinic tradition under the terrible persecution of the Roman emperor Hadrian in the 2nd century. Rabbi Yehudah ben Bava was murdered by the Romans, but these five scholars, headed by Rabbi Meir, rebuilt the infrastructure of Torah in the Land of Israel. Eventually, Rabbi Elazar ben Shamua was also executed by the Roman authorities, for the "crime" of teaching Torah.

יְהִי כְבוֹד תַּלְמִידְךָ חָבִיב עָלֶיךָ כְּשֶׁלָּךְ *Let the honor of your student be as dear to you as your own*

THE RELATIONSHIP BETWEEN STUDENTS AND TEACHERS, AS WELL AS THE relationship between fellow students, can easily determine one's course in life and even one's relationship with faith and Jewish observance. A teacher of Torah who is disrespectful of his students, impatient with their questions and

14. Rabbi Yochanan HaSandlar says: Every assembly that is dedicated to the sake of Heaven will have an enduring effect; but one that is not for the sake of Heaven will not have an enduring effect.

15. R' Elazar ben Shamua says: Let the honor of your student be as dear to you as your own; the honor of your colleague as the reverence for your teacher; and the reverence for your teacher as the reverence for Heaven.

---

rigid in response to their behavior, is a failure as a teacher, no matter how great a scholar he may be. The Talmud records a paradigm of a teacher, Rabbi Preida, a great scholar who answered a certain question of his student four hundred times until the student finally mastered the idea. Hillel's admonition (2:6) that a rigid, haughty, perfectionist teacher is in the wrong profession serves as the basis for these wise words of Rabbi Elazar ben Shamua. Respect for students as people and as individuals is a necessary tool in a teacher's arsenal.

❦ ❦ ❦

I recall a certain rosh yeshivah who invited a number of colleagues to his home for a working lunch. His wife prepared an elegant meal for the guests as befitted their stature. A week later, when the same rosh yeshivah invited a number of his students to his home, to discuss a matter that had arisen in the yeshivah, his wife prepared meager refreshments. The rosh yeshivah gently reminded her that "students are also honored guests."

❦ ❦ ❦

A student should be made to feel that his honor is as dear to the teacher as the teacher's own honor. If the student has that feeling, he will reciprocate. He will honor his fellow students and classmates and not subject them to the harassment, bullying and cliquishness that are unfortunately a part of average school life, even in yeshivos. The fellow student will be treated not only as a friend, but as a potential and actual teacher, for the truth is that one's friends and peers are often one's main teachers and exert an enormous influence on one's life in school and thereafter.

ומוֹרָא רַבָּךְ כְּמוֹרָא שָׁמָיִם
And the reverence for your teacher as the reverence for Heaven

FINALLY, RESPECT FOR THE TEACHER ENTAILS A SENSE OF AWE THAT STEMS from recognition of greatness and gratitude, akin to the sense of awe that one is commanded to have for Heaven itself. Such respect is basic to Judaism's vision of the world. The teacher must be a hero, a source of inspiration and guidance, a model for imitation. However, the teacher should not rely only on the advice of Rabbi Elazar ben Shamua and on the student's willingness to see him that way. Rather, the teacher must behave in such an exemplary fashion that he will *earn* that level of awe from his students.

[טז] **רַבִּי** יְהוּדָה אוֹמֵר: הֱוֵי זָהִיר בְּתַלְמוּד, שֶׁשִּׁגְגַת תַּלְמוּד עוֹלָה זָדוֹן.

[יז] **רַבִּי** שִׁמְעוֹן אוֹמֵר: שְׁלֹשָׁה כְתָרִים הֵם: כֶּתֶר תּוֹרָה, וְכֶתֶר כְּהֻנָּה, וְכֶתֶר מַלְכוּת; וְכֶתֶר שֵׁם טוֹב עוֹלֶה עַל גַּבֵּיהֶן.

רַבִּי יְהוּדָה
Rabbi Yehudah

Mishnah 16 RABBI YEHUDAH BAR ILLA'I WAS ANOTHER OF THE FIVE students of Rabbi Akiva who were later ordained by Rabbi Yehudah ben Bava. He was the main colleague of Rabbi Meir, and his halachic disputes with Rabbi Meir are spread throughout the Mishnah. He was famous for his piety and his poverty, as were his many students. Rabbi Yehudah was regarded as רֹאשׁ הַמְדַבְּרִים, *the leading spokesman,* for the Jewish people and the cause of Torah. He was on good terms with the Roman government and expressed a tolerant attitude toward its rule and physical and political achievements. Because of this attitude of moderation, the Romans appointed him the head of the Jewish society, in effect eclipsing the office of the *Nasi,* Rabban Shimon ben Gamliel II. A generation later, however, at the time of Rabbi Yehudah HaNasi, the son of Rabban Shimon, the Romans returned leadership of Israel to the *Nasi.* In deference to the honor of the *Nasi,* however, Rabbi Yehudah was called the מְדַבְּרָנָא דְאוּמָּתָא יִשְׂרָאֵל, *spokesman of the people of Israel,* not the *Nasi,* even though he was the head of the Sanhedrin and the main yeshivah, and thus the de facto *Nasi.*

הֱוֵי זָהִיר בְּתַלְמוּד
Be meticulous in study

RABBI YEHUDAH POINTS OUT THE DIFFICULTIES INHERENT IN DECIDING important Torah issues. Mistaken theories, wrong interpretations of Torah law and a cursory attitude toward the complexities involved in Torah studies and decisions — even if unintentional and without malice or agenda — can lead to serious breaches of Torah law and conduct. In Jewish torts law, gross negligence is liable as though it were willful behavior. This principle lies at the heart of Rabbi Yehudah's dictum, for the misinterpretation of Torah law, due to erroneous study and poor understanding of the texts, is tantamount to gross negligence, and brings with it heavy liabilities. Extreme care must be taken in teaching and studying Torah, so that false doctrine and erroneous interpretations can be eliminated. We all know that with sufficient skills in mental gymnastics, one can pull an elephant through the eye of a needle. In fact one of the requirements for being a member of the Sanhedrin was to know how perverse logic can be used to "prove" that a dead rodent is ritually pure, which it certainly is not. Such a premise, of course, is absurd, and a member of the Sanhedrin must know it in order to be vigilant against it. The ability to decide correctly and

16. Rabbi Yehudah says: Be meticulous in study, for a careless misinterpretation is considered tantamount to willful transgression.

17. Rabbi Shimon says: There are three crowns — the crown of Torah, the crown of priesthood, and the crown of kingship; but the crown of a good name surpasses all of them.

---

not foolishly, to think clearly and without agenda, to understand and diligently analyze the true meaning of the Torah and Talmud, free from distorted mental cleverness, is the basic requirement for all decisions in Torah matters.

רַבִּי שִׁמְעוֹן ***Rabbi Shimon***

Mishnah 17 THIS RABBI SHIMON IS THE GREAT AND HOLY RABBI Shimon ben Yochai, also a disciple of Rabbi Akiva and one of the five scholars later ordained by Rabbi Yehudah ben Bava. Just as his colleague Rabbi Yehudah was moderate in his attitude toward Rome and its rule, Rabbi Shimon was bitterly hostile toward it, seeing in it only greed, exploitation, and hypocrisy. When his attitude became known to the Romans, he went into hiding to escape arrest and certain execution. With his son, Rabbi Elazar, he hid in sandy caves for twelve years, until the situation with the Roman authorities in Israel changed for the better. Emulating the prophet Eliyahu, Rabbi Shimon and his son lived on a diet of carob fruit and water, and achieved an extraordinary sense of spirituality and holiness.

Because of this level of holiness achieved in years of isolation, when Rabbi Shimon returned to society he could not countenance the everyday work pattern and mundane behavior of ordinary people. Wherever his gaze rested, he "burned" such mortals with the laser fire of holiness in his eyes. A voice from Heaven reprimanded him and said: "Have you come forth from your cave to destroy my world? If so, then return to your cave!" Chastened, Rabbi Shimon indeed returned to the cave for another year and then became more tolerant of the human world, finally emerging to become one of the foremost teachers of Torah. Rabbi Shimon is the traditional author of the *Zohar,* the basic book of Kabbalistic thought. Rabbi Shimon's tomb, located on Mount Meron in the Upper Galilee, is visited by masses of Jews every year, especially on Lag B'Omer, the anniversary date of his death.

שְׁלשָׁה כְתָרִים הֵם ***There are three crowns***

THE THREE CROWNS MENTIONED HERE — TORAH, PRIESTHOOD AND Royalty — are not easily acquired. In fact, the priesthood and royalty are matters of genealogy and birth and really have nothing to do with merit or achievement, and the crown of Torah has already been discussed in Avos very often. It is the "fourth" crown, the "crown of a good name" that draws our attention.

[יח] **רַבִּי** נְהוֹרָאִי אוֹמֵר: הֱוֵי גוֹלֶה לִמְקוֹם תּוֹרָה, וְאַל תֹּאמַר שֶׁהִיא תָבוֹא אַחֲרֶיךָ, שֶׁחֲבֵרֶיךָ יְקַיְּמוּהָ בְיָדֶךָ. „וְאֶל בִּינָתְךָ אַל תִּשָּׁעֵן.״

[יט] **רַבִּי** יַנַּאי אוֹמֵר: אֵין בְּיָדֵינוּ לֹא מִשַּׁלְוַת הָרְשָׁעִים וְאַף לֹא מִיִּסּוּרֵי הַצַּדִּיקִים.

[כ] **רַבִּי** מַתְיָא בֶּן חָרָשׁ אוֹמֵר: הֱוֵי מַקְדִּים בִּשְׁלוֹם

וְכֶתֶר שֵׁם טוֹב עוֹלֶה עַל גַּבֵּיהֶן ***But the crown of a good name surpasses all of them***

IF THIS IS A CROWN LIKE THE OTHER THREE, THEN WHY DID RABBI SHIMON state that there are *three* crowns in Jewish life? He should have said that there are *four* crowns. Because of this problem, many have interpreted Rabbi Shimon to mean that the three crowns of Torah, Priesthood and Royalty have their greatest validity only if accompanied by the crown of a good name. A crown, even of achievement but certainly one of heredity, is of little value without the crown of a good name. This is a repetition of the idea expressed many times in Avos and throughout the Talmud that a person's good reputation is sacred and must be guarded at all costs. The crown of a good name supersedes all else in life.

Mishnah 18

רַבִּי נְהוֹרָאִי ***Rabbi Nehorai***

THERE IS OPINION IN THE TALMUD THAT RABBI NEHORAI is really Rabbi Meir, since *Nehorai* is the Aramaic translation of *Meir*, meaning *to illuminate*. If so, then the admonition of this mishnah certainly fits the life of Rabbi Meir, as noted below.

הֱוֵי גוֹלֶה לִמְקוֹם תּוֹרָה ***Exile yourself to a place of Torah***

AS MENTIONED ABOVE, RABBI MEIR WAS FORCED TO LEAVE THE LAND OF Israel and exiled himself to Turkey. Therefore, he pointed out that even in exile one should always attempt to be in an environment of Torah. Over the centuries, Rabbi Nehorai's words were taken to imply that one should leave one's home to study Torah even if institutions of Torah learning are available in one's hometown. Whether this was his true intent is open to debate, but the custom of Torah students leaving their homes to study in distant schools is a long established one in Jewish life.

שֶׁחֲבֵרֶיךָ יְקַיְּמוּהָ בְיָדֶךָ ***For it is your colleagues who will cause it to remain with you***

NO ONE SHOULD RELY EXCLUSIVELY ON HIS OWN INTELLECT AND KNOWLedge to preserve his Torah knowledge; rather one should always seek the company of Torah scholars, for only such a society and environment can guarantee that one's Torah knowledge and abilities will be maintained and even improved. The stimulation of other scholars and the influence of good

18. Rabbi Nehorai says: Exile yourself to a place of Torah — and do not assume that it will come after you — for it is your colleagues who will cause it to remain with you; *and do not rely on your own understanding* (*Proverbs* 3:5).

19. Rabbi Yannai says: It is not in our power to explain either the tranquility of the wicked or the suffering of the righteous.

20. Rabbi Masya ben Charash says: Initiate a greeting to

---

people will prod one to grow in learning and in *mitzvah* observance.

רַבִּי יַנַּאי
Rabbi Yannai

Mishnah 19 RABBI YANNAI WAS A CONTEMPORARY OF HIS COLLEAGUE/ disciple, Rabbi Yehudah HaNasi, and was the head of a large and famous yeshivah in the Galilee. He was active in teaching traditions and laws that were somehow omitted in Rabbi Yehudah HaNasi's final edition of the Mishnah.

אֵין בְּיָדֵינוּ לֹא מִשַּׁלְוַת הָרְשָׁעִים
It is not in our power to explain either the tranquility of the wicked

RABBI YANNAI ADDRESSES THE PROBLEM THAT AFFLICTS ALL BELIEVERS in a just God: How can the righteous suffer so much while the evil people appear to prosper? In essence, the Book of Job/*Iyov* concerns itself exclusively with this issue and its conclusion is simply that God is inscrutable and unknowable and that His conduct is just even when human beings cannot comprehend how this is so. In a sense, Rabbi Yannai seems to sum up in one pithy sentence all of the wisdom of the holy Book of Job/*Iyov*, that it is not within our finite and limited human abilities to understand the seeming prosperity of the wicked and/or the oppression of the righteous and good. There are philosophical problems that are beyond our rational reach of logic, so it becomes a matter of faith in God and Torah. Faith abrogates the necessity for logical answers to difficult questions in life. Rabbi Yannai's statement, therefore, is not a shrug-of-the-shoulders "I don't know" answer. Rather it is a positive declamation of faith and belief in the face of the unknown and the unknowable.

רַבִּי מַתְיָא בֶּן חָרָשׁ
Rabbi Masya ben Charash

Mishnah 20 AS A RESULT OF HADRIAN'S PERSECUTIONS IN THE 2ND century CE, many of the great rabbis were forced to flee from the Land of Israel. Rabbi Masya bearded the lion in its own den. He moved to Rome itself, and there established a noted Torah center. The Jews of Rome enjoyed relative freedom and opportunity at the same time that their brethren in the Land of Israel were being persecuted and oppressed. Even in

כָּל אָדָם, וֶהֱוֵי זָנָב לַאֲרָיוֹת, וְאַל תְּהִי רֹאשׁ לְשׁוּעָלִים.

[כא] **רַבִּי** יַעֲקֹב אוֹמֵר: הָעוֹלָם הַזֶּה דּוֹמֶה לִפְרוֹזְדוֹר בִּפְנֵי הָעוֹלָם הַבָּא, הַתְקֵן עַצְמְךָ בַּפְּרוֹזְדוֹר, כְּדֵי שֶׁתִּכָּנֵס לַטְּרַקְלִין.

[כב] **הוּא** הָיָה אוֹמֵר: יָפָה שָׁעָה אַחַת בִּתְשׁוּבָה וּמַעֲשִׂים טוֹבִים בָּעוֹלָם הַזֶּה מִכֹּל חַיֵּי הָעוֹלָם הַבָּא; וְיָפָה שָׁעָה אַחַת שֶׁל קוֹרַת רוּחַ בָּעוֹלָם

Rome, Rabbi Masya remained influential among the remaining yeshivos and scholars in the Land of Israel, though few of his statements are recorded in the Mishnah or the Talmud.

הֱוֵי מַקְדִּים בִּשְׁלוֹם כָּל אָדָם ***Initiate a greeting to every person***

TO GREET PEOPLE IN A FRIENDLY MANNER IS MORE THAN JUST GOOD SOCIAL manners; it reflects an optimistic and friendly view of life. The Torah unalterably opposes sadness and melancholy as a psychological state of being. Accustoming oneself to greeting people, even strangers, and not only Jews, is a method for developing this positive psychological attitude toward life and its inherent challenges. I am continually shocked by the experience of wishing someone a "Good Shabbos" and receiving no response. Sometimes I am rewarded with a blank stare (like a "what's your problem?" stare), but many times the person just walks by me as though I didn't exist and my greeting was never extended. Not only is this rude, it flies in the face of what Torah behavior should be. Rabbi Masya urged Jews to be the initiators of greetings and courtesy. He wanted us not to stand on ceremony, not to feel that others were obligated somehow to greet us first before we responded in kind. But he certainly never imagined that there would be those who would completely ignore greetings of others when extended. A cheerful "good morning" greeting is beneficial to both the giver and the recipient.

וֶהֱוֵי זָנָב לַאֲרָיוֹת, וְאַל תְּהִי רֹאשׁ לְשׁוּעָלִים ***And be a tail to lions, rather than a head to foxes***

IT IS CERTAINLY MORE WORTHY AND PROFITABLE TO BE A UTILITY PLAYER on a major league sports team than to remain a perennial minor leaguer. One should always search for friends and teachers who are greater than oneself. This is how one can grow intellectually and spiritually. The constant search for self-improvement elevates one's sights and social framework in life. On the other hand, remaining contented and stagnant in a group that does not aspire to greater accomplishments, especially in spiritual life, guarantees mediocrity, self-righteousness, and zero growth. Life is a ladder and we must always try

every person; and be a tail to lions, rather than a head to foxes.

21. Rabbi Yaakov says: This world is like a lobby before the World to Come; prepare yourself in the lobby so that you may enter the banquet hall.

22. He used to say: Better one hour of repentance and good deeds in this world than the entire life of the World to Come; and better is one hour of spiritual bliss in the World

---

to continue climbing higher. Following the lions of Israel and avoiding the fawning of the foxes is a necessary step in attaining spiritual growth and meaningful living.

רַבִּי יַעֲקֹב
Rabbi Yaakov

Mishnah 21 BECAUSE THE RABBIS CITED IN THIS CHAPTER ALL LIVED in the time of the Hadrianic persecutions, this Rabbi Yaakov is probably Rabbi Yaakov ben Kurshai. He was a member of the Sanhedrin of Rabban Shimon ben Gamliel II and defended him against an aborted revolt against his leadership. Rabbi Yaakov was a mentor and teacher of Rabbi Yehudah HaNasi.

הָעוֹלָם הַזֶּה דּוֹמֶה לִפְרוֹזְדוֹר בִּפְנֵי הָעוֹלָם הַבָּא
This world is like a lobby before the World to Come

THESE WORDS REFLECT THE TRADITIONAL JEWISH VIEW OF LIFE IN THIS world. This mortal and temporary world should be viewed as the entrance foyer, the outer hall of the great palace of God's eternity. Just as a guest at a royal banquet prepares himself in dress and demeanor before entering the palace, so must we see all our actions in this world as preparation before arriving in the palace of the World to Come. This realization will lend importance to everything we do, and serve to reinforce our attempts to be good and pious people.

יָפָה שָׁעָה אַחַת בִּתְשׁוּבָה וּמַעֲשִׂים טוֹבִים בָּעוֹלָם הַזֶּה
Better one hour of repentance and good deeds in this world

Mishnah 22 IN LINE WITH HIS STATEMENT IN THE PREVIOUS MISHNAH regarding the relationship of life in this world to that of eternal life in the World to Come, Rabbi Yaakov now compares the preparation in this world with the reward in the next. In the World to Come, the "market for opportunity" is nonexistent. One can have a great insight on a Saturday night at 2 a.m. about which securities to buy, but if the stock market is closed one cannot buy them — no matter how strong the desire to do so. The greatest value of life in this world is that the market of good deeds, repentance, and spiritual growth is always open. In all of eternity, no one can achieve the spiritual gain that one hour in this world affords. Such opportunities should not be ignored or squandered. There is an eternal price for

הַבָּא מִכֹּל חַיֵּי הָעוֹלָם הַזֶּה.

[כג] **רַבִּי** שִׁמְעוֹן בֶּן אֶלְעָזָר אוֹמֵר: אַל תְּרַצֶּה אֶת חֲבֵרְךָ בִּשְׁעַת כַּעְסוֹ; וְאַל תְּנַחֲמֵהוּ בְּשָׁעָה שֶׁמֵּתוֹ מֻטָּל לְפָנָיו; וְאַל תִּשְׁאַל לוֹ בִּשְׁעַת נִדְרוֹ; וְאַל תִּשְׁתַּדֵּל לִרְאוֹתוֹ בִּשְׁעַת קַלְקָלָתוֹ.

[כד] **שְׁמוּאֵל** הַקָּטָן אוֹמֵר: „בִּנְפֹל אוֹיִבְךָ אַל

---

misdeeds and wasted opportunities, and there is never-ending reward for positive actions and pious behavior.

וְיָפָה שָׁעָה אַחַת שֶׁל קוֹרַת רוּחַ בָּעוֹלָם הַבָּא
And better is one hour of spiritual bliss in the World to Come

THE REWARD IN THE WORLD TO COME IS FAR GREATER THAN ANY imaginable pleasure in this world. As noted elsewhere, pleasures in this world are equivalent to investing $10,000 in order to achieve a profit of $100. Pleasures of the World to Come, though they may be earned only with a heavy investment of toil, commitment, and sacrifice, are the equivalent of investing that same $10,000 in order to achieve a profit of millions. So preparing oneself in the foyer in order to enter the royal palace is not only good manners and smart advice, it is also very good business sense. The amount to be gained in the World to Come is inestimably larger than anything we can imagine while still in this physical world. Realizing the stakes involved will help us chart a course in life that will gain us proper entry into the royal palace in the World to Come.

רַבִּי שִׁמְעוֹן בֶּן אֶלְעָזָר
Rabbi Shimon ben Elazar

Mishnah 23 RABBI SHIMON BEN ELAZAR WAS A CONTEMPORARY OF Rabbi Yehudah HaNasi, a member of the last generation of the rabbis of the Mishnah.

אַל תְּרַצֶּה אֶת חֲבֵרְךָ בִּשְׁעַת כַּעְסוֹ
Do not appease your fellow in the time of his anger

RABBI SHIMON'S ADVICE IS CERTAINLY SAGE AND PRACTICAL. MANY TIMES in life, despite good and kind intentions, hurt feelings and strife often result from well-meant sentiments that are expressed at an inopportune time. When people are caught up in the throes of emotion — grief, anger, regret at foolish commitments, anguish in times of ruin — they should not be approached and advised. I have often been at houses of mourning where those who are attempting to comfort the mourners mouth banalities and statements that actually hurt the already grief-stricken mourners. When a wound is still open, one must be very careful as to what type of balm to place upon it. Therefore, there is a custom not even to visit mourners before the third day of the *shivah*. In any event, words of comfort before the finality of burial, no matter how well

to Come than the entire life of this world.

23. R' Shimon ben Elazar says: Do not appease your fellow at the time of his anger; do not console him while his dead lies before him; do not question him about his vow at the time he makes it; and do not attempt to see him at the time of his degradation.

24. Shmuel HaKattan says: *When your enemy falls do not*

---

meant, usually fail to register on the mourner. The same is true for apologies made too soon, while the other person is still enraged. The apology will probably be rejected in anger and then the chances for later reconciliation will have been severely lessened.

וְאַל תִּשְׁאַל לוֹ בְּשְׁעַת נִדְרוֹ ***Do not question him about his vow at the time he makes it***

VOWS CAN BE ANNULLED BY THE PROCESS OF RABBINIC JUDGES ASKING IF the one who took the vow really realized the consequences of the vow when it was taken. Upon reflection and contemplation, the answer to that question is almost always no and thus a "door" is opened for the legal annulment of the vow. If, however, such a question is asked too soon, while the one making the vow is still emotionally wedded to the new commitment, the answer might likely be, "Yes, I want to make the vow under all circumstances." Such a response will cut off any chances of later annulment after sober reflection of the consequences of the vow sets in.

וְאַל תִּשְׁתַּדֵּל לִרְאוֹתוֹ בְּשְׁעַת קַלְקָלָתוֹ ***And do not attempt to see him at the time of his degradation***

THE TORAH IS VERY SENSITIVE TOWARD A HUMAN BEING'S SENSE OF shame. Since humans are representative of their Creator, shaming a human being is tantamount to an affront to the Creator; therefore one should avoid gloating at another's downfall, a lesson that the next mishnah emphasizes. Here, Rabbi Shimon warns us not to attempt to witness one's downfall and punishment. Even those who are punished by God or the court are entitled to privacy. I do not feel that this rule applies to extraordinary circumstances, such as the Nuremberg trails of the Nazi criminals. Rather, it applies to the failures, losses, and even punishments of ordinary humans that occur in the regular course of our lives. In all events, one must respect another person's privacy and be sensitive to his pain and failure.

שְׁמוּאֵל הַקָּטָן ***Shmuel HaKattan***

Mishnah 24 SHMUEL HAKATTAN WAS A MEMBER OF THE SECOND generation of *Tannaim*, a colleague of the disciples of Rabban Yochanan ben Zakkai. There are various reasons why he was called *HaKattan*, the "small" Shmuel. Some take this title literally: that he was a short person. Others say that he was called thus because of his spiritual

תִּשְׂמָח, וּבִכָּשְׁלוֹ אַל יָגֵל לִבֶּךָ. פֶּן יִרְאֶה יהוה וְרַע בְּעֵינָיו, וְהֵשִׁיב מֵעָלָיו אַפּוֹ."

[כה] **אֱלִישָׁע** בֶּן אֲבוּיָה אוֹמֵר: הַלּוֹמֵד יֶלֶד,

---

greatness, in the Jewish tradition of often using euphemisms with opposite meanings to describe individuals, the people of Israel, and certain events, both joyous and sad. The rabbis of the Talmud considered Shmuel to be so great that they ranked him in the chain of Ezra and Hillel, regarding the transmission of Torah and the possession of sterling qualities of piety and holiness. They stated that he was worthy that God's Presence should rest upon him, but that his generation was not worthy of such an event. Because of his fame and piety, there are those who go so far as to say that he was called Shmuel HaKattan — the small Shmuel — to differentiate him from the great prophet Shmuel, the august leader of Israel in Biblical times, who anointed Saul and David as the first kings of Israel.

Aside from his teaching in this mishnah, Shmuel HaKattan is noted as the one who compiled the 19th blessing of the *Amidah*. This blessing is known as *Birkas HaMinim,* the blessing asking for God's help against the slanderers who collaborate with the enemies of the Jewish people. In the time of the Mishnah, this blessing was used to identify traitors and uproot them from the synagogue, in order to prevent their missionary work among Jews. Any person who refused to recite this blessing was assumed to be a slanderer and was excluded from worship in the synagogue. This practice eventually forced a complete separation between Jews and Christians. The *Birkas HaMinim* has undergone many changes in wording and traditions over the centuries. In its present form it deals more with Jewish traitors and informers, and in Ashkenazic liturgy there no longer is any reference to *minim*, the early code word for "Jewish" Christians.

בִּנְפֹל אוֹיִבְךָ אַל תִּשְׂמָח
When your enemy falls, do not be glad

SHMUEL HAKATTAN WAS THE NATURAL CHOICE TO COMPOSE *BIRKAS HaMinim* because of his great piety and complete lack of any personal animus toward others. This is illustrated in his constant use of this maxim, which is a verbatim quote of a verse in Proverbs/*Mishlei.* One of the most difficult tasks in life is to separate people from their ideologies. False and dangerous ideologies must be fought and defeated, but the people should be convinced, persuaded, and won over. We should never gloat over the defeat of enemies but rather view their downfall as God's will and not necessarily a vindication of our personal vendetta. Jews have always been on the side of eradicating sin and evil, but not forceful in persecuting those who committed those sins and errors. Even the justified punishment of Nazi war criminals (as though any human punishment can ever be sufficient!) brings no joy or solace to us, only a grim

be glad, and when he stumbles let your heart not be joyous, lest HASHEM see and it displease Him, and He turn His wrath from him [to you] (Proverbs 24:17-18).

25. Elisha ben Avuyah says: One who studies [Torah] while

---

feeling that eventually evil destroys its perpetrators. So Shmuel HaKattan, the arch-defender of the Jewish faith from distortions and false interpretations, reminds us constantly of this wisdom of Solomon never to gloat over the defeat of human opponents, but also never to compromise with falsehood and mendacity. He quotes the verse verbatim because he lived by it. The "small Shmuel" is certainly a great man and a lasting influence in Jewish life and thought.

אֱלִישָׁע בֶּן אֲבוּיָה
Elisha ben Avuyah

Mishnah 25 ELISHA BEN AVUYAH IS THE MOST ENIGMATIC AND TRAGIC figure in the Mishnah. A great Torah scholar and mentor of Rabbi Meir and other leading scholars, a man of charisma and vision, he attempted to enter the "orchard" of mysticism and higher spirituality. Like someone staring at the sun, Elisha, great though he was, was incapable of coping with the intensity of that vision and he suffered negative effects. Later in his life, he saw someone die while performing a *mitzvah* for which the Torah promised "long life." The Sages interpret that promise to refer to the quality of life in the World to Come, but Elisha took it literally. He also saw the execution by the Romans of the great and holy scholar, Rabbi Chutzpis HaMeturgaman. These events shook him to the core of his being and his faith.

In our terms, we can say that he was overwhelmed by the problem of why bad things happen to good people and such questions as how did God allow Auschwitz to happen. Because of his already weakened faith from the experience of the "orchard," he was unable to now cope with these problems that he had been able to deal with and overcome in the past. Although Elisha maintained his Torah knowledge and study, he abandoned Torah observance. All of his students left him, except for Rabbi Meir, who continued to study Torah with him. When questioned about this, Rabbi Meir responded: "I eat the fruit and cast away the peel."

Elisha ben Avuyah came to be called "*Acher*" — a different person, someone else — by his former colleagues. Rabbi Meir never gave up on trying to rehabilitate his teacher. But it was Elisha who gave up on himself. He was convinced that even if he repented, Heaven somehow would not accept him. Only after his mentor's death was Rabbi Meir finally able to successfully intercede on his behalf so that Elisha was afforded some sense of peace in his grave.

Although Elisha's apostasy was known to all by the time the Mishnah was compiled, his inclusion in Avos is in the tradition of Rabbi Meir's statement that

לְמָה הוּא דוֹמֶה? לִדְיוֹ כְתוּבָה עַל נְיָר חָדָשׁ. וְהַלּוֹמֵד זָקֵן, לְמָה הוּא דוֹמֶה? לִדְיוֹ כְתוּבָה עַל נְיָר מָחוּק.

[כו] **רַבִּי** יוֹסֵי בַּר יְהוּדָה אִישׁ כְּפַר הַבַּבְלִי אוֹמֵר: הַלּוֹמֵד מִן הַקְּטַנִּים, לְמָה הוּא דוֹמֶה? לְאוֹכֵל עֲנָבִים קֵהוֹת, וְשׁוֹתֶה יַיִן מִגִּתּוֹ. וְהַלּוֹמֵד מִן הַזְּקֵנִים, לְמָה הוּא דוֹמֶה? לְאוֹכֵל עֲנָבִים בְּשׁוּלוֹת, וְשׁוֹתֶה יַיִן יָשָׁן.

[כז] **רַבִּי** מֵאִיר אוֹמֵר: אַל תִּסְתַּכֵּל בַּקַּנְקַן, אֶלָּא בְּמַה שֶׁיֵּשׁ בּוֹ; יֵשׁ קַנְקַן חָדָשׁ מָלֵא יָשָׁן,

---

"the fruit can be eaten and the peel cast away." The fact that Elisha ben Avuyah's statement was incorporated into the Mishnah is one of the important lessons of Avos. Even though he tragically became "*Acher*" he is remembered in the eternal book of Mishnah as Elisha ben Avuyah.

הַלּוֹמֵד יֶלֶד ***One who studies [Torah] while [he is still] as a child***

IN A SENSE, ELISHA'S TEACHING SERVES AS THE BASIS FOR THE NEXT TWO *mishnayos*. Just as they will discuss the relative benefits of age and youth as far as a teacher is concerned, so too does this mishnah come to discuss this same subject from the perspective of the student. The Sages always emphasized the importance of גִּירְסָא דְיַנְקוּתָא, the knowledge gained while one is still young, and when the mind and memory are still fresh. There is no substitute for youth. Teaching the young imparts knowledge that is indelible in their minds. It is clear ink written on smooth new parchment. Important as it is to teach and study Torah at all stages and ages of life, it eventually becomes like writing on parchment that has been scraped and erased. It is harder for the ink to attach itself to the parchment, it blurs and sometimes runs and there is no certainty that it will hold fast for long.

Elisha teaches an important lesson in education and schooling. Primary school teachers, those who deal with young students, are many times the most important teachers one will ever have. It is natural that a young scholar entering the teaching profession aspires to teach at the highest level possible to the most advanced students. But one who teaches young children, simply, ably, and honestly, is often the ultimate hero of their educational experience. My wife taught fourth grade for twenty-five years. I, on the other hand, have always taught on a high school or post-high school, even graduate school level. I envy her achievements and lasting influence on her students, which I believe have

[he is still] a child, to what can he be likened? — to ink written on fresh [clean] paper. And one who studies [Torah] as an old man, to what can he be likened? — to ink written on smudged paper.

26. Rabbi Yose bar Yehudah of Kfar HaBavli says: One who learns [Torah] from the young, to what can he be likened? — to one who eats unripe grapes or drinks unfermented wine from his vat. But one who learns [Torah] from the old, to what can he be likened? — to one who eats ripe grapes or drinks aged wine.

27. Rabbi Meir says: Do not look at the vessel, but at what is in it; there is a new jug filled with old wine,

---

been far greater than mine. I realize that talent and personality are also involved, but teaching younger children very often makes a more meaningful and lasting impression on their lives than teaching the very same students when they are a decade older.

רַבִּי יוֹסֵי בַּר יְהוּדָה ***Rabbi Yose bar Yehudah***

Mishnah 26 RABBI YOSE BAR YEHUDAH, THE SON OF RABBI YEHUDAH bar Illa'i, is mentioned a number of times in the Midrash, in conjunction with trips and events with his colleague Rabbi Yehudah HaNasi.

הַלּוֹמֵד מִן הַקְּטַנִּים ***One who learns [Torah] from the young***

YOUTH MUST BE SERVED BUT NOT AT THE EXPENSE OF WISDOM, EXPERIence, and practicality. Learning from the young is compared to eating raw fruit before it ripens, and drinking wine that is not aged and full-bodied. In modern society, the bulk of marketing is directed at the young. The old attempt to imitate the young, physically, socially, and even spiritually. I am always reminded of Mark Twain's ironic comment regarding his father: "When I was 16 my father was the dumbest man on the planet. But you would be surprised to know how much the old man learned by the time I was 30." The Talmud placed great store in life's experiences as an educational tool. Learning from those who have been tempered by life and have the perspective of years is likened to eating fully ripened grapes and drinking wine that is properly aged.

אַל תִּסְתַּכֵּל בַּקַּנְקַן, אֶלָּא בְּמַה שֶׁיֵּשׁ בּוֹ ***Do not look at the vessel, but at what is in it***

Mishnah 27 THIS MISHNAH EXPRESSES AN OPINION CONTRARY TO that of Rabbi Yose in the previous one. The author of this mishnah, Rabbi Meir, was the close friend and colleague of Rabbi Yose's father. Rabbi Meir states that age, outward appearance, even life experience

וְיָשָׁן שֶׁאֲפִילוּ חָדָשׁ אֵין בּוֹ.

[כח] **רַבִּי** אֱלְעָזָר הַקַּפָּר אוֹמֵר: הַקִּנְאָה וְהַתַּאֲוָה וְהַכָּבוֹד מוֹצִיאִין אֶת הָאָדָם מִן הָעוֹלָם.

[כט] **הוּא** הָיָה אוֹמֵר: הַיִּלּוֹדִים לָמוּת, וְהַמֵּתִים לִחְיוֹת, וְהַחַיִּים לִדּוֹן – לֵידַע לְהוֹדִיעַ וּלְהִוָּדַע שֶׁהוּא אֵל, הוּא הַיּוֹצֵר, הוּא הַבּוֹרֵא, הוּא

---

are not necessarily the only determining factors in judging a person's wisdom and Torah erudition. There are variant texts of this mishnah that attribute its authorship to Rabbi Yehudah HaNasi himself or to Rabbi Elazar, and not Rabbi Meir.

Whoever the author is, the import of the message is clear. There are "new vessels" — young people, who contain "old wine" — the metaphor for Torah knowledge and human wisdom. And there are "old vessels" — people of age and alleged life experience — who are really empty vessels. Old fools are the worst fools. Externals often deceive. We should endeavor to glimpse the true inside of the person.

Nevertheless, the Talmud demands that we respect age, even if great wisdom is not present. The famous statement recorded in the Talmud, "Even if wisdom is not present within me, age is present here," has practical validity. In such a case, the respect is for age, and not for wisdom. I think that is Rabbi Meir's intent. An old person is not necessarily a wise person, but is entitled to respect, nonetheless. The Talmud quotes a great rabbi who rose in respect for an elderly gentile, saying, "How many experiences in life he must have passed through!" This remains the operative form of Jewish behavior towards our elders.

The opinions quoted in these two *mishnayos* are an example of how the Mishnah is never reticent in quoting differing opinions of Torah scholars on important subjects. All of these opinions are Torah, "the words of the living God." All have eternal value and meaning.

רַבִּי אֱלְעָזָר הַקַּפָּר
Rabbi Elazar HaKappar

Mishnah 28 RABBI ELAZAR HAKAPPAR IS A MYSTERIOUS FIGURE. THIS is the only place in the Mishnah where his name is mentioned, although he is sometimes quoted in the Talmud.

and an old jug that does not even contain new wine.

28. Rabbi Elazar HaKappar says: Jealousy, lust, and glory remove a man from the world.

29. He [Rabbi Elazar HaKappar] used to say: The newborn will die; the dead will live again; the living will be judged — in order that they know, teach, and become aware that He is God, He is the Fashioner, He is the Creator, He is

---

הַקִּנְאָה וְהַתַּאֲוָה וְהַכָּבוֹד מוֹצִיאִין אֶת הָאָדָם מִן הָעוֹלָם
Jealousy, lust, and glory remove a man from the world

WE READ EARLIER OF THE ILLS OF JEALOUSY, LUST AND PHYSICAL DESIRES, and the pursuit of power and honor. Rabbi Elazar reiterates the warning against succumbing to these drives, and adds that they have the pernicious quality of being able to drive the person "out of this world." Not only do these faults make the person an anti-social being that his fellows will abhor and shun, but they literally turn him into a wild being, of uncontrollable behavior and in constant disaffection, frustration and disappointment. Such a person is out of this world as far as society is concerned. Since it is impossible to satisfy these desires — there will always be a more successful person to be jealous of, a further physical desire to pursue, an honor not yet achieved — one is driven out of this world. It is akin to drinking saltwater; it creates thirst but cannot quench it. Therefore, Rabbi Elazar's advice is of utmost practicality in helping chart one's course in life. The Torah bids us to live in *this* world; we should make every attempt not to drive ourselves "out of this world."

הוּא הָיָה אוֹמֵר
He used to say

Mishnah 29 RABBI ELAZAR OUTLINES THE THREE STAGES OF THE human life cycle. We are born mortal and thus we are all destined to die. But death is not the end of the story, for the soul lives on and even the body will yet be revived at the time of the resurrection of the dead. And finally, we will have to account for our actions and achievements.

לֵידַע לְהוֹדִיעַ וּלְהִוָּדַע שֶׁהוּא אֵל
In order that they know, teach, and become aware that He is God

AN UNDERSTANDING AND APPRECIATION OF THIS LIFE CYCLE LEADS ONE to realize that God is the life sustaining force within us. He is omniscient and all seeing. He understands us. He formed and created us, and breathes within us daily His spirit of eternity. He is judge and jury, witness and counsel, prosecutor and defense attorney. Everyone must account to Him for his or her life and behavior, actions and deeds. And God is not comparable to any human judge. He is not swayed by bias or sympathy, by corruption or venality. He never twists the law, nor does He play favorites in His courtroom. There is no forgetting or overlooking of facts and evidence in the heavenly court.

הַמֵּבִין, הוּא הַדַּיָּן, הוּא הָעֵד, הוּא בַּעַל דִּין, הוּא עָתִיד לָדוּן. בָּרוּךְ הוּא, שֶׁאֵין לְפָנָיו לֹא עַוְלָה, וְלֹא שִׁכְחָה, וְלֹא מַשּׂוֹא פָנִים, וְלֹא מִקַּח שֹׁחַד; שֶׁהַכֹּל שֶׁלּוֹ. וְדַע, שֶׁהַכֹּל לְפִי הַחֶשְׁבּוֹן. וְאַל יַבְטִיחֲךָ יִצְרְךָ שֶׁהַשְּׁאוֹל בֵּית מָנוֹס לָךְ – שֶׁעַל כָּרְחֲךָ אַתָּה נוֹצָר; וְעַל כָּרְחֲךָ אַתָּה נוֹלָד; וְעַל כָּרְחֲךָ אַתָּה חַי; וְעַל כָּרְחֲךָ אַתָּה מֵת; וְעַל כָּרְחֲךָ אַתָּה עָתִיד לִתֵּן דִּין וְחֶשְׁבּוֹן לִפְנֵי מֶלֶךְ מַלְכֵי הַמְּלָכִים, הַקָּדוֹשׁ בָּרוּךְ הוּא.

❦ ❦ ❦

רַבִּי חֲנַנְיָא בֶּן עֲקַשְׁיָא אוֹמֵר: רָצָה הַקָּדוֹשׁ בָּרוּךְ הוּא לְזַכּוֹת אֶת יִשְׂרָאֵל, לְפִיכָךְ הִרְבָּה לָהֶם תּוֹרָה וּמִצְוֹת, שֶׁנֶּאֱמַר: „יהוה חָפֵץ לְמַעַן צִדְקוֹ, יַגְדִּיל תּוֹרָה וְיַאְדִּיר.”

These ideas are expressed vividly in the Rosh Hashanah/Yom Kippur prayers where the yearly Days of Awe and Judgment are described in detail, but Rabbi Elazar is dealing here with the ultimate day of judgment of one's soul after death, as a part of the life cycle, and not only of the yearly cycle.

Rabbi Elazar stresses the completeness and exactitude of Heavenly judgment. The old joke about the accountant who couldn't balance the books and was off by a few cents and left a nickel on the desk for the client to even things out does not apply to the Heavenly Court of Judgment. Exquisite exactitude is the rule in God's courtroom. The words *din* , law, and *cheshbon* , reckoning, are the operative ones in the judgment procedure. *Din* refers to judgment of one's actual behavior and deeds. *Cheshbon* refers to what could have been accomplished with the person's time, talents, wealth and other blessings of life had they been utilized properly. We are judged not only on

the Discerner, He is the Judge, He is the Witness, He is the Plaintiff, He will judge. Blessed is He before Whom there is no iniquity, no forgetfulness, no favoritism, and no acceptance of bribery, for everything is His. Know that everything is according to the reckoning. And let your Evil Inclination not promise you that the grave will be an escape for you — for against your will you were created; against your will you were born; against your will you live; against your will you die; and against your will you are destined to give an account before the King Who rules over kings, the Holy One, Blessed is He.

❧ ❧ ❧

Rabbi Chanania ben Akashia says: The Holy One, Blessed is He, wished to confer merit upon Israel; therefore He gave them Torah and *mitzvos* in abundance, as it is said: *HASHEM desired, for the sake of its [Israel's] righteousness, that the Torah be made great and glorious* (*Isaiah* 42:21).

---

what we did, but also on what we could have done had we but applied ourselves to the task.

שֶׁעַל כָּרְחֲךָ אַתָּה נוֹצָר
For against your will you were created

THE SCRUPULOUS EXACTITUDE OF JUDGMENT IS TRULY TOUGH LOVE, BUT it is the responsibility that the Torah places upon us. We are brought into this world without having the choice to decline living. The rabbis taught that our souls agree that we would have been far better off never having to live in this world, but once God placed us here, we are obligated to make something of ourselves. We live by Divine will, we die by His will, and we will be compelled to account for our deeds. Since death is not the end of the story, the grave is not an escape hatch from responsibility and accountability. This sense of eternity, of the day of judgment, of infinite accountability, lends drama and importance to all of our acts in life. It is what makes life itself so compelling and vital.

פרק חמישי
CHAPTER FIVE

כָּל יִשְׂרָאֵל יֵשׁ לָהֶם חֵלֶק לָעוֹלָם הַבָּא, שֶׁנֶּאֱמַר: „וְעַמֵּךְ כֻּלָּם צַדִּיקִים, לְעוֹלָם יִירְשׁוּ אָרֶץ, נֵצֶר מַטָּעַי, מַעֲשֵׂה יָדַי לְהִתְפָּאֵר.״

All Israel has a share in the World to Come, as it is said: *And your people are all righteous; they shall inherit the land forever; a branch of My plantings, My handiwork, in which to take pride* (Isaiah 60:21).

[א] **בַּעֲשָׂרָה** מַאֲמָרוֹת נִבְרָא הָעוֹלָם. וּמַה תַּלְמוּד לוֹמַר? וַהֲלֹא בְמַאֲמָר אֶחָד יָכוֹל לְהִבָּרְאוֹת? אֶלָּא לְהִפָּרַע מִן הָרְשָׁעִים, שֶׁמְּאַבְּדִין אֶת הָעוֹלָם שֶׁנִּבְרָא בַּעֲשָׂרָה מַאֲמָרוֹת, וְלִתֵּן שָׂכָר טוֹב לַצַּדִּיקִים, שֶׁמְּקַיְּמִין אֶת הָעוֹלָם שֶׁנִּבְרָא בַּעֲשָׂרָה מַאֲמָרוֹת.

Chapter Five

MOST OF THIS CHAPTER HAS AN INTERNAL ORDER BASED ON NUMBERS — the only chapter of the tractate with such an arrangement of topics. The Mishnah first lists events and ideas that are based on the number ten. It then discusses insights based on the number seven, and then thoughts based on the number four. Then the chapter reverts to the general style of Avos, of individual statements on varying moral teachings. In this chapter, numbers are deemed supremely important, but numbers alone are not the main message. It is the profundity of the concepts that lie behind these numbers that inspire us in studying this chapter.

בַּעֲשָׂרָה מַאֲמָרוֹת נִבְרָא הָעוֹלָם
With ten utterances the world was created

Mishnah 1 TEN REPRESENTS THE DIVINE COMMANDMENTS OF SINAI. In Kabbalistic thought it represents the ten *sefiros,* the levels of heavenly holiness and closeness, so to speak, to God.

In spite of all the detail that appears in the first chapter of *Genesis,* the Torah does not really describe the process of creation — how the universe came into existence, how it is maintained, and what is its ultimate fate. The process of creation was a series of utterances from God: *"Let there be light, and there was light." "Let there be luminaries in the heavens,"* etc. What light? How did it come into being? What were the luminaries that were suspended in *the firmament of the heaven* — and what is the heaven? And what is the meaning of the firmament that *separated between the waters that were beneath . . . and the waters that were above?*

The Torah does not address itself to any of these questions and the many others like them. Why, then, did the Torah not begin by saying simply that God created everything, and move on to tell the story of humankind? Our mishnah addresses this question. Why does the Torah say ten times that God, so to speak, spoke and created, instead of saying once that He spoke and created? And why did God, so to speak, trouble to speak ten times, when the omnipotent Creator could have created everything with just one utter-

5/1

1. With ten utterances the world was created. What does this come to teach us? Indeed, could it not have been created with one utterance? This was to exact punishment from the wicked, who destroy the world that was created with ten utterances, and to bestow goodly reward upon the righteous, who sustain the world that was created with ten utterances.

---

ance? The mishnah teaches a basic lesson of Judaism and does so in its usual pithy and unforgettable manner.

This world was not created by random forces. The universe that we live in is far too exquisite and precise to have come into being haphazardly. God's guiding hand is in everything that we see about us, from the colors of a rose to the seemingly infinite abyss of space. A world of such beauty, a universe of such vastness and grandeur, all testify to the Creator Who fashioned it and sustains it. That Creator brought the universe and the world into being in stages, one stage building upon the other. It could have all been created in one blinding flash of a millisecond, full-blown and complete — with "one utterance," but instead it was created in stages, in levels — in "ten utterances." This teaches that we are to build ourselves and our spiritual personalities in the same way — slowly, carefully, incrementally, not through overnight wonders.

The Talmud teaches that even though there were people who were able to gain the World to Come in an instant, in a flash of total repentance, self-sacrifice, and action, those people died immedialy from the exertion. Sudden and instantaneous spiritual creations, no matter how positive, apparently are not consistent with survival in this world. The only way to grow and survive and benefit others is by climbing the ladder of goodness and holiness one step after another.

We live in a "Ten Utterances" world, not a "One Utterance" creation. Therefore, those who consistently pursue the path of righteousness justify by their behavior the painstaking and vastly intricate levels of time and complexity that the Creator, so to speak, invested in our universe. For the attainment of righteousness also demands "many utterances." And those whose evil behavior destroys others and themselves thereby help to dismantle a world that came into being through painstaking care and attention.

❦ ❦ ❦

Longing for the logs

I still remember that as a child I built a complex structure out of Lincoln Logs, a plaything that was very popular before the toy industry became overrun by batteries and graphics. It took me days to do it and I was enormously proud of my achievement. It was before Pesach and my mother had

[ב] **עֲשָׂרָה** דוֹרוֹת מֵאָדָם וְעַד נֹחַ, לְהוֹדִיעַ כַּמָּה אֶרֶךְ אַפַּיִם לְפָנָיו; שֶׁכָּל הַדּוֹרוֹת הָיוּ מַכְעִיסִין וּבָאִין, עַד שֶׁהֵבִיא עֲלֵיהֶם אֶת מֵי הַמַּבּוּל.

[ג] **עֲשָׂרָה** דוֹרוֹת מִנֹּחַ וְעַד אַבְרָהָם, לְהוֹדִיעַ כַּמָּה אֶרֶךְ אַפַּיִם לְפָנָיו; שֶׁכָּל הַדּוֹרוֹת

---

a cleaning woman come into the house to help her. In her zeal to render the house spotless, the cleaning woman unthinkingly destroyed my Lincoln Logs structure. I still feel that pain within me sixty years later.

❦ ❦ ❦

It is no wonder, therefore, that the rabbis of the Talmud comment on God's pain, so to speak, when evil reigns in His world and when immoral behavior governs life. Should a world of such painstaking labor and accomplishment be destroyed by people who cannot control their base drives?! The rabbis take the liberty of saying metaphorically that God, so to speak, moans and says: "My head hurts, my arm hurts." A world of such greatness, of "ten utterances," should be so abused by evildoers! Our world is far too great a creation to be abandoned to those who are evil. The purpose of Israel is to maintain and glorify the world that was created with "ten utterances."

עֲשָׂרָה דוֹרוֹת מֵאָדָם וְעַד נֹחַ
There were ten generations from Adam to Noah

Mishnah 2 THE TEN GENERATIONS FROM THE FIRST MAN UNTIL THE great flood are to a great extent anonymous. The Torah says little about them, about their leaders and about the progress of their civilization. What does emerge from the Torah is that these humans lost their way, forgot the truth about creation and the Creator, and descended into a sea of immorality, corruption, robbery, abuse, and paganism. Idolatry became the norm. The Midrash indicates that it was a purposeful rebellion against God. Rambam contends that their grievous error began with a logical assumption. At first people philosophized that since God had created the heavenly bodies and other forces as His "agents" in maintaining the world, it was proper to honor them, just as it is a mark of respect to a king to honor his ministers. Eventually this error mushroomed until people forgot about God and began to worship the various forces of nature. However idolatry began, the human race sank into the animal world, losing its Godly form and holy purpose. Nevertheless, the Lord had patience, waiting for over sixteen centuries for the human race to right itself, before bringing the tragedy of the flood upon it.

There are two lessons here. The obvious one is the Godly virtue of patience. Not being hasty in judgment and action is one of the core lessons of Avos, being repeated numerous times in this tractate. Humans should learn

2. There were ten generations from Adam to Noah — to show the degree of His patience; for all those generations angered Him increasingly, until He brought upon them the waters of the flood.

3. There were ten generations from Noah to Abraham — to show the degree of His patience; for all those genera-

---

to emulate our Creator in this trait of patience and restraint. The Lord waited ten generations before punishing and destroying. Even though there was no improvement between, let us say, the seventh and eighth generations, still He waited. Perhaps there would be a change in the ninth generation. Since the Lord is omniscient, He knew that humans were not going to change their ways, yet He waited patiently for ten generations, so to speak, through the continuing spiritual and moral decline of the human race. He waited not for His sake, but rather to set an example for the post-flood humans about the necessity of patience and forbearance in all of their human affairs. If God, Who always knows the eventual outcome, has patience, ordinary humans who can never be sure of the outcome of events or the reactions of people, should certainly exercise patience.

The second lesson concerns the value of one person, a lonely figure of righteousness engulfed in a mob of malicious and mendacious evildoers. Noah and his family would overcome their environment; they would survive the flood and repopulate the world. God's patience in outwaiting the evil of the ten generations is somehow rewarded by the appearance of the righteous person — the crown and purpose of all creation. The world can exist for the sake of one good person who will appear and push the process of civilization forward.

Judaism teaches that God is impressed, so to speak, by quality, not by quantity or publicity. And Judaism also teaches that there will always be such a good person and we have no right to give up on the struggle against evil and mendacity. Even if all is washed away because of human failure, the righteous idea and person survive to begin the process of building goodness and civilization again. These two lessons lend great import to the Torah's record of the ten generations from Adam to Noah.

עֲשָׂרָה דוֹרוֹת מִנֹּחַ וְעַד אַבְרָהָם
There were ten generations from Noah to Abraham

Mishnah 3 NOAH WAS A SUCCESS AS A PERSON, BUT LESS SO AS A father and leader of society. Many, probably most, of his own grandchildren — the "survivor" generation — soon sank back into the pre-flood swamp of idolatry and immorality. Tyrants arose to oppress humans and to deny God. Gigantic projects were planned — the Tower of Babel for example — in order to worship the new man-made deities. Nimrod

הָיוּ מַכְעִיסִין וּבָאִין, עַד שֶׁבָּא אַבְרָהָם אָבִינוּ וְקִבֵּל שְׂכַר כֻּלָּם.

[ד] **עֲשָׂרָה** נִסְיוֹנוֹת נִתְנַסָּה אַבְרָהָם אָבִינוּ וְעָמַד בְּכֻלָּם, לְהוֹדִיעַ כַּמָּה חִבָּתוֹ שֶׁל אַבְרָהָם אָבִינוּ.

---

is the precursor of Lenin and Stalin — the cult of personality that crushes millions on the way to imagined world domination and improvement. The new religions of atheism, paganism, worship of humans, the killings of many for the benefit of the few — the world of Chairman Mao, Pol Pot, Saddam Hussein, Kim Il Sung, etc. — were aided and abetted by the example of Nimrod and his like during the ten generations after Noah and the flood.

The world was apparently without hope of betterment, and people — even good, fine, upstanding people — made peace with the idea that Nimrod and his successors would always triumph. There was no alternative but to go along and to stifle within one's bosom any dreams of a better world.

And then someone "roused himself and shone forth from the East," smashed his father's idols, was miraculously saved from Nimrod's furnace and embarked on a mission that would change humanity forever. The father of human civilization, of all nations and peoples, the progenitor of the Jewish people and Judaism, the preacher of monotheism and goodness among humans, Abraham bursts on the world scene. The unbelievable power of one person, of acts of kindness and goodness, to alter the world permanently for the better is nowhere better illustrated than in the lives of our father Abraham and our mother Sarah, for they were unique, and were able to impart their message and character traits to later generations for all time.

עַד שֶׁבָּא אַבְרָהָם אָבִינוּ וְקִבֵּל שְׂכַר כֻּלָּם
Until our forefather Abraham came and received the reward of them all

IN THE MODERN WORLD, THERE ARE LOTTERIES IN ALMOST EVERY COUNTRY, and when no one wins the first lottery, the jackpot is added to the next lottery. If nine consecutive drawings went by with no winner, the tenth lottery winner would receive an enormous prize. This is the idea that the mishnah points out in regard to Abraham. No one in any of the previous generations won the lottery of righteous conduct, so to speak, so that the reward awaiting Abraham was enormous: the founding of the Jewish people, the bequeathing of the Land of Israel to him and his descendants, the covenant of circumcision, recognition as "the Godly leader in our midst." All of this and more was now his share, the cumulative reward of the ten generations that produced no winners. Thus Abraham becomes the symbol of good triumphant over an evil world, the rock of righteousness in a morally corrupt and cruel society, the

tions angered Him increasingly, until our forefather Abraham came and received the reward of them all.

4. Our forefather Abraham was tested with ten trials and he withstood all of them — to show the degree of our forefather Abraham's love for God.

---

hospitable host in an environment of hatred and exclusion of the stranger. Is not such a person truly worthy of winning the great cumulative jackpot of ten generations of losers?

עֲשָׂרָה נִסְיוֹנוֹת
Ten trials

Mishnah 4 THE TRUE MEASURE OF A PERSON IS HOW HE REACTS TO pressure, disappointment, danger, and difficulty. There are those who grow from such experiences, and there are those who falter because of them. For most people, it is better not to be tempted and not to be tested. In our daily morning prayers we ask God not to subject our faith and moral deportment to tests and undue stress, but no one really escapes being tested. The marketplace and the office, the street and the culture of society, the media and the human failings of supposed heroes, all rise to challenge our Jewish convictions, faith, and lifestyle.

Our tests in life are numerous and complex, sometimes blatant, mostly subtle. In fact, the rabbis attest that the more righteous and pious a person attempts to become, the more likely it is that he will be constantly tested. Thus, we can appreciate that the tests of Abraham, too, were many and varied. In fact, there is no unanimity among the commentators as to what his particular ten tests were. If we will add up all the varying tests offered by the different commentators we will arrive at a number far higher than ten. All agree, however, that the *Akeidah* — God's command that Abraham sacrifice his son Isaac on the altar at Mount Moriah — was one of the tests, if not the primary one.

The Jewish people internalized the test of the *Akeidah* within their national life. It is no exaggeration to say that the Jewish people have always lived in the shadow of the *Akeidah,* and it is the greatness of Israel that it has survived and even prospered in a world of this constant test. Israel has emerged greater from every *Akeidah* in its history.

וְעָמַד בְּכֻלָּם
And he withstood all of them

IN MY OPINION, THE IMPORTANT LESSON OF THIS MISHNAH LIES IN THESE words. Abraham stood tall after every test. He became greater. Thus he could be tested again in the surety that he would not be broken by the continued challenges thrust upon him. This was the essential difference between Abraham and Noah. Noah overcame one great challenge in his lifetime — the building of the Ark and the flood — but was unable to deal with the

[ה] **עֲשָׂרָה** נִסִּים נַעֲשׂוּ לַאֲבוֹתֵינוּ בְּמִצְרַיִם וַעֲשָׂרָה עַל הַיָּם. עֶשֶׂר מַכּוֹת הֵבִיא הַקָּדוֹשׁ בָּרוּךְ הוּא עַל הַמִּצְרִים בְּמִצְרַיִם וְעֶשֶׂר עַל הַיָּם.

[ו] **עֲשָׂרָה** נִסְיוֹנוֹת נִסּוּ אֲבוֹתֵינוּ אֶת הַקָּדוֹשׁ בָּרוּךְ הוּא בַּמִּדְבָּר, שֶׁנֶּאֱמַר: „וַיְנַסּוּ אֹתִי זֶה עֶשֶׂר פְּעָמִים, וְלֹא שָׁמְעוּ בְּקוֹלִי.״

---

challenges of the post-flood world. He lived for well over three hundred years after the flood, but he retired from the fray after his one great challenge. Not so Abraham who influenced mankind primarily because of his ability to became even greater from every challenge and test.

Throughout history, simply being a Jew has been a major test. It is a test that no Jew escapes, not those who attempt to completely assimilate nor those who disdain the outside world and attempt to isolate themselves from it. Built into the Jewish DNA, so to speak, is this tenacious attribute of our father Abraham, the ability and willingness to face tests and challenges and overcome them. Abraham, who is the symbol of goodness, kindness, and tolerance, and who could therefore be mistaken as just a "good guy," is in reality the tenacious person of faith, strong in heart and stubborn in behavior, who cannot be shaken from his belief in God and the positive future of human destiny, even by ten tests.

עֲשָׂרָה נִסִּים ***Ten miracles***

Mishnah 5 THE TEN PLAGUES THAT DESTROYED THE EGYPTIAN RULE over the people of Israel are so wondrous in their intensity and effects that they are beyond our abilities to describe accurately or to appreciate. But what we *can* understand is that the Jews were spared from those plagues. This is the explanation of the ten miracles that occurred to our forebears in Egypt. Normally, when a plague occurs, God forbid, it makes no distinctions between sections of the population. It destroys everyone and everything. Not so in ancient Egypt. The Jews intermingled completely with the Egyptians in their work projects if not in their dwelling places, and were nevertheless spared ten times from the effects of awful physical plagues and punishments.

וַעֲשָׂרָה עַל הַיָּם ***And ten at the Sea***

THERE WERE ALSO TEN MIRACLES AT THE SPLITTING OF THE SEA OF REEDS. We read in the Pesach Haggadah that hundreds of disasters befell the Egyptians on that fateful day when the Sea split for the Jewish people. As with Abraham's tests, the commentators here have different versions of what were the ten primary miracles at the Sea. The most obvious miracle is that the Sea

5. Ten miracles were performed for our ancestors in Egypt and ten at the Sea. Ten plagues did the Holy One, Blessed is He, bring upon the Egyptians in Egypt and ten at the Sea.

6. [With] ten trials did our ancestors test the Holy One, Blessed is He, in the Wilderness, as it is said: *They have tested Me these ten times and they did not heed My voice* (*Numbers* 14:22).

---

split, saving Israel from certain annihilation or a return to slavery, allowing the Jews to escape and subsequently drowning the Egyptian army in the roiling waters.

This historic event is celebrated and commemorated every seventh day of Pesach and remains the basis for the existence and survival of Israel to this very day. The mishnah mentions the ten miracles at the Sea in order to equate this event with the actual Exodus from Egypt and the ten miracles that accompanied the ten plagues. The first day of Pesach, the Exodus itself, and the seventh day of Pesach, the day of deliverance of the Jewish people at the Sea, are the bookends that encapsulate the ideas and experience of Jewish deliverance.

עֲשָׂרָה נִסְיוֹנוֹת נִסּוּ אֲבוֹתֵינוּ ***[With] ten trials did our ancestors test***

Mishnah 6 AS WAS THE CASE REGARDING THE OTHER "TENS," THERE are different counts in the rabbinic writings regarding the identity of these ten testings of God. In any event, they are all summed up in the last words of the verse quoted in this mishnah: *and they did not heed My voice*. The Jewish streak of stubbornness, which in our later history would prove to be such an asset to our survival, was a distinct liability in the generation that wandered in the Wilderness after the Exodus. The Jews of the desert could not completely shake off the chains and bondage of Egyptian society and influence. They were a great generation of people who accepted the Torah and were the דוֹר דֵּעָה, the most knowledgeable generation in Jewish history. Yet, they were also grumblers, complainers, ungrateful, and stubbornly attached to their past in Egypt. Therefore they tested God, so to speak, ten times, never really being confident of their new status as a free people with a bright and holy future.

Basically, they were frightened of the future and wary of entrusting their fate to the God of Israel. When someone is in a bad mood, then the food (even heavenly manna) is not good, the leadership (even the incomparable Moses and Aaron) is to be blamed for all otherwise normal problems and shortcomings, and positive events (such as the report of Joshua and Caleb regarding the Land of Israel) are misinterpreted as being threatening and malicious. As a result of this misanthropic nature, all blame is then eventually reflected back at

[ז] **עֲשָׂרָה** נִסִּים נַעֲשׂוּ לַאֲבוֹתֵינוּ בְּבֵית הַמִּקְדָּשׁ: לֹא הִפִּילָה אִשָּׁה מֵרֵיחַ בְּשַׂר הַקֹּדֶשׁ; וְלֹא הִסְרִיחַ בְּשַׂר הַקֹּדֶשׁ מֵעוֹלָם; וְלֹא נִרְאָה זְבוּב בְּבֵית הַמִּטְבְּחַיִם; וְלֹא אִירַע קֶרִי לְכֹהֵן גָּדוֹל בְּיוֹם הַכִּפּוּרִים; וְלֹא כִבּוּ הַגְּשָׁמִים אֵשׁ שֶׁל עֲצֵי הַמַּעֲרָכָה; וְלֹא נִצְּחָה הָרוּחַ אֶת עַמּוּד הֶעָשָׁן; וְלֹא נִמְצָא פְּסוּל בָּעֹמֶר, וּבִשְׁתֵּי הַלֶּחֶם, וּבְלֶחֶם הַפָּנִים; עוֹמְדִים צְפוּפִים, וּמִשְׁתַּחֲוִים רְוָחִים; וְלֹא הִזִּיק נָחָשׁ וְעַקְרָב בִּירוּשָׁלַיִם מֵעוֹלָם; וְלֹא אָמַר אָדָם לַחֲבֵרוֹ: „צַר לִי הַמָּקוֹם שֶׁאָלִין בִּירוּשָׁלַיִם.״

---

the God Who liberated them from Egypt to make them His chosen people, and Whom they accused of bringing them into the desert to let them die there. This attitude is the source of the disastrous ten tests that spelled the doom of that otherwise potentially greatest of all Jewish generations.

The rabbis of *mussar* concentrated on the character flaw of ingratitude as the source for this black mood. A person so afflicted is never grateful for what he has and instead is depressed because of what he does not yet possess. The testing of God, so to speak, stemmed from the streak of ingratitude that was part of the psychological makeup of that generation. Ingratitude brings depression, which in turn intensifies ingratitude. The ten tests in the desert clearly confirm this sad cycle of human behavior.

עֲשָׂרָה נִסִּים נַעֲשׂוּ לַאֲבוֹתֵינוּ בְּבֵית הַמִּקְדָּשׁ
Ten miracles were performed for our ancestors in the Holy Temple

Mishnah 7 THE COMMENTATORS DISAGREE AS TO WHETHER THESE TEN miracles occurred only during the time of the First Temple or occurred in Second Temple as well.

There are two types of miracles in this list: those that deal with defying the laws of physical nature and those that deal with a denial of human nature. Anyone who is even remotely familiar with the Torah is accustomed to miracles as exceptions to nature, to such an extent that the miraculous aspect of these events tends to fade and becomes almost taken for granted. Thus, it is miraculous, but not surprising, that there were no flies where meat and blood abounded, no rotting carcasses in a slaughter house, no rain extinguishing the Altar fire, and so on — these and the other miracles defy the ordinary laws of nature. Let us now turn to the second category of miracles, those that defy human nature.

7. Ten miracles were performed for our ancestors in the Holy Temple: (a) No woman miscarried because of the aroma of the sacrificial meat; (b) the sacrificial meat never became putrid; (c) no fly was seen in the place where the [sanctified] meat was butchered; (d) no seminal emission occurred to the High Priest on Yom Kippur; (e) the rains did not extinguish the fire on the Altar pyre; (f) the wind did not disperse the vertical column of smoke from the Altar; (g) no disqualification was found in the Omer, the Two Loaves, or the Show Bread; (h) the people stood crowded together, yet prostrated themselves in ample space; (i) neither serpent nor scorpion ever caused injury in Jerusalem; (j) never did any man say to his fellow, "The space is insufficient for me to stay overnight in Jerusalem."

עוֹמְדִים צְפוּפִים, וּמִשְׁתַּחֲוִים רְוָחִים
The people stood crowded together, yet prostrated themselves in ample space

MIRACLES REGARDING HUMAN NATURE ARE SO EXTRAORDINARY AS TO command our attention and respect, if not our awe and wonderment. In addition to the physical miracle that space expands to accommodate the needs of the large crowds in Jerusalem, the commentators see a moral lesson in these miracles.

The Rabbis taught that if we stand erect and inflexible, insisting on our rights alone and not willing to compromise in deference to the needs of others, we will find ourselves in a very crowded and uncomfortable world. However, if we can bow to the rights of others and compromise our own personal interests in the interests of public harmony and a peaceful society, then we will find that life truly affords us a great deal of elbow room. But to get humans to behave in such a fashion is a truly miraculous feat. As the holiest national entity, the Temple allows for this type of miraculous human attitude to appear and flourish. Miracles are of little practical avail in this world if they do not lead to the improvement of human character and behavior.

וְלֹא אָמַר אָדָם לַחֲבֵרוֹ: "צַר לִי הַמָּקוֹם שֶׁאָלִין בִּירוּשָׁלַיִם"
Never did any man say to his fellow, "The space is insufficient for me to stay overnight in Jerusalem."

IT IS UNDERSTANDABLE THAT THE FINAL, CULMINATING MIRACLE LISTED IN connection with the Temple is that no one who came to worship at the Temple ever complained about a lack of space in Jerusalem. People are by nature complainers. Whether it is the food, the accommodations, the weather, etc., there is always room for complaint. But the influence of the Holy Temple and its constant attendant physical miracles caused one to see things in the great perspective of Jerusalem, instead of only in the small viewpoint of the comfort or lack thereof of one's hotel room. When one sees the big picture that Jerusalem truly represents, then there is no room for complaints of any kind. All the inconveniences become too trivial to be worthy of notice.

[ח] **עֲשָׂרָה** דְבָרִים נִבְרְאוּ בְּעֶרֶב שַׁבָּת בֵּין הַשְּׁמָשׁוֹת, וְאֵלּוּ הֵן; פִּי הָאָרֶץ, וּפִי הַבְּאֵר, פִּי הָאָתוֹן, וְהַקֶּשֶׁת, וְהַמָּן, וְהַמַּטֶּה, וְהַשָּׁמִיר,

---

❦ ❦ ❦

To ascend to Jerusalem

On my first visit to Israel in 1967, my wife and I took a cab from the airport to Jerusalem. The cabs then were not Mercedes or Volvos, but rather decrepit 1953 DeSotos, an American brand that has long since ended in the scrap heap of extinct automobile models. As the DeSoto chugged its way up the then old, winding road to Jerusalem, the cab experienced a number of breakdowns, overheating, and finally a flat tire. As I climbed out to help unload the luggage so that the tire could be changed, my frustration at the turn of the events was visible on my face. The driver looked at me sternly and then smiled and said, "You think it is easy to ascend to Jerusalem?" His remark put the entire experience into perspective. My forebears would have walked across Eastern Europe in the snow barefoot to see a Jewish community in the Land of Israel, and to be able to physically ascend to Jerusalem. All of my frustration drained from me, and was replaced with a sense of inner joy.

❦ ❦ ❦

Let no one ever say that the accommodations in Jerusalem or the travel thereto are inadequate. And even if one is upset, one should never communicate that feeling to others. The mishnah purposely states that no one ever *said to his fellow* that he was uncomfortable in Jerusalem. Even if one felt that way, the miracle was that this negativism was kept private and not allowed to influence others. No one ever *said* it — what a wondrous miracle!

עֲשָׂרָה דְבָרִים נִבְרְאוּ בְּעֶרֶב שַׁבָּת בֵּין הַשְּׁמָשׁוֹת
Ten things were created on the eve of the first Sabbath

Mishnah 8 THE MISHNAH DESCRIBES THESE TEN "LAST-MINUTE" CREations of God as the finishing touches, so to speak, to the universe as we know it. In reality, the mishnah deals with the nature of miracles and their place in our worldview. There are very different views in Jewish tradition regarding the nature of miracles. Rambam [Maimonides] is of the opinion that nature will remain unchangeable even in Messianic times and that the Lord instituted this immutable rule when He created the universe. Therefore, all miracles are merely natural events that were programmed into nature's computer, so to speak, at the moment of creation, and were then set to occur at a specific time and place in the course of human history. Anyone who has visited an automobile assembly line and seen how gigantic computers run the plant, supply the exact parts to the exact location

8. Ten things were created on the eve of the first Sabbath. They are: The mouth of the earth, the mouth of the well, the mouth of [Bilaam's] donkey, the rainbow [shown to Noah], the manna, the staff, the shamir worm,

---

on the assembly line at the right time, has an idea of how the Rambam visualized this concept of natural, pre-programmed miracles.

Ramban [Nachmanides] and others, however, dissented from this Maimonidean principle, and held that nature can change (for example, they maintained that it changed after the flood, and will yet change again in the Messianic Era, etc.), and that miracles are examples of Divine intervention; the laws of nature were established as part of creation, but they can be varied by God's will. Thus, miracles are not necessarily pre-programmed, but rather are current changes in nature for specific purposes of punishment and salvation.

At first glance, our mishnah seems to support the view of Rambam, for otherwise there would have been no necessity for God to create these exceptions to nature as part of the process of creation. Naturally, those who disagree with Rambam interpret the mishnah differently.

וְהַקֶּשֶׁת ***The rainbow [shown to Noah]***

AFTER THE FLOOD, GOD SHOWED NOAH A RAINBOW AS A SYMBOL OF HIS guarantee that He would never again destroy the world with a flood. The rainbow, which is the division of the spectrum of light into its component colors, represents the many different types of people in the world. This miracle is the symbol of God's commitment to the human race, in spite of all its continuing failings. This covenant between the human race and its Creator is a thing of light and beauty. It reaffirms that somehow we will always muddle through, and that our commitment to God should be as firm as His is to us.

The beauty of the rainbow symbolizes the creativity, talent, and flash of genius that God invested in our world and in mankind. Yet, the Talmud teaches us that in a generation where a great and holy person lives, there is no need for the rainbow to appear; the presence of such a person is itself mankind's guarantee of survival. The great Rabbi Yehoshua ben Levi, upon arriving in heaven, was challenged by Rabbi Shimon ben Yochai, "Did the rainbow appear in your lifetime? If it did, then you are not the great ben Levi I expected here." The good person, the ultimate pinnacle of God's creation, is more than a rainbow. It is that person who by his being and behavior testifies to the fact that humans are created in the form of God and are capable of transcendent acts of goodness, kindness and piety. Thus, the symbol of the rainbow provides us a goal to which to aim, a level of behavior to which to aspire — a lasting miracle with a message to each and every one of us.

ה/ח

הַכְּתָב, וְהַמִּכְתָּב, וְהַלּוּחוֹת. וְיֵשׁ אוֹמְרִים: אַף הַמַּזִּיקִין, וּקְבוּרָתוֹ שֶׁל מֹשֶׁה. וְאֵילוֹ שֶׁל אַבְרָהָם אָבִינוּ. וְיֵשׁ אוֹמְרִים: אַף צְבַת בִּצְבַת עֲשׂוּיָה.

וְיֵשׁ אוֹמְרִים: אַף הַמַּזִּיקִין
Some say also the destructive spirits

IN ADDITION TO THE TEN LAST-MINUTE ADDITIONS TO CREATION LISTED above, some hold that there were other such creations. Included in this latter list are *mazikin,* creatures that do harm. The mishnah is not specific as to what these creatures are, but we can all testify that unfortunately there is no shortage of destructive creatures in our world and our lives. From unseen viruses to visible thugs and terrorists, *mazikin* are omnipresent in our lives. But their very presence and existence can also aid us in having a positive posture in life. The presence of lurking dangers makes us realize how truly fragile and exposed we are to harm. It reinforces the realization of our constant dependence upon God and the utmost necessity of faith and hope in order to withstand the *mazikin.* Therefore, in a perverse way, their existence contributes to a better human being and a better world. Nevertheless, we would all prefer a world without *mazikin.* Perhaps this is why this opinion is given as "some say," rather than as the opinion of the author of the mishnah itself.

וּקְבוּרָתוֹ שֶׁל מֹשֶׁה
The burial place of Moses

THE BURIAL PLACE OF OUR TEACHER MOSES IS UNKNOWN AND UNKNOWable. The Lord thereby prevented the rise of a cult of Moses worshipers. One shudders at the thought that Moses's tomb would be a great tourist attraction and be turned into the mercantile- and carnival-like atmosphere that afflicts the tombs of many great Jews. In His infinite wisdom and mercy, God spared Moses and us that scene. True, Jews visit the graves of the righteous; indeed, there are regular organized pilgrimages to the graves of great *tzaddikim,* but Moses's grave would be too great a challenge for Jews to handle. There have been occasions in our history when such grave worship has resulted in problems of faith and theology for Judaism. In the main, such pilgrimages have been kept within normative, halachically acceptable bounds, but the temptation to deify Moses would prove to be irresistible for some people. The Talmud teaches that one reason Jacob did not wish to be buried in Egypt was his fear that the Egyptians might worship his grave. The Lord therefore precluded having such a challenge arise among us in reference to Moses.

וְאֵילוֹ שֶׁל אַבְרָהָם אָבִינוּ
And the ram of our forefather Abraham

WHEN GOD TOLD ABRAHAM NOT TO SACRIFICE ISAAC ON THE *AKEIDAH,* and that the original command to do so was a test, Abraham brought a ram upon the altar, in place of Isaac. This symbolizes the spirit of Jewish sacrifice throughout all times and places. The Midrash teaches that one horn of that ram of sacrifice was fashioned into the mighty shofar that was sounded at Sinai when the Ten Commandments were presented to Israel. The other horn will be the script, the inscription, and the Tablets. Some say also the destructive spirits, the burial place of Moses, and the ram of our forefather Abraham. And some say also tongs, which must be made with other tongs.

---

the shofar of redemption that will be sounded to usher in the Messianic era. Thus Abraham's ram symbolizes the knowledge, piety, and hopes of the Jewish people. Jews have made great sacrifices to preserve these two shofars. Many an altar in this world has been sprinkled with innocent Jewish blood, but the miracle of Jewish survival and achievement is symbolized by the ram of Abraham, that miracle of God's creation.

אַף צְבַת בִּצְבַת עֲשׂוּיָה
Also tongs, which must be made with other tongs

A FURTHER OPINION IN OUR MISHNAH DEALS WITH THE MIRACLE OF human ingenuity that has fashioned such a wondrous technologically advanced world. The first tool, the creative spark of man's genius, was fashioned and created by God. After that, man used his ingenuity and inventiveness to make all the other tools that exist in this world. Animals, especially those of the ape families, have been able to create rudimentary tools, but they cannot advance from fashioning these simple tools to build more complex ones, to build upon previous achievements. Only the human race has been able to do so in a consistent and persistent fashion.

This original tool was granted to us by God's miracle of creation. Man needed the first tool, the first tongs, and from that simple beginning man has been able to devise the technology that is the marvel of our current existence, but the mishnah tells us always to remember where that first tool came from — for without a sense of morality and recognition of our Creator, our technology can destroy us. The miracle of the first tool in civilization should always remain with us.

Mishnah 9 HAVING CONCLUDED EIGHT *MISHNAYOS* DEALING WITH series of ten, the mishnah moves on to two series of seven. According to the Midrash, all sevens are holy in one way or another. Seven represents the days of the week, the holy Sabbath, the Sabbatical *Shemittah* year, the days of purification, the days of celebrating a marriage, and, conversely, the days of mourning at the loss of a loved one. But none of these representations of seven appear in this mishnah. The tens of the previous *mishnayos* dealt with historical events, while the sevens will describe human failings and their sad consequences. It is interesting to note that the mishnah purposely avoided the usual representations of the numbers ten and seven and chose rather to dwell on history and human characteristics. I believe that this is because the message of Avos is not so much one of philosophy and theology as it is of practical living and human improvement. There are no greater aids to wise practical living than learning from experience — history, if you will — and

[ט] **שִׁבְעָה** דְבָרִים בְּגֹלֶם, וְשִׁבְעָה בְּחָכָם. חָכָם אֵינוֹ מְדַבֵּר לִפְנֵי מִי שֶׁגָּדוֹל מִמֶּנּוּ בְּחָכְמָה וּבְמִנְיָן; וְאֵינוֹ נִכְנָס לְתוֹךְ דִּבְרֵי חֲבֵרוֹ; וְאֵינוֹ נִבְהָל לְהָשִׁיב; שׁוֹאֵל כְּעִנְיָן, וּמֵשִׁיב כַּהֲלָכָה; וְאוֹמֵר עַל רִאשׁוֹן רִאשׁוֹן, וְעַל אַחֲרוֹן אַחֲרוֹן; וְעַל מַה שֶּׁלֹּא שָׁמַע אוֹמֵר: „לֹא שָׁמַעְתִּי"; וּמוֹדֶה עַל הָאֱמֶת. וְחִלּוּפֵיהֶן בְּגֹלֶם.

[י] **שִׁבְעָה** מִינֵי פֻרְעָנִיּוֹת בָּאִין לָעוֹלָם עַל שִׁבְעָה גוּפֵי עֲבֵרָה: מִקְצָתָן מְעַשְּׂרִין וּמִקְצָתָן אֵינָן מְעַשְּׂרִין, רָעָב שֶׁל בַּצֹּרֶת בָּא, מִקְצָתָן רְעֵבִים וּמִקְצָתָן שְׂבֵעִים; גָּמְרוּ שֶׁלֹּא לְעַשֵּׂר, רָעָב שֶׁל מְהוּמָה וְשֶׁל בַּצֹּרֶת בָּא; וְשֶׁלֹּא לִטֹּל אֶת הַחַלָּה, רָעָב שֶׁל כְּלָיָה בָּא.

---

studying and improving character traits.

שִׁבְעָה דְבָרִים בְּגֹלֶם
Seven things characterize an uncultivated person

IN ITS LITERAL SENSE, A *GOLEM* IS SOMETHING RAW, UNFORMED, UNFINISHED, lacking final polish. This is the meaning implied in all of the beloved Jewish stories regarding lifelike creatures created by holy men through supernatural means, such as the famous *Golem* of Prague. In Jewish tradition and popular usage, a *golem* came to mean a fool, someone who is "unfinished," or, in common parlance, "just doesn't get it." It is in this latter sense that our mishnah employs the word *golem.* A fool speaks out of turn, never admits error, is disorganized in speech and thought, has an answer and opinion for everything — even for subjects that he knows nothing about — interrupts others who are speaking, and does not respect the opinions of those who are wiser and more experienced. A wise person, on the other hand, is courteous and respectful of others and of their opinions, patient, honest, loyal to truth and quick to retract error, is orderly in thought and presentation of ideas and lessons, always focused on the topic being discussed, and appreciative of the wisdom of elders and wise people.

As I have discussed earlier, the rabbis of the Mishnah considered a fool to be dangerous. Perhaps such a person is truly to be pitied, but he certainly should be avoided. The great Yiddish aphorism applies here: "When a fool throws a stone into a well, even seven wise men will be unable to remove it." The mishnah, therefore, details the seven characteristics of a wise person and states that the reverse of them identifies a *golem,* a fool.

9. Seven traits characterize an uncultivated person and seven a learned one. A learned person does not begin speaking before one who is greater than he in wisdom or in years; he does not interrupt the words of his fellow; he does not answer impetuously; he asks relevant questions, and replies appropriately; he discusses first things first and last things last; about something he has not heard he says, "I have not heard"; and he acknowledges the truth. And the reverse of these [traits] characterizes an uncultivated person.

10. Seven types of punishment come to the world for seven kinds of transgressions. (a) If some people tithe and others do not, a famine caused by lack of rain ensues; some go hungry and some are satisfied; (b) if all decided not to tithe, [general] famine caused by armed bands and drought ensues; (c) [if they also decided] not to separate *challah,* a famine caused by fatal drought ensues.

By outlining the qualities of a wise person and a fool, the mishnah creates a measuring rod for one's personal use in determining how much of the wise man and how much of the fool remains within each and every one of us. It is from such a mishnah that the immense practicality of the teachings of Avos shines through.

שִׁבְעָה מִינֵי פֻּרְעָנִיּוֹת בָּאִין לָעוֹלָם
Seven types of punishment come to the world

Mishnah 10 THERE ARE SEVEN CATEGORIES OF SERIOUS SIN, WHICH lead to seven different types of tragic consequences in the Jewish world. The punishments are always described as being meted out exactly measure for measure — *middah keneged middah.* So, if some tithe their crops and others don't, the result is a mixed famine, in which some will have food and some won't. If, however, it becomes officially sanctioned and approved not to tithe, there will be a devastating hunger that affects everyone. It will be a hunger of confusion and anarchy, of people violently clawing at each other for a scrap of bread. It will be a hunger that mocks all public policy and all public order, because it will cause a breakdown of the very society that decided that it no longer needed to tithe and be charitable to others.

וְשֶׁלֹּא לִטֹּל אֶת הַחַלָּה
[If they also decided] not to separate challah

SOMETIMES THE REBELLION AGAINST TORAH LAW AND TRADITION IS SO great that it results in a raging famine that kills off many. *Challah* is a small, almost infinitesimal bit of dough that had to be given to the *Kohen.* One could rationalize that giving tithes — a tenth of the produce — was an

[יא] **דֶּבֶר** בָּא לָעוֹלָם – עַל מִיתוֹת הָאֲמוּרוֹת בַּתּוֹרָה שֶׁלֹּא נִמְסְרוּ לְבֵית דִּין, וְעַל פֵּרוֹת שְׁבִיעִית; חֶרֶב בָּאָה לָעוֹלָם – עַל עִנּוּי הַדִּין, וְעַל עִוּוּת הַדִּין, וְעַל הַמּוֹרִים בַּתּוֹרָה שֶׁלֹּא כַהֲלָכָה; חַיָּה רָעָה בָּאָה לָעוֹלָם – עַל שְׁבוּעַת שָׁוְא, וְעַל חִלּוּל הַשֵּׁם; גָּלוּת בָּאָה לָעוֹלָם – עַל עוֹבְדֵי עֲבוֹדָה זָרָה,

---

economic hardship, but no such justification could be advanced for a refusal to give *challah*. Only a callous rebellion against the Torah could prompt a public decision that *challah*-giving is no longer necessary. Such brazenness elicits a wrathful response — a famine that devastates society.

מִיתוֹת הָאֲמוּרוֹת בַּתּוֹרָה שֶׁלֹּא נִמְסְרוּ לְבֵית דִּין ***Death penalties prescribed by the Torah that were not carried out by the court***

Mishnah 11 PLAGUES AND EPIDEMICS OCCUR AS A RESULT OF SYMPATHY to criminals and not to victims, of a faulty judicial system, of a tolerance of all types of wrongdoing in society. Plagues are indiscriminate in their choice of victims, as the Talmud (*Bava Kamma* 60a) states, "Once permission is granted to the destroyer to destroy, there is no distinction between the guilty and the innocent." It is the apathy of society; its unwillingness to distinguish between right and wrong, between the criminal and the victim; the complacent moral relativism that makes everyone equal, the terrorist and the innocent victim, that brings about an indiscriminate type of punishment — plagues and epidemics that sweep away all without apparent rhyme or reason.

פֵּרוֹת שְׁבִיעִית ***Fruits of the Sabbatical year***

THE FRUITS OF THE *SHEMITTAH*/SABBATICAL YEAR HAVE A DEGREE OF holiness, and certain rules of halachah govern their use and consumption. Above all else, the Sabbatical year reminds us that we are not the owners, but only the temporary trustees of what we call "ours." By disregarding the laws and concept of *Shemittah,* society invites a strong reminder that God controls the world; plagues and epidemics are a stark reminder that man is powerless against His will. Learning the lesson of *Shemittah* allows us to be spared more painful demonstrations of God's dominion.

חֶרֶב ***The sword [of war]***

WAR IS SEEMINGLY OMNIPRESENT IN HUMAN SOCIETY. EVEN THOUGH ALL of mankind pays lip service to the ideal of peace, times of peace have been few and far between in human history. To have peace within a society and between different nations and societies, there must exist a system of law and judgment that is fair, efficient, unbiased, and effective. Without such a system, the seeds of strife can always grow and flourish, eventually leading to violence and murder. Corrupting the judicial system is the most serious of societal crimes.

11. (d) Pestilence comes to the world for death penalties prescribed by the Torah that were not carried out by the court, and for [illegal use of] fruits of the Sabbatical year; (e) the sword [of war] comes to the world for the delay of justice, for the perversion of justice, and for rendering decisions contrary to the halachah; (f) wild beasts come upon the world for vain oaths and for desecration of God's Name; (g) exile comes to the world for idolatry,

---

Delaying judgment and retribution, twisting the law to make it inequitable, deciding matters of Jewish law incorrectly and politically, either through malice or ignorance — all undermine the trust in justice that is the bedrock of a peaceful society. Judaism stresses the importance of judges, rabbis, and leaders who are trustworthy, industrious and unbiased to all. Without such people and their influence, we will always face struggle and war, the sword and violence, both from within our community and from our enemies without.

חַיָּה רָעָה בָּאָה לָעוֹלָם
Wild beasts come upon the world

THE PUNISHMENT OF WILD ANIMALS ATTACKING INNOCENT HUMANS CAN be understood, as much of Avos can, both literally and figuratively. Most of us never expect to confront a wild animal in our lifetime, but some people behave like wild animals and, unfortunately, we will certainly encounter them at one time or another. Our roads and streets are filled with "wild animals" that exhibit road rage, and tens of thousands of people are killed every year because of them. There are muggers and addicts that kill and maim, and rational people would agree that terrorists, suicide bombers and those who dispatch them are wild animals of the worst sort.

Rebellion against God, swearing falsely in His Name, and defaming Him and the Torah and the people of Israel because of greed and callousness, unlooses wild forces within society. A wild animal, in its human form, is always an angry individual. A true servant of God learns to conquer, or at least control, anger, and to overcome greed and cupidity. Swearing falsely in God's Name and other acts of desecrating God's Name almost always result from uncontrolled greed and/or unchecked anger. These faults blind us to the consequences of such behavior and assure us that we will get away with our misdeeds. The wild animal among us serves to remind us that such misplaced optimism can be fatal in the long run.

גָּלוּת בָּאָה לָעוֹלָם
Exile comes to the world

FINALLY, EXILE IS A RESULT OF THE PUBLIC VIOLATION OF THE THREE fundamental principles of Judaism — monotheism, the sanctity of life, and moral sexual conduct. These concepts are so dear to Judaism that only regarding them does the Torah demand that these principles be upheld even

וְעַל גִּלּוּי עֲרָיוֹת, וְעַל שְׁפִיכוּת דָּמִים, וְעַל שְׁמִטַּת הָאָרֶץ.

[יב] **בְּאַרְבָּעָה** פְּרָקִים הַדֶּבֶר מִתְרַבֶּה: בָּרְבִיעִית, וּבַשְּׁבִיעִית, וּבְמוֹצָאֵי שְׁבִיעִית, וּבְמוֹצָאֵי הֶחָג שֶׁבְּכָל שָׁנָה וְשָׁנָה. בָּרְבִיעִית, מִפְּנֵי מַעְשַׂר עָנִי שֶׁבַּשְּׁלִישִׁית; בַּשְּׁבִיעִית, מִפְּנֵי מַעְשַׂר עָנִי שֶׁבַּשִּׁשִּׁית; בְּמוֹצָאֵי שְׁבִיעִית, מִפְּנֵי פֵּרוֹת שְׁבִיעִית; בְּמוֹצָאֵי הֶחָג שֶׁבְּכָל שָׁנָה וְשָׁנָה, מִפְּנֵי גֶּזֶל מַתְּנוֹת עֲנִיִּים.

---

at the cost of our own lives. The mishnah here lists the sins which caused the First Temple to be destroyed and the Babylonian exile to occur.

The Midrash states that the seventy-year Babylonian exile was in punishment for the seventy *Shemittah* years that were not observed in the First Temple Era. However, the almost two-millennia exile of Israel after the destruction of the Second Temple stems from the sin of baseless hatred and dissension within Jewish society. Why is this sin not mentioned in this mishnah? There are many reasons advanced in the commentaries. One simple reason is that much of Avos is *Mishnah Rishonah,* the early notations of the laws that were compiled in private notebooks before the destruction of the Second Temple, beginning centuries before Rabbi Yehudah HaNasi redacted the Mishnah for public study. There are many places where he quoted the *Mishnah Rishonah* verbatim, and this may be such a case, especially in a mishnah like ours where the author is not named.

From the severity of the sins described here, it is reasonable to see exile as the worst of all punishments. The words of the Baal Shem Tov on exile ring constantly in my ears: "Exile is forgetting." There is no worse punishment in human life than forgetting — forgetting family, home, tradition, God Himself. Living as I do in Israel, I realize all of the shortcomings that still exist in our little state. But living here does not allow one, no matter how secular and rebellious that person is, the luxury of forgetting that one is a Jew. We have to fight the disease of exile — forgetting — with tenacity, creativity, and wisdom. The punishment of exile is truly a cruel one.

Mishnah 12 THE NUMBERS IN THE MISHNAH NOW CHANGE TO FOUR, which is also a favorite number in Jewish tradition. There are the four sons of the Pesach Seder, the four questions, the four cups of wine, and the four matriarchs.

for immorality, for bloodshed, and for working the earth during the Sabbatical year.

12. At four periods [of the seven-year Sabbatical cycle] pestilence increases: in the fourth year, in the seventh year, in the year following the Sabbatical year, and annually at the conclusion of the [Succos] festival. In the fourth year [of the *Shemittah* cycle] for [neglecting] the tithe of the poor in the third; in the seventh year for [neglecting] the tithe of the poor in the sixth; [immediately] following the Sabbatical year for [violating the laws of] the Sabbatical produce; annually, at the conclusion of the festival [of Succos], for robbing the poor of their gifts.

בְּאַרְבָּעָה פְרָקִים הַדֶּבֶר מִתְרַבֶּה
At four periods . . . pestilence increases

THOUGH THE NUMBER HAS CHANGED, THE THEME OF THIS MISHNAH continues the ideas expressed in the previous one — that bad human behavior leads to bad natural occurrences. Thus after the cycle of the years of the various tithings — *maasros* — and after the *Shemittah* year, the Jews of Israel were particularly vulnerable to plagues and natural disasters. God promised that if Israel were to fulfill its charity obligations, it would be showered with innumerable blessings, and we read in the prophet Malachi (3:10) that God pleaded with Israel to "test" Him by living up to its obligations regarding tithes and charity. But there always is present in society an inclination to cut corners — if not even cheat — on obligations that require unselfishness. It is not easy to part with one's material wealth for purely altruistic causes and reasons.

❦ ❦ ❦

Whose dime?

The story is told about a young boy who was given two dimes by his mother. With one he was to buy himself a candy bar (you can tell this is an old story) and the other was to be placed in the synagogue's charity box. As he traipsed merrily along, playing with the coins, one of the dimes fell into the gutter and disappeared into the yawning mouth of the sewer catch basin. The boy thought for a moment, assessed the situation, raised his face heavenward and exclaimed: "Well, Lord, there went Your dime!"

❦ ❦ ❦

If we always think that it is God's dime that can be dispensed with, we invite the problems and plagues mentioned in this mishnah into our society and very being. There are times — the four times mentioned here — when we are particularly vulnerable to such plagues. Nowadays, in the absence of the Temple and full Jewish settlement and return to the Land of Israel, these four times are no longer as relevant, but this does not excuse us from our obligations

[יג] **אַרְבַּע** מִדּוֹת בָּאָדָם. הָאוֹמֵר: „שֶׁלִּי שֶׁלִּי וְשֶׁלְּךָ שֶׁלָּךְ,״ זוֹ מִדָּה בֵינוֹנִית, וְיֵשׁ אוֹמְרִים: זוֹ מִדַּת סְדוֹם; „שֶׁלִּי שֶׁלָּךְ וְשֶׁלְּךָ שֶׁלִּי,״ עַם הָאָרֶץ; „שֶׁלִּי שֶׁלָּךְ וְשֶׁלְּךָ שֶׁלָּךְ,״ חָסִיד; „שֶׁלְּךָ שֶׁלִּי וְשֶׁלִּי שֶׁלִּי,״ רָשָׁע.

---

to the poor. In fact, this probably makes us vulnerable now at all times of the year if we do not live up to our obligations to charities and to those who are less fortunate than we.

אַרְבַּע מִדּוֹת בָּאָדָם
There are four character types among people

Mishnah 13 IT IS INTERESTING THAT THE MISHNAH DID NOT STATE that there are four different types of *people*, but rather that there are four different inclinations of *character* and behavior. I think that we can all agree that one time or another, a person reflects all of these differing, even contradictory, character traits within himself. We are very complex beings and consistency is a very difficult trait to maintain. Sometimes we are noble, pious, and generous, and sometimes we are evil, niggardly, and cruel. These four different natures are therefore to be found within all of us, constantly struggling for our attention and for control of our actual behavior.

שֶׁלִּי שֶׁלִּי וְשֶׁלְּךָ שֶׁלָּךְ
My [property] is mine and yours is yours

MOST PEOPLE SUBSCRIBE TO THIS PHILOSOPHY, AND ON THE SURFACE IT appears to be a most logical and fair view of life. By agreeing that what is yours is yours, one avoids being a thief and a jealous person, and the mishnah considers it to be an average and acceptable character trait. However, the mishnah gives a second opinion that this trait is a bad one, a characteristic of the extraordinarily wicked city of Sodom. The "Sodom" reason for this opinion is based on the belief that what is mine is mine. In reality, nothing in this world is really mine. People should look at themselves as God's surrogates, and view everything as entrusted to them to use wisely and promote the general good. Sodom was the symbol of "mine" in the world. That city legislated against helping others, blamed the poor and the stranger for their lot in life, and degenerated into a viciously cruel society. If people really believe that "mine is mine," then there is an everpresent danger of wickedness, exploitation, and serfdom. This opinion warns us that a selfish society, though it may see itself as being legally justified and normal, is in reality a great threat to its very own existence.

שֶׁלִּי שֶׁלָּךְ וְשֶׁלְּךָ שֶׁלִּי
Mine is yours and yours is mine

THERE IS A CONCEPT OF COMMUNAL PROPERTY, WHICH WAS VERY POPULAR in the 19th and 20th centuries. "What is mine is yours and what is yours is mine" was extolled as being the wave of the future and the solution to mankind's woes. Marxism was the philosophical and political distillation of this unnatural pro-

13. There are four character types among people: (a) One who says, "My [property] is mine, and yours is yours" is an average character type, but some say this is characteristic of Sodom; (b) "Mine is yours, and yours is mine" is an unlearned person; (c) "Mine is yours, and yours is yours" is scrupulously pious; (d) "Yours is mine, and mine is mine" is wicked.

---

gram of economics and human behavior. When carried to the extreme, this program resulted in monstrous states of terror, inefficiency, and human sadness and privation. Though unchecked exploitative *laissez faire* capitalism results in the evils of Sodom, Marxist theory, which ignores human nature and economic reality, results in the pursuit of an unattainable utopia that eventually is held up to ridicule and shame. The collapse of Communism in the world and the slow but steady demise of the old kibbutz collectives in Israel indicate the ignorance of human behavior inherent in a "mine is yours and yours is mine" society. Utopian schemes are always initially popular; everyone longs for a system that can give us a better world. But disregarding the truth that human beings treasure private property is not a sign of wisdom or progress. It leads to a fool's paradise which soon turns into a living hell.

שֶׁלִּי שֶׁלָּךְ וְשֶׁלְּךָ שֶׁלָּךְ
Mine is yours and yours is yours

THIS PHILOSOPHY REPRESENTS THE NOBILITY OF HUMAN CHARACTER AND pious behavior. To look out for the needs of others and share the gifts that the Lord has granted us has been a hallmark of Jewish life from the time of our father Abraham. But from him we also learned the great lesson in life to always be a giver and never a taker. "Not a thread or a shoelace do I want from you!" said Abraham to the king of Sodom, who wished to reward the Patriarch for saving Sodom from a crushing military defeat. What is yours is yours, and I do not want to depend on others for financial help. There is no greater achievement in life than making one's own way independently. The Talmud is replete with admonitions against being a taker. "Make your Sabbath [table] look like a weekday one, and do not seek the help of other human beings" (*Shabbos* 118a). "Rather skin hides in the public marketplace and do not say that I am entitled to donations because I am a great scholar" (*Pesachim* 113a). The long and bitter exile of Israel, with its attendant grinding poverty, has dulled these sensitivities somewhat, but our mishnah clearly points the way to piety: to share with others and never to take for oneself.

שֶׁלְּךָ שֶׁלִּי וְשֶׁלִּי שֶׁלִּי
Yours is mine and mine is mine

THE CULMINATION OF ALL EVIL IS A PURELY SELFISH, NARCISSISTIC NATURE. Everything is mine, even what does not legally or morally belong to me. Tyrants, dictators, murderers, and terrorists are all cursed with this nature and worldview. Though there may be surface justification for such behavior in

[יד] **אַרְבַּע** מִדּוֹת בְּדֵעוֹת: נוֹחַ לִכְעוֹס וְנוֹחַ לִרְצוֹת, יָצָא שְׂכָרוֹ בְּהֶפְסֵדוֹ; קָשֶׁה לִכְעוֹס וְקָשֶׁה לִרְצוֹת, יָצָא הֶפְסֵדוֹ בִשְׂכָרוֹ; קָשֶׁה לִכְעוֹס וְנוֹחַ לִרְצוֹת, חָסִיד; נוֹחַ לִכְעוֹס וְקָשֶׁה לִרְצוֹת, רָשָׁע.

[טו] **אַרְבַּע** מִדּוֹת בְּתַלְמִידִים: מָהִיר לִשְׁמוֹעַ וּמָהִיר לְאַבֵּד, יָצָא שְׂכָרוֹ בְּהֶפְסֵדוֹ;

---

ideological and national terms, the truth is that, at bottom, such behavior stems from pure selfishness and the inability and/or refusal to recognize the rights, lives, and property of others. This trait is even worse than the attitude of Sodom, which refuses to help others with its own wealth, but nevertheless recognizes the right of others to their own property. The truly evil person recognizes no such rights at all. Unrestrained selfishness eventually leads to violence and tragedy.

אַרְבַּע מִדּוֹת בְּדֵעוֹת
There are four types of temperament

Mishnah 14 AS THE DEFINING PERSONALITY TRAITS OF A PERSON, THE mishnah identifies his reaction to adversity and handling of anger. In previous chapters we have seen how strongly the rabbis felt that anger is the one trait that must be completely tamed, for otherwise life is not worth living. Rage saps all joy out of life and diminishes any satisfaction in its accomplishments.

קָשֶׁה לִכְעוֹס וְנוֹחַ לִרְצוֹת, חָסִיד
One who is hard to anger and easy to pacify is pious

A PERSON WHO IS DIFFICULT TO PROVOKE, WHO CAN HOLD THE DEMON of temper in check, and even if momentarily angered recovers good spirits and tolerance very quickly, is a truly blessed individual. A combination of a wise attitude toward life and training from earliest youth in self-control can achieve much toward helping one to become such a blessed person. There is an element of holiness in a person who controls his anger, and such a person is therefore called *chassid,* someone of spiritual piety. People who are slow to anger and quick to forgive imitate the traits of our Creator and thus are truly pious.

Earlier, the mishnah lists two intermediate personality traits regarding anger. One is someone who is slow to anger but also slow to give it up; and the other is the trait of being quick to anger, but getting over it just as quickly. But whatever positive element can be found in either of these two intermediate traits is nullified by the negative part of the trait. Usually, people who cannot easily let go of their anger feel that the world somehow owes them something

14. There are four types of temperament: (a) One who is angered easily and pacified easily, his gain is offset by his loss; (b) one who is hard to anger and hard to pacify, his loss is offset by his gain; (c) one who is hard to anger and easy to pacify is pious; (d) one who is easily angered and hard to pacify is wicked.

15. There are four types of students: (a) One who grasps quickly and forgets quickly, his gain is offset by his loss;

---

and they are in a constant state of subdued but gnawing frustration. People who are quick to anger are childish in their attitude toward life.

נוֹחַ לִכְעוֹס וְקָשֶׁה לִרְצוֹת, רָשָׁע ***One who is easily angered and hard to pacify is wicked***

THE WORST OF ALL POSSIBLE TRAITS — IT IS TRULY A CURSE — IS A PERSON who is quick to anger and slow to be pacified. Angry people are hard to live with. They inflict a great deal of harm on themselves and on those close to them. They usually are guilty of verbal abuse, if not worse. A home of quick-tempered people is a dangerous and volatile place in which to live. A person of such vile temper is called a *rasha*, an evil person. The rabbis never make excuses for bad and uncivil behavior.

אַרְבַּע מִדּוֹת בְּתַלְמִידִים ***There are four types of students***

Mishnah 15 TRUE GENIUSES ARE USUALLY BLESSED WITH THE TWIN traits of a very quick mind that readily grasps what is being taught or read and a strong retentive memory. Such a combination of traits is truly a blessed gift from the Creator. When a person has one of these two gifts but not the other one, the negative aspect of the missing skill is mitigated by the other skill. The question left unanswered by the mishnah is whether either of these traits can be acquired or developed, or is it all a matter of genetic structure.

In the yeshivah world, it has long been axiomatic that diligence in study, true mental effort, intense focus and concentration on Torah knowledge to the exclusion of all else, will eventually allow one to rise to Torah scholarship and even greatness. There is no doubt that effort, constant review of the subject matter, and acquired experience in good study methods and habits certainly play a vital role in the development of intellect and the acquisition of knowledge. Diligence is worth many points on the IQ scale. In combination with a naturally quick mind and a good memory, the above traits of diligence and good study habits are the basis for the achievements of great Torah scholars; but the honor roll of scholars is well peppered with diligent students who far surpassed expectations.

The reason why some are gifted and others are sub-par intellectually is a

קָשֶׁה לִשְׁמוֹעַ וְקָשֶׁה לְאַבֵּד, יָצָא הֶפְסֵדוֹ בִּשְׂכָרוֹ; מָהִיר לִשְׁמוֹעַ וְקָשֶׁה לְאַבֵּד, זֶה חֵלֶק טוֹב; קָשֶׁה לִשְׁמוֹעַ וּמָהִיר לְאַבֵּד, זֶה חֵלֶק רָע.

[טז] **אַרְבַּע** מִדּוֹת בְּנוֹתְנֵי צְדָקָה: הָרוֹצֶה שֶׁיִּתֵּן וְלֹא יִתְּנוּ אֲחֵרִים, עֵינוֹ רָעָה בְּשֶׁל אֲחֵרִים; יִתְּנוּ אֲחֵרִים וְהוּא לֹא יִתֵּן, עֵינוֹ רָעָה בְּשֶׁלּוֹ; יִתֵּן וְיִתְּנוּ אֲחֵרִים, חָסִיד; לֹא יִתֵּן וְלֹא יִתְּנוּ אֲחֵרִים, רָשָׁע.

---

mystery that is beyond our ability to understand. Only God understands why He apportions intellectual gifts as He does. It is axiomatic, however, that He expects people to utilize whatever capacity He has given them. In the expression of the sages, "The Holy one, Blessed is He, counts not pages, but hours." He expects no more than one is capable of giving, nor does he accept less.

What should be clear is that different methods and orders of curriculum are necessary for different types of students. In education and schools, in spite of all protestations to the contrary, one size does not fit all.

אַרְבַּע מִדּוֹת בְּנוֹתְנֵי צְדָקָה ***There are four types of donors to charity***

Mishnah 16 GIVING CHARITY IS A JEWISH TRAIT, INHERITED FROM OUR father Abraham, and the concept of charity and goodness toward others is a constant theme of Avos. But there are many conflicting emotions present in charity-giving. In effect, the giving of charity and one's attitude toward it is a major test of personality and faith.

הָרוֹצֶה שֶׁיִּתֵּן וְלֹא יִתְּנוּ אֲחֵרִים ***One who wishes to give himself but wants others not to give***

THERE ARE PEOPLE WHO WANT THE WHOLE CREDIT FOR THEMSELVES AND do not allow others to share in the project. Though their zeal for charity is commendable, they are inconsiderate of others by excluding them from participation in the *mitzvah*. As someone who has raised funds my entire life for charitable and educational causes, I have often dreamt of finding the one individual who would simplify my task by single-handedly giving me the large sum of money needed for whatever project I was involved in. The Lord always helped me in that I never found such a person. I had to visit many people and made new friends and acquaintances — and many people were privileged to share in the worthy project of helping others and strengthening Torah learning.

יִתְּנוּ אֲחֵרִים וְהוּא לֹא יִתֵּן ***That others should give but that he should not give***

THERE IS A TYPE OF PERSON WHO DOES NOT GIVE ANY MONEY HIMSELF, but refers the needy to others who will. I have always had a sneaking resentment toward such conduct. This person has a "bad eye" — he begrudges *himself*. His help in referring the collector to others may be valuable

(b) one who grasps slowly and forgets slowly, his loss is offset by his gain; (c) one who grasps quickly and forgets slowly, this is a good portion; (d) one who grasps slowly and forgets quickly, this is a bad portion.

16. There are four types of donors to charity: (a) One who wishes to give himself but wants others not to give, he begrudges others; (b) that others should give but that he should not give, he begrudges himself; (c) that he should give and that others should give is saintly; (d) that he should not give and that others should not give is wicked.

---

and successful, but in effect it eases his conscience and rationalizes his own lack of generosity. Eventually such a person becomes a habitual non-giver. Just as giving charity is a matter of training and consistency, so is not giving. Many times in my rabbinic career has a poor man come to me for help because someone else excused himself from giving by saying, "Go see the rabbi. He will take care of you." Such people truly begrudge themselves the opportunity for character improvement and the pleasure of goodness.

❦ ❦ ❦

Who will help?

People often confuse their true roles in charity-giving. I once visited a very wealthy man for whom I had done many favors. I thought that he owed me a great deal in return, and I asked him for a substantial donation for my yeshivah. The man wrote out a check and handed it to me. In my opinion the amount was at least one if not two zeroes short. My disappointment must have been reflected on my face. The man looked at me and said: "Cheer up. Rabbi, God will help." I replied: "That is my speech — God will help — not yours. Your task is to give generously!"

❦ ❦ ❦

יִתֵּן וְיִתְּנוּ אֲחֵרִים
That he should give and that others should give

PEOPLE WHO ARE THEMSELVES GIVERS ARE ENTITLED TO REFER TO OTHERS so that they may also give. In fact, that is the highest and healthiest form of charitable giving. It is a badge of piety to give and include others in the giving process as well.

לֹא יִתֵּן וְלֹא יִתְּנוּ אֲחֵרִים
That he should not give and that others should not give

THE WORST OF ALL TRAITS IS NOT TO GIVE CHARITY AND TO DISCOURAGE others from giving. This is a conscience-salving mechanism, for if no one gives then the miser is no longer perceived as being especially miserly. But not giving charity "on principle" and asking others to also adhere to that wicked principle is shameful and evil behavior.

[יז] **אַרְבַּע** מִדּוֹת בְּהוֹלְכֵי בֵית הַמִּדְרָשׁ: הוֹלֵךְ וְאֵינוֹ עוֹשֶׂה, שְׂכַר הֲלִיכָה בְּיָדוֹ; עוֹשֶׂה וְאֵינוֹ הוֹלֵךְ, שְׂכַר מַעֲשֶׂה בְּיָדוֹ; הוֹלֵךְ וְעוֹשֶׂה, חָסִיד; לֹא הוֹלֵךְ וְלֹא עוֹשֶׂה, רָשָׁע.

[יח] **אַרְבַּע** מִדּוֹת בְּיוֹשְׁבִים לִפְנֵי חֲכָמִים: סְפוֹג, וּמַשְׁפֵּךְ, מְשַׁמֶּרֶת, וְנָפָה.

הוֹלֵךְ וְאֵינוֹ עוֹשֶׂה ***One who goes but does not practice***

Mishnah 17 IN THE TIME OF THE MISHNAH, WHEN THE ORAL LAW WAS still transmitted from teacher to student, and books were not yet available, the focal place of Torah learning was the *beis midrash* — the public study hall where Torah lectures and discussion groups were centered. There may have been people who attended the study hall but did not practice its teachings or reflect its knowledge in their everyday life and behavior. Nevertheless, even they benefited by going to the *beis midrash* and attending its sessions. The power of regular Torah study is such that it subconsciously sinks into a person's psyche and improves him spiritually, even if it appears imperceptible. There is reward, therefore, for simply "going to the *beis midrash.*"

In popular Jewish usage, the phrase *s'char halichah,* reward for going, is applied to all efforts to attend worthwhile gatherings and/or Torah lectures or to embark on worthwhile endeavors, even if they are never seen through to fruition or even if one sleeps through the entire lecture or meeting. I personally know people who attend lectures given by great Torah scholars here in Jerusalem and sleep through the entire proceedings, but bring their tape recorder along to capture the lecture. I once asked one of these people why he bothers to attend the lecture himself when he could just have the lecture recorded by a friend. (As you may know, I am a great protagonist of recorded tape lectures.) He replied that he wanted to have the reward of *s'char halichah* — the compensation for at least "just going" — something that could not be achieved by sending a tape recorder.

עוֹשֶׂה וְאֵינוֹ הוֹלֵךְ ***One who practices but does not go***

THERE ARE THOSE WHO ESCHEW ATTENDING THE *BEIS MIDRASH,* BUT nevertheless observe the commandments and attempt to raise themselves spiritually in the privacy of their homes. Though they are certainly rewarded for their efforts and piety, they cheat themselves of the spirit, camaraderie, and inspiration that only a public study hall can provide.

הוֹלֵךְ וְעוֹשֶׂה ***One who goes and practices***

THIS IS THE IDEAL SITUATION — TO ATTEND THE STUDY HALL REGULARLY and incorporate the lessons learned and the inspiration acquired into one's

17. There are four types of people who go to the study hall. (a) One who goes but does not practice [what he learned] has the reward for going; (b) one who practices but does not go has the reward for practicing; (c) one who goes and practices is pious; (d) one who does not go and does not practice is wicked.

18. There are four types among students who sit before the sages: a sponge, a funnel, a strainer, and a sieve —

---

daily behavior and human actions. One who does so is, or will surely become, a *chassid*, a pious individual who strives for self-improvement. The converse — not attending and not observing the commandments or attempting to gain spiritual growth — is not viewed as mere laziness, but as evil. Life is a ladder with no stationary rungs. Either we try to climb higher or we inevitably slip lower. Thus "not going" and "not practicing" inexorably lead to bad behavior and evil attitudes.

אַרְבַּע מִדּוֹת בְּיוֹשְׁבִים לִפְנֵי חֲכָמִים
There are four types among students who sit before the sages

Mishnah 18 STUDENTS ARE IMPRESSED BY THEIR TEACHERS, ESPECIally those who are charismatic, intellectual masters. There are different reactions to such people of authority. There are students who, like a sponge, absorb everything, not only the subject being taught, but even the mannerisms of the teacher. Others are like a funnel, who absorb nothing from their classroom experience. Still others are like a strainer that collects only the dregs of the wine and lets the precious liquid itself slip through. I am well acquainted with students who copied all the externals of their teacher — the angle of the head and the hat, the mannerisms, the idioms, etc. — but retained little of the knowledge that he was trying to impart to them. Adolescents tend to imitate such meaningless characteristics, but such unconscious mimicry can be very counterproductive to personality development and true inner spiritual growth.

מְשַׁמֶּרֶת, וְנָפָה
A strainer, and a sieve

BEING LIKE A STRAINER — RETAINING WHAT IS BAD AND REJECTING WHAT is good — is the worst of all possible options for a student, even worse than being a funnel. Rather, one should strive to be like a sieve that retains the finest flour and lets the dust fall away. One should separate the knowledge to be gained from a great teacher from the idiosyncrasies that such a person may have. The wise student is able to do so. However, it is almost to be expected that a devoted student will imitate the teacher in every possible way. Here again, the oft-repeated Torah stress on balance is most applicable. Well-balanced people who sit at the feet of great scholars and teachers are sieves and not funnels, strainers or even sponges.

סְפוֹג, שֶׁהוּא סוֹפֵג אֶת הַכֹּל; וּמַשְׁפֵּךְ, שֶׁמַּכְנִיס בְּזוֹ וּמוֹצִיא בְזוֹ; מְשַׁמֶּרֶת, שֶׁמּוֹצִיאָה אֶת הַיַּיִן וְקוֹלֶטֶת אֶת הַשְּׁמָרִים; וְנָפָה, שֶׁמּוֹצִיאָה אֶת הַקֶּמַח וְקוֹלֶטֶת אֶת הַסֹּלֶת.

[יט] **כָּל** אַהֲבָה שֶׁהִיא תְלוּיָה בְדָבָר, בָּטֵל דָּבָר, בְּטֵלָה אַהֲבָה; וְשֶׁאֵינָהּ תְּלוּיָה בְדָבָר, אֵינָהּ בְּטֵלָה לְעוֹלָם. אֵיזוֹ הִיא אַהֲבָה שֶׁהִיא תְלוּיָה בְדָבָר? זוֹ אַהֲבַת אַמְנוֹן וְתָמָר. וְשֶׁאֵינָהּ תְּלוּיָה בְדָבָר? זוֹ אַהֲבַת דָּוִד וִיהוֹנָתָן.

[כ] **כָּל** מַחֲלֹקֶת שֶׁהִיא לְשֵׁם שָׁמַיִם, סוֹפָהּ לְהִתְקַיֵּם; וְשֶׁאֵינָהּ לְשֵׁם שָׁמַיִם, אֵין סוֹפָהּ לְהִתְקַיֵּם.

כָּל אַהֲבָה שֶׁהִיא תְלוּיָה בְדָבָר
Any love that depends on a specific cause

Mishnah 19 THE MISHNAH SPEAKS OF TWO DIFFERENT FORMS OF LOVE. The first is a love that is purely dependent on physical attraction, economic advantage, or some other self-interest. The feeling seems to be directed at a person, but what the lover truly craves is pleasure, wealth, or position. The object of the "love" is really being exploited for the money, power, etc. that the "beloved" one allegedly represents. The classic example of such bogus love is Amnon's infatuation with Tamar. It was based purely on lust (see *II Samuel* Ch. 13). When the passion wanes, as it must in life, then the love that had been so obsessive and urgent suddenly disappears. True love is really a spiritual state of being. If it is reduced to purely physical, monetary or other mundane considerations, no matter how attractive they may seem to be, then it loses its spirituality. It is no longer love, but something else entirely.

וְשֶׁאֵינָהּ תְּלוּיָה בְדָבָר, אֵינָהּ בְּטֵלָה לְעוֹלָם
But if it does not depend on a specific cause, it will never cease

TRUE LOVE IS NOT DEPENDENT ON EXTERNAL CIRCUMSTANCES AND changing times. It is not infatuation, nor is it simply physical desire. It is a commitment, a broadening of one's own perspective and soul to include another human being, an emotion that when present stands the test of time. King Solomon in *Song of Songs* (8:7) states that "Great waters cannot extinguish [the flame of] love." True love speaks of loyalty and concern, character development and spiritual growth. Since human beings long for such a relationship, it is no wonder that the literature of the world is replete with stories about the pursuit of true love. The mishnah establishes the line of

(a) a sponge, which absorbs everything; (b) a funnel, which lets in from one and lets out from the other; (c) a strainer, which lets the wine flow through and retains the sediment; (d) and a sieve, which allows the flour dust to pass through and retains the fine flour.

19. Any love that depends on a specific cause, when that cause is gone, the love is gone; but if it does not depend on a specific cause, it will never cease. What sort of love depended on a specific cause? — the love of Amnon for Tamar. And what did not depend upon a specific cause? — the love of David and Jonathan.

20. Any dispute that is for the sake of Heaven will have a constructive outcome; but one that is not for the sake of Heaven will not have a constructive outcome. What

---

demarcation that separates true love from false imitations of that emotion. David and Jonathan loved each other even when their self-interests should have militated to make them rivals, if not enemies. There were no other considerations present in their relationship except their respect for and loyalty to each other at all occasions.

The basis of Judaism is love. Not ephemeral and unreal superhuman love as preached by other faiths, but the true and hard love that must be constantly cultivated by faith, loyalty and good and kind behavior, as exemplified in the demands of Judaism regarding marriage, family, love of Torah and love of the Creator. It is no coincidence that the Lord commands us to love "the Lord your God." Attaining such a love allows one to be freed of the bonds of shrewd considerations and outside forces that often sour relationships and turn them into the sickness of the ruined lives of Amnon and Tamar.

כָּל מַחֲלֹקֶת שֶׁהִיא לְשֵׁם שָׁמַיִם
Any dispute that is for the sake of Heaven

Mishnah 20 HUMAN BEINGS DO NOT ALWAYS AGREE WITH EACH other, whether the matters are petty or important. Jews are certainly a contentious lot, as proven by our history, both past and current, yet some disagreements are healthy. Disputes that clarify issues, establish halachah, create positive discussion, and are conducted civilly — even lovingly — are of great benefit to Israel. Such disputes do not involve attacks on personalities, discourteous behavior, personal gain or honor. They have a higher motive. They are called disputes that are for the sake of heaven, and their purpose is for truth and right to prevail.

אֵיזוֹ הִיא מַחֲלֹקֶת שֶׁהִיא לְשֵׁם שָׁמַיִם? זוֹ מַחֲלֹקֶת הִלֵּל וְשַׁמַּאי. וְשֶׁאֵינָהּ לְשֵׁם שָׁמַיִם? זוֹ מַחֲלֹקֶת קֹרַח וְכָל עֲדָתוֹ.

[כא] **כָּל** הַמְזַכֶּה אֶת הָרַבִּים, אֵין חֵטְא בָּא עַל יָדוֹ;

מַחֲלֹקֶת הִלֵּל וְשַׁמַּאי
The dispute between Hillel and Shammai

AS AN EXAMPLE OF SUCH A POSITIVE DISPUTE, THE MISHNAH CITES THE debates between the House of Hillel and the House of Shammai, which are recorded throughout the Mishnah and the Talmud. Although these great academies held firm opinions about hundreds of matters over which they disagreed, they were allies, not personal adversaries; all of them were working "for the sake of heaven." When scholarship and events proved one of the opinions to be more correct, the other school was ready to retract its opposition. The rabbis could confidently say, therefore, that both sides of the dispute represent the living God of Israel. Because of this attitude of mutual respect — even though the halachah long ago decided which opinion to follow — the two opinions, often diametrically opposed to one another, march in tandem throughout the history of Torah scholarship. Devoid of any personal biases and prejudices, the disputes of Hillel and Shammai, and of their disciples live on as the paradigm of positive debate within Torah knowledge and Jewish life.

Despite their example, to achieve the level of *l'sheim Shamayim* [for the sake of Heaven] in disputation is a difficult task. Rabbi Yisrael Lipkin of Salant stated the problem pithily: "One must always be certain that one's *l'sheim Shamayim* is *l'sheim Shamayim";* one may even be convinced that one is acting for the sake of heaven, when in reality one's reactions are colored by personal interests or resentments. Personal motives are often disguised and wrapped in the mantle of seeming religious piety.

זוֹ מַחֲלֹקֶת קֹרַח וְכָל עֲדָתוֹ
The dispute of Korach and his entire company

A PRIME EXAMPLE OF A DISPUTE THAT LEAVES NO LASTING BENEFIT, ONLY bitter feelings and tragic consequences, is the dispute mounted by Korach and his followers against Moses (see *Numbers* 16-17). Intoxicated by his wealth, jealous of Moses's stature and position, Korach rallies the malcontents and naysayers of the generation of the Sinai desert to his side and confronts Moses and Aaron in open rebellion against their God-given authority. Korach is driven by base motives — jealousy, illusions of grandeur, lust for power, and personal animosities. These character weaknesses blind him to the damage that his behavior will bring to Israel and to the fatal consequences of his actions to himself and his family. There is no lasting good to this type of dispute. It will always remain an example of shameful behavior and terrible judgment.

sort of dispute was for the sake of Heaven? — the dispute between Hillel and Shammai. And which was not for the sake of Heaven? — the dispute of Korach and his entire company.

21. Whoever influences the masses to become meritorious shall not be the cause of sin; but one who influences

---

❧ ❧ ❧

Degrees of right

My father taught me in the name of his great teacher and mentor, Rabbi Shimon Shkop, an insight into this dispute. The Torah tells us "there will never be such a dispute again in Israel as the dispute of Korach against Moses" (Numbers 17:5). But, unfortunately, there have been many bitter disputes within the Jewish people since then. The meaning, therefore, is that the dispute against Moses was the only one in Jewish history where one side, that of Moses, was 100 percent correct and innocent and the other side, that of Korach, was 100 percent wrong and unjustified. This dispute does not have a lasting outcome, for no lesson remains for later generations to benefit from. In all other later disputes in communal Jewish life, conducted within the framework of Torah faith and tradition, the ratio of 100 to zero was never again present. This is a good lesson to bear in mind when dealing with the pain of the numerous disputes that dot the Jewish communal landscape continually.

❧ ❧ ❧

כָּל הַמְזַכֶּה אֶת הָרַבִּים
Whoever influences the masses to become meritorious

Mishnah 21 SINCE THE PREVIOUS MISHNAH DISCUSSED THE GREATNESS of Moses, this mishnah continues in that vein to give us another appreciation of our beloved mentor and master instructor. Bringing public good to the many is the highest service a Jew can perform. The rewards for such altruistic behavior are immediate and far-reaching. Serving the public by bringing Torah to the masses is a firewall that protects the person from sin and temptation. Influencing the masses to adopt correct attitudes and behavior brings great merit to all concerned. Moses reached the pinnacle of human spiritual attainment and prophecy because he influenced the Jewish people, and through them the entire world, to strive for morality and Godliness in their lives.

Such merit is like compound interest; it builds upon itself. To the end of all time, Moses's merit is constantly increased by the good deeds that others do because of his teachings and holy example. Moses is remembered every day in Jewish life and his influence still pervades our people millennia after his death. Our civilization and spiritual progress is all due to him, so he is the beneficiary of all the good that characterizes Jewish life daily. We are all in Moses's debt, and we express our gratitude to him by following the Torah that is called *Toras Moshe*, the Torah of Moses. By so doing, we add merit to him

וְכָל הַמַּחֲטִיא אֶת הָרַבִּים, אֵין מַסְפִּיקִין בְּיָדוֹ לַעֲשׂוֹת תְּשׁוּבָה. מֹשֶׁה זָכָה וְזִכָּה אֶת הָרַבִּים, זְכוּת הָרַבִּים תָּלוּי בּוֹ, שֶׁנֶּאֱמַר: „צִדְקַת יהוה עָשָׂה, וּמִשְׁפָּטָיו עִם יִשְׂרָאֵל.” יָרָבְעָם בֶּן נְבָט חָטָא וְהֶחֱטִיא אֶת הָרַבִּים, חֵטְא הָרַבִּים תָּלוּי בּוֹ, שֶׁנֶּאֱמַר: „עַל חַטֹּאות יָרָבְעָם אֲשֶׁר חָטָא, וַאֲשֶׁר הֶחֱטִיא אֶת יִשְׂרָאֵל.”

[כב] **כָּל** מִי שֶׁיֵּשׁ בְּיָדוֹ שְׁלֹשָׁה דְבָרִים הַלָּלוּ, הוּא מִתַּלְמִידָיו שֶׁל אַבְרָהָם אָבִינוּ; וּשְׁלֹשָׁה דְבָרִים אֲחֵרִים, הוּא מִתַּלְמִידָיו שֶׁל בִּלְעָם הָרָשָׁע.

---

and to ourselves. So, too, should we also strive in our lives to be a positive and proactive influence for the public good. It will enhance our merit and create the conditions for immortality.

וְכָל הַמַּחֲטִיא אֶת הָרַבִּים
But one who influences the masses to sin

BEING A PUBLIC AND INFLUENTIAL SINNER, BRINGING NEGATIVITY AND falsehood into society, being an example of rejection of the Torah and its precepts, guarantees eternal damnation and heavenly disapproval. The sins of the many are assigned, as well, to the one who got the ball rolling, so to speak. After the death of King Solomon, Yarovam ben Nevat was the founding first king of the Northern Tribes of Israel, who broke away from the Davidic dynasty to form their own nation. Yarovam was an outstanding Torah scholar, a man of charisma and power and great influence. He was anointed as the king of Israel by no less a personage than the prophet Achiyah the Shilonite. Yet none of this stood Yarovam in good stead when, for personal reasons of pique and hubris, he led the Northern Kingdom down the terrible road of state-sponsored paganism. Jealous of the king of Judah and of the Temple being in Jerusalem under Judah's control, Yarovam constructed temples of idolatry in his kingdom to lull the masses into rebellion against God.

All of the many successors to Yarovam on the throne of the Northern Kingdom were also evil people, pagan worshipers, and idolaters. Yet, whenever their sins are mentioned in the Books of *Kings*, Yarovam's sin is also mentioned, over and over again. He sinned and caused others to sin, others whom he never knew and who lived centuries after his death. Such is the severity of judgment against one who influenced the public negatively and seduced them to sin. Even the later destruction of the Northern Kingdom that

the masses to sin will not be given the means to repent. Moses was meritorious and influenced the masses to be meritorious, so the merit of the masses was to his credit, as it is said: *Carrying out God's justice and His ordinances with Israel* (*Deuteronomy* 33:21). Yarovam ben Nevat sinned and caused the masses to sin, so the sin of the masses is charged against him, as it is said: *For the sins of Yarovam that he committed and that he caused the people of Israel to commit* (*I Kings* 15:30).

22. Whoever has the following three traits is among the disciples of our forefather Abraham; and [whoever has] three different traits is among the disciples of the evil Bilaam.

Yarovam originally founded hundreds of years earlier is seen as a direct result of his sins: "The sins of Yarovam that he committed and that he caused the people of Israel to commit." That stain is indelible.

This is the concept in the Torah of visiting the sins of the fathers on later generations, even to the fourth generation. If the children tragically keep on the evil road established by their father's example, the sins of the father are now still present and active within the children, and then their punishment becomes cumulative. In life, there are many exceptions to the general rule that evil begets evil and good begets good. But there is no doubt that evil parents, evil leaders and rulers, evil teachers and professors, all are guilty of creating generations of evil in human society. People should always ask themselves, "How will my behavior, speech, attitudes, and comportment influence my children, my grandchildren, my students, my employees, my constituents?" We are not only responsible for ourselves but we are held responsible, for better or worse, for many others as well.

מִתַּלְמִידָיו שֶׁל אַבְרָהָם אָבִינוּ . . . מִתַּלְמִידָיו שֶׁל בִּלְעָם הָרָשָׁע
The disciples of our forefather Abraham . . . the disciples of the evil Bilaam

Mishnah 22 THE MISHNAH POINTS OUT THAT THE VAST DIFFERENCES that are mentioned here between the two groups are between the *students* of Abraham and Bilaam. Apparently between Abraham and Bilaam themselves the differences are not that noticeable at first glance. Bilaam puts on a good act. He is a prophet and wears the mantle of piety and subservience to God. In his inner soul, however, he is evil and is contemptuous of God's wishes and directions. Abraham, on the other hand, is completely obedient to the Lord and is the eternal example of human kindness and generosity of spirit and wealth. But the enormous difference between these two individuals becomes unmistakenly apparent only when generations pass and we are able to measure the disciples and descendants of one against

ה/כב

עַיִן טוֹבָה, וְרוּחַ נְמוּכָה, וְנֶפֶשׁ שְׁפָלָה, תַּלְמִידָיו שֶׁל אַבְרָהָם אָבִינוּ. עַיִן רָעָה, וְרוּחַ גְּבוֹהָה, וְנֶפֶשׁ רְחָבָה, תַּלְמִידָיו שֶׁל בִּלְעָם הָרָשָׁע. מַה בֵּין תַּלְמִידָיו שֶׁל אַבְרָהָם אָבִינוּ לְתַלְמִידָיו שֶׁל בִּלְעָם הָרָשָׁע? תַּלְמִידָיו שֶׁל אַבְרָהָם אָבִינוּ אוֹכְלִין בָּעוֹלָם הַזֶּה, וְנוֹחֲלִין הָעוֹלָם הַבָּא, שֶׁנֶּאֱמַר: „לְהַנְחִיל אֹהֲבַי יֵשׁ, וְאֹצְרֹתֵיהֶם אֲמַלֵּא." אֲבָל תַּלְמִידָיו שֶׁל בִּלְעָם הָרָשָׁע יוֹרְשִׁין גֵּיהִנֹּם, וְיוֹרְדִין לִבְאֵר שַׁחַת, שֶׁנֶּאֱמַר: „וְאַתָּה אֱלֹהִים תּוֹרִדֵם לִבְאֵר שַׁחַת, אַנְשֵׁי דָמִים וּמִרְמָה לֹא יֶחֱצוּ יְמֵיהֶם, וַאֲנִי אֶבְטַח בָּךְ."

---

the other. It is the disciple, the child, the student, who often defines the true character of the mentor and/or the parent. Therefore, the mishnah bids us to look at the disciples, at the results of the teachings and labor of Abraham and Bilaam. By so doing, we will have the correct measure of the teacher as well.

עַיִן טוֹבָה, וְרוּחַ נְמוּכָה, וְנֶפֶשׁ שְׁפָלָה
A good eye, a humble spirit, and a meek soul

THESE ARE THE CHARACTERISTICS OF THE DISCIPLES OF ABRAHAM. I HAVE discussed the idea represented by a *good eye* in Chapter 2:13. Here it means the ability to be optimistic, tolerant, generous, and removed from the diseases of selfishness and jealousy. Humility allows a person to minimize life's frustrations and to be a friend to all. A humble person is grateful and appreciative of life and what it has granted, and is not fazed by differences of opinion or even insults slung at oneself. Humility is emphasized in Avos (see 4:4) and in all facets of Jewish life, because it is the road to serenity and happiness. A natural corollary to this goal is meekness and unpretentiousness of spirit and behavior. Such people are happy to see others succeed and never feel themselves unduly threatened by the publicity and noise that others may encourage and pursue.

❦ ❦ ❦

When the meek prevailed

In my Jerusalem neighborhood there is a small bakery and mini-cafe operated by a pleasant, God-fearing, industrious Jew. His business always appeared to be successful and his cheerful demeanor encouraged his customers to come back again. But then a large wholesale bakery opened a branch store and mini-cafe only a block from the "little guy's" enterprise. Everyone came in to console him because it appeared obvious that this giant competitor would seriously diminish his business. However, he cheerfully

5/22 Those who have a good eye, a humble spirit, and a meek soul are the disciples of our forefather Abraham. Those who have an evil eye, an arrogant spirit, and a greedy soul are the disciples of the wicked Bilaam. How are the disciples of our forefather Abraham different from the disciples of the wicked Bilaam? The disciples of our forefather Abraham enjoy [the fruits of their good deeds] in this world and inherit the World to Come, as it is said: *To cause those who love Me to inherit an everlasting possession [the World to Come], and I will fill their storehouses [in this world]* (*Proverbs* 8:21). But the disciples of the evil Bilaam inherit *Gehinnom* and descend into the well of destruction, as it is said: *And You, O God, shall lower them into the well of destruction, men of bloodshed and deceit shall not live out half their days; but as for me, I will trust in You* (*Psalms* 55:24).

---

responded to the situation, saying, "The Lord has provided for me till now. If I merit His help, He will continue to do so in the future." And God did help him. The new interloper, owned by the giant company, soon closed for lack of patrons and neighborhood pressure against its operation. The meek and humble spirit of the little guy prevailed. Now, I am aware that this is not how the average mom and pop store vs. giant supermarket story usually ends. Economics, like nature, has its rules, and according to Maimonides, the Lord is loath to interfere in those rules. Nevertheless, it was heartening to see that there are people of meek spirit and serenity of soul in our truly difficult and competitive society. It was doubly heartening to see that this meekness of spirit actually can prevail sometimes in our world.

❧ ❧ ❧

תַּלְמִידָיו שֶׁל בִּלְעָם הָרָשָׁע
The disciples of the evil Bilaam

THE DISCIPLES OF BILAAM ARE NEGATIVE PEOPLE, JEALOUS OF OTHERS' success and arrogant to a major degree. They are pompous and boastful. (Bilaam himself, before delivering his prophecy, introduces himself in the most grandiose terms and manner.) Their vanity precedes their wisdom and therefore they are never really happy people. Serenity in life and gratitude for what one has are far removed from Bilaam's disciples. Their inner turbulence, born of their dissatisfaction with themselves and their station in life, spills over into resentment of others and unwillingness to help the less fortunate. In spite of all their apparent successes, the disciples of Bilaam have unpleasant and turbulent lives. They suffer not only in the World to Come, but in this world, as well. The mishnah promises his disciples a sad fate: being lowered into

[כג] **יְהוּדָה** בֶּן תֵּימָא אוֹמֵר: הֱוֵי עַז כַּנָּמֵר, וְקַל כַּנֶּשֶׁר, רָץ כַּצְּבִי, וְגִבּוֹר כָּאֲרִי לַעֲשׂוֹת רְצוֹן אָבִיךָ שֶׁבַּשָּׁמָיִם.

[כד] **הוּא** הָיָה אוֹמֵר: עַז פָּנִים לְגֵיהִנֹּם, וּבֹשֶׁת פָּנִים לְגַן עֵדֶן. יְהִי רָצוֹן מִלְּפָנֶיךָ יהוה אֱלֹהֵינוּ

---

the well of destruction, to a sad and bitter end and punishment for their souls. Their lives are really hell in this world and hell in the World to Come, whereas the disciples of Abraham are blessed in this world and in the World to Come. The Lord promises that He has more than sufficient treasures and resources to reward the righteous, the disciples of Abraham.

The verse used in this mishnah to indicate God's reward to the righteous is also used in the conclusion of the Six Orders of the Mishnah, which states that the Lord has 310 worlds to grant every righteous person. The number 310 is derived from the numerical value of the letters of the word יֵשׁ that appears in this verse. The true difference between the disciples of Abraham and those of Bilaam is therefore reflected both in this temporary worldly existence of ours and, more importantly, in the eternal World to Come.

יְהוּדָה בֶּן תֵּימָא ***Yehudah ben Teima***

Mishnah 23 HE LIVED AT THE TIME OF THE BAR KOCHBA REBELLION in 2nd-century Judea. Very little is known about him except that the Talmud mentions him as a "master of Mishnah." Very few statements of his are preserved in the Talmud, though a longer ethical message of his is found in *Avos D'Rabbi Nassan.*

There is opinion among the commentators that this mishnah and the succeeding ones in this chapter are later additions to Avos, and not part of the original chapter. This is based on certain traditions and on the fact that this chapter until now has not named any authors for its statements, and was obviously intended to follow a numerical order — ten, seven, four, three — so that these concluding *mishnayos* do not follow this pattern of the chapter. Be that as it may, the words of Rabbi Yehudah ben Teima have been treasured throughout the Jewish experience.

הֱוֵי עַז כַּנָּמֵר ***Be bold as a leopard***

THIS MISHNAH, ADORNED BY FIGURES OF THE LEOPARD, THE EAGLE, THE deer, and the lion has decorated many Jewish synagogue walls in all countries of the Jewish exile. The traits enumerated here have validity only if they are employed to do the will of our Father in heaven. Otherwise, in personal behavior and relationships with other human beings, these traits — unyielding boldness and arrogance, swiftness and lightness, strength of body

23. Yehudah ben Teima says: Be bold as a leopard, light as an eagle, swift as a deer, and strong as a lion, to carry out the will of your Father in Heaven.

24. He [Yehudah ben Teima] used to say: The brazen goes to *Gehinnom,* but the shamefaced goes to the Garden of Eden. May it be Your will, HASHEM, our God

---

and spirit, the ability to run and flee — may not always be positive traits. Balance in all traits and behavior — the principle of Judaism discussed several times in the course of this commentary — applies here as well. For a holy purpose, these characteristics are admirable and necessary. In ordinary human life, they can lead to discord, dishonesty, and even violence. One must therefore always check the holiness of the "holy" purpose being pursued. As I quoted previously, one's *l'sheim Shamayim,* for the sake of Heaven, has to be truly *l'sheim Shamayim.*

The descendants of our father Abraham, the Jewish people, are noted for being bashful, merciful, and generous to others, traits that were inherited from him. But there are times when brazenness prevails and for a good result. Rabbi Tzadok HaKohen of Lublin, one of the great Chassidic masters and seminal thinkers of late 19th-century Congress Poland, writes that *chutzpah* will prevail even against Heaven (!) during the beginning of the Messianic Era, which he described as being "in our days." He says that the attempt of the *maapilim* — those who tried to force their way from the Sinai desert into the Land of Israel against Moses's instructions not to do so — failed and they died, but in the future — "in our days" — such an attempt will be successful (*Tzidkas HaTzaddik; Eliyahu Ki Tov* ed., Jerusalem, 1987, section 46, p. 36). Although Reb Tzadok was known as a fierce and public opponent of the Zionist movement of his day, his teaching is almost a prophecy as to how the return of millions of Jews to the Land of Israel would happen in the next century. Only time will tell us what "in our days" really means.

עַז פָּנִים לְגֵיהִנֹּם
The brazen goes to Gehinnom

Mishnah 24 IN THE PREVIOUS MISHNAH, YEHUDAH BEN TEIMA URGED that one be bold in the service of God. Now he says forcefully that in other contexts, boldness and brazenness — *chutzpah* and *azus panim* — should be avoided almost at all costs. The brazen are condemned to Hell and it is the meek and shamefaced that are rewarded in Paradise. (There is an opinion that this phrase in the mishnah is no longer that of Rabbi Yehudah ben Teima, and may therefore conceivably be an opposing opinion to his, even as regards brazenness and boldness in holy pursuits.)

וֵאלֹהֵי אֲבוֹתֵינוּ שֶׁיִּבָּנֶה בֵּית הַמִּקְדָּשׁ בִּמְהֵרָה בְיָמֵינוּ וְתֵן חֶלְקֵנוּ בְּתוֹרָתֶךָ.

[כה] **הוּא** הָיָה אוֹמֵר: בֶּן חָמֵשׁ שָׁנִים לַמִּקְרָא, בֶּן עֶשֶׂר שָׁנִים לַמִּשְׁנָה, בֶּן שְׁלֹשׁ עֶשְׂרֵה לַמִּצְוֹת, בֶּן חֲמֵשׁ עֶשְׂרֵה לַגְּמָרָא, בֶּן שְׁמוֹנֶה עֶשְׂרֵה לַחֻפָּה, בֶּן עֶשְׂרִים לִרְדּוֹף, בֶּן שְׁלֹשִׁים לַכֹּחַ,

---

יְהִי רָצוֹן . . . שֶׁיִּבָּנֶה בֵּית הַמִּקְדָּשׁ
May it be Your will . . . that the Holy Temple be rebuilt

THE COMMENTATORS DISCUSS WHY THIS PHRASE REGARDING THE rebuilding of the Temple is placed here in the middle of this mishnah. Many hold that this is a later insertion into the original text of the mishnah, and that Rabbi Yehudah ben Teima is not its author. Others have advanced ingenious solutions to connect this phrase to the previous words of the mishnah and even to Rabbi Yehudah ben Teima himself. It has been suggested that this text was inserted here — submerged, so to speak, in the surrounding subject matter — so that the Romans would not notice it and interpret the desire for the rebuilding of the Temple as an expression of rebellion and sedition against their rule.

It was certainly intended to reinforce Jewish faith and hope in the eventual rebuilding of the Temple, especially after the disaster of Bar Kochba and the razing of the Temple ruins by the Roman emperor Hadrian after the rebellion was crushed. No matter what the circumstances, Jews have never given up on Jerusalem and the Temple.

This segment of the mishnah has been incorporated into the final section of the *Amidah* prayer and is recited thrice daily by Jews. Implicit in this prayer is that "our share in the Torah" cannot be completely appreciated and acquired as long as the full redemption of Israel has not yet occurred and the Temple rebuilt and restored. It is this realization of our incompleteness without the Temple, even in Torah study and observance, that makes this prayer so vital and relevant.

הוּא הָיָה אוֹמֵר
He used to say

Mishnah 25 THIS PHRASE INDICATES THAT THIS PARAGRAPH BELONGS to Rabbi Yehudah ben Teima. Many commentators, however, attribute these ideas and words to Shmuel HaKattan, whom we met in Chapter Four (4:24).

בֶּן עֶשֶׂר שָׁנִים לַמִּשְׁנָה
A ten-year-old begins Mishnah

THE MISHNAH DEALS WITH DIFFERENT STAGES OF LIFE, EACH OF WHICH has its own purpose. The first stages in life — 5, 10, 13 and 15 years — deal with education and training in Torah. It is a curriculum of *mitzvos* and knowledge. Throughout Jewish history, a struggle has raged regarding this order of study.

and the God of our forefathers, that the Holy Temple be rebuilt, speedily in our days, and grant us our share in Your Torah.

25. He [Yehudah ben Teima] used to say: A five-year-old begins Scripture; a ten-year-old begins Mishnah; a thirteen-year-old becomes obliged to observe the commandments; a fifteen-year-old begins to study Gemara; an eighteen-year-old goes to the marriage canopy; a twenty-year-old begins pursuit [of a livelihood]; a thirty-year-old attains full strength;

In actual practice, few schools and parents wait until 10 to begin Mishnah or 15 to begin Talmud. From the 16th-century Maharal of Prague to 19th-century Rabbi Samson Raphael Hirsch, to Rabbi Yaakov Kamenetsky in our own time, many have urged that the system of Jewish education follow the program outlined in this mishnah. The vast majority of Torah authorities throughout the centuries, however, have departed from this system on the grounds that the breadth and depth with which Scripture was studied in the period of the Mishnah corresponds to our current study of Mishnah and Talmud (see *Nefesh HaChaim*).

As of this writing, the vast majority of Jewish children enrolled in Torah schools do not enjoy five years of intensive Bible study and an additional five years of intensive Mishnah study. It is my humble opinion that thorough knowledge of Mishnah prepares a student wonderfully for the rigors and complexities of studying Talmud. It would be a service to children — depending, of course, on their ability — if parents could arrange for them to be proficient in Bible and Mishnah. Such proficiency would greatly increase their chance of success and enjoyment in the study and comprehension of Talmud.

בֶּן שְׁמוֹנֶה עֶשְׂרֵה לַחֻפָּה
An eighteen-year-old goes to the marriage canopy

RABBI YEHUDAH NOW TURNS FROM THE EDUCATION OF THE YOUNG TO the years of adulthood. The mishnah encourages early marriage, and, indeed, throughout Jewish history, until the late 19th century, Jews married early. The Talmud's advice about conquering and channeling physical desire undoubtedly played a great role in establishing this pattern. Also, younger people are more flexible and can adjust more easily than those who are already older, an important consideration since marriage is a relationship that demands great flexibility and constant personal and emotional adjustment. The trend in our time is to postpone marriage until after schooling or other projects. In prewar Lithuanian yeshivos, many of the students did not marry until their late 20's or 30's. This was often not so much a matter of choice as of societal circumstances. It is hard to generalize about the optimum age for marriage in current society. I still think that the earlier the better, though again circum-

בֶּן אַרְבָּעִים לַבִּינָה, בֶּן חֲמִשִּׁים לְעֵצָה, בֶּן שִׁשִּׁים לְזִקְנָה, בֶּן שִׁבְעִים לְשֵׂיבָה, בֶּן שְׁמוֹנִים לִגְבוּרָה, בֶּן תִּשְׁעִים לָשׁוּחַ, בֶּן מֵאָה כְּאִלּוּ מֵת וְעָבַר וּבָטֵל מִן הָעוֹלָם.

[כו] **בֶּן** בַּג בַּג אוֹמֵר: הֲפָךְ בָּהּ וַהֲפָךְ בָּהּ, דְּכֹלָּה בָהּ; וּבָהּ תֶּחֱזֵי, וְסִיב וּבְלֵה בָהּ, וּמִנָּהּ לָא תָזוּעַ, שֶׁאֵין לְךָ מִדָּה טוֹבָה הֵימֶנָּה. בֶּן הֵא הֵא אוֹמֵר: לְפוּם צַעֲרָא אַגְרָא.

---

stances of family and finances have a great role to play in the matter. Yet in spite of all current societal practices, in certain sections of the Jewish population early marriage is still the norm.

בֶּן עֶשְׂרִים לִרְדּוֹף ***A twenty-year-old begins pursuit [of a livelihood]***

THE OTHER NUMBERS THAT APPEAR IN THIS MISHNAH — THE DECADES from 20 to 100 — are in reality descriptions of physical and psychological stages of life. Aging gracefully is no mean feat. Acceptance of the fact that as we age we change is a key to living the good life. A 60-year-old person should not behave like an adolescent, either in action, outlook, or goals. We all pray for long years and good health. We should also ask for the wisdom to deal with our years properly and with good sense and cheer. Age should bring perspective and vision to a person. The Talmud teaches that Torah scholars are more settled and correct in their knowledge and advice as they age, while people devoid of Torah become less stable and ever more driven by circumstances as they become older. The cycle of life has many parts and divisions to it. All of them should be studied and assimilated into our psyche in order to deal with life and aging.

בֶּן בַּג בַּג . . . בֶּן הֵא הֵא ***Ben Bag Bag . . . Ben Hei Hei***

Mishnah 26 SOME COMMENTATORS SAY THAT BECAUSE BEN BAG BAG and Ben Hei Hei lived short lives, they are called only by their fathers' names. The same explanation is given for the use of the names Ben Azzai and Ben Zoma, whose teachings were presented in Chapter Four. There is a tradition that both Ben Bag Bag and Ben Hei Hei were Roman converts to Judaism and that they were called by these strange names to protect their identities from the Roman authorities who forbade conversion to Judaism on pain of death. Abraham and Sarah are seen as the "parents" of all converts to Judaism. Each of them had an extra letter — a hei — added to their names by the Almighty, and therefore a convert would be called "Ben Hei Hei" — the son

a forty-year-old attains understanding; a fifty-year-old can offer counsel; a sixty-year-old attains seniority; a seventy-year-old attains a ripe old age; an eighty-year-old shows strength; a ninety-year-old becomes stooped over; a hundred-year-old is as if he were dead, passed away and ceased from the world.

26. Ben Bag Bag says: Delve in it [the Torah] and [continue to] delve in it, for everything is in it; look deeply into it; grow old and gray over it; do not stir from it, for you can have no better portion than it. Ben Hei Hei says: The reward is in proportion to the exertion.

---

of the two *heis,* Abraham and Sarah. Since the numerical value of the letter hei is five and the numerical value of the letters beis and gimmel that spell Bag Bag is also five, converts were also called "Ben Bag Bag." These two convert scholars lived at the time of the Hadrianic persecution of the Torah leaders of Israel and therefore had ample reason to remain incognito.

הֲפָךְ בָּהּ וַהֲפָךְ בָּהּ
Delve in it [the Torah] and [continue to] delve in it

ONE SHOULD TURN THE TORAH OVER AGAIN AND AGAIN IN ONE'S MIND and in one's heart, constantly studying it and reviewing it. There are always new insights and new wisdom to be gained from dealing with it. Everything is in the Torah. Whatever one searches for in intellect, inspiration, and knowledge can be found in the Torah, so one should constantly explore it and see current events in the light of its wisdom and experience of life.

That is why we read the Torah over again every year and never tire of it, for it always provides us with fresh insights on our lives and circumstances. The goal of the rabbinic sermon on Shabbos, in my opinion, is to help point out those insights and relate the Torah's words to our current personal and national lives in a meaningful fashion. Unless we see the Torah as current events and not merely as ancient teachings and history, we will never gain the full benefit of its study and knowledge. Therefore one ages gracefully with the Torah. It directs us and enhances our being at every age and stage of life. One should never forsake the Torah, for it is "our lives and the length of our days." It is irreplaceable and incomparable.

לְפוּם צַעֲרָא אַגְרָא
The reward is in proportion to the exertion

THIS IS NOT ONLY THE FINAL MISHNAH OF THIS CHAPTER, BUT ALSO THE conclusion of Tractate Avos, since Chapter Six, as we shall explain below, is a collection of extraneous teachings (*beraisos*) that are not part of the tractate. This final mishnah sums up the Torah's attitude toward life. According to the sacrifice and pain, the blood, tears and sweat, is the reward and the gain.

רַבִּי חֲנַנְיָא בֶּן עֲקַשְׁיָא אוֹמֵר: רָצָה הַקָּדוֹשׁ בָּרוּךְ הוּא לְזַכּוֹת אֶת יִשְׂרָאֵל, לְפִיכָךְ הִרְבָּה לָהֶם תּוֹרָה וּמִצְוֹת, שֶׁנֶּאֱמַר: „יהוה חָפֵץ לְמַעַן צִדְקוֹ, יַגְדִּיל תּוֹרָה וְיַאְדִּיר."

There is no gain without pain; there is no free lunch in this world. On the verse "Man was created for toil," the Rabbis comment, "Happy is the person whose toil is in Torah"; toil there must be, better that it be in the mastery of Torah than in the countless pursuits that offer nothing permanent.

Life is a serious business and strenuous effort is necessary to accomplish goals. This is true in the world of our careers and work. It is true in the realm of our families, where constant attention and focus is necessary.

❦ ❦ ❦

Rabbi Chanania ben Akashia says: The Holy One, Blessed is He, wished to confer merit upon Israel; therefore He gave them Torah and *mitzvos* in abundance, as it is said: *HASHEM desired, for the sake of its [Israel's] righteousness, that the Torah be made great and glorious* (*Isaiah* 42:21).

It is certainly true in the world of our spiritual self. Without great effort and zeal, there cannot be any meaningful spiritual growth and development. We all know that no matter how brilliant our minds may be, a successful scholastic career requires effort and good study habits. Torah is acquired primarily by great effort and not only great intellectual prowess. Thus, the whole lesson of Jewish life is elegantly phrased in the words of Ben Hei Hei.

פרק ששי
CHAPTER SIX

כָּל יִשְׂרָאֵל יֵשׁ לָהֶם חֵלֶק לָעוֹלָם הַבָּא, שֶׁנֶּאֱמַר: „וְעַמֵּךְ כֻּלָּם צַדִּיקִים, לְעוֹלָם יִירְשׁוּ אָרֶץ, נֵצֶר מַטָּעַי, מַעֲשֵׂה יָדַי לְהִתְפָּאֵר.״

All Israel has a share in the World to Come, as it is said: *And your people are all righteous; they shall inherit the land forever; a branch of My plantings, My handiwork, in which to take pride* (Isaiah 60:21).

שָׁנוּ חֲכָמִים בִּלְשׁוֹן הַמִּשְׁנָה. בָּרוּךְ שֶׁבָּחַר בָּהֶם וּבְמִשְׁנָתָם.

[א] **רַבִּי** מֵאִיר אוֹמֵר: כָּל הָעוֹסֵק בַּתּוֹרָה לִשְׁמָהּ זוֹכֶה לִדְבָרִים הַרְבֵּה; וְלֹא עוֹד, אֶלָּא

Chapter Six:
The Acquisition of Torah

THIS CHAPTER IS NOT PART OF AVOS, PER SE. IT IS RATHER A LATER addition (probably 4th or 5th century CE) of *beraisos,* teachings and rulings of the rabbis that were not included in the Mishnah itself, when it was compiled in its final form by Rabbi Yehudah HaNasi, around 190 CE.

The style, general message, and contents of this chapter are similar to that of the first five chapters, but the main emphasis of the chapter — almost its exclusive message — regards Torah study, Torah knowledge, and the ways in which this study and knowledge can be made an integral part of our daily lives. Consequently, this chapter is known as פֶּרֶק קִנְיַן תּוֹרָה [*Perek Kinyan Torah*], *the Chapter of the Acquisition of Torah,* its knowledge, systems, attitudes, and values. Torah is a treasure that must be acquired by every individual Jew, but to do so requires effort and sacrifice; it is not free for the taking.

Just as an art collector may have agents scouring the galleries of the world to find the paintings he or she may wish to own, so too must a Jew search for Torah. Our agents in this quest for Torah are our teachers, our parents, our spiritual leaders, our books, our traditions. But above all, once Torah is discovered and found, one must be willing to pay the price demanded in order to acquire it. This chapter discusses both the methods of searching for Torah and the "cost" to acquire it.

The chapter of *Kinyan Torah* follows logically from the final statements in the fifth and last chapter of the Mishnaic tractate of Avos. That last chapter concluded with the statements of Ben Bag Bag and Ben Hei Hei. Those statements respectively dealt with the value of Torah wisdom and study above all else — for everything in life is included in its words and values — and also with the fact that the achievement of its rewards is dependent on the effort expended to know and understand it. As mentioned above, these are the two basic subjects covered in the chapter of *Kinyan Torah.* Thus, this chapter is a natural follow-up to the subject matter of the tractate's actual conclusion.

The Sages taught [this chapter] in the language of the Mishnah. Blessed is He Who chose them and their teaching.

1. Rabbi Meir said: Whoever engages in Torah study for its own sake merits many things; furthermore, [the

---

שָׁנוּ חֲכָמִים בִּלְשׁוֹן הַמִּשְׁנָה
The Sages taught [this chapter] in the language of the Mishnah

Introduction IT IS NOT ONLY SUBJECT MATTER THAT IS IMPORTANT. Literary style and language forms also play an important role in the transmission of Torah. The Talmud taught that "one is obligated to teach his students with the same language and expression that he heard from his teacher." The tradition in many yeshivos, therefore, was to repeat not only the words of the teacher, but his voice inflections and nuances of style as well! The sound of the hauntingly sweet melody of my teacher of Talmud when I was but 11 years old still echoes in my ears. One must always see a mental picture of one's mentors when teaching Torah to the next generation. Therefore, the language forms of this collection of *beraisos* closely resemble those of the Mishnah. In fact, some of them are reported to us in the name of some of those great teachers of the Mishnah.

בָּרוּךְ שֶׁבָּחַר בָּהֶם וּבְמִשְׁנָתָם
Blessed is He Who chose them and their teaching

BECAUSE OF THIS TYPICALLY JEWISH REVERENCE FOR THE TEACHERS OF the past, the chapter begins appropriately by blessing God Who chose to provide us with the great teachers of the Mishnah and also chose to impart their Torah wisdom to all future generations. This introductory acknowledgment of Divine favor lends an aura of holiness and eternity to their words of wisdom and counsel.

כָּל הָעוֹסֵק בַּתּוֹרָה לִשְׁמָהּ
Whoever engages in Torah study for its own sake

Mishnah 1 THE CONCEPT OF SERVING GOD WITHOUT ULTERIOR MOTIVES or hoped-for reward has been emphasized previously in Avos, as in the teaching of Antigonos Ish Socho in Chapter 1:3. Pious Jews throughout the ages tried to live up to this lofty demand. *Lishmah* is nobility for nobility's sake alone. In a sense, giving charity silently and anonymously is an example of such a trait in action, for there will be no earthly recognition, although there will be Heavenly reward. But even hope for heavenly reward alone is not quite yet *lishmah*. Therefore, some saintly people went even further. There are many stories and legends of holy Jews who were interested only in serving God, and not in the reward for their good deeds. In order to fulfill the goal of performing a *mitzvah lishmah* at least once in their lifetime, they went so far as to waive their eternal reward for the performance of a commandment and granted that reward to another.

If *lishmah* is the goal in the performance of all other commandments, it is especially desirable in reference to the study and teaching of Torah. Many great works of Torah scholarship were published anonymously, and only after

ו/א

שֶׁכָּל הָעוֹלָם כֻּלּוֹ כְּדַאי הוּא לוֹ. נִקְרָא רֵעַ, אָהוּב. אוֹהֵב אֶת הַמָּקוֹם, אוֹהֵב אֶת הַבְּרִיּוֹת, מְשַׂמֵּחַ אֶת הַמָּקוֹם, מְשַׂמֵּחַ אֶת הַבְּרִיּוֹת. וּמַלְבַּשְׁתּוֹ עֲנָוָה וְיִרְאָה; וּמַכְשַׁרְתּוֹ לִהְיוֹת צַדִּיק, חָסִיד, יָשָׁר, וְנֶאֱמָן; וּמְרַחַקְתּוֹ מִן הַחֵטְא, וּמְקָרַבְתּוֹ לִידֵי זְכוּת. וְנֶהֱנִין מִמֶּנּוּ עֵצָה וְתוּשִׁיָּה, בִּינָה וּגְבוּרָה, שֶׁנֶּאֱמַר: „לִי עֵצָה וְתוּשִׁיָּה, אֲנִי בִינָה, לִי גְבוּרָה.״ וְנוֹתֶנֶת לוֹ מַלְכוּת, וּמֶמְשָׁלָה, וְחִקּוּר דִּין; וּמְגַלִּין לוֹ רָזֵי תוֹרָה;

---

the books attained great fame were the authors finally found out and their names exposed. Two examples of this phenomenon in modern times are Rabbi Yisrael Meir Kagan and his work, *Chafetz Chaim,* and Rabbi Avraham Yeshaya Karelitz and his work, *Chazon Ish.* One of the great works of Jewish ethics, *Orchos Tzaddikim,* published in the 14th century, still has no clearly identified author. I imagine that this anonymity is the ultimate expression of *Torah lishmah.*

Torah should be studied for its own sake, even if no practical purpose or result of that study is immediately discernible. For it is the study of Torah itself, without any practical considerations, that supports life on this earth and binds Jews to their Creator in an eternal fashion. Unlike other types of study, where practical results are the criterion for determining the worth of the student — degrees, published works, valuable research, economic progress, etc. — Torah study is its own reward. In many yeshivos, therefore, the idea of studying for rabbinical ordination was looked at askance. In the Lithuanian yeshivos of the 19th and early-20th centuries, rabbinical ordination was never granted by the yeshivah itself, but rather by individual rabbis privately. This system still prevails in many yeshivah institutions, though rabbinical ordination by the institution itself has now become a staple of Jewish life.

שֶׁכָּל הָעוֹלָם כֻּלּוֹ כְּדַאי הוּא לוֹ ***[The creation of] the entire world — all of it — is worthwhile for him alone***

IN VIEW OF THE ABOVE, RABBI MEIR'S STATEMENT THAT ALL OF GOD'S creation is worthwhile for the sake of even a single individual who studies *Torah lishmah* is understandable. The Jewish view is that the existence of one worthy person is sufficient to justify the existence of our finely tuned and enormously complex universe. Thus, one who studies *Torah lishmah* not only receives personal merit and achieves many great things for himself, but contributes in a vastly disproportionate manner to the preservation of human life and of the world itself.

creation of] the entire world — all of it — is worthwhile for him alone. He is called, "Friend, Beloved." He loves the Omnipresent, he loves [His] creatures, he gladdens the Omnipresent, he gladdens [His] creatures. [The Torah] cloaks him in humility and fear [of God]; it makes him fit to be righteous, devout, fair, and faithful. It moves him away from sin and draws him near to merit. From him people enjoy counsel and wisdom, understanding and strength, as it is said: *Mine are counsel and wisdom, I am understanding, mine is strength (Proverbs* 8:14). [The Torah] gives him kingship and dominion and analytical judgment; the secrets of the Torah are revealed to him;

נִקְרָא רֵעַ, אָהוּב
He is called, "Friend, Beloved"

ONE WHO STUDIES TORAH SINCERELY AND FOR ITS OWN SAKE BECOMES a friend to all, a beloved person, for the influence of *Torah lishmah* is so pervasive that love of God and love of one's fellow humans automatically exudes from such a person. It is only when knowledge is exploited to achieve other agendas — power, wealth, political gain, personal honor, etc. — that it can result in baseless hatred and negative traits.

וּמַלְבַּשְׁתּוֹ עֲנָוָה וְיִרְאָה
[The Torah] cloaks him in humility and fear [of God]

STUDYING *TORAH LISHMAH* PROVIDES ONE WITH AN IMMUNITY VACCINE against intellectual and personal arrogance. It is a protective garment that shields one from the base elements of human character. It helps encourage righteous and selfless behavior, trustworthiness and compassion for others. Without it, a great deal of knowledge and wisdom, a good and facile mind, a valid reputation as a scholar, can all too often lead to hubris and arrogance. Righteousness and piety stem from inner holiness and personality strengths. They are not external qualities, nor do they depend upon external dress or manners for vindication. *Torah lishmah* saves one from temptations and sin and brings one closer to attaining eternal merit and reward.

וְנֶהֱנִין מִמֶּנּוּ עֵצָה וְתוּשִׁיָּה
From him people enjoy counsel and wisdom

SUCH AN EXEMPLARY PERSON IS SOUGHT AFTER BY OTHERS FOR ADVICE and counsel, for a good word and an understanding heart. Jews always poured out their hearts and troubles to the great Torah scholars because they knew that they would find in them an attentive ear and a willingness to help. This very generosity of spirit invests the scholar with power and influence in the community. He is able to judge things realistically and dispassionately. He is sensitive to falsehoods and illegitimate claims. He is aware of the truth and seeks to enforce it in all situations. He is able to fathom the secrets of the Torah, to do what is just and correct, to view the forest and not just the trees. He understands the nuances of the public policies of the Torah, is able to

וְנַעֲשֶׂה כְּמַעְיָן הַמִּתְגַּבֵּר, וּכְנָהָר שֶׁאֵינוֹ פוֹסֵק; וְהֱוֶה צָנוּעַ, וְאֶרֶךְ רוּחַ, וּמוֹחֵל עַל עֶלְבּוֹנוֹ. וּמְגַדַּלְתּוֹ וּמְרוֹמַמְתּוֹ עַל כָּל הַמַּעֲשִׂים.

[ב] **אָמַר** רַבִּי יְהוֹשֻׁעַ בֶּן לֵוִי: בְּכָל יוֹם וָיוֹם בַּת קוֹל יוֹצֵאת מֵהַר חוֹרֵב, וּמַכְרֶזֶת

---

read its "x-rays," so to speak, and not merely judge by superficial impressions or purely literal readings of the law.

וְנַעֲשֶׂה כְּמַעְיָן הַמִּתְגַּבֵּר . . . וּמוֹחֵל עַל עֶלְבּוֹנוֹ ***He becomes like a steadily strengthening fountain . . . and forgiving of insult to himself***

SUCH A PERSON IS AN INEXHAUSTIBLE FOUNT OF KNOWLEDGE AND GOOD advice, a powerful spring of sweet water that constantly refreshes others while yet always replenishing itself. He is modest and withdrawn, never seeking public fame, though invariably acclaim will certainly pursue such a holy individual. Because of his modesty, he forgives slights easily, shrugs off disrespectful behavior, and continues the course of pursuing the study of *Torah lishmah.*

The Talmud teaches that overly sensitive individuals "have no life" in this world. This is certainly true of people in public life who, if they take every "constructive criticism" to heart and feel embittered and unappreciated, "have no life" no matter how mighty or wealthy they may be. *Torah lishmah* enables a person to rise above the vagaries and pettiness of everyday life and to focus on the service of God and man. It makes us oblivious to seeming insults and slights and gives us a view of all life from the heights — an aerial view, if you will — that is illuminating and inspiring. It elevates the entire concept of life and living and creates greatness and nobility of character and person. *Torah lishmah* is the ultimate level of Jewish achievement. Even if we do not attain it, we should be aware of its presence and challenge.

רַבִּי יְהוֹשֻׁעַ בֶּן לֵוִי ***Rabbi Yehoshua ben Levi***

Mishnah 2 HE WAS A FAMOUS SCHOLAR, TEACHER, AND HOLY MAN who lived in the first half of the 3rd century in the Land of Israel. He was a contemporary of Rabbi Yochanan and Rabbi Shimon ben Lakish, whose yeshivah in Tiberias in the Galilee was then the main Torah center in the Land of Israel. Rabbi Yehoshua's yeshivah was located in Lod in Judea, west of Jerusalem. His mentors were Bar Kappara, Rabbi Yehudah ben Pedayah and Rabbi Pinchas ben Yair. He was known as a person of moderation and peace, he even forbade cursing the enemies of Israel. His reputation as a holy person led the rabbis of the Talmud to state that during his lifetime there was no necessity for the rainbow to appear in the heavens to signify God's covenant with humankind, that He would never again

he becomes like a steadily strengthening fountain and like an unceasing river. He becomes modest, patient, and forgiving of insult to himself. [The Torah] makes him great and exalts him above all things.

2. Rabbi Yehoshua ben Levi said: Every single day a Heavenly voice emanates from Mount Horeb, proclaiming

---

destroy the entire world with a flood, as He did in the time of Noah (*Genesis* 9:8-17).

The mere presence of such a human being as Rabbi Yehoshua ben Levi in human society was itself sufficient proof of the ongoing bond between God and His human creatures. Rabbi Yehoshua was well respected by the Roman authorities in Israel as well, visiting the ruling authorities in Caesarea a number of times on behalf of the Jewish residents of Judea.

His devotion to Torah study was unwavering, and he stated (*Makkos* 10a) that those who are engaged in the study of Torah give soldiers fighting a war the strength to stand and prevail in battle. He even saw in the study of Torah the ability to cure one's physical ills. He stated (*Eruvin* 54a) that a person with a headache should engage in Torah study. Even one who feels ill throughout his entire body should concentrate on Torah study. This background of Rabbi Yehoshua ben Levi is sufficient for us to fully understand the idea of the supremacy of Torah he expresses in this *baraisa*.

בְּכָל יוֹם וָיוֹם בַּת קוֹל יוֹצֵאת
Every single day a Heavenly voice emanates

THERE IS A CONSTANT, DAILY ECHO THAT EMANATES FROM SINAI AND informs us of the importance of Torah. All things Godly have eternity built into them. The Divine Torah given on Sinai left its echo for all time in the world we inhabit. It is up to us, however, to hear that sound. Just as there are innumerable frequencies of sound filling the airwaves of the world — they are all present in the room that you are currently sitting in while reading this book — and one has to tune one's radio to the correct frequency of the broadcast one desires to hear, so must one attune one's spiritual ear to hear this echo from Sinai.

This idea was expressed by the great Rebbe of Kotzk, in a comment on God's command to Abraham, לֶךְ לְךָ, *Go forth* from your land to the land that I will show you (*Genesis* 12:1). This message, the Kotzker said, was sent out through the "airwaves" of the world, open to anyone who wished to hear and respond to it. It was the fateful decision of Abraham to tune into that message and act upon it that changed his life and created the Jewish people. So too, this echo of Sinai that bemoans the degradation of Torah is broadcast to all human beings. It is for us to listen and respond to its message.

There is an active form of degradation, a mocking of Torah and its adher-

ו/ב

וְאוֹמֶרֶת: „אוֹי לָהֶם לַבְּרִיּוֹת, מֵעֶלְבּוֹנָהּ שֶׁל תּוֹרָה!" שֶׁכָּל מִי שֶׁאֵינוֹ עוֹסֵק בַּתּוֹרָה נִקְרָא נָזוּף, שֶׁנֶּאֱמַר: „נֶזֶם זָהָב בְּאַף חֲזִיר, אִשָּׁה יָפָה וְסָרַת טָעַם." וְאוֹמֵר: „וְהַלֻּחֹת מַעֲשֵׂה אֱלֹהִים הֵמָּה וְהַמִּכְתָּב מִכְתַּב אֱלֹהִים הוּא חָרוּת עַל הַלֻּחֹת," אַל תִּקְרָא „חָרוּת" אֶלָּא „חֵרוּת," שֶׁאֵין לְךָ בֶּן חוֹרִין אֶלָּא מִי שֶׁעוֹסֵק בְּתַלְמוּד תּוֹרָה.

---

ents — the type of behavior common to the radical Jewish secularists of the 19th and 20th centuries. And there is a more subtle type of degradation that results when the Torah is ignored and treated as being irrelevant to the needs of modern-day society. Rabbi Yehoshua ben Levi speaks to both types of degradation. He teaches that a Jew who feels the pain of spirit when he sees that the Torah is not observed, studied, raised to the highest priority in life, as it should be, literally hears that echo from Sinai and is tuned to the correct frequency of holy living. Someone who is deaf to that echo, who is not personally challenged by the demands of the Torah and Jewish living, contributes passively to the sad abuse of Torah and its values in everyday human life.

נִקְרָא נָזוּף
Is called "Rebuked"

THERE ARE THOSE WHO SEEMINGLY ACCEPT THE TORAH IN THEIR LIVES, but only on a superficial and conditional level. They may pay lip service to its ideals and observances, they may even dress the part of observant Jews, but in their inner beings they have not internalized its values and attitudes. Rabbi Yehoshua ben Levi calls them *rebuked,* i.e., people who are excluded from the company of the truly righteous, because their very insincerity is in itself a rejection and degradation of the Torah.

Someone who truly does not concern himself with Torah and its values in his personal life and dealings with others automatically removes himself from the company of the holy people of Israel. A person whose attachment to Torah is only external and whose piety is merely a sham portrayal for the benefit of others is likened to a pig with a golden bauble in its snout. The Torah — the golden bauble — is degraded by being in the pig's snout, for the pig remains a pig in spite of its beautiful adornment. Similarly, one who does not honor the Torah through study and correct behavior and holy attitudes, automatically dishonors it. For Torah sets standards for living and functioning in family and society. Without adherence to those standards one runs the risk of being the pig with a piece of gold jewelry in its otherwise ugly snout.

and saying, "Woe to them, to the people, because of [their] insult to the Torah!" For whoever does not occupy himself with the Torah is called "Rebuked," as it is said: *Like a golden ring in a swine's snout is a beautiful woman who turns away from good judgment* (*Proverbs* 11:22). And it says: *The Tablets are God's handiwork and the script was God's script charus (engraved) on the Tablets* (*Exodus* 32:16). Do not read *charus* (engraved), but *cherus* (freedom), for you can have no freer man other than one who engages in Torah study.

שֶׁאֵין לְךָ בֶּן חוֹרִין אֶלָּא מִי שֶׁעוֹסֵק בְּתַלְמוּד תּוֹרָה

For you can have no freer man other than one who engages in Torah study

THERE IS ANOTHER ASPECT TO TORAH, ITS ABILITY TO CREATE A TRULY free person. Judaism is a staunch defender of personal freedom and autonomous freedom of choice. This requires that there be a defender of man's ability to make such choices and that man not be enslaved to his passions, momentary whims, or current societal political correctness. That defender is the Torah itself. The very Torah that seems to impose so many restrictions upon our behavior is in reality the vehicle by which one may achieve true personal freedom. For it is the Torah and, paradoxically, its numerous restrictions that provide the very basis for individual freedom. The Torah's discipline frees us from the slavery of our very nature. Just as all free societies require laws, police, self-discipline, and a sense of purpose in order to prevent anarchy and violence, so too does the individual have to appreciate the necessity of Torah law and restrictions guaranteeing the ultimate freedom of the individual Jew.

We should not allow ourselves to become prisoners of the pursuit of wealth or fame, of the demands of power and avarice. We can be in control of our physical desires and temper them with the investment of holiness in all physical acts and behavior. "Keeping up with Joneses," "everybody does it," "be liberated" — such slogans of life may entice us, but ultimately they truly enslave us. They are countered by the opening statement of the Ten Commandments, in which God identifies Himself as the One Who freed Israel from Egyptian bondage so that it should serve Him.

The Torah frees us from the temporary and tawdry, and uplifts us to see the eternal and meaningful things in life. Therefore, it is only through the Torah, its standards and observances, its wisdom and guidance, that the true spirit of freedom can be achieved in one's life. Torah teaches us that in discipline lies freedom and in adherence to God's commandments one finds the inner sense of purpose and peace that transcends all human problems and constraints. The "owner of our work" is not necessarily our human boss, but is rather the Creator of us all. Knowledge of that elementary fact of life grants freedom of perspective and eventual freedom of soul and spirit.

וְכָל מִי שֶׁעוֹסֵק בְּתַלְמוּד תּוֹרָה הֲרֵי זֶה מִתְעַלֶּה, שֶׁנֶּאֱמַר: ,,וּמִמַּתָּנָה נַחֲלִיאֵל, וּמִנַּחֲלִיאֵל בָּמוֹת.״

[ג] **הַלּוֹמֵד** מֵחֲבֵרוֹ פֶּרֶק אֶחָד, אוֹ הֲלָכָה אַחַת, אוֹ פָּסוּק אֶחָד, אוֹ דִבּוּר אֶחָד, אוֹ אֲפִילוּ אוֹת אַחַת – צָרִיךְ לִנְהָג בּוֹ כָּבוֹד. שֶׁכֵּן מָצִינוּ בְּדָוִד מֶלֶךְ יִשְׂרָאֵל, שֶׁלֹּא לָמַד מֵאֲחִיתֹפֶל אֶלָּא שְׁנֵי דְבָרִים בִּלְבָד,

---

וְכָל מִי שֶׁעוֹסֵק בְּתַלְמוּד תּוֹרָה הֲרֵי זֶה מִתְעַלֶּה
And anyone who engages in Torah study becomes elevated

THE TORAH UPLIFTS A PERSON AND RAISES HIS NATURE AND BEING. THE gift of Torah that the Lord bestowed upon Israel is the primary tool available for the improvement of human nature and for guidance in achieving civilized behavior. The great 19th-century Lithuanian-based *Mussar* movement used Torah as its guidebook for strengthening Jewish ethical behavior and reforming the ills that had crept into Jewish life. The great pietists of Israel would always refer to the Torah for instruction in matters of ethical behavior.

All of life is the attempt to scale the great mountain of spiritual challenge and societal harmony. Just as mountain climbers need tools and safety ropes to scale a peak, so too does the Torah provide Jews the necessary tools and safety ropes in our attempt to scale spiritual heights. Even if we slip and lose our footing, and we may sometimes feel that we are dangling near disaster, the Torah's safety rope will keep us from falling completely. It is this idea that King David discusses in *Psalms* (24:3): *Who shall ascend the mountain of the Lord?* The mountain is there and we must all attempt to ascend it. The same Torah that demands of us to accept that challenge also provides the means and support necessary to successfully achieve that goal. The fact that not every Jew who claims Torah as his or her guide in life may succeed in climbing that mountain successfully, in no way diminishes the value of Torah as the means by which that goal can be achieved. Much of life's success and spiritual achievement depends on the climber himself; a mountain climber may have the best equipment possible for the climb and still fail.

הַלּוֹמֵד מֵחֲבֵרוֹ פֶּרֶק אֶחָד
He who learns from his fellow even a single chapter

Mishnah 3 A PRINCIPLE THAT IS REITERATED MANY TIMES IN AVOS and in Jewish life generally is that of הַכָּרַת הַטּוֹב, being appreciative of favors and goodness, past and current, that have been extended by others. The beginning of all feelings and expressions of gratitude and appreciation should naturally be directed to the Creator of us all, but we are bidden to express our appreciation to our fellow human beings, as well. Special appreciation is reserved for those who have raised and educated us. Respect

And anyone who engages in Torah study becomes elevated, as it is said: *From Mattanah to Nachaliel and from Nachaliel to Bamos* (*Numbers* 21:19).

3. He who learns from his fellow even a single chapter, a single halachah, a single verse, a single Torah statement, or even a single letter, must treat him with honor. For thus we find in the case of David, King of Israel, who learned nothing from Achitophel except for two things,

---

for parents and teachers lies at the core of all Jewish attitudes. Many times, however, our definition of a teacher is restricted to those mentors who taught us for many years, or who explained complicated subjects, or helped us master skills that we now utilize in our careers. But we often neglect to remember teachers who taught us small things, incidental knowledge, and even those who taught us the basic tools of education and literacy while we were yet very young.

❦ ❦ ❦

The melamed's advantage

I am eternally grateful to my Irish spinster second-grade public school teacher, Miss McCarthy, for teaching me how to read and write English acceptably, though I must admit that I did not appreciate her strictness and punctiliousness at that time. On a more serious note, it is said that the great Rabbi Chaim Soloveitchik, even after gaining enormous fame as one of the foremost Talmudists of the last centuries, still rose to his feet in honor of the relatively unlearned melamed (elementary-school teacher) who taught him the Hebrew alphabet. He said that "everything he taught me has remained unquestionably true — an aleph is still an aleph, a beis is still a beis, etc. — while now I know that many of the Talmudic lessons that I learned from greater scholars were in error." Thus gratitude to all those who have taught us something new in life and in living deserves priority in Jewish behavior.

❦ ❦ ❦

בְּדָוִד . . . שֶׁלֹּא לָמַד מֵאֲחִיתֹפֶל אֶלָּא שְׁנֵי דְבָרִים בִּלְבָד
David . . . who learned nothing from Achitophel except for two things

AMONG ALL OF HIS OTHER ATTRIBUTES, KING DAVID WAS A GREATER TORAH scholar than Achitophel. Nevertheless David showered him with praise and accolades for having taught him two rules in Torah. Achitophel's two rules were not unimportant ones. He taught that one should not study Torah alone, in isolation from others; Torah thrives on the give and take between scholars and students, on debate and questions and discussion. Only in such an atmosphere can correctness and truth win out over pure intellectual pyrotechnics, which often are seemingly brilliant, but ultimately incorrect. Achitophel's second rule is that prayer and the synagogue — the place

וְקְרָאוֹ רַבּוֹ, אַלּוּפוֹ, וּמְיֻדָּעוֹ, שֶׁנֶּאֱמַר: „וְאַתָּה אֱנוֹשׁ כְּעֶרְכִּי, אַלּוּפִי וּמְיֻדָּעִי.״ וַהֲלֹא דְבָרִים קַל וָחֹמֶר: וּמַה דָּוִד מֶלֶךְ יִשְׂרָאֵל, שֶׁלֹּא לָמַד מֵאֲחִיתֹפֶל אֶלָּא שְׁנֵי דְבָרִים בִּלְבָד, קְרָאוֹ רַבּוֹ אַלּוּפוֹ וּמְיֻדָּעוֹ — הַלּוֹמֵד מֵחֲבֵרוֹ פֶּרֶק אֶחָד, אוֹ הֲלָכָה אֶחָת, אוֹ פָּסוּק אֶחָד, אוֹ דִבּוּר אֶחָד, אוֹ אֲפִילוּ אוֹת אֶחָת, עַל אַחַת כַּמָּה וְכַמָּה שֶׁצָּרִיךְ לִנְהָג בּוֹ כָּבוֹד! וְאֵין כָּבוֹד אֶלָּא תוֹרָה, שֶׁנֶּאֱמַר: „כָּבוֹד חֲכָמִים יִנְחָלוּ״; „וּתְמִימִים יִנְחֲלוּ טוֹב״ וְאֵין טוֹב אֶלָּא תוֹרָה, שֶׁנֶּאֱמַר: „כִּי לֶקַח טוֹב נָתַתִּי לָכֶם, תּוֹרָתִי אַל תַּעֲזֹבוּ.״

[ד] **כָּךְ** הִיא דַרְכָּהּ שֶׁל תּוֹרָה: פַּת בַּמֶּלַח תֹּאכֵל,

---

of public prayer — must be approached with respect and awe. Since prayer and the synagogue comprise such a regular daily role in Jewish life, the temptation to lose the reverence and awe due them is great; as the saying goes, familiarity breeds contempt and lightheartedness. Therefore, Achitophel's rule is very important.

David, the great king of Israel, the author of the Psalms, the warrior and savior of the Jewish people, the Torah scholar par excellence of his generation, could perhaps be excused for neglecting to thank Achitophel publicly for teaching him merely two out of thousands of Torah rules. Yet, David made a public and lavish acknowledgment of appreciation to Achitophel for his two teachings. This lesson of appreciation to others for their help and guidance should never be lost on us. The honor of the Torah demands such an attitude and behavior pattern from all Jews. The Lord described Torah as the ultimate good: *For I have granted you the good portion* (*Proverbs* 4:2). In fact, it is the key to all "good." It leads to all honor and when one has that honor — the ultimate good — then the necessity of expressing gratitude to those who helped us achieve it is obvious.

כָּךְ הִיא דַרְכָּהּ שֶׁל תּוֹרָה
This is the way of Torah

Mishnah 4 JUDAISM DOES NOT GLORIFY POVERTY AS AN END IN ITSELF, but it does demand sacrifice. Thus poverty is not acceptable as an excuse for ignorance of Torah or non-observance of its precepts. One has to sacrifice to study Torah, and that applies equally to rich and poor, old and young, the gifted and the average. Hillel serves as the example of the

yet called him his teacher, his guide, his intimate, as it is said: *You are a man of my measure, my guide and my intimate* (*Psalms* 55:14). One can derive from this the following: If David, King of Israel, who learned nothing from Achitophel except for two things, called him his teacher, his guide, his intimate — one who learns from his fellowman a single chapter, a single verse, a single statement, or even a single letter, how much more must he treat him with honor! And honor is due only for Torah, as it is said: *The wise shall inherit honor* (*Proverbs* 3:35); *and the perfect shall inherit good* (ibid. 28:10). And only Torah is truly good, as it is said: *I have given you a good teaching, do not forsake My Torah* (ibid. 4:2).

4. This is the way of Torah: Eat bread with salt, drink

---

student of Torah who is penniless and alone, yet rises to become the great scholar and leader of Israel. Rabbi Eliezer, Rabbi Yehudah HaNasi and other great teachers of Israel were very wealthy, yet they attained their Torah greatness only through sacrifice and hard effort. When it comes to Torah, there is no free lunch. Thus the words of the mishnah may be understood to mean that even if one is forced to eat crusts of bread and measures of water and sleep on the floor and experience pain and want in life, the study of Torah will yet bring happiness and reward in this world and in the next world. Belief in the worth and happiness of Torah life and study is central to Jewish belief and society. Thus, although poverty is not a required condition for Torah greatness, neither is its presence an excuse for not toiling in the vineyard of Torah.

Especially in an affluent and developed society, it is psychologically unwise that Torah be somehow identified with institutionalized poverty. Yet, the pursuit of wealth at the expense of Torah study and observance should be avoided. As in everything in Judaism, balance is a key ingredient. Thus the words of the mishnah refer to the wealthy as well as the poor. Historically, great Torah scholars have come from both backgrounds; the common requirement under all financial circumstances is sacrifice, study, and diligent effort.

❧ ❧ ❧

A piquant interpretation

The great Rabbi Meir Shapiro created Yeshivas Chachmei Lublin in Lublin, Poland in the 1920's. He built a massive building with all of the then modern conveniences including electricity, indoor plumbing, a dining room

וּמַיִם בַּמְּשׂוּרָה תִּשְׁתֶּה, וְעַל הָאָרֶץ תִּישָׁן, וְחַיֵּי צַעַר תִּחְיֶה, וּבַתּוֹרָה אַתָּה עָמֵל; אִם אַתָּה עוֹשֶׂה כֵּן, „אַשְׁרֶיךָ וְטוֹב לָךְ": „אַשְׁרֶיךָ" – בָּעוֹלָם הַזֶּה, „וְטוֹב לָךְ" – לָעוֹלָם הַבָּא.

[ה] **אַל תְּבַקֵּשׁ** גְּדֻלָּה לְעַצְמְךָ, וְאַל תַּחְמֹד כָּבוֹד; יוֹתֵר מִלִּמּוּדֶךָ עֲשֵׂה.

וְאַל תִּתְאַוֶּה לְשֻׁלְחָנָם שֶׁל מְלָכִים, שֶׁשֻּׁלְחָנְךָ גָּדוֹל מִשֻּׁלְחָנָם, וְכִתְרְךָ גָּדוֹל מִכִּתְרָם; וְנֶאֱמָן

---

that served three wholesome meals a day, a library with tens of thousands of books and a comfortable dormitory. These were all advantages that no other yeshivah in Poland had at that time. His critics (all those who attempt to construct something new in Jewish society will encounter critics) asked him why he violated the literal meaning of this mishnah. He retorted: "You read the mishnah incorrectly. The mishnah should not be read as a statement but rather as a question. "Is this the way of Torah? To eat crusts of bread, to drink water by the measure, to sleep on the floor and live in pain and poverty?" This clever retort is certainly not the simple explanation of the mishnah, but it illustrates the above point that poverty is not a necessity for successful Torah study.

❦ ❦ ❦

אַשְׁרֶיךָ וְטוֹב לָךְ
You are praiseworthy and it is well with you

THE SENSE OF WELL-BEING AND SPIRITUAL ACCOMPLISHMENT THAT THE study of Torah brings is immeasurable. It is not merely the sense of self-satisfaction that intellectual accomplishment brings that is important; that feeling can come with the study of any discipline or science. Torah is more than that. It has been said, in a somewhat accurate oversimplification of very complex subjects, that prayer represents a Jew's conversation with God, while studying Torah is God's conversation with Jews. It is that particular feeling of closeness to the Creator that Torah study fosters, and it brings happiness and satisfaction to the student of Torah over and above any joy that comes with pure intellectual accomplishment. Thus, the reward, the happiness that Torah study brings to its students is not reserved only for the World to Come, but is palpably present in this world as well.

אַל תְּבַקֵּשׁ גְּדֻלָּה לְעַצְמְךָ
Do not seek greatness for yourself

Mishnah 5 HONOR IS AN ADDICTION. ITS PURSUIT DESTROYS PEOPLE who are otherwise worthy, valuable and important. Therefore, this mishnah's warning is clear and trenchant. The greatest leaders of Israel — Moses, Saul, Hillel and others throughout Jewish history, all fled

water in small measure, sleep on the ground, live a life of deprivation — but toil in the Torah! If you do this, *You are praiseworthy and it is well with you* (*Psalms* 128:2). *You are praiseworthy* — in this world; *and it is well with you* — in the World to Come.

5. Do not seek greatness for yourself, and do not crave honor; let your performance exceed your learning. Do not lust for the table of kings, for your table is greater than theirs, and your crown is greater than their crown, and your

---

from power and honor and had their leadership roles thrust upon them. In our current world of constant elections and unabashed pursuit of station and office, the words of the mishnah may seem incongruous, but it is merely reinforcing the idea mentioned before in Avos, that Torah knowledge is not to be exploited for personal gain. Coveting honors and position because of Torah knowledge is essentially anti-Torah behavior. It is the underlying theme of the opening mishnah of this chapter, which extols the greatness of *Torah lishmah,* the study of Torah without ulterior motives. *Torah lishmah* is the antidote to the pursuit of power, position and honor.

יוֹתֵר מִלִּמּוּדְךָ עֲשֵׂה
Let your performance exceed your learning

TORAH STUDY IS THE BASIS FOR ALL JEWISH SURVIVAL AND THE *TORAH lishmah* student is entitled to support and respect. Yet, study in an ivory tower is also not the fulfillment of the Jewish mission. A Jew must do more than what he or she knows and understands. That is the basis for the Jewish acceptance of the Torah at Sinai — נַעֲשֶׂה וְנִשְׁמַע, we will do first and understand later. A Jew is obligated to do God's will even though he lacks knowledge and understanding. By "doing," one achieves the Torah's purpose, and that is the greatest honor a Jew can achieve. If a Jew realizes this, then he also realizes that "his table is greater than that of kings and his crown [of exemplary Jewish behavior] is greater than the crown of kings and rulers."

A Jew's behavior must be above reproach. Looking for shortcuts and leniencies for one's own behavior and interests — even if they can somehow be justified legally and intellectually — misses the point of true Torah living. "Doing" implies behavior that will not be subject to societal misinterpretation and criticism. As such, legal niceties and intellectual hair-splitting, while mentally rewarding and challenging, are not the way to go in terms of behavior. As taught before in Avos, one must flee from the possibility of sin and even from the *appearance* of sinning. That can only be accomplished by doing more than one knows and understands.

הוּא בַּעַל מְלַאכְתְּךָ, שֶׁיְּשַׁלֶּם לְךָ שְׂכַר פְּעֻלָּתֶךָ.

[ו] **גְּדוֹלָה** תוֹרָה יוֹתֵר מִן הַכְּהֻנָּה וּמִן הַמַּלְכוּת,
שֶׁהַמַּלְכוּת נִקְנֵית בִּשְׁלֹשִׁים מַעֲלוֹת,
וְהַכְּהֻנָּה נִקְנֵית בְּעֶשְׂרִים וְאַרְבָּעָה, וְהַתּוֹרָה
נִקְנֵית בְּאַרְבָּעִים וּשְׁמוֹנָה דְבָרִים, וְאֵלּוּ הֵן:
בְּתַלְמוּד, בִּשְׁמִיעַת הָאֹזֶן, בַּעֲרִיכַת שְׂפָתַיִם,

וְנֶאֱמָן הוּא בַּעַל מְלַאכְתְּךָ, שֶׁיְּשַׁלֶּם לְךָ שְׂכַר פְּעֻלָּתֶךָ ***Your Employer can be relied upon to pay you the wage of your labor***

THE MISHNAH EMPHASIZES THAT OUR "EMPLOYER" CAN BE TRUSTED TO pay our wages at the end of the day. This statement is repeated a number of times in Avos. It provides assurance that no good deed goes unnoticed or unrewarded. In fact, that is one of the reasons that "your crown is greater" (see next *baraisa*), for earthly crowns always lie uneasy on the heads of rulers. There is no guarantee that the crown and the table of kings will provide any actual or permanent rewards. Many glittering promises do not actuate, but the Torah comes with a guarantee that its rewards are certain, plentiful, and eternal, because the Eternal One of Israel stands behind them. Our trust in God, His judgments and rewards, is the basic foundation of Jewish behavior and of its world perspective.

גְּדוֹלָה תוֹרָה יוֹתֵר מִן הַכְּהֻנָּה וּמִן הַמַּלְכוּת ***Torah is even greater than priesthood or royalty***

Mishnah 6 AS DISCUSSED BEFORE, THERE ARE SEPARATE "CROWNS" for Jewish royalty, the priesthood and the scholars of Torah, which are distinguished by the privileges and obligations that they confer upon the persons who don them. There is a fundamental difference, however, between the crowns of royalty and the priesthood on one hand and the crown of Torah scholarship on the other. The first two are natural rights of inheritance, dynastic in nature, and independent of any personal achievement. Not so in the case of the crown of Torah. It is not inherited, nor does it come easily or automatically to those who aspire to it. As the name of this chapter implies — "*Kinyan Torah*/ Acquisition of Torah" — Torah is attained by personal sacrifice, effort, and tenacity. It is this method of acquiring Torah that makes its crown unique and greater among the other crowns of royalty and the priesthood. Since the very nature of the attributes under discussion are so different — those of priesthood and royalty refer to prestige and entitlements, whereas those of Torah refer to the aspirant's need for strenuous effort — the numbers given in this mishnah are not meant to be a criterion of the comparison. The mishnah will go on to list the forty-eight methods, character traits and disciplines by which Torah may be acquired.

The concept of twenty-four advantages regarding the priesthood refers to the gifts that the *Kohanim* receive as their due according to Torah law. They are

Employer can be relied upon to pay you the wage of your labor.

6. Torah is even greater than priesthood or royalty, for royalty is acquired along with thirty prerogatives, and the priesthood with twenty-four [gifts], but the Torah is acquired by means of forty-eight qualities, which are: Study, attentive listening, articulate speech,

---

derived from verses that appear in Numbers (Chapter 18) and are discussed thoroughly in the Talmud. The thirty advantages of royalty are derived from verses that appear in the book of I Samuel (Chapter 8). The thirty legal and juridical rights and limitations regarding kings are listed in Tractate *Sanhedrin* 18a. All of the above are outlined in the commentary of the Gaon of Vilna to Avos. But the *baraisa* itself describes the forty-eight ways that are needed for the acquisition of Torah. A discussion of all forty-eight will make for a long chapter, but it is worth it! So let me begin:

בְּתַלְמוּד
Study

THERE IS NO SUBSTITUTE FOR ACTUAL STUDY, FOR LEARNING. NOT PRAYER nor piety equal the power of real study in the quest for attaining Torah knowledge. It has been pointed out numerous times earlier in Avos that study, in Jewish terms, means having a teacher, someone who imparts knowledge and tradition to the student. Some texts of Avos have the alternate reading: בְּלִמּוּד, by learning through being taught. Study from books and other non-human means requires some sort of original guidance and instruction from a personal teacher in order to be truly effective.

בִּשְׁמִיעַת הָאֹזֶן
Attentive listening

IN MY YEARS AS A STUDENT AND AS A TEACHER, I HAVE FOUND THAT listening is really a talent and an art. To enable our ears to truly hear what is being said by the teacher requires effort and concentration. Passive listening rarely contributes to increased knowledge on the part of the listener. In *Deuteronomy* (27:9), Moses tells Israel, *Pay attention and listen*. Without first paying attention to what is being said it is unlikely that one will truly listen. One of the fundamental complaints within families is "you don't listen to me." Listening and hearing are two different concepts and descriptions. The acquisition of Torah requires not merely hearing, but more importantly, listening intensively. The ear can be the conduit to our mind and heart. All three — the ear, the mind, and the heart — must always be kept open if Torah knowledge and values are to be gained.

בַּעֲרִיכַת שְׂפָתָיִם
Articulate speech

TORAH STUDY DEMANDS CORRECT PRONUNCIATION AND CAREFUL CHOICE of language and diction. Care in teaching, reviewing, and studying the text and the language of Torah is part of the tradition of Israel. The Talmud itself points out instances in Jewish history (such as regarding the details of the eternal war of Israel against Amalek) where wrong pronunciations and incorrect punctuation of Hebrew words led even great men to encounter problems and tragedies. One has to train one's lips to speak correctly when Torah study is involved. This is true for the student, but it is especially true for the teacher. A teacher's carelessness in pronunciation, grammar, diction, and punctuation can undermine the student's understanding. Any student of the Talmud knows that much of the Oral Law is based on the nuances of spelling and pronunciation of the words of the Written Law. As such, particular attention should be paid to these skills when dealing with the forms and texts that constitute the literature of our Torah studies.

This concept of articulate speech especially deals with the requirement of review, which is an essential component of all Torah learning. As any student will tell you, *chazarah* /review is the most difficult discipline to master. One of the ways to remember what one has learned is to repeat it aloud to oneself or to others. All successful *chazarah* requires repetition of the lesson in a carefully articulate, spoken manner to oneself or to others. In my student days, if I was not able to repeat the day's lesson clearly and flowingly to myself, it was a sign that I did not truly understand that lesson. Thus, articulation became not only an aid to my study; it served as the measuring rod of my understanding.

But articulate speech is the measure of the teacher, as well as of the student. Rabbi Chaim Soloveitchik, who was a master of Talmudic analysis and clarity of thought, is reputed to have said: "A teacher who cannot explain a difficult concept in an understandable and clear fashion indicates that he himself does not quite understand the subject." In any event, this attribute is a necessary ingredient for the success of all teachers and students of Torah.

בְּבִינַת הַלֵּב ***Intuitive understanding***

OUR HEARTS HAVE AN INTUITION AS TO RIGHT AND WRONG. *BINAH* REFERS to truly deep understanding, to weighing things correctly, to intuitively appreciating what is correct and proper. The Torah does not operate in a vacuum; it has an outlook — a הַשְׁקָפָה, *perspective* — on life. Understanding what that perspective is remains a key to true understanding of the Torah. It is possible to twist knowledge and arrive at conclusions that defy logic and Torah values. *Intuitive understanding* is a line of defense against such occurrences.

בְּשִׂכְלוּת הַלֵּב ***Discernment***

THOUGH THE TORAH IS DIVINE WISDOM, IT IS DEALT WITH BY HUMAN intellect and logic. Good common sense makes for better understanding and appreciation of Torah. Patently illogical halachic decisions fly in the face of the Torah values that they are meant to represent. There is an inner intuition to Torah study that points the student in the right direction of understanding and

intuitive understanding, discernment, awe, reverence, modesty,

---

application of its principles in practical life. This intuition is called *sichlus halev*, the logic or discernment of the heart. In Proverbs, King Solomon warns constantly of the harm that a fool can do in society. A fool who believes that he is a Torah scholar is truly a menace to Torah, for his foolish and illogical decisions can undo any respect that Torah had attained in the community. Torah and Jewish tradition do not easily suffer fools or foolishness

בְּאֵימָה, בְּיִרְאָה
Awe, reverence

TORAH STUDY MUST BE APPROACHED WITH TREPIDATION AND REVERENCE. The Torah must not be considered as another "subject" in the school's curriculum. It is comparable to no other educational discipline or knowledge. Previously in Avos, we saw that the Torah and its teachers and students are compared to fire. Fire warms, but it also burns. One must respect the danger of fire in order to properly harness it for productive use. So too, the Torah must be approached with respect, with awe, with restraint and dignity. Taking liberties with it, disrespecting its divinity and scholarship, treating the personages of the Torah and the Talmud as our equals, all lead to an eventual depreciation of Torah and its values. They are a sad estrangement from the ever-flowing waters of Jewish tradition.

❦ ❦ ❦

People of the book

Harry A. Wolfson, a Slabodka Yeshivah alumnus who became a professor of Hebrew classics at Harvard University, was once asked by a none-too-friendly non-Jewish faculty colleague: "What makes you Jews so special? Why are you the people of the book?" Wolfson replied: "We are the only people that I know of who, when picking up a book that fell to the floor, kiss it!" Fear, awe, reverence, are the keys to meaningful Torah study.

❦ ❦ ❦

בַּעֲנָוָה
Modesty

HUMILITY IS A BASIC CHARACTER TRAIT THAT THE TORAH DEMANDS FROM us. And it is the study of Torah itself that contributes to humility. The Torah is so broad and deep, and must be understood on so many different levels, that complete mastery of it is virtually impossible for any one human being. The Talmud describes the study of Torah as encompassing an area "broader than the oceans." The great rabbis have taught us that the ultimate purpose of Torah study and knowledge is to make us realize that as much as we know, there is still so much that we do not know. I have found in my personal experience that the higher the level of attainment in Torah studies, the greater the frustration one feels at what still remains unknown or not understood.

❦ ❦ ❦

The more you know, the less you know

In fact, the greater and more proficient the student of Torah, the more aware he becomes that there is so much more to it that he has not yet fathomed. When

one studies the great works of Torah scholarship of the previous generations of Israel, one stands meekly and humbly at the feet of those giants. Rambam writes that when he thinks about the Torah greatness of Rabbi Yosef ibn Migash, his father's mentor, his head aches from wonder and humility. The renowned genius and founder of the Mussar movement, Rabbi Yisrael Lipkin of Salant, writes that he did not approach the ankles of his inspirational teacher, Rabbi Yosef Zundel of Salant. Such are the realizations and personal attitudes that made humility the staple commodity in the characters of the great scholars of Israel. In a very inexact comparison, I can state that when I was 16 I knew little but thought that I understood much. When I was 60, I knew much more, but understood much less.

❦ ❦ ❦

Torah and its Giver abhor arrogance in any human being and certainly more so in someone who aspires to Torah scholarship and greatness. Setting one's sights very high in such matters, realizing that one may not always attain those heights of knowledge, remaining determined and not frustrated, and above all being humble about oneself and one's achievement — together these form the healthy pattern for successful Torah study and accomplishment.

בְּשִׂמְחָה
Joy

BECAUSE OF THE POSSIBILITY OF FRUSTRATION IN TORAH STUDIES, IT would seem likely that the student would become depressed, but just as the Torah does not coexist with arrogance, it also cannot exist for long in an atmosphere of sadness, frustration, and depression. The Talmud teaches that joy, happiness, and contentment are necessary for a true Torah personality to emerge. I recall my Eastern European teachers, each of whom had suffered greatly and experienced exile and wandering, yet had a great joy of life. When teaching Torah they were always upbeat, optimistic, full of humor and joyful purpose.

One of the most startling points of difference — *lehavdil* — that I noticed about my professors as compared to my *rebbeim* was how downbeat the former were on the world, its societies, and peoples. They always were trying to build a new and utopian world, and had nothing but sadness and criticism for the present world that we all had to live in. They exuded sadness, anger, and frustration. This helped me to then make up my mind that I would try to bring happiness to others and to myself by somehow making Torah my life's work. Torah gladdens the hearts of humans. But it also resides only with personalities who are themselves confident, happy, and enthusiastic about life and knowledge. The Chassidic world is popularly credited with bringing joy into the masses of the Jewish societies of Eastern Europe three centuries ago. But the world of the true Torah scholar was always a joyful and happy one throughout

6/6 joy, purity, ministering to the sages, closeness with

---

all of Jewish history. It is not by chance that the day of celebration of the Torah at the conclusion of the holiday of Succos is called Simchas Torah — the Rejoicing in Torah. Torah and happiness are inseparable components of Jewish life.

בְּטָהֳרָה
Purity

HOLINESS OF BEHAVIOR, THOUGHT, AND ATTITUDE IS NOT A NECESSARY requirement for obtaining a higher degree in the world of universities and professional schools. In fact, some of the leading intellectual figures in the Western world over the past centuries have been downright awful people in their personal deportment and human relations with others. In Judaism, this loose standard of conduct is unacceptable when it comes to the acquiring of Torah. The rabbis of the Talmud taught that to someone without merit (meaning holiness, purity, selflessness) Torah is poison and not the elixir of life.

The blessing that we recite before chanting the words of the prophets in the Sabbath and festival services — the *haftarah* — thanks the Lord for granting us good people as our prophets. The nations of the world were also granted prophets — Bilaam, for example — but they were not necessarily good persons. And therefore any good influence that they could have had on their societies was mitigated by the negativity of their own persona. Torah is a very volatile substance that does not easily find its place in any and every receptacle. A sense of holiness of subject and mission, of soaring spirituality and immortality, must accompany the actual intellectual exercise of studying Torah. Throughout our history, those who have approached the study and knowledge of Torah without an attitude of holiness have in the end been found wanting and their teachings have been rejected by the faithful core of Israel. Intellect, research, knowledge are all essential ingredients in studying Torah. But without the basic ingredient of personal holiness, Torah will not flourish.

בְּשִׁמּוּשׁ חֲכָמִים
Ministering to the sages

THE TALMUD INTERPRETS THIS PHRASE TO MEAN STUDY OF THE ORAL LAW — Talmud, Mishnah, Midrash, etc. — itself. In its plain sense, however, the phrase refers to being in the company of scholars and actually tending to their needs. This is an idea repeated often earlier in Avos. "Sitting in the dust before the feet of the wise men" was taught to us already at the beginning of our Avos experience. Torah is acquired not in a monastic cell, isolated and free of human contact, but rather through the personal relationship with scholars. Torah is not only books and knowledge; it is people and human behavior. Seeing great men doing ordinary, everyday things, teaches us great moral lessons and life-guiding messages. While not approving of such behavior, the Talmud records the attempt of a disciple to be present even during intimate moments of his teacher, claiming that "this, too, is Torah, and I have to study it!"

Some of my greatest moments is life occurred during my service as the "chauffeur" for Rabbi Yosef Kahaneman, the Ponevezher Rav, during his winters in Miami Beach, when I was a rabbi there. Seeing how he interacted with all types of people, hearing his clever observations and witticisms, observing his respectful and loving treatment of his wife, and admiring his rock-hard honesty and morality in fund-raising matters and techniques, all combined to teach me a great deal of Torah that I had never learned before. Jewish tradition has always taught that "one's eyes should constantly see his teacher's visage before him." Serving and ministering to the wise men of Torah is a spiritually uplifting and importantly practical learning experience.

בְּדִקְדּוּק חֲבֵרִים
Closeness with colleagues

AGAIN, TORAH SHOULD NOT BE STUDIED IN A SOCIAL VACUUM. FRIENDS, learning partners, a group setting, all combine to create a necessary atmosphere for growth and achievement in Torah studies. The bond of friendship and human warmth created while studying together lasts for a lifetime, long after the participants have gone their separate ways in life. Whenever I return to Chicago, I always feel a surge of emotion and warmth when I meet former classmates, even if I have not had any contact with them for decades.

The Talmud relates Torah knowledge — *devar halachah* — to remembering friends. Rabbi Avraham Kook explains this comparison by stating that Torah itself is an old friend of each and every Jew. When a Jew comes to study Torah, even if he has not done so for many years or perhaps even never before in his life, instinctively he has the feeling that he is meeting an old friend after many years of separation. True friendship will always stand the test of passing time. A successful yeshivah should be measured not only by the stature of the scholars who stand at its helm. No less important in determining the success of a yeshivah is the social atmosphere and bonds of friendship that exist between its students.

One of the proudest accomplishments of my twenty-year tenure as head of a yeshivah in Monsey, New York is that over thirty sets of brothers-in-law were formed in the yeshivah during that time. In the Talmud, we regularly find the debate on halachic issues conducted by pairs of friends and colleagues. Rabbi Yochanan and his brother-in-law Reish Lakish, Rav and Shmuel, Abaye and Rava, Ravina and Rav Ashi, are only some of the magnificent friendship pairs that created the Talmud.

❦ ❦ ❦

The right partner

I imagine that the best illustration of how yeshivah students feel about the subject is in this rueful joke common to all yeshivos: When Yaakov and Eisav were in their mother Rivkah's womb, each struggled to get out — Eisav to visit pagan places and Yaakov to frequent holy places. We can understand why

6/6 colleagues, sharp discussion with students, deliberation,

---

Eisav preferred places of idolatry to the womb, but Jewish tradition tells us that an angel teaches Torah to the fetus in his mother's womb. Why would Yaakov struggle to leave such a paradise? The answer is that even if the rosh yeshivah/teacher is an angel, but if the chavrusa/study partner is an Eisav, then you have to leave that yeshivah!" In any event, closeness with colleagues is a vital necessity for any meaningful acquisition of Torah knowledge and values.

❦ ❦ ❦

פִּלְפּוּל הַתַּלְמִידִים
Sharp discussion with students

THIS LITERALLY MEANS "WITH THE FIERY PEPPERY DISCUSSIONS OF THE students." The word *pilpul* has had many nuances of interpretation and definition over the centuries. In its original and positive sense, however, *pilpul* means a give-and-take discussion of the particular Torah topic under study, marshalling different sources and analyses, the better to understand the complexities of the issue involved. It is this form of *pilpul* that is almost universally in use in the yeshivos of today, at the beginning of the 21st century. The criticsm of *pilpul* that is found in the works of many of the great scholars of Israel refers to the abuse of *pilpul* by the use of sophistry and illogical theses. This is not the *pilpul* described in this *baraisa.*

The discussion of students among themselves and their questions and comments to their teachers regarding their lectures and ideas are enormously productive for Torah education. The rabbis of the Talmud spoke of מִלְחַמְתָּהּ שֶׁל תּוֹרָה, *the battle of Torah.* The fiery discussions, the attack on and defense of ideas and interpretations, the struggle of thoughts and creativity, all add up to teach us the benefit of *pilpul hatalmidim, sharp discussion with students.* Implicit in this idea is the point that the teacher has to be open and receptive to what his students have to say about the subject and his presentation of the material. Teaching Torah is not a take it or leave it affair. Many a great teacher in Israel has changed his mind or even withdrawn his lecture's premise, based on the comments and responses of his students. "From my students I have learned the most," was the statement of Rebbi (*Makkos* 10a), more than from his colleagues and teachers. The Talmud even dares to say that God Himself, so to speak, agrees that His children Israel have "conquered" Him in certain Torah matters! Listening to one's students is the best way to teach them.

בְּיִשּׁוּב
Deliberation

TORAH STUDY REQUIRES CONCENTRATION, SERENITY, AND ORDER. IT IS difficult in our world to concentrate on any given issue or subject for an appreciable amount of time. The distractions of life are too many — whoever allowed the mobile phone to come into being? But successful Torah study demands complete attention to the subject. A Polish nobleman once asked the great Rebbe of Kotzk, Rabbi Menachem Mendel Morgenstern, "Wherein lies your greatness? You appear quite ordinary to me!" The Rebbe answered: "I am

ו/ו בְּמִשְׁנָה, בְּמִעוּט סְחוֹרָה, בְּמִעוּט דֶּרֶךְ אֶרֶץ, בְּמִעוּט תַּעֲנוּג, בְּמִעוּט שֵׁנָה, בְּמִעוּט שִׂיחָה, בְּמִעוּט שְׂחוֹק,

---

able to concentrate exclusively on one subject for three hours consecutively." There are few people in our world who can match that feat.

Serenity of mind and soul are also necessary for proper Torah study. Such serenity is also difficult to achieve in our noisy, information-filled world. I think that this may be part of the reason that much of the Torah-studying society divorces itself from the modern means of communication. It simply destroys the ability to concentrate exclusively on the subject at hand. Important decisions in life should be made with a cool head and a steady soul. Studying Torah requires that same type of steadiness of mind and heart.

בְּמִקְרָא, בְּמִשְׁנָה ***[Knowledge of] Scripture, Mishnah***

PART OF THE *DELIBERATION* MENTIONED IMMEDIATELY ABOVE IS KNOWLEDGE of the basic texts of Torah. Without a deep and wide knowledge of Scripture and Mishnah, the study of Talmud is more difficult, possibly faulty, and often incorrect. The order of study that we learned earlier in Avos — age 5 for Scripture, 10 for Mishnah, 15 for Talmud — has not been adhered to over the past few centuries. Despite the important reasons for doing so, the educational decision to teach Talmud to young children, before they are proficient in Scripture and Mishnah, has had in many instances serious educational consequences. Be that as it may, however, the order of study — Scripture to Mishnah to Talmud — is still a guideline for the knowledge needed for maximum success in learning. Knowledge of the basic texts of Judaism remains the key to opening the gate of greater Torah knowledge and accomplishment.

בְּמִעוּט סְחוֹרָה ***Limited business activity***

THE *BARAISA* MENTIONS SIX AREAS OF LIFE WHERE ONE SHOULD LIMIT one's indulgence in order to succeed in acquiring Torah knowledge. The Torah advocates moderation. There are certain areas and pursuits in life that, if not contained and regulated, easily become all consuming.

The pursuit of commerce and wealth certainly is addictive if it is not balanced by the perspective of family and Torah living. One must earn a living, but that requirement must be balanced with other equally important facets of life. Torah knowledge and its attendant benefits cannot be acquired unless one is willing to minimize the drive to pursue wealth at all costs. The rabbis counseled that one find a "clean and easy" profession or trade. That excellent advice is not always simple to implement. Yet, there are many Jews who are able to engage in regular and intensive Torah study and still engage in meaningful and productive work and careers. The key to this success is the word *limited*. In a society that knows no satisfaction with what it has and

[knowledge of] Scripture, Mishnah, limited business activity, limited sexual activity, limited pleasure, limited sleep, limited conversation, limited laughter, slowness to

---

always has to have more, the *baraisa* cautions that in most areas of life, less is more. Only by agreeing to the concept of "less" can one hope to acquire the blessings of Torah.

The counsel of moderation also extends to pleasures, leisure, even civic activity and studies of the world. These too must have limitations placed upon them. In modern society, the pursuit of happiness is a full-time job and in most instances falls far short of its aim. Pleasure and enjoyment are necessary ingredients of life, but they can lead to obsessive behavior. All of the addictions of the modern world — tobacco, alcohol, gambling, drugs, sports, etc. — are due to the unmitigated and unrestrained pursuit of pleasure.

Time, too, must be managed. We all need sleep, but most people can probably do very well with less sleep than they think they need. After all, time is the most precious commodity in our lives. It is just about the only thing that is not replaceable. The great men of the *Mussar* movement in 19th-century Lithuania had a mournful poem about time (in Hebrew, it rhymed; in English it does not — but its message is clear in any language): "A person is disturbed by the loss of money but not by the loss of time. Eventually his money cannot help him but time lost will never return."

בְּמִעוּט שִׂיחָה
Limited conversation

CAREFUL CONVERSATION AND MEASURED SPEECH ARE REQUIREMENTS for Torah living. In the first chapter of Avos, the desirable quality of wisely applied silence was discussed. Though we are not bidden to be mutes, we are again asked to measure our patterns of speech by the standard of "less." Say little and do much is a maxim of traditional Judaism. Conversation for the sake of conversation is an addictive form of behavior, especially in our world of constant noise and sound, of talk-shows and incessant 24-hour a day news networks. In a culture that is afraid of silence, the requirement of applying the doctrine of "less" is more essential than ever. Guarding one's tongue and lips from wrong speech and/or excessive words is a necessary concomitant to the acquisition of Torah.

בְּמִעוּט שְׂחוֹק
Limited laughter

HUMOR IS ONE OF THE GREAT HUMAN DEFENSE MECHANISMS, AND JEWS are famous for their ability to inject humor into life. It is no accident that Jews are so heavily over-represented in the world of professional comedy. Jewish humor, especially Yiddish humor, was the hallmark of Jewish society for centuries. But there is a great difference between humor and שְׂחוֹק, which

בְּאֶרֶךְ אַפַּיִם, בְּלֵב טוֹב, בֶּאֱמוּנַת חֲכָמִים, בְּקַבָּלַת

---

refers to lightheartedness and a general attitude of not taking matters seriously. Such attitudes often lead to cynicism and mockery of others. This idea of less laughter is a reinforcement of the idea of "deliberation," which was discussed earlier. There are moments in life when a person may justifiably give oneself over to joy and laughter. But they are not many, and here too, therefore, one must apply the rule of "less," which governs the activities and situations mentioned in this section of the *baraisa.* The rabbis taught that in the time of the complete redemption of Israel at the Messianic Era, "then our mouths will be filled with complete laughter and our tongues with joy." But perhaps even then, after the initial outpouring of emotional joy, the rule that less is more will yet apply.

בְּאֶרֶךְ אַפַּיִם
Slowness to anger

PATIENCE IS THE MOTHER OF ALL VIRTUES. CERTAINLY AS REGARDING THE study of Torah, patience is essential for accomplishment, and frustration is the enemy of any accomplishment in the study of Torah. Hasty conclusions as to Torah decisions and the meaning of Talmudic texts leads to false halachah and shallowness of understanding. Persistence on the part of the student and patience on the part of the teacher is the formula for successful learning. The Talmud tells us of a teacher who was willing to repeat the lesson four hundred times in order to help the student grasp and understand it. Throughout Avos we have seen how this virtue of patience was emphasized in all areas of life, but it is nowhere so required as in study and education. Patience is listed as one of God's Thirteen Attributes of Mercy. In our emulation of our Creator, patience is the key to achieving all other virtues and Godly attributes.

בְּלֵב טוֹב
A good heart

A GOOD HEART WAS HIGHLY PRAISED EARLIER. A GOOD HEART CARRIES with it many other good things, again as discussed earlier, but in Torah study, a good heart is a necessity. It prevents unwarranted jealousy and competition between scholars and students of Torah and it creates an atmosphere of cooperation and encouragement between Torah scholars for the benefit of the spread and understanding of Torah. It was the goodheartedness of Rabbi Moshe Isserles (*Rema*) in adding his notes and glosses to the *Shulchan Aruch* of Rabbi Yosef Caro that guaranteed that the book would become the basic book of Jewish law for the entire Jewish world. True scholarship can occur only when there is a willingness to share information, to consider the opinions of others, and to feel satisfaction in the scholarly accomplishments of others. All of these qualities are included under the general heading of a having a good heart.

6/6 anger, a good heart, faith in the Sages, acceptance of

בְּאֱמוּנַת חֲכָמִים
Faith in the Sages

THERE ARE WIDE SWINGS OF INTERPRETATION REGARDING THIS FASCINATING and vital issue. In its simplest and most widely accepted form, the term refers to belief in the tradition of halachah, in the divinity of the Oral Law, and in the methods and people that created the Talmud and the other great works of rabbinic Torah scholarship throughout the ages. All new innovations in Jewish life must therefore be measured by the standards of past tradition. This does not preclude innovation and creativity in halachah particularly or Jewish society generally, but rather it serves as a brake on radical changes that defy tradition and will eventually drive Jews out of the pale of tradition and Torah life.

Ideas in Torah and Jewish life must be of such a truthful nature that they will stand the test of time. Short-term good ideas may turn out to be long-term disasters. *Emunas chachamim* [faith in the Sages] is the tool by which all good ideas must be measured and approved. With its somewhat inhibiting force, *emunas chachamim* prevents hasty decisions and currently politically correct but nevertheless wrong policies from being followed. All of Jewish history has borne out the wisdom of this necessary quality.

The concept of *emunas chachamim* has been applied to accepting the advice and decrees of the great men of Torah in one's own generation, even when one disagrees with them. As the Sages put it, "Even if they say right is left and left is right." In many instances the sages may differ among themselves, and then one must decide which sage one must follow, but at the same time, one must not be hypocritical and skip around from question to question, and scholar to scholar, always looking for a rabbi who will agree with one's personal preference.

Furthermore, there arises the question as to what are the limits, if any, of the concept of *emunas chachamim.* Is *emunas chachamim* restricted to matters of Torah law, or is it valid for political, diplomatic, military, public policy, and economic matters, as well? And what about the authority of the sages regarding personal advice and counsel on family or career issues? These questions confuse many in the Jewish world and have created a wide spectrum as to when and how to apply the requirement of *emunas chachamim.* The intense politicization and partisanship that have so divided Jewish society over the past century also has weakened the concept of *emunas chachamim.*

Suffice it to say that *emunas chachamim* is based on the concept that the sages are as free as humanly possible from prejudices and biased thinking, because they base their opinions on their Torah tradition, knowledge, its values, and personalities that it molds. It is their best assessment of the situation at that moment, and that assessment is distilled through their

הַיִּסּוּרִין, הַמַּכִּיר אֶת מְקוֹמוֹ, וְהַשָּׂמֵחַ בְּחֶלְקוֹ,

Torah-based intellect and intuition. Furthermore, it is based on faith that their piety and dedication to find the truth in the service of God will somehow earn them Divine guidance. Given the above, it should be clear that scholarship alone is not enough; to be worthy of such confidence, the sage must be permeated with Torah knowledge, purity of character, total faith in its Giver, and fear of Heaven.

Emunas chachamim, however, does not imply that the sages are infallible. Based on the verse that says of God, [He] *makes wise men retreat and makes their wisdom foolish (Isaiah* 44:25), the Talmud asserts that great men may also sometimes err, if there is a Heavenly reason for such occurrences. The idea that wise men are infallible contributes to eventually weakening the concept of *emunas chachamim* instead of strengthening it. The fact that the rabbis of Europe did not foresee the Holocaust is constantly thrown up at me when I discuss the necessity of observing the concept of *emunas chachamim* in Jewish life. To me, that is the perfect and tragic example of turning the hearts of the wise men backwards for some unfathomable Heaven-ordained reason. Man is only man — even the greatest of us — and God is God and that is just the way it is. Therefore, *emunas chachamim* must also fit into that stark statement of fact, and people must be aware that the same God Who ordains the course of history guides the counsel of His sages to shepherd His plans to fruition.

I wish to hazard a final observation on the subject. Since there are many genuine sages in the Jewish world at any given time, and since these various wise men often maintain disparate views about important issues, Jews who choose to follow the opinion of one rabbi should not anathemize those Jews who follow the different view of another rabbi. Rabbi Naftali Tzvi Yehuda Berlin, the Netziv of Volozhin, in his commentary to the Torah, *Haamek Davar* (Introduction to *Genesis),* points out that in Second Temple times, Jews who followed one sage's opinion in their service of God were branded as heretics by some Jews who followed the opinion of other sages. Eventually this led to such baseless hatred and violence among Jews that the Second Temple was destroyed because of it. Rabbi Avraham ben HaRambam made the same type of observation centuries before the Netziv, when he defended his sainted father against the Jewish forces in Montpelier that had incited the Church to destroy Rambam's books because they considered some of his views to be unacceptable. Eventually, this act of zealotry led to allowing the Church and the king of France to burn fourteen wagonloads of the Talmud (all handwritten) in Paris. This in turn led to the closing of the yeshivos of the Tosafists and finally to the expulsion of the Jews from France.

6/6 suffering, one who knows his place, one who is happy with his

---

Emunas chachamim is intended to be a positive tool for the acquisition of Torah and the enhancement of the prestige and station of Torah scholars within the Jewish community. It was never meant to be employed as a weapon against other faithful Jews. It should be a unifier, not a divisive force, in Jewish society.

בְּקַבָּלַת הַיִּסּוּרִים
Acceptance of suffering

THE BOOK OF JOB/*IYOV* IS DEVOTED TO THE DIFFICULT QUESTION OF HOW to accept adversity in life. Its basic theme is that there is no good answer that humans can understand as to why adversity strikes some so harshly and spares others. Thus, the entire issue is reduced to a matter of faith and trust in the Lord. Adversity has a purpose. It is not malicious or random punishment; it is part of God's plan. The rabbis therefore said that "one whose head hurts should renew his efforts in the study of Torah." The ability to accept adversity and continue to serve God is the hallmark of the Torah scholar. It has also been the identifying characteristic of the Jewish people throughout the long ages of exile and despair. Life contains troubles and problems. The Biblical verse (*Job* 3:7) teaches us that "humans are born to toil," to which the rabbis of the Talmud (*Berachos* 17a) commented: "Fortunate is the one whose toil is related to Torah study." By the acceptance of this toil and adversity and relating it to Torah study and progress, one acquires another important aid in becoming a Torah personality.

הַמַּכִּיר אֶת מְקוֹמוֹ
One who knows his place

THERE IS A SUBTLE SHIFT OF LANGUAGE NOW IN THE *BARAISA*. UNTIL NOW it described the *attribute*, now it describes the *person*. On this change, Rabbi Yaakov Emden (Yaavetz) comments that the attributes that will now be listed are acquired after one has internalized the previous attributes. In other words, we are no longer discussing the *means* of acquiring Torah, but what a Torah personality looks like. Recognizing one's place, having an accurate assessment of one's knowledge, influence and worth, leads to the true sense of modesty that is the essence of Torah values and behavior. Recognizing one's place also has practical implications in everyday life. Overblown views of one's talents and abilities lead to disappointment and frustration. Conversely, underestimating one's value also leads to lack of fulfillment and accomplishment. Our frequently expressed rule of Torah balance allows for a correct assessment of one's self and an ability to recognize one's true place in society and life.

❧ ❧ ❧

וְהָעוֹשֶׂה סְיָג לִדְבָרָיו, וְאֵינוֹ מַחֲזִיק טוֹבָה לְעַצְמוֹ, אָהוּב,

---

Know your seat

As an aside and not as interpretation of the words of this baraisa, I wish to comment on one's physical "place" in the synagogue. I have witnessed many incidents of extreme unpleasantness in the synagogue over the issue of "my seat." The responsa and commentaries of the rabbis over the ages are replete with disputes over the rights to specific seats in the synagogue. And then there is the tendency of some people to demand seating at the head of the synagogue, while others cannot find a seat too far back from the ark. I have been involved in the construction of two major synagogue buildings in my rabbinic career. When asked by the architects designing those structures for my input regarding the seating arrangements in the sanctuary, I answered, only half facetiously, that they needed to provide only two rows of seating — the front row and the back row. In any event, it takes goodwill, patience and a sense of the general good of the congregation to recognize one's true place in the synagogue's seating plan.

❦ ❦ ❦

וְהַשָּׂמֵחַ בְּחֶלְקוֹ
One who is happy with his lot

IMMERSION IN TORAH ALLOWS ONE TO FEEL SATISFIED WITH ONE'S SHARE of material goods and pleasures, which is how the rabbis defined true wealth. Torah accomplishment and values channel satisfaction into our inner being and allow us to go through life without falling victim to anger and disappointment at not having greater wealth. Pursuit of wealth, power and honor is an addiction, a thirst that can never be slaked. Again, the line of balance between necessary ambition and drive on the one hand and excess desires and constant dissatisfaction on the other hand is the goal of the Torah's lifestyle.

❦ ❦ ❦

The value of money

I am reminded of an incident that I saw as a small child in the home of my grandparents in Chicago. My grandfather was a distinguished rabbi and rosh yeshivah who was paid a very meager wage, but that never seemed to disturb him. Somehow, he and his family always had food on the table and a roof over their heads. One day he told my mother that a stranger approached him in the synagogue at the end of the prayer service and gave him $5 (not an insignificant sum in those years) as an honorarium, even though my grandfather could not recall what service he had ever rendered that person. Then he told my mother that while walking home from the synagogue, a poor man approached him and begged for his help for food and rent. My grandfather beamed and said: "It must have been the prophet Elijah who gave me the $5 so I would be able to give it to that poor man and help him in his dire straits." My grandfather truly felt that he had no need personally for those $5.

lot, he makes a limitation on his speech, he does not take credit for himself, he is beloved, he loves the Om-

---

❧ ❧ ❧

וְהָעוֹשֶׂה סְיָג לִדְבָרָיו
He makes a limitation on his speech

THIS VIRTUE HAS BEEN MENTIONED BEFORE, BUT HERE AN ADDED NUANCE of advice is present. The warning about limitless speech follows the admonition regarding recognizing one's place. It is more in the nature of an earlier lesson in Avos against demanding that others accept one's opinion carte blanche, "for it is their (the listeners') prerogative and not yours." One's speech should be controlled even when presenting an idea or an opinion that one truly believes to be correct and necessary. Extra words, vehement words, verbosity instead of conciseness, have torpedoed the presentation of many a good idea. This is especially true in teaching students. The rabbis always cautioned teachers to present their words of Torah concisely, clearly, and accurately. Recognizing one's own limitations — one's place, so to speak — will lead to correct speech within norms and limitations.

וְאֵינוֹ מַחֲזִיק טוֹבָה לְעַצְמוֹ
He does not take credit for himself

SELF-CONGRATULATION LEADS TO ARROGANCE AND HUBRIS. AS WE HAVE seen, many of these forty-eight attributes of acquiring Torah are restatements of ideas previously described in Avos. Everyone should feel proud of doing one's job well and successfully, but no one should feel entitled to special reward and recognition for doing what is, after all, only one's duty. In the military, medals are awarded for actions above and beyond the call of duty. The study and support of Torah is our duty in life — "for this is the purpose for which you were created." The line between pride of accomplishment and unwarranted self-congratulation is indeed a very fine one. But it is one that must be negotiated successfully for the acquisition of Torah to be valid and complete.

אָהוּב
He is beloved

TORAH, ITS KNOWLEDGE AND CORRECT BEHAVIOR, LEADS TO A PERSON becoming loved. The great scholars of Israel were always heroes in Jewish life, beloved by their people. Even centuries or millennia later, such great scholars as Hillel, Rabbi Akiva, Rashi, Rambam, etc. are beloved figures. I was amazed and deeply moved at the emotional outpouring of Jews who watched my documentary film about the life of Rashi. They all regarded him as a member of their own family, a beloved grandfather, and their love for him was not dimmed by the passage of over nine and a half centuries. That is what Torah, in its truest and most pristine form, can do for a person: make one beloved immortally.

ו/ו

אוֹהֵב אֶת הַמָּקוֹם, אוֹהֵב אֶת הַבְּרִיּוֹת, אוֹהֵב אֶת הַצְּדָקוֹת, אוֹהֵב אֶת הַמֵּישָׁרִים, אוֹהֵב אֶת הַתּוֹכָחוֹת, וּמִתְרַחֵק מִן הַכָּבוֹד, וְלֹא מֵגִיס לִבּוֹ בְּתַלְמוּדוֹ,

---

אוֹהֵב אֶת הַמָּקוֹם, אוֹהֵב אֶת הַבְּרִיּוֹת
He loves the Omnipresent, he loves [His] creatures

TO BE BELOVED, ONE MUST BE ABLE TO LOVE AS WELL. THE PRIMARY commandment of the Torah is to love God. The great rule of the Torah is to love one's fellow human beings. By its very nature, love is unconditional and above rational explanation. It is a deep emotion. In *Song of Songs* (8:7), Solomon stated, "Great waters cannot extinguish the flame of love." The word "love" in our time has suffered the fate of many other noble words in the language — it has been demeaned and cheapened. It can be used now for chocolates and baseball teams, furniture and house design. The *baraisa* here uses it for the lasting objects of our affection — God, fellow human beings, acts of righteousness and charity, justice and truth, constructive criticism and self-improvement. One's attitude toward them must be one of unconditional, emotional love. Charity given grudgingly is still charity, but charity given out of love is a taste of heaven itself. To love justice means to love it even if the court or judge decides against your personal interests. To be able to accept fair and constructive criticism and not blame the messenger is also an expression of love.

Just as there is love of persons close to us — parents, siblings, spouses, children, grandchildren, etc. — so too is there love of ideals and noble faith. A Jew is bidden always to do the right thing, to be noble and just and good and faithful. Someone who is able to love others and to love ideals and goodness is a person who eventually becomes beloved to others as well. The acquisition of Torah creates within us the situation of loving others and being beloved by them. Perhaps this is one of Torah's greatest gifts to human beings. The cities of Sodom banned love of others in their societies. That was the source of their eventual downfall and destruction. There is no worse fate than having to live in a loveless world.

וּמִתְרַחֵק מִן הַכָּבוֹד
He distances himself from honor

IT IS INSUFFICIENT NOT TO PURSUE HONOR DIRECTLY. THE ADDICTION TO honor is potentially so powerful and damaging that one must actively distance oneself from its effects. Although self-respect is necessary for productive life, reliance on constant popular praise is like drinking saltwater. It makes one thirstier and thirstier. So too, the balance of maintaining one's own dignity and self-respect on one hand, and on the other hand, not falling prey to the elixir of outside honor, is not easy to achieve. There are times when one should accept personal honor if thereby the honor and

6/6

nipresent, he loves [His] creatures, he loves righteous ways, he loves justice, he loves reproof, he distances himself from honor, he is not arrogant with his learning,

---

support of Torah values and institutions can be enhanced. However, caution should always be the byword when matters of honor are involved. The Torah is compared to water, always seeking the lowest and most humble. Honor that is an expression of unwarranted arrogance and leads to further feelings of hubris is abhorrent to Jewish life and its value system. The true Torah personality treats honor as a volatile and dangerous ingredient. One should not rush to handle it, and if one must, it should be done gingerly.

וְלֹא מֵגִיס לִבּוֹ בְּתַלְמוּדוֹ
He is not arrogant with his learning

THOSE WHO ACQUIRE TORAH SHOULD NOT FALL INTO THE TRAP OF HUBRIS and false pride that often afflicts those with superior intellect. Accordingly, this is a continuation of the previous admonition to flee from the trap of honor and arrogance. Puffed-up pride due to intellectual accomplishment is the antithesis of Torah values.

Another translation of this term is "He does not treat his Torah knowledge casually, matter-of-factly." This interpretation deals with the problem of human nature. All things and accomplishments, no matter how great and exalted, emotionally uplifting and spiritually rewarding, tend to lose their uniqueness and freshness when they occur regularly. As one becomes accustomed to beauty and wonder, the initial excitement fades and they become ordinary and taken for granted. I have a friend who lives in a home overlooking a spectacularly beautiful mountain valley with a river rushing in its midst. Whenever I visit there, I am overcome by the beauty of the place and spend time staring out the broad picture window that fronts on that scene. My friend did, too, during his first weeks and months in his home, but no more. I am always astonished that my friend, who sees this beauty all the time, hardly ever even glances out the window.

Treating the extraordinary as ordinary is a human failing. The acquisition of Torah knowledge is an extraordinary achievement and gift. It should never be treated lightly or considered as something ordinary. This is part of the rabbis' lesson to us — that Torah knowledge is not guaranteed — "it is not an inheritance that automatically falls to you." When achieved, it should therefore be treasured and appreciated on a continuing and constant basis.

ו/ו

וְאֵינוֹ שָׂמֵחַ בְּהוֹרָאָה, נוֹשֵׂא בְעֹל עִם חֲבֵרוֹ, וּמַכְרִיעוֹ לְכַף זְכוּת, וּמַעֲמִידוֹ עַל הָאֱמֶת, וּמַעֲמִידוֹ עַל הַשָּׁלוֹם, וּמִתְיַשֵּׁב לִבּוֹ בְּתַלְמוּדוֹ, שׁוֹאֵל

וְאֵינוֹ שָׂמֵחַ בְּהוֹרָאָה
He does not enjoy halachic decision-making

SOME PEOPLE HAVE OPINIONS ABOUT EVERYTHING, EVEN ABOUT AFFAIRS that are not their concern. Aside from the plain meaning of these words, that a judge or a rabbi should not feel triumphant or joyful at his power to make decisions that affect the lives of others, there is another aspect to these words. A person should not be quick to volunteer advice and counsel to others in areas that are not one's expertise and especially when he was not asked. The Torah's lifestyle abhors busybodies. There is an element of prideful glee when one instructs others, and we must do all we can to temper that emotion. Proper advice, properly asked for and properly rendered, is a great act of kindness. However, when any of these "propers" turn improper, then it can be disastrous.

The Talmud points out that our good friend in Torah life, balance, is important here as elsewhere. The rabbis criticized a scholar who is qualified to render advice and decisions, halachic and otherwise, but refuses to do so because of misplaced modesty, or because he lacks a sense of responsibility toward those who need him. The rabbis also criticized even more bitterly those who are not really worthy of rendering such decisions, yet jump into the fray. Thus, the correct balance and an honest self-appraisal of one's abilities, knowledge, responsibilities, and influence is the necessary ingredient for following this admonition of the *baraisa.*

נוֹשֵׂא בְעֹל עִם חֲבֵרוֹ
He shares his fellow's yoke

TO HELP CARRY ANOTHER'S BURDEN IS AN ACT OF RIGHTEOUSNESS THAT knows no dimensions or limitations. Teachers, friends, family, rabbis, doctors, lawyers, accountants and others, whether they be professionals or not, are all engaged in helping someone else carry a burden. Even if they are being paid for their services, they are still doing a great service, if they render it honestly, sincerely, and with wisdom and compassion. Judaism is the antithesis of Sodom, where helping others was disdained and eventually forbidden. Our father Abraham was the sworn opponent of Sodom even as he prayed for the physical survival of its citizens. Goodness knows no bounds or particular address. Rabbi Yisrael Lipkin of Salant expressed this lesson in his usual brilliant, pithy, and concise fashion: "Caring for the other person's *olam hazeh* (worldly, physical needs and concerns) is my *olam haba* (my merit for achieving the reward of the World to Come)."

Many times just being there at a time of grief or need is also a valuable contribution to the well-being of others. In my experience as a congregational rabbi and *rosh yeshivah* there were many situations when I could be of no practical assistance to people suffering pain, loss, and anguish, but my merely

he does not enjoy halachic decision-making, he shares his fellow's yoke, he judges him favorably, he sets him on the truthful course, he sets him him on the peaceful course, he thinks deliberately as he studies, he asks and

---

being with them — simply the presence of someone who cared about them — provided aid and comfort. No one should have to be alone at times of sadness, crisis, and pain. The Lord is always with us in all of our travails, but fellow human beings should also be present to help carry the burdens of life.

וּמַכְרִיעוֹ לְכַף זְכוּת
He judges him favorably

THIS REFERS NOT ONLY TO GIVING SOMEONE THE BENEFIT OF THE DOUBT and not engaging in unjustified and unwarranted suspicion of others' motives and behavior, but it has a positive message as well. Overly suspicious and cynical natures create unwholesome human beings. One is bidden to help others do the right thing. By judging them favorably and charitably, by reducing cynicism and apathy in the community, we can encourage them to do the right thing. On the other hand, foolish naivete regarding the intentions of others is suicidal. Helping others wisely and attempting to truly understand them helps create this balance in our relationship with others.

וּמַעֲמִידוֹ עַל הָאֱמֶת
He sets him on the truthful course

TRUTH AND PEACE ARE VALUES THAT HELP THE WORLD EXIST, AS EXPLAINED in the first chapter of Avos. To imbue someone with these values is a true expression of friendship to individuals and to society generally. Part of carrying the burden of others' problems is to help them attain a life of truth and peace.

The word וּמַעֲמִידוֹ literally means "to stand him up straight." It is the pursuit of peace and the attainment of inner peace that makes us walk erect through life, no matter what the obstructing circumstances. The Talmud uses the expression "he stretched forth his hand and raised him up" as representative of the ultimate goodness that one can bestow upon another person. In a world where many strive to put others down, someone who attempts to raise them up is truly an admirable role model. The goals of peace and truth are absolutes and hence difficult to achieve or even approach, but they represent the innermost desires of our souls to live at peace with ourselves and others and to live up to the demands of truth. At all ages and circumstances, we may need others to pick us up and help us proceed in life. The person who has acquired Torah and internalized its lessons and values can help others in their pursuit of peace and truth in our world.

וּמִתְיַשֵּׁב לִבּוֹ בְּתַלְמוּדוֹ
He thinks deliberately as he studies

HIS LEARNING STABILIZES HIS PERSONALITY. HE BECOMES A MEASURED thinker, he looks before he leaps; his actions conform to his knowledge and to the value system of the Torah. He reviews his knowledge and internalizes the morality and piety that the Torah taught him. He is not hasty in judgment and

וּמֵשִׁיב, שׁוֹמֵעַ וּמוֹסִיף, הַלּוֹמֵד עַל מְנָת לְלַמֵּד, וְהַלּוֹמֵד עַל מְנָת לַעֲשׂוֹת, הַמַּחְכִּים אֶת רַבּוֹ,

---

not extreme in behavior. By constantly comparing what he knows to what he does, he achieves a serenity in life and deportment that marks him as a true Torah personality. This trait of thinking deliberately allows him to attain the level of יִשּׁוּב, *deliberation*, mentioned earlier. By attaining deliberation, a person then can acquire even more learning, thereby entering the never-ending cycle of Torah and Jewish life.

שׁוֹאֵל וּמֵשִׁיב
He asks and responds

THE GIVE AND TAKE OF TORAH LEARNING LIES IN ITS ESSENTIAL QUESTION-and-answer format. All questions are valid — even those to which we know we may never receive a satisfactory answer. Faith is often the only answer, but the question need not disappear. We can all live with questions; apathy is the great enemy of spiritual growth and Torah attainment. The Talmud's example of the great Hillel's patience was his ability to deal with even foolish or frivolous — or purposely provocative — questions. Children and students, old and young, should be encouraged to ask questions. Teachers and parents, public officials and religious leaders should be prepared to respond, even when the honest answer is "I don't know." It is the exchange of ideas, the refinement of concepts that uniquely characterizes all Torah learning. This sort of debate has been the traditional way to engage in Torah study throughout the ages.

שׁוֹמֵעַ וּמוֹסִיף
He listens and adds [***to the discussion***]

TO BE ABLE TO LISTEN IS A GREAT GIFT. TO HEAR WHAT SOMEONE ELSE is really saying and not to jump to conclusions is the mark of a wise person. By listening carefully one will be able to add wisdom to the conversation and/or lesson. To contribute one's thoughts and opinions without first hearing out the other person is not only boorish, but it precludes any true advancement of knowledge on the part of the impatient listener. Stepping on other people's lines has destroyed many a promising acting career. Listening intently and clearly to the words of other people automatically gives the listener the right to add to those words, to debate them, and thereby to increase knowledge of Torah for all concerned.

One should always remember that the attentive ear must precede the open mouth. I once saw a sign that advised: "Do not operate mouth unless brain is in gear." Listening attentively and respectfully to others, especially to elders and teachers, is the clutch pedal that helps put the brain into gear.

הַלּוֹמֵד עַל מְנָת לְלַמֵּד
One who learns in order to teach

TORAH LISHMAH IS THE GOAL OF TORAH, AND LEARNING IN ORDER TO transmit Torah knowledge to others is its highest goal. The true purpose of *Torah lishmah* is to magnify and glorify its presence among Israel and the

responds, he listens and adds [to the discussion], one who learns in order to teach, one who learns in order to practice, one who makes his teacher wiser, one who

---

world. I feel that implicit in this message is that one must learn not only the knowledge of Torah but also the knowledge of how to teach Torah to others. Many a student has been turned away from the pursuit of intensive Torah study by teachers of Torah who were competent scholars but incompetent teachers. The *baraisa* here conveys a subtle but vital message: Part of one's Torah training must be the acquisition of the proper and necessary skills to teach others. As mentioned earlier, Rabbi Chaim Soloveitchik was reputed to have said that one never really understands a particular subject in Talmud if he cannot explain it to others. A Torah scholar who cannot communicate, either by writing or speaking, is like a brilliant diamond lost in the sands of time. What is demanded of him is not only knowledge of subject matter, but the ability to effectively transmit it.

וְהַלּוֹמֵד עַל מְנָת לַעֲשׂוֹת
One who learns in order to practice

OVER AND OVER AGAIN IN AVOS, WE ARE EXHORTED TO PROPER BEHAVIOR and action. Knowledge is the precondition to all meaningful Jewish life. But knowledge alone, without meaningful, consistent, moral behavior and deeds is sterile and unproductive. The rabbis teach that the goal of Torah study is לְעַסוּקֵי שְׁמַעְתָּא אַלִּיבָּא דְהִלְכְתָא, to use learning in order to know what the halachah requires in given circumstances. For after all is said and done — and a lot more is usually said than done — what is *done* is mightily and primarily important. Training oneself to act — on behalf of Torah and Israel, on behalf of others, on behalf of knowledge and truth — is part of the curriculum of Torah study. In Jewish life, there are no members of the audience; we are on stage and performing at all times. We should, therefore, attempt to make our performance memorable and inspiring.

הַמַּחְכִּים אֶת רַבּוֹ
One who makes his teacher wiser

HOW DOES ONE MAKE ONE'S TEACHER WISER? ENRICHMENT COURSES and in-service conferences may certainly help, but the *baraisa* seems to have a simpler and less expensive solution. Students who critique and debate the teacher, who are not sycophants and yes-people, who listen seriously and question wisely, make for a wiser instructor. I had great teachers who refused to allow their students to take written notes during the lecture. When one is busy taking notes, it is difficult to ask probing questions and to truly analyze and internalize the teacher's thoughts.

The tradition in Eastern European yeshivos was to surround the teacher physically and verbally during the lecture, to engage in the give-and-take of "the war of Torah." Many a time our great teachers changed their minds, withdrew their earlier logical premises, changed course in the middle of the

ו/ו **וְהַמְּכַוֵּן אֶת שְׁמוּעָתוֹ, וְהָאוֹמֵר דָּבָר בְּשֵׁם אוֹמְרוֹ. הָא לָמַדְתָּ, כָּל הָאוֹמֵר דָּבָר בְּשֵׁם אוֹמְרוֹ, מֵבִיא גְאֻלָּה לָעוֹלָם, שֶׁנֶּאֱמַר: „וַתֹּאמֶר אֶסְתֵּר לַמֶּלֶךְ בְּשֵׁם מָרְדְּכָי.״**

---

discussion, in the search for truth and accuracy. Thus we students, inferior as we were in intellect and knowledge to our great teachers, made them wiser, greater, better teachers, more advanced scholars. It has often been said in this work that one never really understands the complexity of a given subject until one is forced to teach and explain it to others. Torah is not to be learned by rote and meek acceptance of others' opinions. It is rather a raging sea of ideas and facts that requires thought, organization, debate, creativity, imagination and discussion. Contrary students often make for greater teachers.

Another aspect of this quality is that the student should respect his teacher's wisdom and realize that the teacher may also have thought of the great question that one is about to spring on him and already taken it into account when preparing the lecture. The goal of the debate between student and teacher is not personal triumph, but rather a joint effort to arrive at the truth. Since teachers are usually a generation older than their students, the students often are too young to factor in the importance of life experience and maturity of mind. Youth is certainty and self-righteousness. Ideally, maturity in years strips away these "attributes." So there is this balance of the student questioning and debating the teacher while at the same time attributing wisdom and accuracy to the teacher.

וְהַמְּכַוֵּן אֶת שְׁמוּעָתוֹ
One who ponders over what he has learned

BEING CAREFUL IN UNDERSTANDING THE LESSON IS THE KEY TO TRUE Torah scholarship. Just as one requires *kavanah* — concentration, intensity, thoughtfulness — in prayer, so too is *kavanah* required in Torah study. It is more than a requirement, it is Torah study itself. A superficial approach to Torah study is doomed to be ineffective.

The word *kavanah* also means adjustment, balance, perspective. Torah can only be appreciated in its entirety. Concentrating on only one portion, one idea of Torah, often leads to distortions and misrepresentations. The great rule of learning is אֵין כּוֹתְבִין תּוֹרָה פָּרָשִׁיּוֹת פָּרָשִׁיּוֹת, one may not write a Torah scroll of individual chapters, choosing those that are to the writer's liking. The balanced whole view of Torah, of justice and mercy, of tenacity and compassion, of loyalty to the law and tradition, is part of the necessary *kavanah* of the study of Torah.

ponders over what he has learned, one who repeats something in the name of the one who said it. For you have learned this: Whoever repeats a thing in the name of the one who said it brings redemption to the world, as it is said: *And Esther said to the king in the name of Mordechai* (Esther 2:22).

Finally, *kavanah* also means being in line — in correct anticipation and aim — with the history and traditions of Torah and one's teachers. I can testify from personal experience that there is no greater feeling of accomplishment and intellectual joy for a Torah student than to find that one's understanding or explanation of a Torah subject coincides with the opinion of a great Torah sage of previous times. Torah study requires original thought and creativity, but it also requires vindication by the past and a firm framework of tradition.

וְהָאוֹמֵר דָּבָר בְּשֵׁם אוֹמְרוֹ ***One who repeats something in the name of the one who said it***

INTELLECTUAL HONESTY IS THE BEDROCK OF TORAH STUDY AND VALUES. Plagiarism is a crime, a dishonest act. Therefore, any student of the Talmud is well aware of the lengths to which it goes in order to attribute the saying under discussion to the correct teacher. Sometimes, however, a saying or a teaching becomes so popular and well known that it enters the "public domain." When that happens it is often attributed to a wide variety of potential authors or, more commonly, no longer attributed to anyone in particular. Such is the price of fame, even of sayings and teachings of great scholars.

❦ ❦ ❦

Secret sources

In referring to a redemption that flows from this intellectual honesty, the baraisa cites the example of Mordechai and Esther. But there is a longer-range redemption involved in the accurate attribution of authorship. So, you will ask, why are there no footnotes or credits to this book of mine? In my defense I can only quote a famous parable of the Maggid of Dubno, Rabbi Yaakov Krantz, who, when asked why he gave no sources in his public discourses, answered: "A poor man was invited to attend the wedding of a very rich relative. The wedding required formal dress which the poor man naturally did not own. So, he went around town borrowing the necessary items from different people, shoes from one, a shirt from another, a suit from a third and so on. When he arrived at the wedding in his newly found splendor, his rich relative asked him in amazement where he got all those fancy clothes. The poor man replied: 'Why should I enumerate to you in

[ז] **גְּדוֹלָה** תוֹרָה, שֶׁהִיא נוֹתֶנֶת חַיִּים לְעוֹשֶׂיהָ בָּעוֹלָם הַזֶּה וּבָעוֹלָם הַבָּא, שֶׁנֶּאֱמַר: ,,כִּי חַיִּים הֵם לְמֹצְאֵיהֶם, וּלְכָל בְּשָׂרוֹ מַרְפֵּא.'' וְאוֹמֵר: ,,רִפְאוּת תְּהִי לְשָׁרֶךָ, וְשִׁקּוּי לְעַצְמוֹתֶיךָ.'' וְאוֹמֵר: ,,עֵץ חַיִּים הִיא לַמַּחֲזִיקִים בָּהּ וְתֹמְכֶיהָ מְאֻשָּׁר.'' וְאוֹמֵר: ,,כִּי לִוְיַת חֵן הֵם לְרֹאשֶׁךָ, וַעֲנָקִים לְגַרְגְּרֹתֶיךָ.'' וְאוֹמֵר: ,,תִּתֵּן לְרֹאשְׁךָ לִוְיַת חֵן, עֲטֶרֶת תִּפְאֶרֶת תְּמַגְּנֶךָּ.'' וְאוֹמֵר: ,,כִּי בִי יִרְבּוּ יָמֶיךָ, וְיוֹסִיפוּ לְךָ שְׁנוֹת חַיִּים.'' וְאוֹמֵר: ,,אֹרֶךְ יָמִים בִּימִינָהּ, בִּשְׂמֹאולָהּ עֹשֶׁר וְכָבוֹד.'' וְאוֹמֵר: ,,כִּי אֹרֶךְ יָמִים וּשְׁנוֹת חַיִּים, וְשָׁלוֹם יוֹסִיפוּ לָךְ.''

---

detail the actual owner of the item of clothing item by item? Suffice it to say that from the top of my head to the sole of my shoe, nothing is truly mine!'" So too, did the Maggid conclude, that in our generations everyone knows that whatever thoughts of value we meager rabbis say, "from the top of our heads to the soles of our shoes, nothing is really ours!" That is my defense as well. Anything of worth here in this volume is not necessarily original with me. However, the sources I have used are so many and varied that enumerating them would be counterproductive to the thrust and readability of this book. Nevertheless, the redemption will come to Israel and the world by adherence to the standards of intellectual honesty and accuracy of the transmission of our holy Torah and tradition.

❦ ❦ ❦

גְּדוֹלָה תוֹרָה, שֶׁהִיא נוֹתֶנֶת חַיִּים לְעוֹשֶׂיהָ
Great is Torah, for it confers life upon its practitioners

Mishnah 7 THE GREATNESS OF TORAH IS THAT IT IS THE TREE OF LIFE. It infuses life into our existence, it justifies our innate feelings of immortality, and it serves as the defining measure of life itself. All the verses quoted in this *baraisa* refer to the Torah's life-giving force. At the end of Chapter Three, I noted the striking parable about keeping our leaf intact and attached to the tree of the Torah, the Tree of Life itself. The Torah itself places before us the choice between life and death — and it commands us to choose life. In our prayers we describe the Torah as "our lives and the length of our days." It is ironic in the extreme that Adam and Eve chose to eat from

7. Great is Torah, for it confers life upon its practitioners, both in this world and in the World to Come, as it is said: *For they [the teachings of the Torah] are life to those who find them, and a healing to his entire flesh* (Proverbs 4:22). And it says: *It shall be healing to your flesh and marrow to your bones* (ibid. 3:8). And it says: *It is a tree of life to those who grasp it, and its supporters are praiseworthy* (ibid. 3:18). And it says: *They are a tiara of grace for your head and necklaces for your neck* (ibid. 1:9). And it says: *It will give to your head a tiara of grace, a crown of glory it will deliver to you* (ibid. 4:9). And it says: *Indeed, through me [the Torah] your days shall be increased, and years of life shall be added to you* (ibid. 9:11). And it says: *Lengthy days are at its right, and at its left are wealth and honor* (ibid. 3:16). And it says: *For lengthy days and years of life, and peace shall they add to you* (ibid. 3:2).

---

the Tree of Knowledge and ignored the possibility of eating from the Tree of Life. It is not surprising therefore that their descendants so often still take risks and make life-threatening sacrifices to eat from the Tree of Knowledge and its accompanying material wealth.

In its essential state, the Torah is both the Tree of Knowledge and the Tree of Life, for life without knowledge is meaningless, but knowledge without the proper perspective on life is dangerous and cruel, both to the individual and to the general society of human beings. Perhaps this is part of what the rabbis intended to convey to us when they said (*Eichah Rabbah* 2:13): "If someone tells you that there is wisdom in the general world, you should believe it. But if someone tells you there is Torah in the general world, you should not believe it." Torah — that Godly combination of knowledge and life — is in short supply and minimal circulation in the general world. It remains the task of Israel, the recipient and guardian of Torah, to strive to advance the ideas and cause of Torah in order to move humankind toward a better and more harmonious and productive world society.

[ח] **רַבִּי** שִׁמְעוֹן בֶּן יְהוּדָה מִשּׁוּם רַבִּי שִׁמְעוֹן בֶּן יוֹחַאי אוֹמֵר: הַנּוֹי, וְהַכֹּחַ, וְהָעֹשֶׁר, וְהַכָּבוֹד, וְהַחָכְמָה, וְהַזִּקְנָה, וְהַשֵּׂיבָה, וְהַבָּנִים — נָאֶה לַצַּדִּיקִים וְנָאֶה לָעוֹלָם, שֶׁנֶּאֱמַר: „עֲטֶרֶת תִּפְאֶרֶת שֵׂיבָה, בְּדֶרֶךְ צְדָקָה תִּמָּצֵא.״ וְאוֹמֵר: „עֲטֶרֶת זְקֵנִים בְּנֵי בָנִים, וְתִפְאֶרֶת בָּנִים אֲבוֹתָם.״ וְאוֹמֵר: „תִּפְאֶרֶת בַּחוּרִים כֹּחָם, וַהֲדַר זְקֵנִים שֵׂיבָה.״ וְאוֹמֵר „וְחָפְרָה הַלְּבָנָה וּבוֹשָׁה הַחַמָּה, כִּי מָלַךְ יהוה צְבָאוֹת בְּהַר צִיּוֹן וּבִירוּשָׁלַיִם, וְנֶגֶד זְקֵנָיו כָּבוֹד.״ רַבִּי שִׁמְעוֹן בֶּן מְנַסְיָא אוֹמֵר: אֵלּוּ שֶׁבַע מִדּוֹת, שֶׁמָּנוּ חֲכָמִים לַצַּדִּיקִים, כֻּלָּם נִתְקַיְּמוּ בְּרַבִּי וּבְבָנָיו.

[ט] **אָמַר** רַבִּי יוֹסֵי בֶּן קִסְמָא: פַּעַם אַחַת הָיִיתִי

רַבִּי שִׁמְעוֹן בֶּן יְהוּדָה
Rabbi Shimon ben Yehudah

Mishnah 8 HE WAS A DISCIPLE OF THE GREAT RABBI SHIMON BAR Yochai and was a contemporary of Rabbi Yehudah HaNasi. He came from Kfar Acco in the western Galilee. It would be difficult to improve on this list of qualities and attributes that he lists in this *baraisa;* he lists virtually every human desire. Who would not wish for beauty, strength, wealth, honor, wisdom, long, healthy life and its accompanying achievements, and children? Yet, all of these things have value only if they are used properly and appreciated nobly. Rabbi Shimon supports his list with Scriptural verses that link these attributes to the scholars and the righteous. The linkage of the righteous with these verses emphasizes that in the right person, these attributes are a blessing. In the wrong person, however, they are a liability, if not a curse for society as a whole.

❦ ❦ ❦

Meaningless attributes

An old Jewish anecdote relates the story of the matchmaker who suggests someone to a young woman searching for a mate. "He is an orator, a writer, a scholar, an activist, just a great person," gushes the matchmaker. The young woman responds: "What is his main downside quality?" Sheepishly, the matchmaker says, "He is a bit of a fool." The girl moans: "Oy, an orator, a fool; a writer, a fool; a scholar, a fool; an activist, a fool!" Gifts and talents in life are precious, but they should be entrusted to those who will not abuse them.

❦ ❦ ❦

8. Rabbi Shimon ben Yehudah says in the name of Rabbi Shimon ben Yochai: Beauty, strength, wealth, honor, wisdom, old age, hoary age, and children — these befit the righteous and befit the world, as it is said: *Ripe old age is a crown of splendor, it can be found in the path of righteousness* (*Proverbs* 16:31). And it says: *The crown of the aged is grandchildren, and the splendor of children is their fathers* (ibid. 17:6). And it says: *The splendor of young men is their strength, and the glory of old men is hoary age* (ibid. 20:29). And it says: *The moon will grow pale and the sun be shamed, when God, Masters of Legions, will have reigned on Mount Zion and in Jerusalem, and honor shall be before His elders* (*Isaiah* 24:23). Rabbi Shimon ben Menasia said: These seven qualities that the Sages attributed to the righteous were all realized in Rebbi and his sons.

9. Rabbi Yose ben Kisma said: Once I was walking on

כֻּלָּם נִתְקַיְּמוּ בְּרַבִּי וּבְבָנָיו
Were all realized in Rebbi and his sons

RABBI SHIMON BEN MENASIA SINGLED OUT RABBI YEHUDAH HANASI AND his family as the prime example of all the above attributes being invested in the right people and being used for supremely beneficial purposes. To have great wealth and be unmoved by it, to possess temporal power and influence and not abuse it, to see all blessings of life in perspective and balance — that is being truly gifted and great. In the time of the Classical Era, Rabbi Yehudah HaNasi and his family represented this achievement and the nobility of public life. It is one thing to advocate greatness in theory. It is a greater thing altogether to actually witness such greatness in the flesh. Rabbi Shimon reminds us, therefore, that such greatness did in fact exist in Jewish society and that, difficult as it may seem, it is attainable in other times, as well.

רַבִּי יוֹסֵי בֶּן קִסְמָא
Rabbi Yose ben Kisma

Mishnah 9 WE KNOW LITTLE ABOUT RABBI YOSE BEN KISMA EXCEPT that he apparently opposed the Bar Kochba rebellion, predicting that it would end in defeat and disaster for the Jewish community and the Torah scholars in the Land of Israel. He warned Rabbi Chanina ben Teradyon to desist from openly defying the Roman ban against teaching Torah publicly, but his warning went unheeded, and Rabbi Chanina was burned to death by the Romans.

Although the obvious meaning of "ben Kisma" is that Kisma was the father of Rabbi Yose, there are other interpretations of the name. Some say that

מְהַלֵּךְ בַּדֶּרֶךְ, וּפָגַע בִּי אָדָם אֶחָד. וְנָתַן לִי שָׁלוֹם, וְהֶחֱזַרְתִּי לוֹ שָׁלוֹם. אָמַר לִי: „רַבִּי, מֵאֵיזֶה מָקוֹם אַתָּה?" אָמַרְתִּי לוֹ: „מֵעִיר גְּדוֹלָה שֶׁל חֲכָמִים וְשֶׁל סוֹפְרִים אָנִי." אָמַר לִי: „רַבִּי, רְצוֹנְךָ שֶׁתָּדוּר

Kisma was the name of the city where he was born and raised. However, Talmud Yerusalmi says that "Kisma" was a nickname given him because of the following incident early in his life. He was asked to lead the prayer services in the synagogue and he was unable to do so (the services then were recited from memory by the leader of the prayers). When he returned to the same synagogue years later, he led the prayers perfectly. The people of the town then named him "Kisma," meaning sealed, or redeemed. In any event, Rabbi Yose remains an enigmatic person whose greatness in Torah was recognized and treasured by his peers.

פַּעַם אַחַת הָיִיתִי מְהַלֵּךְ בַּדֶּרֶךְ
Once I was walking on the road

THIS STORY HAS MANY LOOSE ENDS. WHOM DID RABBI YOSE MEET? WHY did the man make such an extravagant offer to someone he apparently had never known before? And why did Rabbi Yose reject the man's offer so immediately and forcefully? After all, with such financial backing, perhaps Rabbi Yose could have developed a Torah community there. Far greater scholars than I have offered answers to these questions over the centuries.

My only thoughts about the entire incident are that Rabbi Yose may have sensed that the encounter with this stranger was a Heaven-sent test of his true loyalty to Torah study. It is one thing to dedicate oneself to Torah study when there are no tempting or viable options available. No one is looking for him to fill an important position, no one is offering him vast sums of money that he can use as he sees fit, when he is alone on the road, fending for himself in a world unappreciative of Torah scholars. There the pain may be great but the temptations are small. And suddenly — out of nowhere — arises the great moment of temptation. Had he accepted the stranger's offer, Rabbi Yose might have felt compromised as to his entire previous life and his dedication to Torah study under previous conditions of need. People, who almost always are willing to judge Torah scholars strictly if not even harshly, would have insisted that he became a scholar not out of choice but rather out of *no* choice, that he could be bought for money, that he is an opportunist, that his motives were never really those of *Torah lishmah*.

This concept of *Torah lishmah* is the basis not only of this chapter, *Kinyan Torah,* but of all Jewish life generally. It may be that it is this concern for the

the road, when a certain man met me. He greeted me and I returned his greeting. He said to me, "Rabbi, from what place are you?" I said to him, "I am from a great city of scholars and sages." He said to me, "Rabbi, would you be willing to live

---

public image of *Torah lishmah* that lay behind Rabbi Yose's firm and instant rejection of the offer. To him, the offer was more in the nature of temptation and not truly one of opportunity. Hence, the vehemence and directness of his response to the stranger on the road.

Yet the question remains, why didn't he think he could build a Torah community in the new venue? After all, he would have the financial support so necessary for such an endeavor. "Without flour there is no Torah" — and now he would have flour in abundance. For example, the blessed successes of Rabbi Samson Raphael Hirsch in constructing a great Torah community in 19th-century Frankfurt am Main were made possible by the unstinting support of the local Baron Rothschild. Apparently Rabbi Yose could have had his own Baron Rothschild.

There are undoubtedly many complex reasons for Rabbi Yose's refusal. Financial stability, though essential, is never a guarantee of the success of Torah communities and/or institutions. But I think that part of his reasoning may have been his realization that he was a marked man. As noted above, Talmud Yerushalmi comments that the name "Kisma" signifies that he was completed and redeemed in the eyes of the Jewish world. Such a reputation demanded of him higher standards than others would set for themselves. Rabbi Yose would not be granted any benefit of the doubt. Perhaps he would be unsuccessful in building a new Torah community; there are never any guarantees in life. He would then no longer be Kisma. He would have lost his place in the great Torah community where he currently resided. And having struggled so greatly to reach that level of *Torah lishmah* in his community of scholars, he would not now risk its loss.

The great scholars of Torah in 19th- and early-20th-century Eastern Europe, in the main, did not emigrate to the Land of Israel or to the United States. It had taken centuries to build the Eastern European Torah society. They would not abandon it in its time of ideological stress and shifting fortunes. With perfect historical hindsight we may look back and question their decision. We may ask what would American or Israeli Jewry look like today had they left and come to those shores. But we have no right to question the motives for their decision. They were after all, *Kisma* — whole, redeemed personalities — who embodied in their lives the realization of the ideal of *Torah lishmah*. They were unwilling to risk losing that role in Jewish life.

עִמָּנוּ בִּמְקוֹמֵנוּ וַאֲנִי אֶתֵּן לְךָ אֶלֶף אֲלָפִים דִּינְרֵי זָהָב וַאֲבָנִים טוֹבוֹת וּמַרְגָּלִיּוֹת?" אָמַרְתִּי לוֹ: „אִם אַתָּה נוֹתֵן לִי כָּל כֶּסֶף וְזָהָב וַאֲבָנִים טוֹבוֹת וּמַרְגָּלִיּוֹת שֶׁבָּעוֹלָם, אֵינִי דָר אֶלָּא בִּמְקוֹם תּוֹרָה." וְכֵן כָּתוּב בְּסֵפֶר תְּהִלִּים עַל יְדֵי דָוִד מֶלֶךְ יִשְׂרָאֵל: „טוֹב לִי תוֹרַת פִּיךָ מֵאַלְפֵי זָהָב וָכָסֶף." וְלֹא עוֹד אֶלָּא שֶׁבִּשְׁעַת פְּטִירָתוֹ שֶׁל אָדָם אֵין מְלַוִּין לוֹ לְאָדָם לֹא כֶסֶף וְלֹא זָהָב וְלֹא אֲבָנִים טוֹבוֹת וּמַרְגָּלִיּוֹת, אֶלָּא תוֹרָה וּמַעֲשִׂים טוֹבִים בִּלְבָד, שֶׁנֶּאֱמַר: „בְּהִתְהַלֶּכְךָ תַּנְחֶה אֹתָךְ, בְּשָׁכְבְּךָ תִּשְׁמֹר עָלֶיךָ, וַהֲקִיצוֹתָ הִיא תְשִׂיחֶךָ." „בְּהִתְהַלֶּכְךָ תַּנְחֶה אֹתָךְ" – בָּעוֹלָם הַזֶּה; „בְּשָׁכְבְּךָ תִּשְׁמֹר עָלֶיךָ" – בַּקֶּבֶר; „וַהֲקִיצוֹתָ הִיא תְשִׂיחֶךָ" – לָעוֹלָם הַבָּא. וְאוֹמֵר: „לִי הַכֶּסֶף וְלִי הַזָּהָב, נְאֻם יהוה צְבָאוֹת."

[י] **חֲמִשָּׁה** קִנְיָנִים קָנָה הַקָּדוֹשׁ בָּרוּךְ הוּא בְּעוֹלָמוֹ, וְאֵלּוּ הֵן: תּוֹרָה – קִנְיָן

שֶׁבִּשְׁעַת פְּטִירָתוֹ שֶׁל אָדָם אֵין מְלַוִּין לוֹ לְאָדָם לֹא כֶסֶף . . . אֶלָּא תוֹרָה וּמַעֲשִׂים טוֹבִים בִּלְבָד

When a man departs from this world, neither silver . . . escort him, but only Torah study and good deeds

THIS STATEMENT ABOUT THE IMMORTALITY OF TORAH AND GOOD DEEDS, while wealth and material possessions never accompany us to the World to Come, is pithy and blunt. Rabbi Yose puts the strange story of his meeting with this seemingly generous stranger into the context of eternity and true value. Only by seeing this event through this viewpoint do we gain insight into the world of true *Torah lishmah* that Rabbi Yose personified.

As the saying goes, "You can't take it with you." But it all depends what "it" really is. A person *does* take good deeds and the sense of a life lived within Torah parameters, for spiritual attainments remain valuable assets in the world of the spirit to which we all journey. Our physical luxuries, however, are valid only in this world of the physical. They have no currency or worth outside of their purely physical nature. All of our possessions will remain here after we are gone, many times to be sadly misused and abused by those who come after us. It is only our soul, finally freed from

with us in our place? I would give you thousands upon thousands of golden *dinars,* precious stones and pearls." I replied, "Even if you were to give me all the silver and gold, precious stones and pearls in the world, I would dwell nowhere but in a place of Torah." And so it is written in the Book of Psalms by David, King of Israel: *"I prefer the Torah of Your mouth above thousands in gold and silver"* (119:72). Furthermore, when a man departs from this world, neither silver, nor gold, nor precious stones, nor pearls escort him, but only Torah study and good deeds, as it is said: *When you walk, it shall guide you; when you lie down, it shall guard you; and when you awake, it shall speak on your behalf (Proverbs* 6:22). *When you walk, it shall guide you* — in this world; *when you lie down, it shall guard you* — in the grave; *and when you awake, it shall speak on your behalf* — in the World to Come. And it says: *Mine is the silver, and Mine is the gold, says HASHEM, Master of Legions (Haggai* 2:8).

10. Five possessions did the Holy One, Blessed is He, acquire for Himself in His world, and they are: Torah, one

---

its bodily restraints and physical worldly cares, that survives, enhanced by the Torah and good deeds that we accomplished during our earthly life.

חֲמִשָּׁה קִנְיָנִים ***Five possessions***

Mishnah 10 THIS CHAPTER HAS DESCRIBED THE ACQUISITION OF Torah by humans, but now it tells us that the Lord, too, makes acquisitions in this world. Even though everything is His, the Torah describes five things that are, so to speak, uniquely owned and acquired by God. All five are uniquely Jewish as well.

תּוֹרָה ***Torah***

THE TORAH WAS ACQUIRED BY ISRAEL, BUT IS ALWAYS REACQUIRED BY God, in the sense that a teacher always reacquires the knowledge that he or she has just imparted to his or her students. The Torah is heaven on earth, but it still remains heaven. The Jewish people were privileged to receive this heavenly treasure, but in essence it remains God's possession.

ו/י

אֶחָד, שָׁמַיִם וָאָרֶץ – קִנְיָן אֶחָד, אַבְרָהָם – קִנְיָן אֶחָד, יִשְׂרָאֵל – קִנְיָן אֶחָד, בֵּית הַמִּקְדָּשׁ – קִנְיָן אֶחָד. תּוֹרָה מִנַּיִן? דִּכְתִיב: „יהוה קָנָנִי רֵאשִׁית דַּרְכּוֹ, קֶדֶם מִפְעָלָיו מֵאָז.” שָׁמַיִם וָאָרֶץ מִנַּיִן? דִּכְתִיב: „כֹּה אָמַר יהוה, הַשָּׁמַיִם כִּסְאִי, וְהָאָרֶץ הֲדֹם רַגְלָי, אֵי זֶה בַיִת אֲשֶׁר תִּבְנוּ לִי, וְאֵי זֶה מָקוֹם מְנוּחָתִי”; וְאוֹמֵר: „מָה רַבּוּ מַעֲשֶׂיךָ יהוה, כֻּלָּם בְּחָכְמָה עָשִׂיתָ, מָלְאָה הָאָרֶץ קִנְיָנֶךָ.” אַבְרָהָם מִנַּיִן? דִּכְתִיב: „וַיְבָרְכֵהוּ וַיֹּאמַר, בָּרוּךְ אַבְרָם לְאֵל עֶלְיוֹן, קֹנֵה שָׁמַיִם וָאָרֶץ.” יִשְׂרָאֵל מִנַּיִן? דִּכְתִיב: „עַד יַעֲבֹר עַמְּךָ יהוה, עַד יַעֲבֹר עַם זוּ קָנִיתָ”; וְאוֹמֵר: „לִקְדוֹשִׁים אֲשֶׁר בָּאָרֶץ הֵמָּה, וְאַדִּירֵי כָּל חֶפְצִי בָם.” בֵּית הַמִּקְדָּשׁ מִנַּיִן? דִּכְתִיב: „מָכוֹן לְשִׁבְתְּךָ פָּעַלְתָּ יהוה, מִקְּדָשׁ אֲדֹנָי כּוֹנְנוּ יָדֶיךָ”; וְאוֹמֵר: „וַיְבִיאֵם אֶל גְּבוּל קָדְשׁוֹ, הַר זֶה קָנְתָה יְמִינוֹ.”

שָׁמַיִם וָאָרֶץ ***Heaven and earth*** HEAVEN AND EARTH, NATURE AND THE WONDERS OF THE UNIVERSE, ARE all God's acquisitions. He fashioned them in their exquisite wonder and complexity; and their secrets, though being constantly but partially unraveled by human intellect, still remain essentially hidden in God's domain.

אַבְרָהָם ***Abraham*** OUR FATHER ABRAHAM, WHO DEVOTED HIS ENTIRE LIFE TO INTRODUCING God and monotheism into a primitive and pagan world, also is one of God's acquisitions. He was God's representative on earth, as the people of Hebron said to him (*Genesis* 23:6), "A prince of God are you in our midst." Thus, when he is recognized as God's prince on earth, he, too, belongs no longer to himself alone, but has been acquired by his Creator to do His service.

יִשְׂרָאֵל ***Israel*** THE JEWISH PEOPLE ARE GOD'S PEOPLE, ACQUIRED BY HIM, SO TO SPEAK, out of the cauldron of Egyptian bondage and Sinaitic revelation. Even though the Jews have freedom of action and intention in their society and world, they never escape being God's people.

possession; heaven and earth, one possession; Abraham, one possession; Israel, one possession; the Holy Temple, one possession. From where do we know this about the Torah? Since it is written: *God acquired me [the Torah] at the beginning of His way, before His works in time of yore* (*Proverbs* 8:22). From where do we know this about heaven and earth? Since it is written: *So says God: The heaven is My throne, and the earth is My footstool; what House can you build for Me, and where is the place of My rest?* (*Isaiah* 66:1). And it says: *How abundant are Your works, God, with wisdom You made them all, the earth is full of Your possessions* (*Psalms* 104:24). From where do we know this about Abraham? Since it is written: *And He blessed him and said: Blessed is Abram of God the Most High, Who acquired heaven and earth* (*Genesis* 14:19). From where do we know this about the people of Israel? Since it is written: *Until Your people passes through, God, until it passes through — this people You acquired* (*Exodus* 15:16), and it [also] says: *But for the holy ones who are in the earth and for the mighty — all my desires are due to them* (*Psalms* 16:3). From where do we know this about the Holy Temple? Since it is written: *Your dwelling place which You, God, have made; the Sanctuary, my Lord, that Your hands established* (*Exodus* 15:17). And it says: *And He brought them to His sacred boundary, to this mountain which His right hand acquired* (*Psalms* 78:54).

בֵּית הַמִּקְדָּשׁ
The Holy Temple

THE TEMPLE IN JERUSALEM ALSO IS GOD'S ACQUISITION, NOT MAN'S. THE Lord has withdrawn the Temple from Israel and mankind twice and will yet restore it once again. There is a difference in opinion in Torah scholarship as to how the Third Temple will appear and whether humans will have any role in its rebuilding. Be that as it may, the Temple belongs to God and its eventual restoration still lies shrouded in His mysterious ways. Our world belongs to its Creator, even as we are able to deal with it and improve or destroy it.

These five Biblical statements remind us of God's acquisitions in this world and of His omnipresence in all of our affairs and struggles.

[יא] **כָּל** מַה שֶׁבָּרָא הַקָּדוֹשׁ בָּרוּךְ הוּא בְּעוֹלָמוֹ לֹא בְרָאוֹ אֶלָּא לִכְבוֹדוֹ, שֶׁנֶּאֱמַר: „כֹּל הַנִּקְרָא בִשְׁמִי וְלִכְבוֹדִי בְּרָאתִיו, יְצַרְתִּיו אַף עֲשִׂיתִיו״; וְאוֹמֵר: „יהוה יִמְלֹךְ לְעוֹלָם וָעֶד.״

❧ ❧ ❧

רַבִּי חֲנַנְיָא בֶּן עֲקַשְׁיָא אוֹמֵר: רָצָה הַקָּדוֹשׁ בָּרוּךְ הוּא לְזַכּוֹת אֶת יִשְׂרָאֵל, לְפִיכָךְ הִרְבָּה לָהֶם תּוֹרָה וּמִצְוֹת, שֶׁנֶּאֱמַר: „יהוה חָפֵץ לְמַעַן צִדְקוֹ, יַגְדִּיל תּוֹרָה וְיַאְדִּיר.״

כָּל מַה שֶׁבָּרָא הַקָּדוֹשׁ בָּרוּךְ הוּא בְּעוֹלָמוֹ לֹא בְרָאוֹ אֶלָּא לִכְבוֹדוֹ
All that the Holy One, Blessed is He, created in His world, He created solely for His glory

Mishnah 11 WE LIVE IN AN EXTREMELY FINE-TUNED UNIVERSE. THE smallest changes in climate, the food chain, and other natural phenomena can alter life on the planet in a significant degree. Thus everything that is in existence here in our universe — everything that the Lord has created and sustained — is important and plays a role in the grand scheme of His handiwork. Thus everything testifies to His glory and honor.

Knowledge of Torah and the application of its teachings to all areas of life, and the performance of the commandments are our highest duty and greatest testimony to the glory of God. But the other great achievements of humans — the symphonies of music, art and architecture, discoveries in science — as well as the natural wonders of the Alps and the Grand Canyon, the myriad hues of color seen in a flower and the grace of the feline families — everything that exists bears testimony to the work of the Creator of all.

11. All that the Holy One, Blessed is He, created in His world, He created solely for His glory, as it is said: *All that is called by My Name, indeed, it is for My glory that I have created it, formed it, and made it* (*Isaiah* 43:7). And it says: *God shall reign for all eternity* (*Exodus* 15:18).

❦ ❦ ❦

Rabbi Chanania ben Akashia says: The Holy One, Blessed is He, wished to confer merit upon Israel; therefore He gave them Torah and *mitzvos* in abundance, as it is said: *HASHEM desired, for the sake of its [Israel's] righteousness, that the Torah be made great and glorious* (*Isaiah* 42:21).

This idea that everything reflects on its Creator has special meaning for human beings. Not only are we bidden to observe in nature and in ourselves the greatness of God, but we are also charged to behave in a way that increases God's glory in the eyes of mankind.

If there is a fitting conclusion to the book of Avos, it is certainly this *baraisa*. All of Avos deals with God's honor, so to speak. In all of our lives, in all of our actions and words, we are obligated to add somehow to the perception of God's honor in our world. This is the concept of *Kiddush Hashem* — the Sanctification of God's Name in the world. By studying and observing the tenets of wisdom that are contained in Avos we are able to advance forward on the road that creates the atmosphere of holiness that leads to *Kiddush Hashem*.